[UN] PRECEDENTED PYONGYANG

DONGWOO YIM

Edited with
Jelena Prokopljević
Rafael Luna

INDEX

Recently, it has become less strange to face various stories about North Korea, especially about Pyongyang, the capital of the nation. Until recently, however, most of information we received was from limited source of major media that tend to frame North Korea with certain perspective, and therefore, we had been mostly exposed to only particular topics, such as military threats, famine and dictator(ship). As the nation is still one of the most seclusive countries in the world, or in history, it is not unfair to say that those framed topics are partly the facts that explain the nation well. However though, the atmosphere has changed in the past five years since the new leader Kim Jung Un has taken over the regime. More international tourists, business people and entrepreneurs are visiting, or being invited to, North Korea, and as a consequence, more photos and essays that show the actual living environment of North Korea, particularly Pyongyang, are unveiled through various social media, such as facebook, twitter and blogs. Although still many major sources of media focus on conventional topics, it is also not hard to read ac-

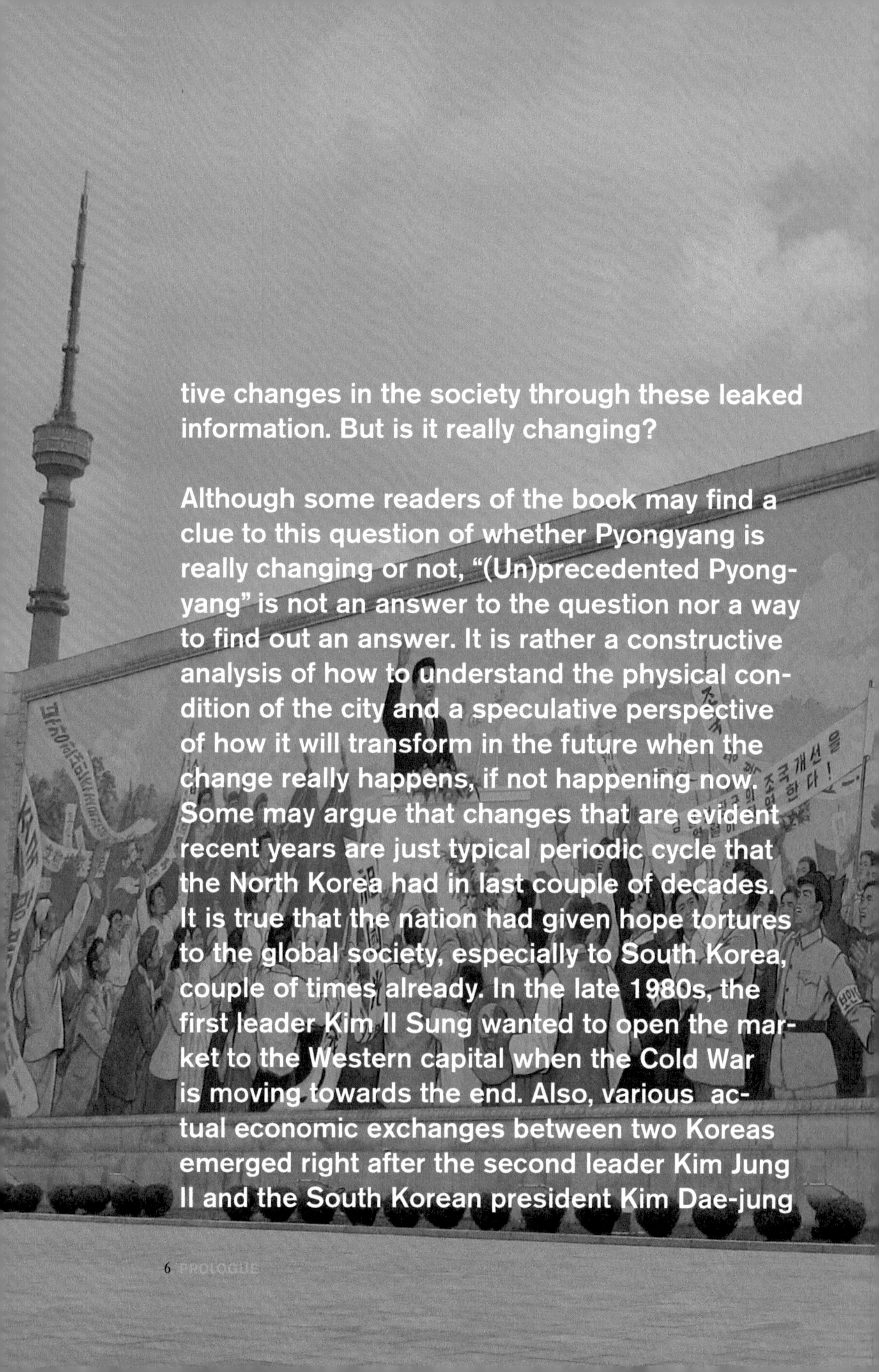

tive changes in the society through these leaked information. But is it really changing?

Although some readers of the book may find a clue to this question of whether Pyongyang is really changing or not, "(Un)precedented Pyongyang" is not an answer to the question nor a way to find out an answer. It is rather a constructive analysis of how to understand the physical condition of the city and a speculative perspective of how it will transform in the future when the change really happens, if not happening now. Some may argue that changes that are evident recent years are just typical periodic cycle that the North Korea had in last couple of decades. It is true that the nation had given hope tortures to the global society, especially to South Korea, couple of times already. In the late 1980s, the first leader Kim Il Sung wanted to open the market to the Western capital when the Cold War is moving towards the end. Also, various actual economic exchanges between two Koreas emerged right after the second leader Kim Jung Il and the South Korean president Kim Dae-jung

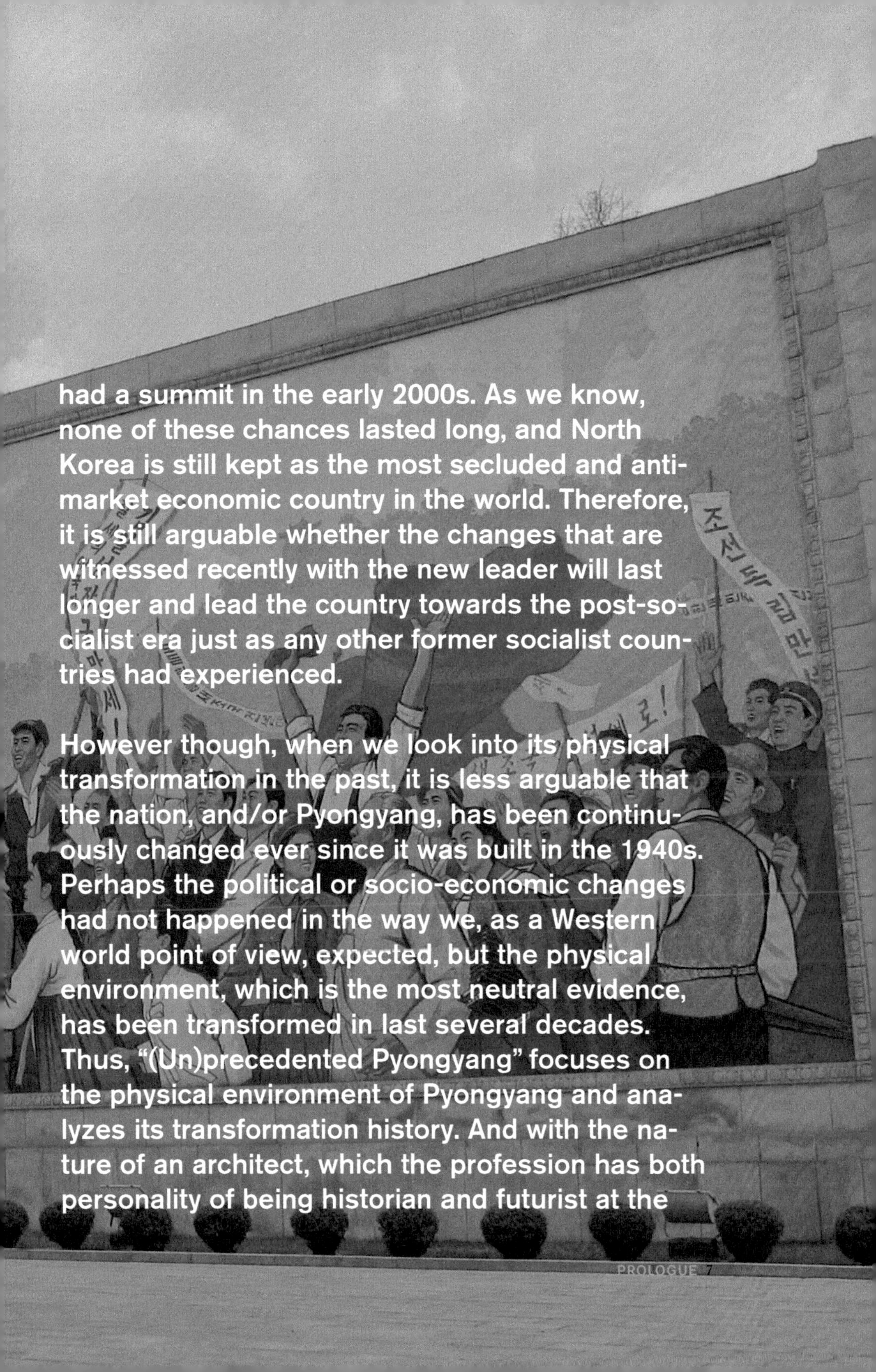

had a summit in the early 2000s. As we know, none of these chances lasted long, and North Korea is still kept as the most secluded and anti-market economic country in the world. Therefore, it is still arguable whether the changes that are witnessed recently with the new leader will last longer and lead the country towards the post-socialist era just as any other former socialist countries had experienced.

However though, when we look into its physical transformation in the past, it is less arguable that the nation, and/or Pyongyang, has been continuously changed ever since it was built in the 1940s. Perhaps the political or socio-economic changes had not happened in the way we, as a Western world point of view, expected, but the physical environment, which is the most neutral evidence, has been transformed in last several decades. Thus, "(Un)precedented Pyongyang" focuses on the physical environment of Pyongyang and analyzes its transformation history. And with the nature of an architect, which the profession has both personality of being historian and futurist at the

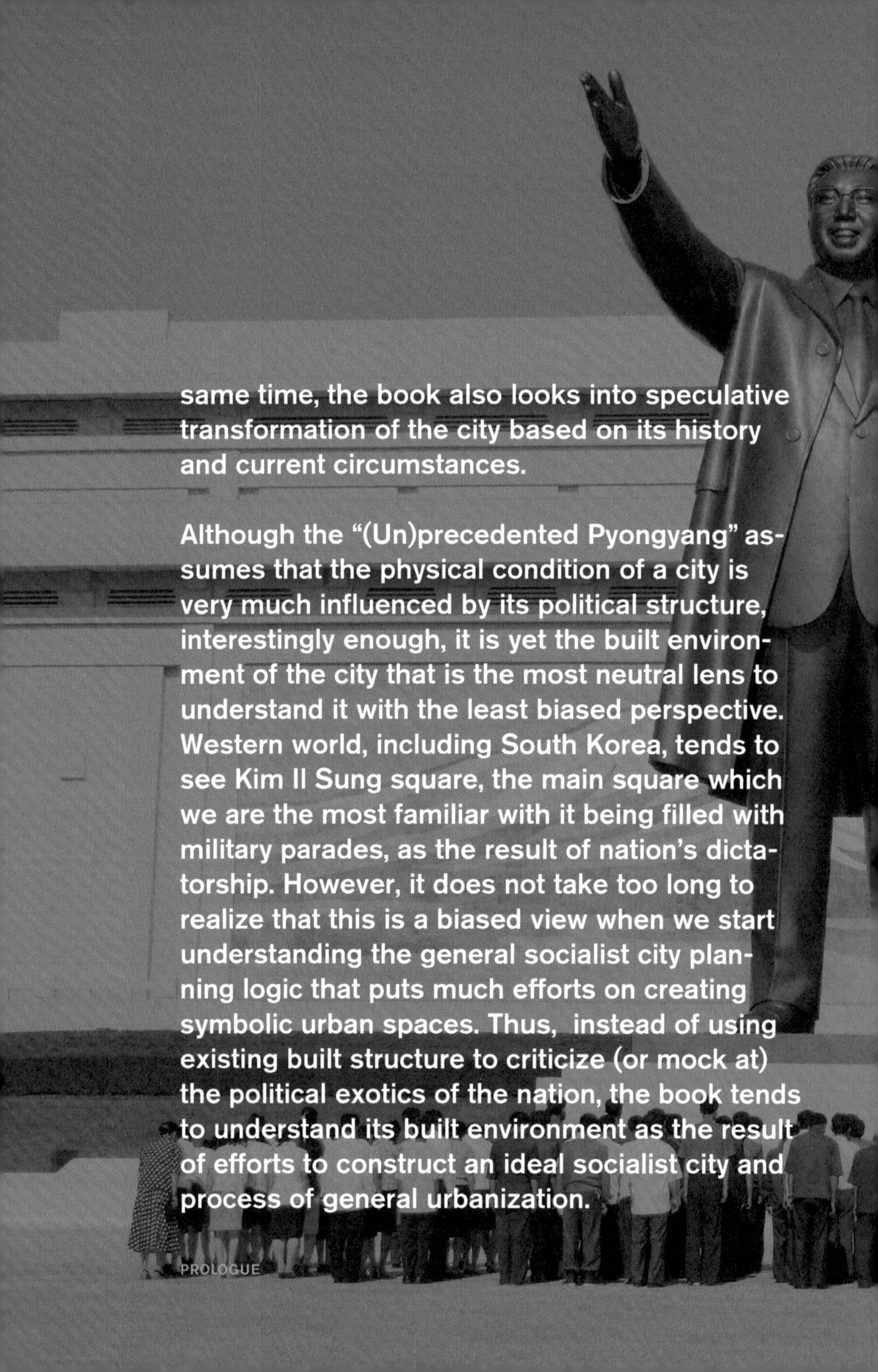

same time, the book also looks into speculative transformation of the city based on its history and current circumstances.

Although the "(Un)precedented Pyongyang" assumes that the physical condition of a city is very much influenced by its political structure, interestingly enough, it is yet the built environment of the city that is the most neutral lens to understand it with the least biased perspective. Western world, including South Korea, tends to see Kim Il Sung square, the main square which we are the most familiar with it being filled with military parades, as the result of nation's dictatorship. However, it does not take too long to realize that this is a biased view when we start understanding the general socialist city planning logic that puts much efforts on creating symbolic urban spaces. Thus, instead of using existing built structure to criticize (or mock at) the political exotics of the nation, the book tends to understand its built environment as the result of efforts to construct an ideal socialist city and process of general urbanization.

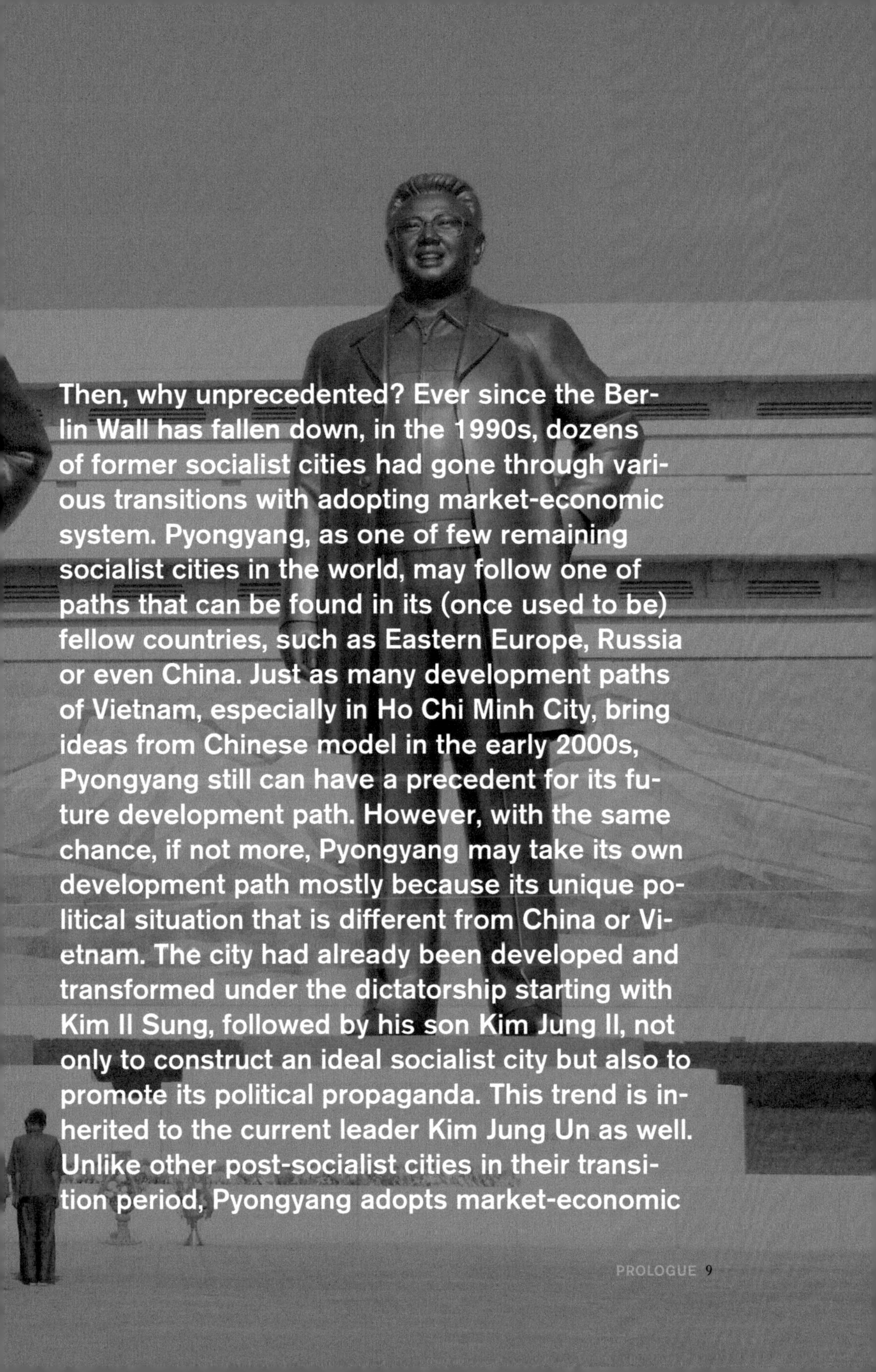

Then, why unprecedented? Ever since the Berlin Wall has fallen down, in the 1990s, dozens of former socialist cities had gone through various transitions with adopting market-economic system. Pyongyang, as one of few remaining socialist cities in the world, may follow one of paths that can be found in its (once used to be) fellow countries, such as Eastern Europe, Russia or even China. Just as many development paths of Vietnam, especially in Ho Chi Minh City, bring ideas from Chinese model in the early 2000s, Pyongyang still can have a precedent for its future development path. However, with the same chance, if not more, Pyongyang may take its own development path mostly because its unique political situation that is different from China or Vietnam. The city had already been developed and transformed under the dictatorship starting with Kim Il Sung, followed by his son Kim Jung Il, not only to construct an ideal socialist city but also to promote its political propaganda. This trend is inherited to the current leader Kim Jung Un as well. Unlike other post-socialist cities in their transition period, Pyongyang adopts market-economic

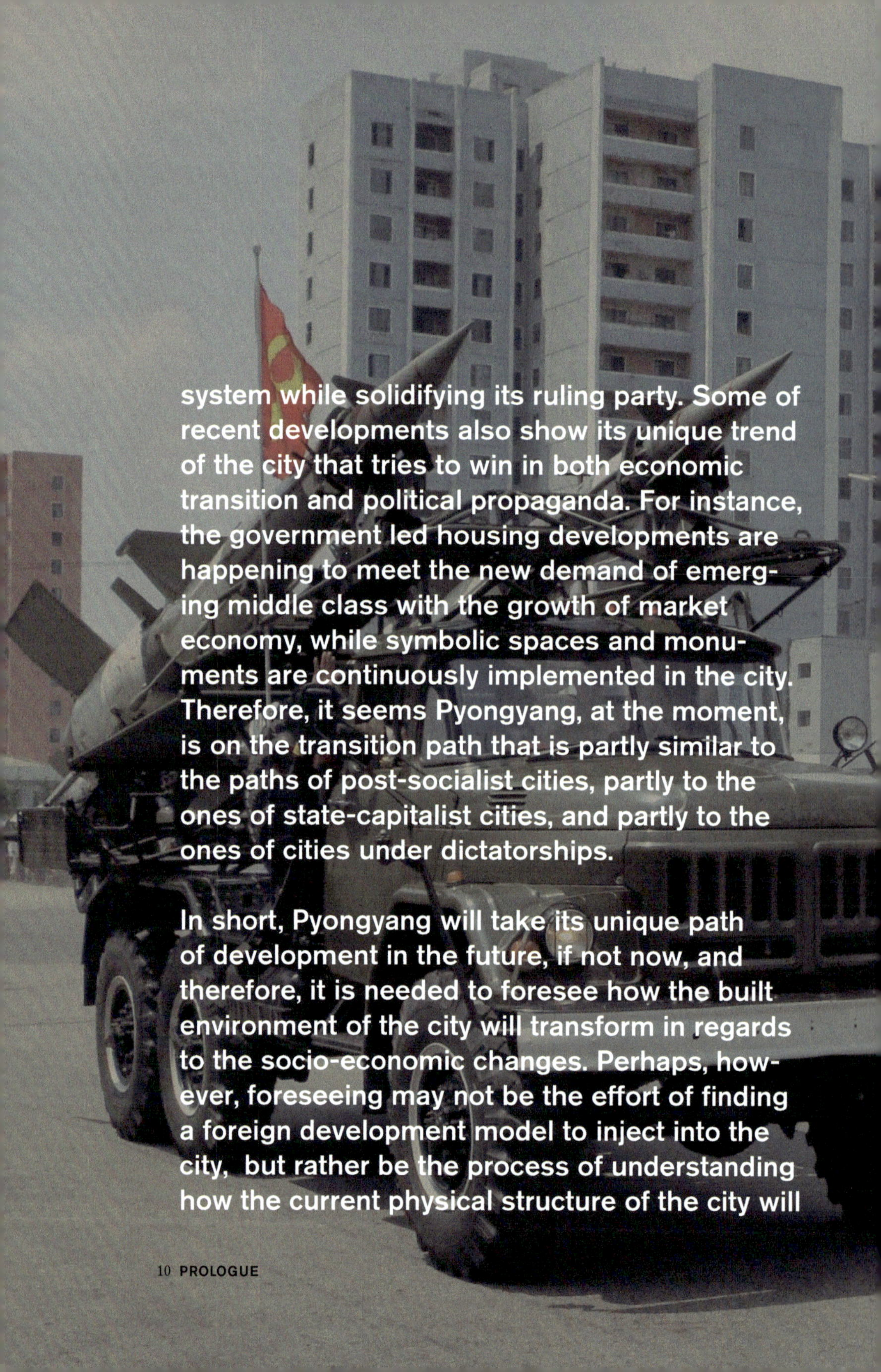

system while solidifying its ruling party. Some of recent developments also show its unique trend of the city that tries to win in both economic transition and political propaganda. For instance, the government led housing developments are happening to meet the new demand of emerging middle class with the growth of market economy, while symbolic spaces and monuments are continuously implemented in the city. Therefore, it seems Pyongyang, at the moment, is on the transition path that is partly similar to the paths of post-socialist cities, partly to the ones of state-capitalist cities, and partly to the ones of cities under dictatorships.

In short, Pyongyang will take its unique path of development in the future, if not now, and therefore, it is needed to foresee how the built environment of the city will transform in regards to the socio-economic changes. Perhaps, however, foreseeing may not be the effort of finding a foreign development model to inject into the city, but rather be the process of understanding how the current physical structure of the city will

respond to the new demand that is largely emerging. And eventually, because of its unique built environment and, presumably, development path, the upcoming urban structure of Pyongyang will have its own DNA that has no precedents in the past.

01
[UN]
PRECEDENTED
PYONGYANG

Ever since the speed of urban development has increased dramatically, transformation became a key word to understand a city. The character and specificities of this process is crucially tied to various economic phenomena operating in the urban environment, such as the flow of capital or fluctuations of dominant activities and corresponding infrastructure and few can deny the impact of economic alterations on the physical form of a city. As many case studies from Eastern European countries, Russia and China suggest, the combination of economic growth and political transition supplied the formula for exceptionally radical and quick urban transformations. Since adopting market-oriented economic systems, former socialist cities have become "blue oceans" for new investments.

Pyongyang, the capital city of North Korea, is one of few socialist cities in the world that has not adopted this new economic model. On the other hand, Pyongyang is comparable to socialist cities of decades ago, in that it exhibits a strong potential to attract huge investments if and when it begins to open its market to other countries. This change has, in fact, already begun to take place, raising the following questions for architects: what growth model can be suggested? where will the new developments happen? and whether the urban transformation will arise from within the existing structure of Pyongyang maintaining its essence or will it replace it with some new, imported model?

FRAMED PYONGYANG

In spite of recent developments in its fledgling tourist industry, North Korea is still the most enclosed country in the world, and even Pyongyang, its capital city, remains under a veil. The information we currently have about Pyongyang primarily comes from media discussions of the country's political or social issues. In contrast to reports of its dictatorship, human rights, nuclear programs, and the trend of nationwide starvation, the actual urban layout of Pyongyang has not received much attention.

Pyongyang was replanned and rebuilt after the Korean War with the goal to become an ideal socialist city, instead of being a closed city under a veil of dictatorship. In the absence of today's political dictatorship Pyongyang provided an experimental field in which socialist architects attempted to apply their ideal urban structures to the real world. Left in complete shambles after the war, the reconstruction of Pyongyang afforded planners the rare opportunity to create practically a new urban scheme from the ground up. In the aftermath of the Korean War (1950-1953), Kim Il Sung, the leader of North Korea, decided to maintain provisionally Pyongyang as the capital city of the DPRK (North Korea). This temporality would end with the 1972 constitution that definitely fixed Pyongyang as the state capital. Its layout reflected the ideology of socialism as well as victory of the war. [1] Thus, in order to fully understand the urban structure of Pyongyang, it is necessary to first consider the larger context of the socialist city model, its historical context, and which are its key differences from the capitalist city.

SOCIALIST CITY

Since the ideology of socialism grew out of the struggles of the urban working class in the industrial era, socialist architects have strived to create the ideal planned city that would improve living and working conditions, hygiene, insulation and connectivity. Marx and Engels themselves believed in the necessity of a new type of city, drawing the link between physical built environment and ideological representation.[2] The main tenets of socialist city planning, based on Marx and Engels' ideas, can be categorized as follows.[3] First, socialists were inherently opposed to uncontrolled growth of mega-cities, as bigger cities were equated to the deterioration of working class livelihood. Moreover, large urban populations were seen as tense battlegrounds between proletariat and bourgeoisie. Socialists even advocated for strong control of immigration to their cities. Second, they rejected the notion of urban redevelopment, dismissing it as a mechanism to re-locate working class people to slum districts–the most densely populated and detestable living environments of all. Also, they believed that this kind of urban redevelopment could only benefit the bourgeoisie and worsen socioeconomic polarization. Third, socialists aimed to synthesize urban and rural areas. For socialists bent on eliminating all signs of class disparities in a society, this separation was troublesome. In capitalist societies, they saw urban elite exploiting farmers, creating a huge vertical –social and spatial- rift between the two classes. Thus, a horizontal relationship between urban and rural areas was understood as a part of the resolution to the problem of class division.

Also, urban planning was a hugely important feature in socialist cities.

Socialists related the urban maladies in capitalist cities to a lack of planning and the excess of speculation. As a result, they argued, the logic of capital accumulation alone came to dominate whole societies. On the contrary, a well-structured master-plan for a city, based on a general, territorial plan of development, could prevent irregular urban problems and improve the living and working environment as a whole. As in all other economic spheres, the realization of these was subject on a strong intervention and control by the government. Thus, unlike capitalist cities, big state-owned companies were in charge of designing a "masterplan" and controlled every aspect of its construction.

SOCIALIST URBAN MORPHOLOGY

After his victory in the October Revolution in 1917, Lenin started to implement Marx and Engels' ideas. He tried to create a city that physically embodied socialism. During the 1920s a large debate took place in the Soviet Union centred on the spatial characteristics of the socialist city. Following the competition for the new industrial town of Magnitogorsk in 1928, N.A Milyutin proposed a Linear City diagram that reflected the basic concept of a socialist city.[4] Out of the nine planning models that Milyutin pointed out, there were three particularly distinctive concepts that affected the physical form of a city: the production areas, the green zones, and the symbolic structures.

The commitment to synthesize urban and rural areas was the key in creating within the city areas of production, as well as those of consumption.[5] Close interaction between industrial and residential areas became the most important factor in rethinking the urban organization, for reasons of improving connectivity and productivity. This strategy eventually developed, during the post WWII reconstruction, into the concept of the "micro-district (Mikrorayon)," which stated that working area as well as other service areas should be located within ten to twenty minutes waking distance from the residential area. This concept has in fact become a central tenet of urban planning in socialist cities, markedly affecting urban morphology.

The second factor in determining the physical form of a socialist city is landscape, which has been generated from the idea of E.Howard's Garden City Movement.[6] Series of landscape structures function not only as a buffer zone between residential and industrial area or transportation infrastructure, but also as a constraint to the expansion of a city. As mentioned above, the limited size of a city was important to socialist city planning, and at least in initial stages of the system development, coupled with the control of immigration. Landscape buffer zones constitute a key structure in making this limitation possible.

A symbolic space as urban structure is the last key factor of socialist urban morphology.[7] James Bater has pointed out that symbolism is a key feature of socialist cities. Indeed, symbolic urban features such as huge squares or representative statues in socialist cities are not easily found in capitalist cities which are developed under the paradigm of real estate, with exception of historic inheritance from the past. So while a capitalist city hesitates to create expansive public spaces within the urban structure, a socialist city insists on large central squares –generally replicas of Moscow Red Square– to propagate its revolutionary ideology or to strengthen its political system through public manifestations. Socialist city promotes public spaces although often without sufficient content to generate continuous use, leaving them for organized events.

PYONGYANG AS A SOCIALIST CITY

After three years of fighting in the Korean War, North Korea started to rebuild its cities through its first three-year reconstruction plan from 1954 to 1956. During this period, several socialist countries supported the reconstruction of North Korean cities by providing resources as well as technological assistance. Pyongyang received support from USSR, China, Hungary and Bulgaria, and not surprisingly, the architectural style and urban structure of Pyongyang showed some similarities to these countries at the beginning of reconstruction.[8]

Based on a master-plan in 1953 that reflected the ideals of socialist city planning, Pyongyang was planned as a one-million population city that would stretch from the Daedong River to the Botong River; 20-25% of the city was planned as development area, and the other portion of the city was planned as green zone. This scheme captured the socialist concepts of constructing a well-planned city. Throughout the decades, Pyongyang realized a number of its socialist urban planning goals. The three major socialist urban morphologies mentioned above were well executed in the city. In order to resolve disparities between cities and balance development between urban and rural areas, architects of Pyongyang aimed to include self-productive units within the city. Today's Pyongyang continues to be planned according to the micro-district system that combines small industry and residential use so that residents can both produce and consume in the same urban unit. The planned density of population is in the range of 300-600 residents/ha., equivalent to a traditional city centre.[9] This well-structured district is located in the area across the Daedong River from the central administration district, and the two areas together comprise a key axis of directionality for the city expansion.

As North Korean leaders insisted that Pyongyang should be developed in well-balanced way in contrast to any other capitalist city in the world, architects carefully injected landscape design into the city. Both riversides were developed as major landscaped areas and most principal boulevards were densely planted with studied varieties of greenery. Additionally, to maximize the effectiveness of workers labor and productivity, they created several leisure parks in the city so that the public could have enough rest and recover. In Pyongyang, most of the leisure parks are located close to historical or memorial areas.

The central part of the city was structured as a place for administration and institutions. Major socialist buildings and national symbols are located in this area, around the main, Kim Il Sung Square. Juche Tower, a symbol of North Korean ideology, is located directly across the river from the square, creating with it a major symbolic spatial axis. Moreover, additional representative buildings and monuments are distributed around Pyongyang in order to serve as physical sites of socialist ideology propaganda.

URBAN TRANSFORMATION

Pyongyang urban reconstruction was based on the master plan designed by Kim Jung Hee in 1953, according to which Pyongyang was structured as a multi-core city. Several different symbolic spaces are distributed evenly throughout the city and each of them become the centre of a district. Also main landscape structures are planned in between districts and function as buffer zones so that they cannot expand freely. This distribution of districts is mainly done to maintain the proper size of the city and to prevent social differentiation that can emerge from marked development in distinct areas. At the same time, each district's central square works as a symbolic space that testifies the centrally controlled society.

In the 1960s, Kim Il Sung ordered the re-definition of the architectural strategy for the further development of Pyongyang.[10] Unlike the 1950s when the urban growth was more focused on reconstruction of infrastructure and housing based on a master-plan, the new wave of development focused on five features that would propagate North Korean socialism as well as the nation's "victory" in war. They consisted in the expansion of major boulevards and construction of high-rise residential buildings along them, large scale civic and cultural facilities, symbolic statues and squares, and leisure and convenient facilities for foreigners.[11]

Once defined, these five strategies became a principal urban development standard with the larger scheme than the master-plan of 1953. However, some of these schemes conflicted with the master-plan. For instance, focusing the growth along main boulevards clashed with the polycentric development. Major boulevards branched out of the central district and dense high-rise residential buildings came to be located along them. Consequently, this destroyed the multi-core system and only certain areas located near the start of the new boulevards could function as core-like districts. Also, denser development of certain areas conflicted with the principle of the equal distribution of residents around Pyongyang. Additionally, even symbolic urban spaces came to congregate in the central areas instead of being distributed throughout the city.

This phenomenon resulted primarily from the rapid growth of the city. Although North Korea, like other socialist countries, at least in the early post war period, controlled migrations of the population, it could not halt illegal immigration into the city and the rapid urbanization of Pyongyang. As the city grew denser, housing shortages became a problem.

To resolve the problem of the rapid growth, Pyongyang developed several high-rise residential areas. At the same time, informal residential areas emerged. They mostly arose in areas originally planned as parks and natural spaces in the 1953 master-plan, and the newly built housing units resembled one or two-story houses typically designed for agricultural areas. This informal development not only broke with the landscape structure in the city, but also rendered micro-districts impossible. Hence, compared to other organized areas that were developed according to the master-plan, the informal development area lost the normative balance between residential units and service facilities. In short, the urban morphology of current-day Pyongyang, as other post-socialist cities, portrays a mixture of the physical forms of the ideal socialist master-plan and the realities of the informal development.

TRANSFORMATION OF A SOCIALIST CITY

As other socialist countries have already experienced, North Korea is also in the midst of transition to adopt the capitalist system in some particular ways. There are several indications that highlight this transition. For instance, the secretive Pyongyang government recently launched an experiment with the free market in 2002, beginning to deregulate prices and hiking salaries.[12] Also, small vendors, which had been controlled strictly by the government, are starting to emerge at major squares, and even underground real estate transactions are taking place.

Collectively, these changes can be seen as early indicators of a market-oriented economic system. The former Soviet Union, its Eastern European satellites, and China underwent this transition two decades ago, and several cities like Moscow, Shanghai, Beijing, have already became booming metropolises in the world. In Europe, 10 former socialist countries are now members of European Union and NATO. As noted earlier, socialist cities have different urban structures and morphologies from capitalist cities. These contrasts not only reflect different political ideologies but also differences in the flow of capital. Hence, when socialist cities start to allow capitalist forms of capital flow, the urban figures also change based on this new logic.

The socialist city center has been the area where most of this transformation unfolded. Because of its strategic location and superior infrastructure, this is the area where most of investments were concentrated. Furthermore, public spaces or institution areas in the city center with weaker capital power tend to be occupied by bigger capitals such as business fields.[13] Therefore, it is the central –administrative or symbolic- area of the city that begins to convert into the central business district, something that a socialist city has not had before.

In summary, the emergence of a variety of retail outlets in the form of street vendors and warehouses are undeniable indicators of Pyongyang's economic transition, and this trend will impact the transformation of its urban morphology. For example, the more evenly distributed activities of the socialist past will become concentrated in certain areas, while denser and higher pedestrian flows will develop around metro stations, principal boulevards, or squares.[14] Moreover, new warehouse-style markets taking place outside the city will start affecting the structuring of suburban areas where few developments have been witnessed under socialism.

Suburbanization is also connected to the restructuring of social classes within the city. In an ideal city, there is no class segregation and government strictly controls periodical movements of its residents. However, as social classes begin to diversify based on personal earnings within the market-oriented system, upper classes tend to relocate to areas that offer better living quality.[15] This observation is closely related to the system of the micro-districts. Aiming to consolidate areas of production and residence within a unique spatial structure the micro-district creates a worse environment for residents than an area mainly focused on residential development. Therefore, social class differentiation leads to the segregation and programmatic restructuring within a city.

PYONGYANG TRANSFORMATION

The urban structure and layout of Pyongyang will likely shift alongside major economic transformations that have already begun to take place. It may be beneficial for the city to develop a new set of plans that would reflect and analyse its transition to a market-oriented system.

What growth models are open to Pyongyang? There are several possible development scenarios for the city. One is the "incremental growth model." Unlike most Chinese cities, the small size of Pyongyang's market and the gradual nature of change suggest that the city will transform step by step. The incremental growth model differs from the ad-hoc master plan that ignores the existing socialist city structure and puts an alien structure onto the city. Just as the urban DNA of today's Pyongyang has resulted from mixing of the original socialist master plan and development scheme, the incremental growth model will also be capable of forging a new DNA of Pyongyang, fusing it with the existing one. Thus the second questions to consider is: where would this incremental growth take place? Studies of other socialists cities that have already been through the transition, suggest that the urban mutation would probably take place in areas where the existing socialist structure and the market-oriented elements collide. For instance, the area extending from the axis between Kim Il Sung Square and Juche Tower is the location where ideal socialist morphology along with well-structured infrastructure co-exist. Because of its advantageous infrastructure and location, this area has a strong potential for attracting new investment in a market-oriented economy system. A desire to improve the residential environment will likely force production facilities, like small scale light industries and manufactures inside the micro-district block, to be relocated outside of the city; further, a new mix-used development, a typical development type in capitalist cities, will fill the gap. Similar types of transformation will unfold, albeit in distinct ways, in areas where informal development schemes arise.

How does a new development interact with existing structures of the area? A significant difference between capitalist and socialist cities is parceling of the land. The property politics in socialist countries establish the public property over the urban soil, distinguishing only the individual right to use of the built space. Though its well distribution of programs, there is no parcel system within a block in Pyongyang, whereas the parcel is the basic element that defines ownership in capitalist cities. However, like the notion of production-consumption within a block, the physical relationship between programs is very strong. Thus, when a new parcel system is introduced for the sake of the market-oriented system, instead of just dividing parcel based on existing programs, the inter-relationship of programs should be carefully considered. For example, a parcel can be composed of both production facilities and residential lots, and it can be developed as a mixed-used program. This not only ensures the maintenance of the existing character of Pyongyang as a socialist city, but also makes possible gradual development within a block instead of a whole block scale development.

In short, after seventy years of socialist rule, the twenty-first century Pyongyang is showing early signs of change, and the developments that are taking place are not completely unprecedented. Even so, it will usher in new paradigms, a new hybrid economic system, and in a new social structure. Therefore, a new structuring of Pyongyang is needed. There may be numerous strategies or scenarios to greet this new era and the scenario of incremental growth I have outlined is one I find particularly important. Pyongyang may or may not exhibit gradual growth patterns in the future. This scenario, however, takes into consideration the existing structures of Pyongyang and anticipates how they will be shaped by new times.

Endnotes

1 Springer, Chris. *Pyongyang: The Hidden History of the North Korean Capital.* Budapest: Entente Bt., 2003.

2 Engels, Friedrich. *The Housing Question.* New York: International Publishers, 1935.

3 Bater, James H. *The Soviet City: Ideal and Reality.* Beverly Hills, CA: Sage Publications, 1980.

4 Treadgold, Donald W. *Twentieth Century Russia.* Chicago: Rand McNally, 1964.

5 Zhao, Liang. *Modernizing Beijing: Moments of Political and Spatial Centrality.* 2005.

6 *Ibid.*

7 Crowley, David, and Susan Emily. Reid. *Socialist Spaces: Sites of Everyday Life in the Eastern Bloc.* Oxford: Berg, 2002.

8 Kim, Wŏn. *Sahoejuŭi Tosi Kyehoek (Socialist Urban Planning).* Seoul: Posŏnggak, 1998.

9 *Ibid.*

10 Kim, Youngkyu. *T'ongil Han'guk*, 1988.

11 Kim, Wŏn. *Sahoejuŭi Tosi Kyehoek (Socialist Urban Planning).* Seoul: Posŏnggak, 1998.

12 Faiola, Anthony. "For North Korea, Openness Proves a Two-Way Street; As Increased Trade and Communication Bring Outside World In, More Citizens Are Spurred to Leave." *The Washington Post*, December 13, 2004. Accessed 2016. http://www.highbeam.com/doc/1P2-228101.html?refid=easy_hf.

13 Andrusz, Gregory D., Michael Harloe, and Iván Szelényi. *Cities after Socialism: Urban and Regional Change and Conflict in Post-socialist Societies.* Oxford: Blackwell, 1996.

14 Axenov, Konstantin, Isolde Brade, and Evgenij Bondarchuk. *The Transformation of Urban Space in Post-Soviet Russia.* Abingdon Oxon: Routledge, 2006.

15 Wu, Fulong, Jiang Xu, and Anthony G. O. Yeh. *Urban Development in Post-reform China: State, Market, and Space.* Abingdon, Oxon: Routledge, 2007.

단결

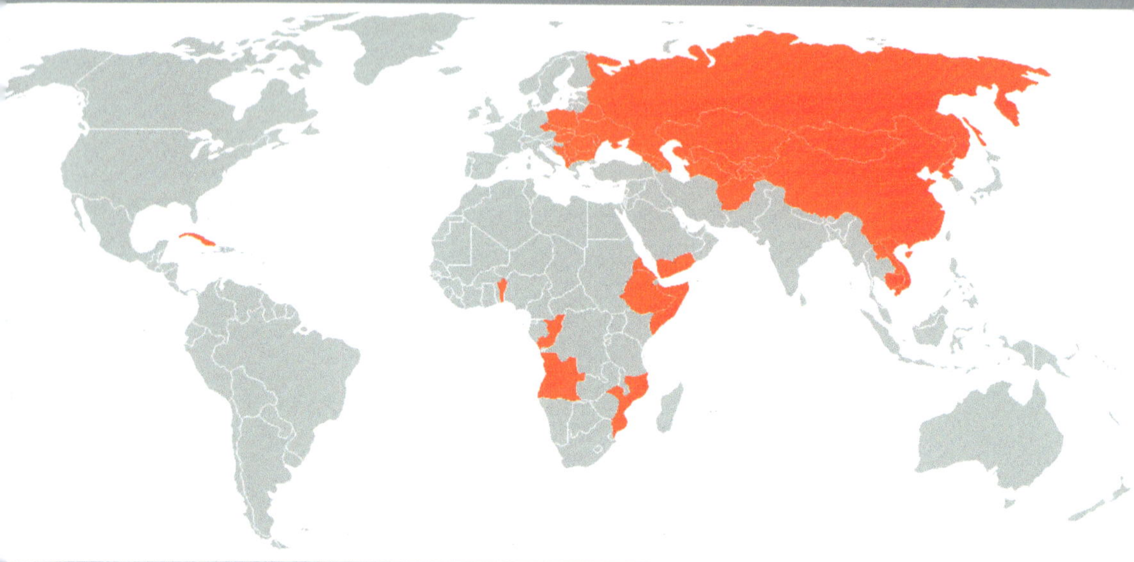

Socialist Countries in 1960s

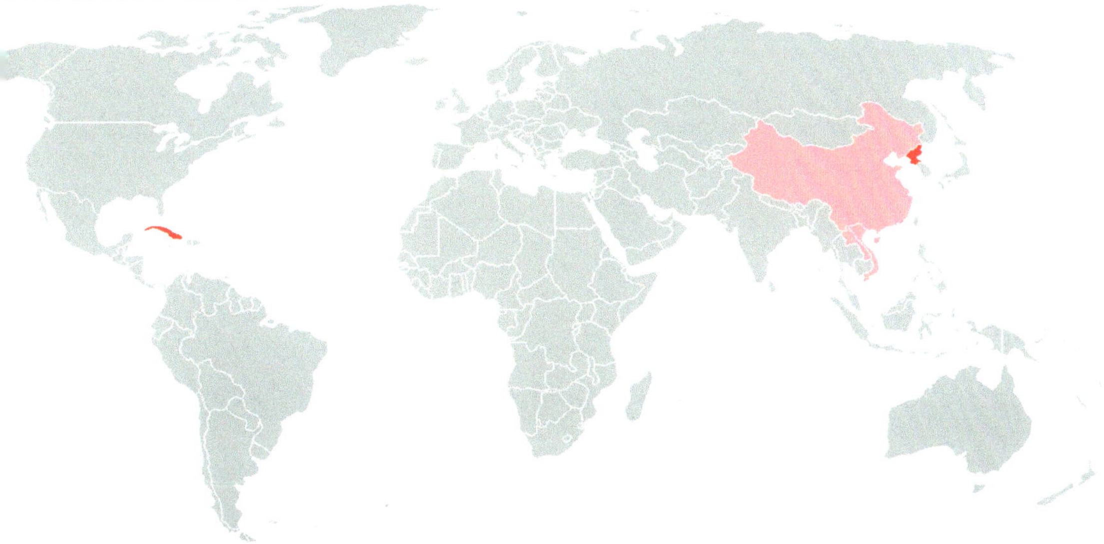

Socialist Countries in 2000s

02
A SOCIALIST CITY

SOCIALIST CITY VS. CAPITALIST CITY

> Since in the capitalist city, private ownership of property was one of the most important sources of taxation, it was regarded as a maxim of planning to increase taxable private lands as much as possible, while minimizing the tax consuming public domain. For urban planning typology this resulted in a demand for broad corridor streets, thoroughfares suitable for development, and a neglect of public areas and green spaces.[1]

A structure of a city is the physical end of a mixture of two factors: constants and variables. The topography, climate, or location of a city that hardly changes throughout periods can be defined as constants, whereas the social structure, political system, or economic structure can be categorized as variables. The comparison between a socialist and a capitalist city cannot be undertaken without a comparison of these variables. What is interesting here is that one is a political system and another is an economic structure. This is because in a socialist city, the political system and its translation into centrally planned economy and the public property over the territory where the individual profit has no direct importance, impacts deeply the urban planning of the city rather than the sole economic structure. On the other hand, instead of a democratic structure, capitalism as essentially an economical structure, with regulations depending on the economic value of the land and the plus-value of its exploitation, has another type of influence on the physical form of a city.

These two alternatives, socialism and capitalism, have been the most influential ideologies and paradigms since early the twentieth century and are still, politically and in different urban initiatives competing with each other. As Banik-Schweitzer mentioned, a city that is based on capitalism has urban morphologies and structures that result from its economic structure. Hence, urban spaces in a capitalist city are configured following the logic of

Bucharest, Romania

capital and its flow transforms the city structure. In contrast, urban spaces in a socialist city are structured based on the logic of socialism without having in mind the land values determined by capital exchange. This no-land-value condition made it possible for a socialist city to create a series of public spaces within major or central parts of the city, areas that would have been estimated as the most valuable in a capitalist city.

Thus, the difference between two ideologies, creates grounds for strikingly physical differences in urban space. As Winner answered in response to the question, "Do artifacts have politics?", the physical form of a city is strongly affected by the dominant paradigm of a society.[2] In his discussion he pointed to the example of a bridge in New York that connected the city to the beach but denied access to buses, resulting in social segregation on the beach, for making it impossible the lower classes without private vehicles to reach the beach. In the case of urban structures, due to their close relation with urban planning and policy, they are not only affected by, but also created, based on the logic of political systems or economic structures.

SOCIALIST CITY

This brings us to our following questions. What exactly is a socialist city? What makes urban structures in a socialist city different from those in a capitalist city? Further, can we affirm that a socialist city has ever fully existed in reality? From their series of studies of urbanization in socialist countries, French and Hamilton (1979) discovered crucial differences between socialist and capitalist urban organization. Three main reasons that cause these differences are different systems of collective ownership of urban land and infrastructure, the tendencies of central planning system, and comprehensive strategies for the development of cities within the national settlement network.[3] Thus, though there may be various common factors, we can distinguish a socialist city that has different physical urban structure from a capitalist city.

> The abolition of private property, removal of privileged classes, and application of equity principles espoused by Marxist/socialist leaders should radically alter urban patterns. In the housing arena, the expectation would be one of non-discriminatory, non-spatially differentiated housing in general. No social or occupational group would have better or more favorably located residential sites so that one would find a randomly distributed housing pattern. Similarly, public services of all kinds, including transportation, should be of equal quality, availability and accessibility. Commuting to work…would be minimized and no group would be more dependent on or penalized by such travel than others. Such amenities as high quality physical environment, including recreational environment, would be equally accessible to all. All such urban conditions would be similarly equitably arranged and available.[4]

The idea of socialist urban planning emerged in conjunction with the idea of socialism and was first applied as part of socialist-utopian settlements from the first half of 19th century. As Marx and Engels began to formulate their theory of socialism starting from the exploration of urban – social and environmental- problems in capitalist cities during the nineteenth century, the possibilities of resolving these problems became one way of articulating and applying their ideology. An industrialized city in nineteenth-century Europe was overcrowded, with dense tissue chaotically organized, and contaminated. The logic of capital dominated the whole city and there was no "planning" strategy to resolve the problems of urban functionality and urban growth. During his stay in Manchester in 1842, Engels came to realize that it was not only congestion, but also the working-class seclusion, to be part of a larger, systematic mechanism for social division that had been built into the very structure of the city.[5] This observation from Manchester served him to ground an important founding tenet of socialist urban planning. Engels saw shortages in the Haussmann style of urban development which may have helped resolve the problem of congestion, but left the matter of social segregation in the city untouched. Thus, one of the most important tasks for socialist urban planners was to de-activate the mechanisms that produced the spatial class-separation within the city in order to achieve a major functionality that would exemplify the socialist idea of class-equality in an urban structure.

This idea of class-equality also leads to the idea of diminishing differ-

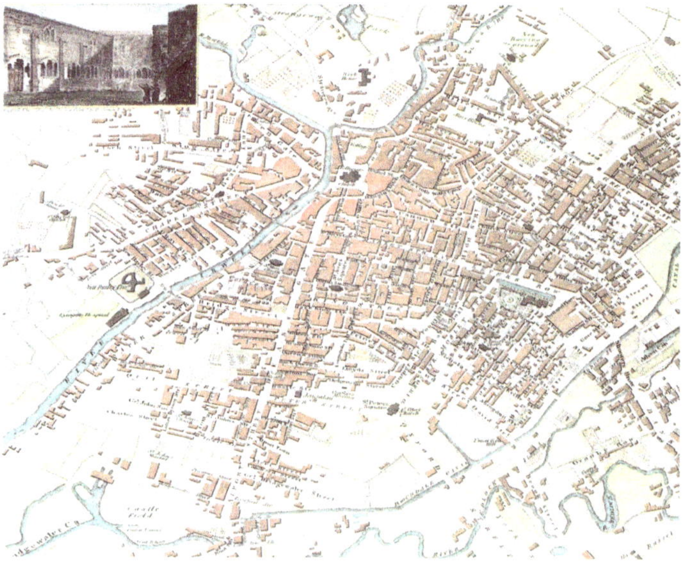

Manchester, 1801

ence between urban and rural areas. Marx analysed the social phenomena of different settlements based on dialectical materialism, and understood that urban and rural areas were not separated areas that do not interact; instead, they were to be interrelated, comprising one entity.[6] In his book "Capital" (1867), Marx points to the 'city' as a space and form generated mainly by financial and industrial capitalists to create and assure their profits through the labour division between urban and rural or physical and intellectual.[7] Like Engels, Marx insisted that this uncontrolled private urban redevelopment conformed a vicious circle that caused and augmented polarization between urban and rural area. Thus, he argued that the control over the finances and territory should be a public domain in order to resolve efficiently the underlying problem of distinction and discrimination between urban and rural areas.

Five guiding ideas of socialist urban planning emerged from Marx and Engels' observations and arguments.[8] First, socialist urban planning was linked to the notion of 'disurbanism' that was first developed by Mikhail Okhitovich. One of the socialist's arguments was that the base for the fast city growth should be the increased immigration from rural areas. Here, proletariat from rural areas inevitably confronts the bourgeoisie as the process of capitalist exploitation starts. Thus, they theoretically preferred smaller cities that included rural and urban components to large metropolis with evident class division. Second, socialist planners criticized urban renovation. As mentioned previously, private urban developments only focus on improving living conditions of the upper class, instead of the workers, a fact directly related to capital flow. Following the urban redevelopment, the land value rises and people who cannot afford the increased rent are forced to move out from the area. It causes a socially and economically motivated spatial segregation in a city. Thirdly, socialists insist on the functional and cultural synthesis of urban and rural areas. According to Marx's dialectical materialism, the two confronting factors, rural and urban,should be combined in a new city structure that has both rural and urban characteristics. Fourth, well-developed urban plan has become an important factor in socialist urban planning. A plan-less development, mostly dominated by the logic of capital, causes urban problems such as congestion, pollution, and poor living environment. Thus, a well-planned development strategy could solve those problems and prevent the endless expansion of a city. Lastly, the state intervention and strict governmental control over the city are key ideas of socialist urban planning. To realize it, socialists insist that public administration should own all lands and means of production so that private capital can no longer dominate the logic of urban development. In short, the ideology of socialism elevated to the logic of the nation, becomes a dominant power that controls all the development strategies in a city.

BUILDING A SOCIALIST CITY

Socialist parties that had gained power through revolution, in many cases parallel to the WWII destruction, chose to reconstruct cities in order to resolve spatial problems caused by the social segregation and formally manifest their ideologies through a physical structure. Unlike capitalist cities, the reconstruction, or rather, a creation of the ideal socialist city was lead by a strong revolutionary party with a powerful support from the people. Through a new physical layout of the city, it aimed to resolve problems that were caused during the preceding capitalist era and to strengthen the unity of the people.[9]

Vladimir Ilich Lenin was the first socialist who actually had a chance to bring the physical structure of socialism to fruition. During his seven years of govern following the October Revolution of 1917, he structured new systems and regulations in the city based on Marx and Engels' ideas. In particular, three reforms he promoted had a huge impact over socialist urban planning strategies: a law on the confiscation of private apartments and tenement houses, the nationalization of banks, industries, and consumers' facilities, and a drastic imposition on the socialization of the land. Especial-

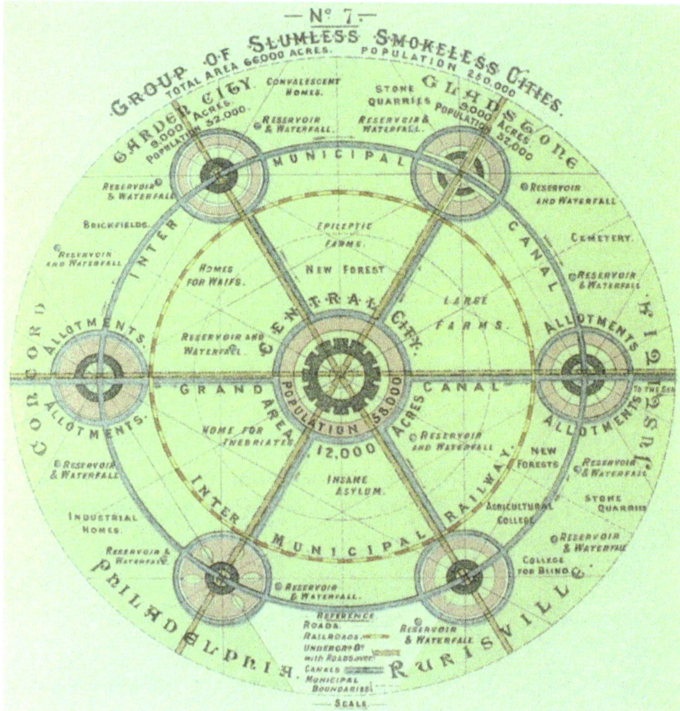

Garden City Diagram, E. Howard

ly, when Lenin said "We must aim at the fusion of industry and agriculture, based on the rigorous application of science, combined with the utilization of collective labor, and by means of a more diffused settlement pattern for the people. We must end the loneliness, demoralization, and remoteness of the village, as well as the unnatural concentration of vast masses of people in the cities," his arguments on rural and urban areas became a strong back bone of socialist urban planning idea to limit the size of a city and to abolish difference between urban and rural areas.[10] In the end, it has become a blueprint for other socialist cities after World War II, including Pyongyang in North Korea.

Obviously, Moscow was the first city that explored and implemented the ideal of socialist city planning strategy. After the revolution, Lenin decided to build a new Soviet capital in Moscow instead of St. Petersburg. Afterwards, a series of debates and discussions were generated in the 1920s on how to rebuild Moscow as a socialist city. And one important theory that had influenced urban planning of Moscow was Ebenezer Howard's Garden City Movement.[11] With his diagram, Howard proposed several key points to solve problems of nineteenth century industrialized cities. The first feature was that the garden city did not allow individual ownership: parcels were to be administrated only by a common authority. The increase of density was to be prevented so that land values could remain stable. Second, the garden city controlled the urban growth and limited its population. The "remaining" land in the city could not become available for new development, but was to be reserved for recreational or agriculture areas. Third, Howard insisted on the importance of balance between town and country.[12] These key features of Garden City Movement were strongly influence to the idea of socialist urban planning. Both "urbanist" and "disurbanist" theories that emerged in the 1920s in Moscow adopted the idea of effective use of green zone in the movement, and the idea of optimizing, or limiting, the size of a city was also borrowed from the Garden City Movement. And most of all, the idea of abolishing difference between urban and rural areas and nationalizing land were not much different from the idea of socialism.[13]

The "Urbanism" group further explored residential interventions focusing on communal city life instead of individual family life. They proposed a super block residential development with communal kitchens, dining halls, and kindergartens separated from apartments. This idea influenced the neighborhood scale conceived as units of housing blocks with all the services needed for communal life.[14] They also proposed standardization of buildings that strongly influenced prefabricated construction in all socialist cities.

On the other hand, the group of "Disurbanists" focused on larger planning strategies of how to abolish the differences between urban and rural areas. They planned a network of several satellite towns with a central administrative town, and introduced "green belts" between them to control the expansion of each settlement. Like the Garden City Movement, they restricted the town size to 32,000 residents. The central administrative town that linked others together was also restricted to 58,000.[15]

Through series of discussions, Moscow adopted a planning strategy called the "General Plan for the Reconstruction of Moscow" in 1935 (Moscow 1935 Master Plan) that included several important socialist urban planning features. It restricted the city population to five million by expanding the city area from 286 km2 to 600 km2. With lower density, the plan proposed 30% of green so that the city not only provided enough public leisure space but also could control expansion of the city and its population. Amongst other reasons, however, Marx and Engels' idea of abolishing the

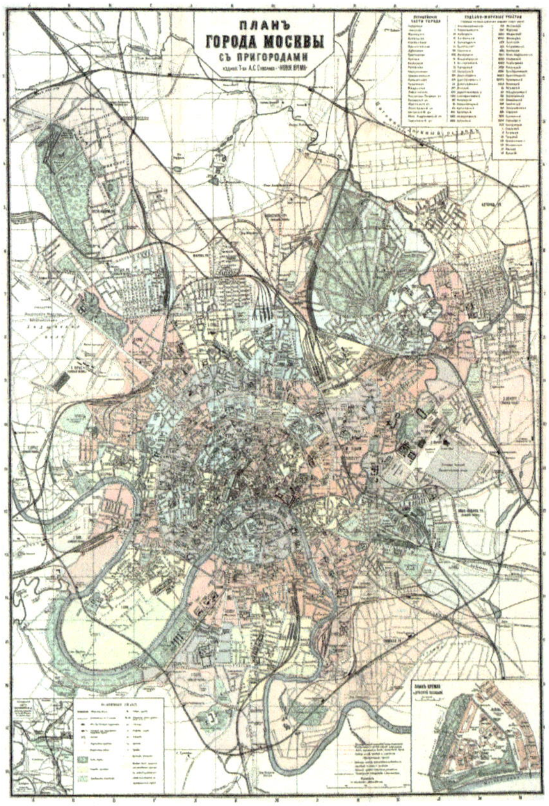

Moscow General Plan, 1935

Moscow Plan, 1917

difference between urban and rural areas through ruralization of a city was the key reason of structuring green spaces in the city. Thus, building farm lands within urban areas was as important as creating urban parks, and this resulted in the physical morphology of Moscow that had both green belt and farm lands. Also the concept of "mikrorayon" (microdistrict) was the basic idea of residential planning in Moscow 1935 Master Plan.

> First used in the 1935 Moscow Plan, the 'microdistrict'(mikrorayon) was defined as a self-contained residential district with an area of 75-125 acres and a population ranging between 5,000 and 15,000 (Sawers, 1978, Bater, 1980, pp. 109-111). Four to five microdistricts, each with a service radius of 300-400 metres, made a residential complex. During the Stalin era, the use of the microdistrict was supplanted by the superblock schema. After Stalin's death, as the new Party leader Nikita Khrushchev was determined to set the Soviet Union on a modified path, the microdistrict idea re-emerged and received wide acceptance almost immediately. [16]

The micro-district was a socialist spatial concept that was to systemize communal life for the public. Within a superblock, public services such as schools, community or retail facilities closely related to communal life were planned together with residential apartments. This maximized the benefits for residents and minimized commuting time for workers. Also, the number of residents of the 'microrayon', planned around 10,000~12,000, was the most effective size to reduce the cost of public services.[17] This system was widely adopted in other socialist cities in their residential development plans.

SOCIALIST URBAN MORPHOLOGY

Including the 1935 Moscow Master Plan, J.H Bater pointed out ten specific guidelines of socialist urban planning: 1) limited city size, 2) state control of housing, 3) planned development of residential areas, 4) spatial equality in the distribution of items of collective consumption, 5) limited commuting to work, 6) stringent land-use zoning, 7) rationalized traffic flow, 8) extensive green space, 9) town planning as an integral part of national planning, 10) symbolism and the central city[18]

Interestingly, several features that Bater pointed out are also seen in capitalist cities as well. This is due to the fact that urban planning strategies in general, whether they are socialist or not, share a host of urban problems, and some of the features cited above provided ways to solve those common issues. Amongst other socialist urban planning features, however, there are three major factors that I would like to highlight which strongly influenced the physical morphology of socialist cities. These include the city of production, city of green, and city of symbolism.

> **City of Production**
> In ancient China, a nation comprised of large, semi-imperial and semi-colonial cities where the governing class gathered (e.g. Beijing), were mostly consumption cities. Besides depriving the working classes, the existence and prosperity of such cities relied entirely on the exploitation of the countryside. "After we entered those large cities, we cannot tolerate such phenomena. To get rid of such phenomena, we have to systematically and rapidly recover and develop production.[19]

After the revolution, the communist party abolished the distinction between capital and labour. Since the party doctrine argued that all socioeconomic and urban problems were the consequence of class segregation and accumulation of capital by powerful minority, it insisted that all inhabitants should be re-educated as the working class able to work for production in some way. This idea is strongly linked to the idea of abolishing the difference between urban and rural areas, as well as abolishing the distinction between intellectual and physical work. The planning of agricultural areas in the city was applied not only to ensure that the city would have rural features, but also in order to donate it productive capacity. Thus, within socialist cities, both agricultural and industrial areas were carefully planned, increasing the presence of the working class, and granting the workers the major role in the city at the expense of other classes. For instance, in China, in the late 1940s, Mao Zedong insisted that the city should be transformed from a city of consumption to a city of production so that the increased number of workers could reinforce the revolution and stabilize the society. He attempted to increase the proportion of workers from 4% to 25% of the population, which was the same as Moscow, while planning more industrial areas and workshops close to residential districts.[20]

In fact, in socialist planning, the relationship between residential and industrial areas is a very important factor that determines the larger structure of the city. In a linear city diagram, N.A. Milyutin, a Soviet planner, placed production enterprises and schools together in the same band, reflecting Engels' conviction that education and labour should be united. This band, placed parallel to the residential zone, interacts strongly with it while minimizing commuting distance. These production enterprises and workshops are also injected into the microdistrict organization to provide a communal working life. In his book *Remaking Chinese Urban Form,* Lu defines the work unit as a revised form of the microdistrict in China, offer-

Potsdamer Platz,1932

ing a variety of social services such as shops, canteens, clinics, nurseries and libraries. He also indicates that a typical work unit brings the workplace, residential facilities, and social facilities in close proximity to one or several walled compounds.[21] Therefore, a microdistrict super block becomes a self-sufficient community in terms of productions and consumption.

City of Green

The International Garden City Society opened a branch in St. Petersburg in 1913 and in Moscow in 1922 after the Communist Revolution. Howard's idea to marry town and country was seen as a perfect match for the Marxist aim to "Abolish the Distinction between Town and Country." Howard's emphasis on planning and social change was also welcomed by the Socialists. His theory had a long and significant influence on Soviet town planning, which in turn influenced town planning in China.[22]

Microdistrict, Gldani, Georgia

As mentioned earlier, the concept of the green city or the park city is one of the major ideals of socialist urban planning. As Howard proposed in his Garden City diagram, socialist planners also conceived the green area as an infrastructure that restricted expansion of each town. Therefore, green areas placed throughout the city not only improved the aesthetic and ecologic environment but also functioned as buffer zones between towns. Landscaped parks as well as agricultural and production areas inside the city were planned as components of the green infrastructure.

In addition to Howard's green infrastructure concept, socialist planners also proposed a green park as an urban public space within the city. For instance, in the Soviet Union, there is a hierarchy of green parks based on their scale and location. Parks of different scales: micro parks, city parks, and forest parks are distributed in corresponding areas such as the micro-district, urban and suburban area.[23] Therefore, the green area is not only a buffer between towns but also an urban leisure space for the public.

As Banik-Schweitzer argued, the green area, created either as a buffer zone or leisure space, has no benefit for taxation and is a "weak space" in a capitalist city. On the other hand, in a socialist city that prioritizes public value over the logic of capital, the green area that provides a place for rest as well as a generally healthier environment for the public is the most important urban space that distinguishes it from a capitalist city. Hence, Leonid Brezhnev, the General Secretary of the Communist Party of the Soviet Union (1964-1982), insisted that creating enough parks, especially micro parks and city parks, was the most effective way to make Moscow the model communist city.[24] Later, various other socialist cities, including Pyongyang, turned their focus to creating city's green areas in order to exemplify their socialist character in consonance with the state ideology.

City of Symbolism

> Many planners aimed for a socialist space that met the population's needs through communal living, eating, childcare, laundry and more. The counter-view sought to build monumental architecture that would serve as symbols of power and representations of the Soviet state and its institutions, with the names and statues of Marx, Engels and other socialist luminaries prominent throughout. What transpired was a combination of pre-revolutionary and NEP-era utopian-idealist schemes for the new city all bundled up in the latest verbiage about the socialist system's concern for the population's well-being.[25]

Most socialist cities are organized in reference to the central squares such as the Red Square in Moscow, Tiananmen Square in Beijing, and Kim Il Sung Square in Pyongyang. Although the creation of symbolic squares was not a main socialist planning strategy listed by any of the early socialist urban planners or mentioned in Marx, Engels or Lenin's theory on the city and society, they have become the most important urban forms that distinguish socialist from capitalist cities. The morphological characteristics of those symbolic urban spaces were influenced by the context of socialist revolution. Socialist parties realized that humongous open spaces were needed for large parades or demonstrations as they established their governments in the wake of social revolution. Large parades and demonstrations were not only to propagate the victory of the revolution, but also to strengthen the ideology of socialism so that the socialist party could stabilize society after the revolution.

Like Red Square and Tiananmen Square, most of these main urban squares in socialist cities were created around areas that held major symbolic value in the preceding era. Their physical locations are decided based on the idea that the people had taken over the city from the old regime. Therefore, they are not just open spaces like urban plazas in medieval or capitalist cities, but major urban morphologies that have strong symbolic and political meaning attached and, as mentioned, the most important state or military parades and demonstrations are held in those spaces. Sometimes grounds

Red Square, 1801

are reconfigured to create this vast, symbolic square for such events. For instance, when the Red Square was created in front of the Kremlin during the Soviet era, Kazan Cathedral and Iverskaya Chapel, along with the Resurrection Gates, were demolished to create ample space for military parades. In parallel with symbolic squares, considerable numbers of statues and monuments are also created to propagate the victory of revolution, and urban plazas and parks are named after the party leaders. These secondary urban features are distributed through the city instead of being concentrated in a unique principal symbolic square; this way they become nodes of each functional area. Because of the hierarchical differences between a major symbolic square and each node, a socialist city inevitably begins to exhibit a spatial hierarchy that conflicts with the garden city idea of evenly distributed towns. In turn, the administrative district, that concentrates the state power and where major symbolic spaces are located, becomes a "city centre" while others become lower-level districts, depending on the distance from the centre. However, in spite of this inherent tension within the ideal concept of the socialist city, most socialist cities concentrated on creating symbolic spaces that eventually became their most distinctive morphological features.

Red Square, 2000s

Endnotes

1 Renate Banik-Schweitzer, *"Urban Visions, Plans, and Projects: 1890–1937"*, in Eve Blau and Monika Platzer, eds, Shaping the Great City: Modern Architecture in Central Europe 1890–1937, Munich, Prestel, 1999.

2 Langdon Winner, 'Do Artifacts Have Politics?', Daedalus,109, no.1(Winter 1980), reprinted in Donald McKenzie and Judy Wajcman, eds, *The Social Shaping of Technology* (London: Open university Press, 1985)

3 Enyedi, György. "Urbanization Under Socialism." In *Cities after Socialism: Urban and Regional Change and Conflict in Post-socialist Societies*. Oxford: Blackwell, 1996.

4 Demko, George J., and Joanna Regulska. "Socialism And Its Impact On Urban Processes And The City." *Urban Geography* 8, no. 4 (1987): 289-92. doi:10.2747/0272-3638.8.4.289.

5 Marcus, S. *Reading the Illegible*. Barrett, G, 2001.

6 Saunders, Peter. *Social Theory and the Urban Question*. New York, NY: Holmes & Meier, 1981.

7 Marx, Karl, Friedrich Engels, Samuel Moore, Edward Aveling, Marie Sachey, and Herbert Lamm. *Karl Marx: Capital: Edited by Friedrich Engels ; And, Manifesto of the CommunistParty by Karl Marx and Friedrich Engels*. Chicago: Encyclopaedia Britannica, 1990.

8 Kim, Wŏn. *Sahoejuŭi Tosi Kyehoek (Socialist Urban Planning)*. Seoul: Posŏnggak, 1998.

9 Fisher, Jack C. *Planning the City of the Socialist Man.* Ithaca, NY: Center for Urban Development Research, Cornell University, 1962.

10 May, Ernst. "City building in the USSR." In *Russia: An Architecture for World Revolution.* Edited by Lissitzky, El. Cambridge: M.I.T. Press, 1970.

11 Zhao, Liang. *Modernizing Beijing: Moments of Political and Spatial Centrality.* 2005.

12 Mumford, Lewis. *The Culture of Cities.* New York: Harcourt, Brace and, 1938.

13 Zhao, Liang. *Modernizing Beijing: Moments of Political and Spatial Centrality.* 2005.

14 French, R. A. *Plans, Pragmatism and People: The Legacy of Soviet Planning for Today's Cities.* London: UCL Press, 1995.

15 *Ibid.*

16 Lu, Duanfang. *Remaking Chinese Urban Form: Modernity, Scarcity and Space, 1949-2005.* London: Routledge, 2006.

17 *Obraztsov, A. "What Will our Future Cities Look Like," Soviet Review, II, No. 4 (April, 1961), 34-37*

18 Bater, James H. *The Soviet City: Ideal and Reality.* London: E. Arnold, 1980.

19 Mao, Zedong. "Turing a City of Consumption to a City of Production." *People's Daily,* March 17, 1949.

20 Zhao, Liang. *Modernizing Beijing: Moments of Political and Spatial Centrality.* 2005.

21 Lu, Duanfang. *Remaking Chinese Urban Form: Modernity, Scarcity and Space, 1949-2005.* London: Routledge, 2006.

22 Zhao, Liang. *Modernizing Beijing: Moments of Political and Spatial Centrality.* 2005.

23 Kim, Wŏn. *Sahoejuŭi Tosi Kyehoek (Socialist Urban Planning).* Seoul: Posŏnggak, 1998.

24 French, R. A., and F. E. Ian. Hamilton. *The Socialist City: Spatial Structure and Urban Policy.* Chichester: Wiley, 1979.

25 Qualls, Karl D. "Accommodation and Agitation in Sevastopol: Redefining Socialist Space in the Postwar 'City of Glory'" In *Socialist Spaces: Sites of Everyday Life in the Eastern Bloc.* Oxford: Berg, 2002.

View from Grand People's House
towards Juche Tower

GEOGRAPHY & INFRASTRUCTURE

03 GEOGRAPHY & INFRASTRUCTURE

MAP OF NORTH KOREA

PY

ASIAN CAPITAL CITIES

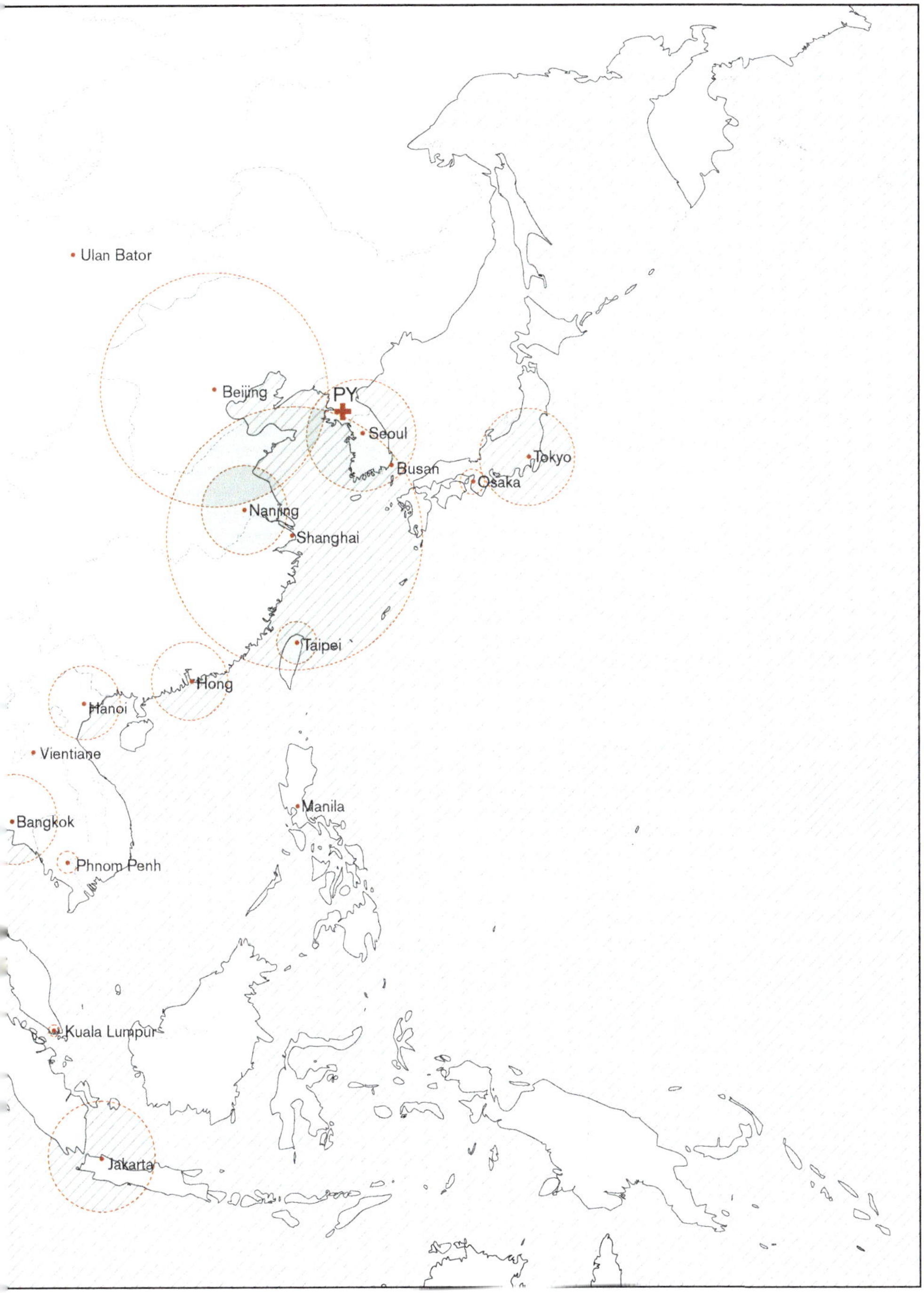
Ulan Bator
Beijing
PY
Seoul
Busan
Tokyo
Osaka
Nanjing
Shanghai
Taipei
Hong
Hanoi
Vientiane
Manila
Bangkok
Phnom Penh
Kuala Lumpur
Jakarta

MAJOR EAST ASIAN CITIES

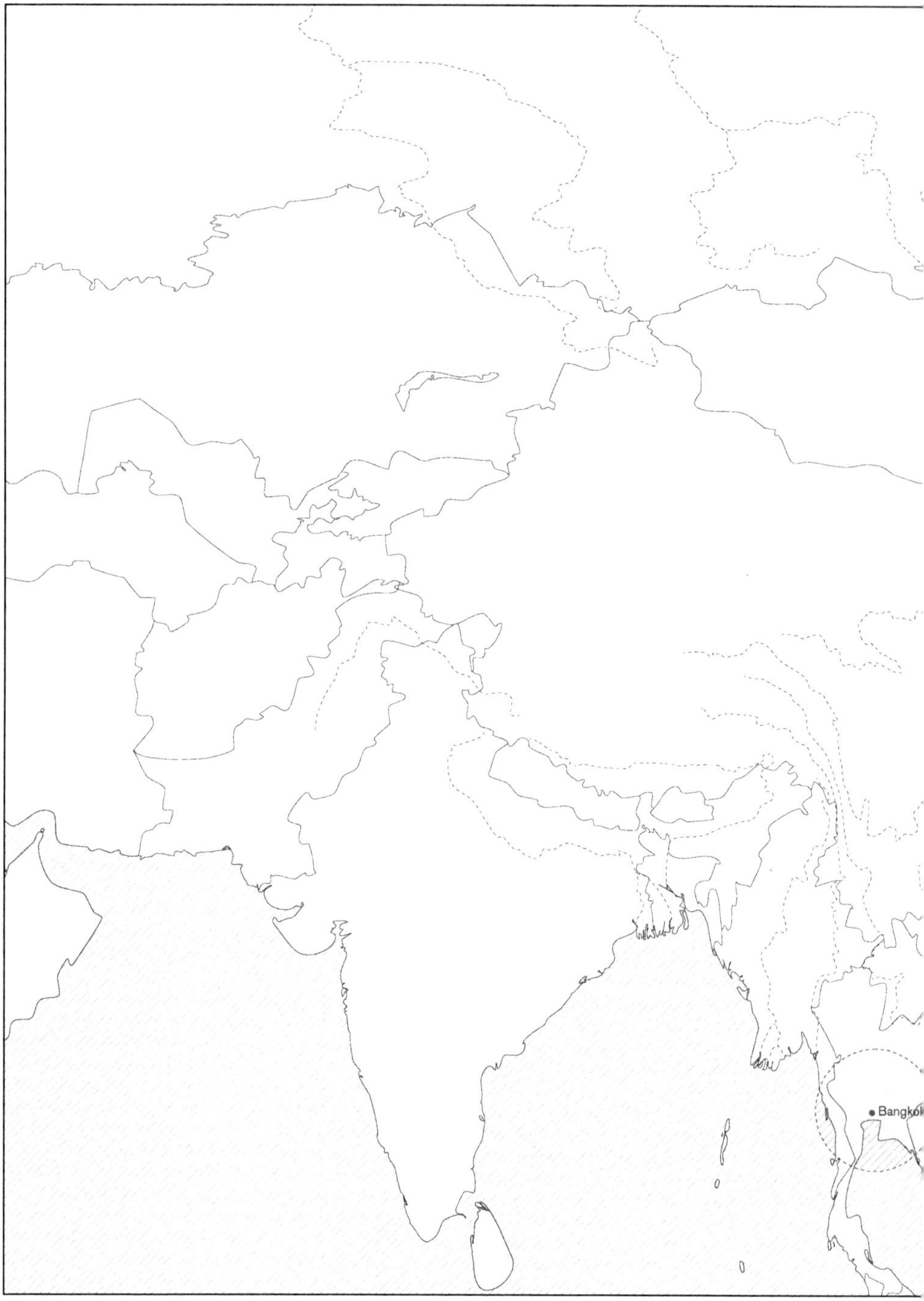

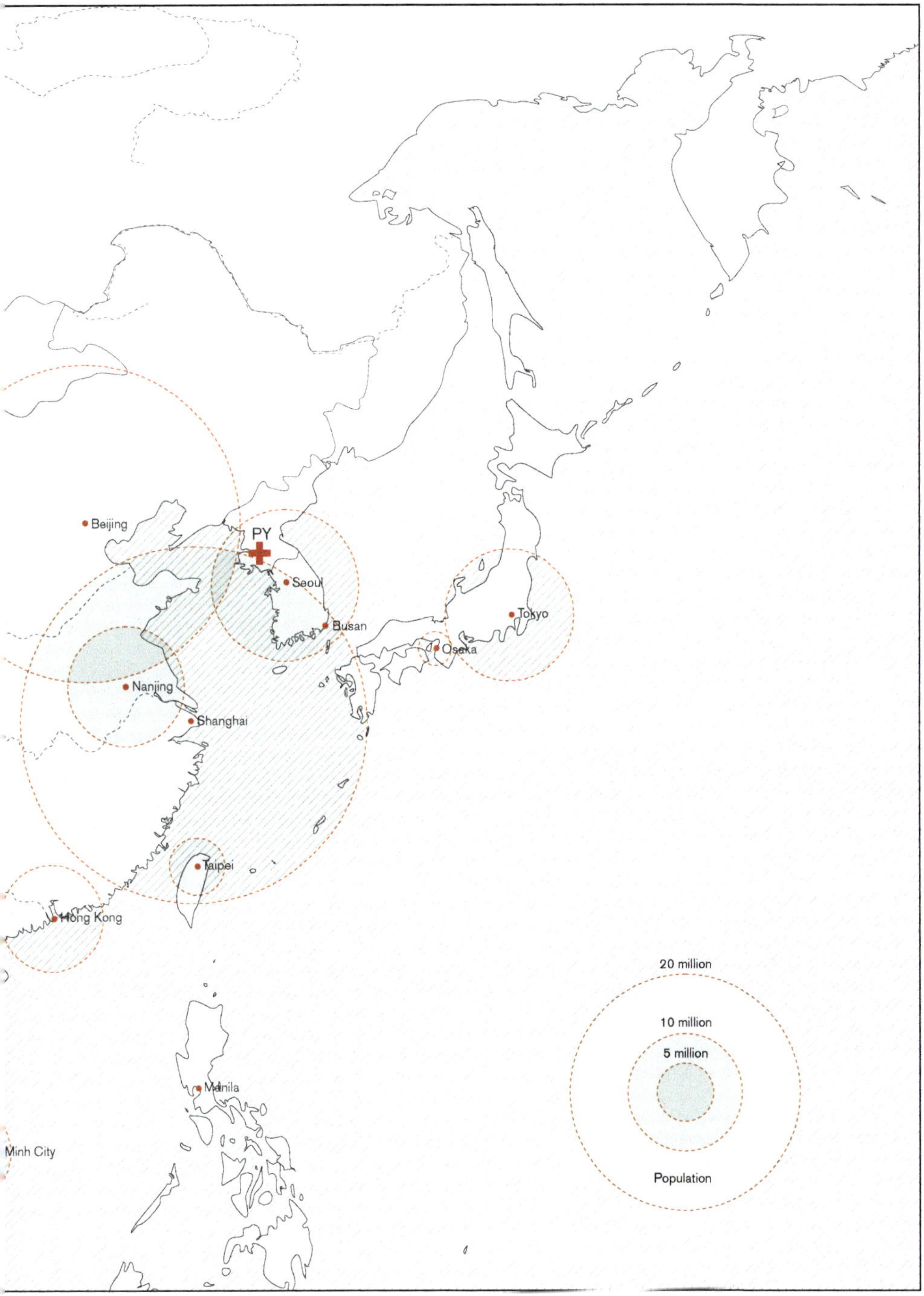
Beijing
PY
Seoul
Busan
Tokyo
Osaka
Nanjing
Shanghai
Taipei
Hong Kong
Manila
Minh City
20 million
10 million
5 million
Population

DISTANCE TO MAJOR CITIES

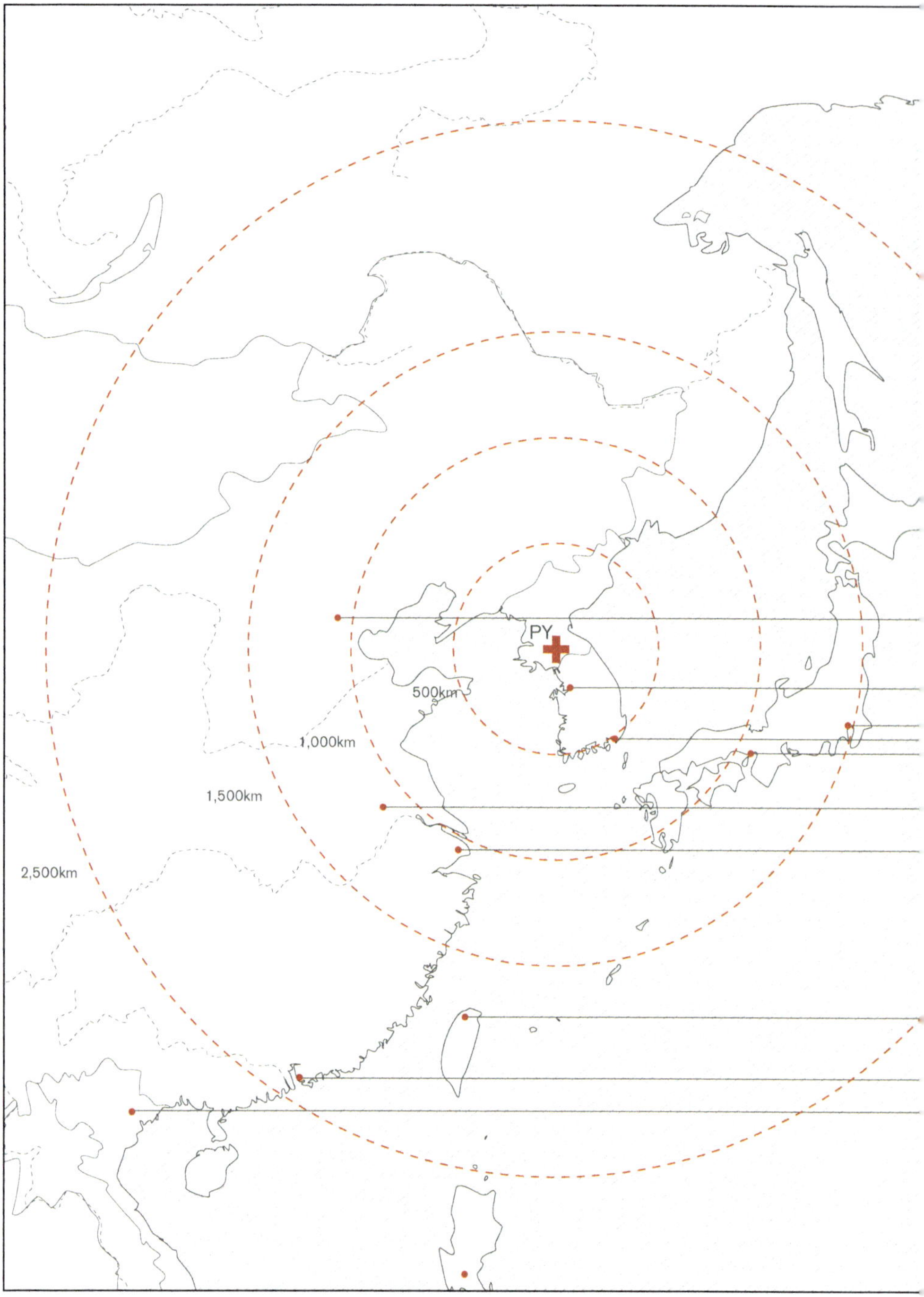

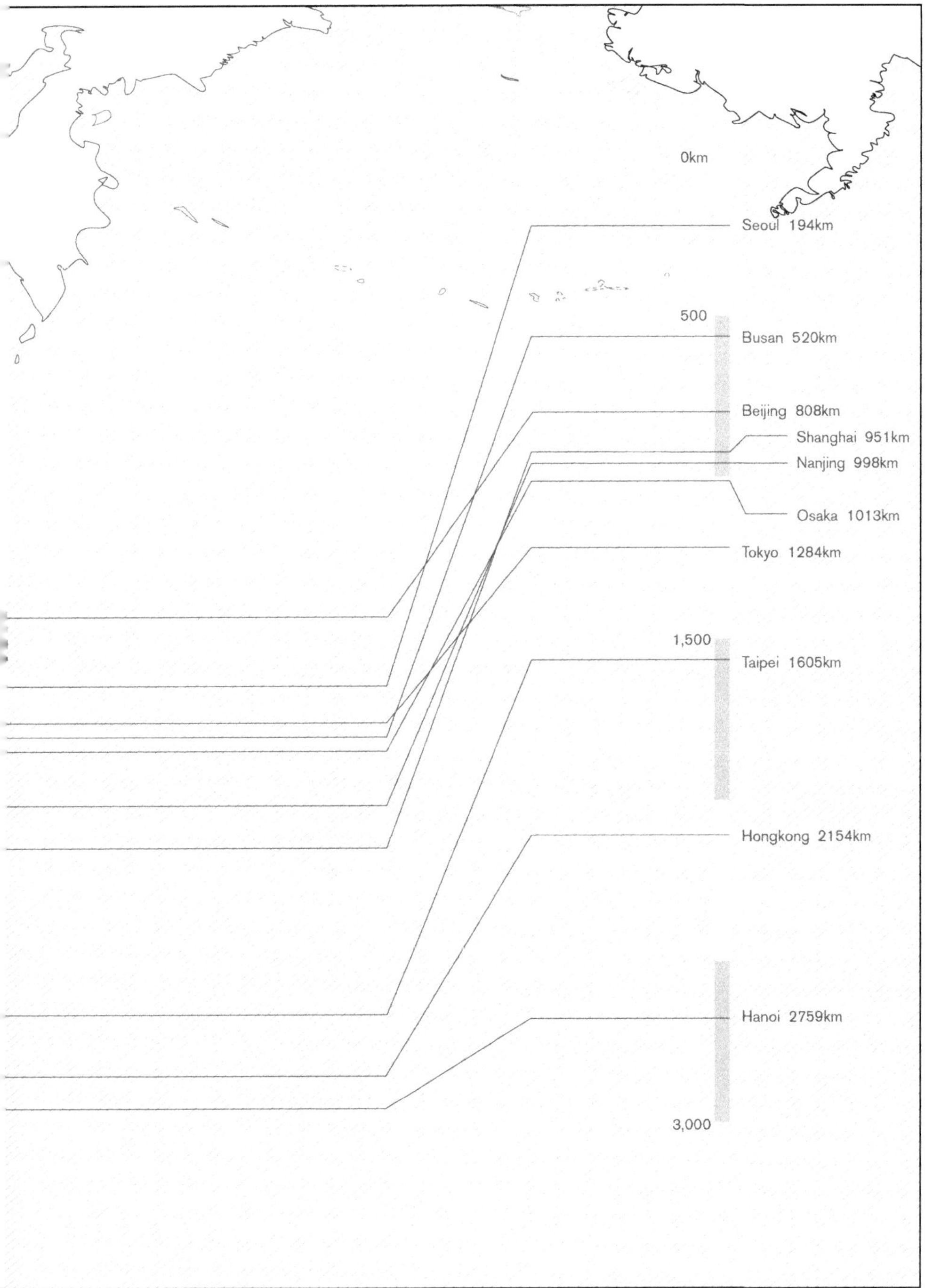
0km
Seoul 194km
500
Busan 520km
Beijing 808km
Shanghai 951km
Nanjing 998km
Osaka 1013km
Tokyo 1284km
1,500
Taipei 1605km
Hongkong 2154km
Hanoi 2759km
3,000

ADMIRAL BOUNDARY

uala Lumpur
Kuwait
Lhasa
Male
Manama
Manila
Moscow
Muscat
Naypyidaw
New Delhi
hnom Penh
Pyongyang
Riyadh
Sanaa
Singapore
Seoul
Taipei
Tashkent
T'bilisi
Iehran
Thimphu
Tokyo
Ulan Bator
Vientiane
Yerevan

AREA COMPARISON

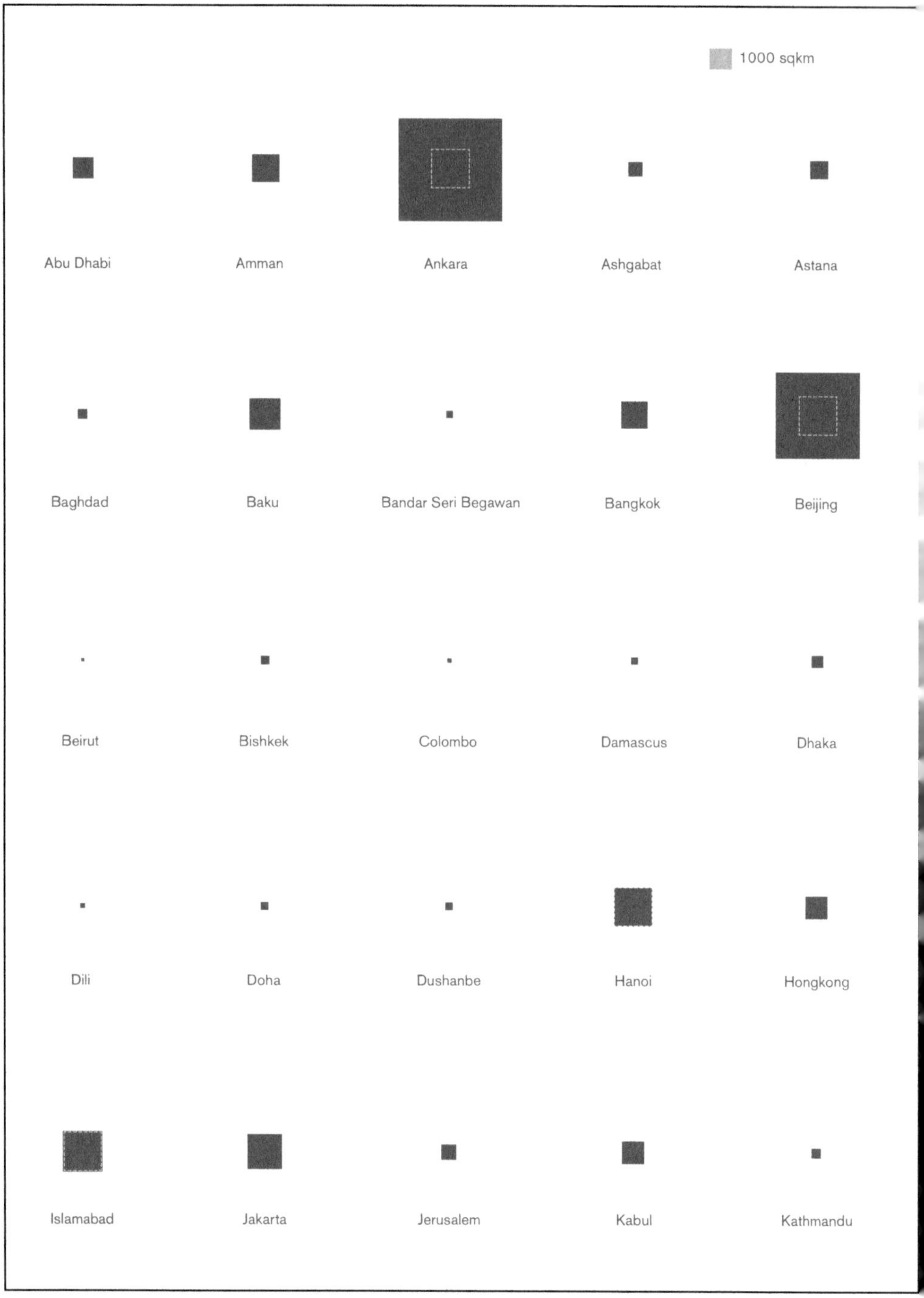

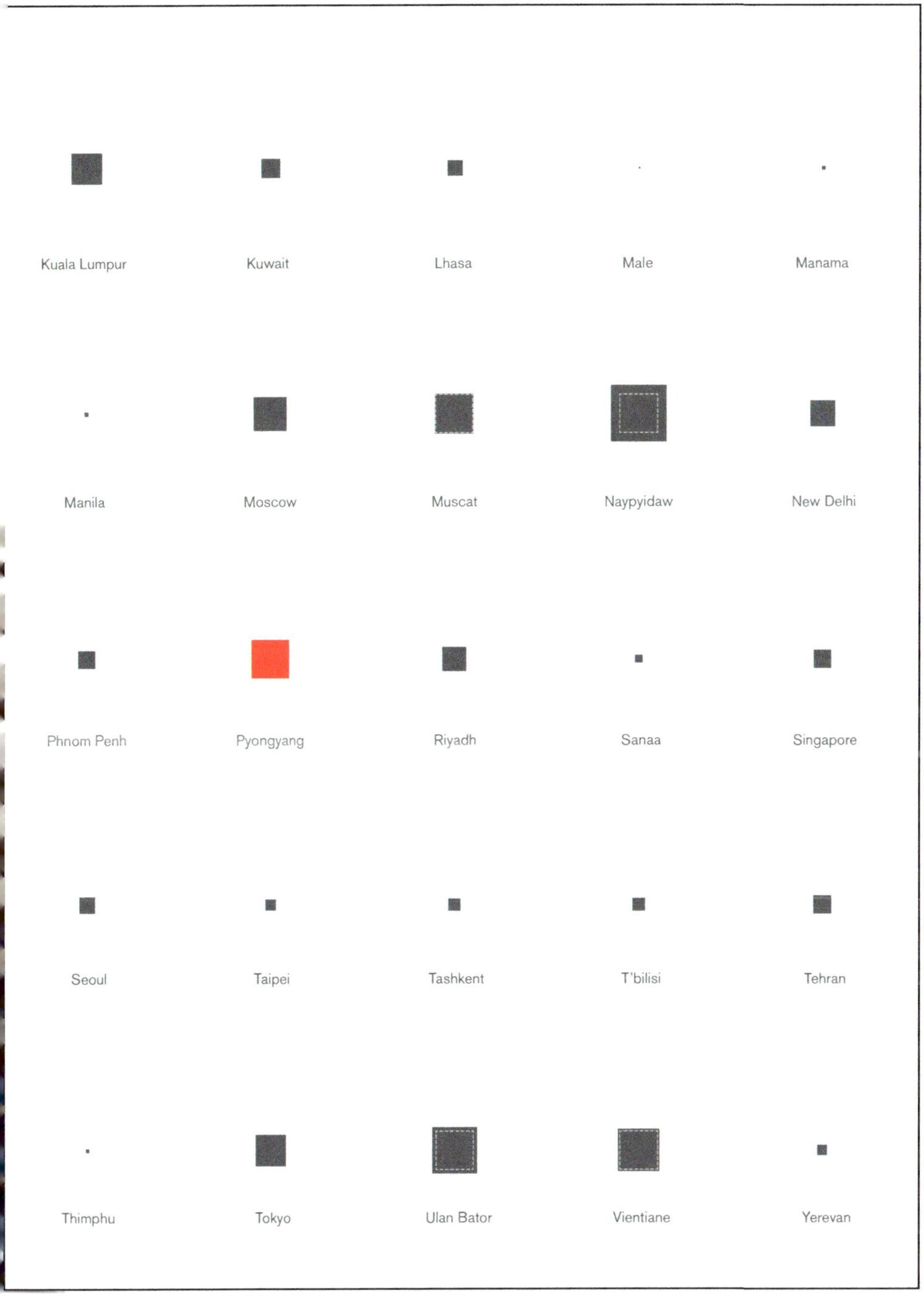
Kuala Lumpur
Kuwait
Lhasa
Male
Manama
Manila
Moscow
Muscat
Naypyidaw
New Delhi
Phnom Penh
Pyongyang
Riyadh
Sanaa
Singapore
Seoul
Taipei
Tashkent
T'bilisi
Tehran
Thimphu
Tokyo
Ulan Bator
Vientiane
Yerevan

POPULATION DATA

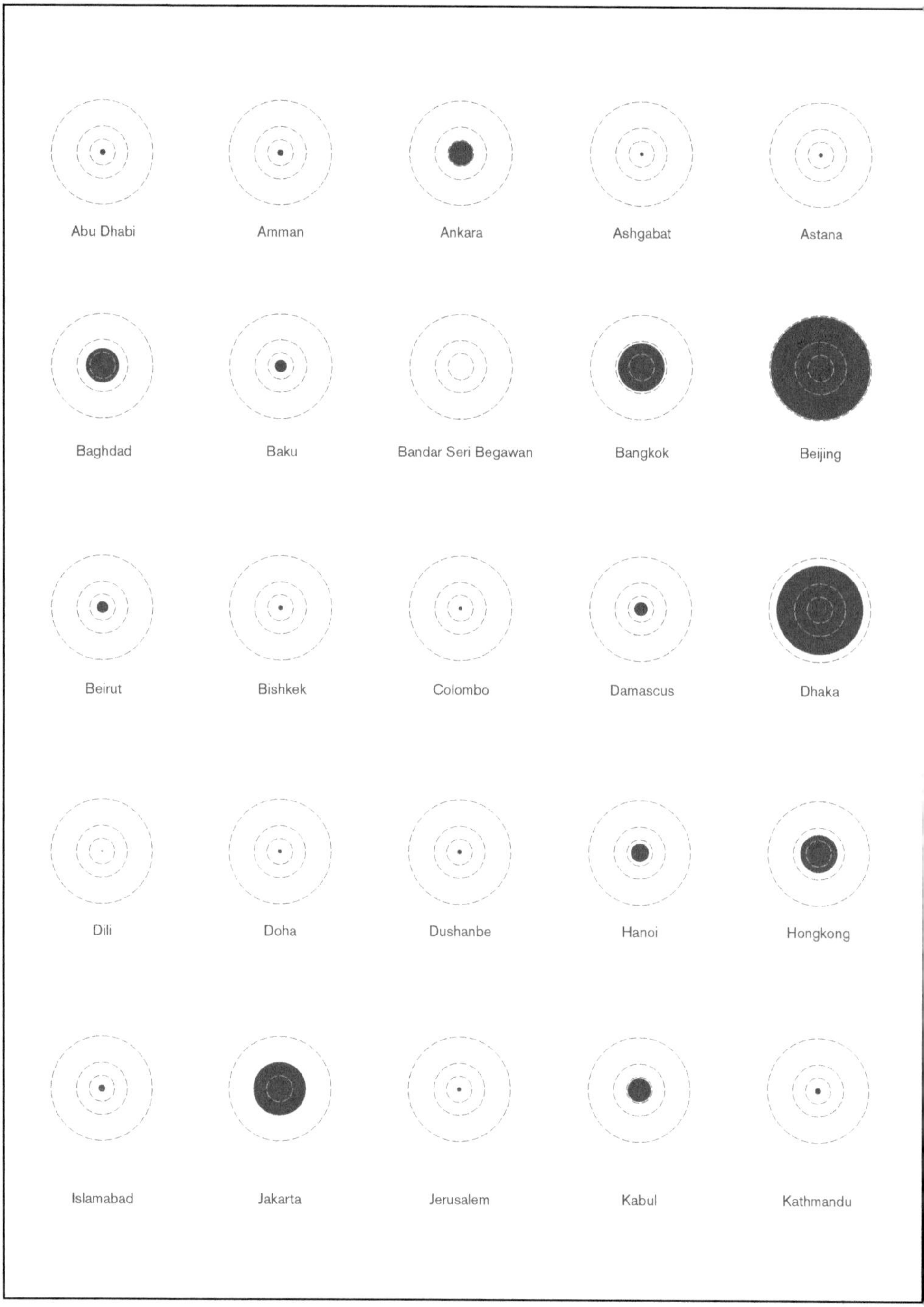

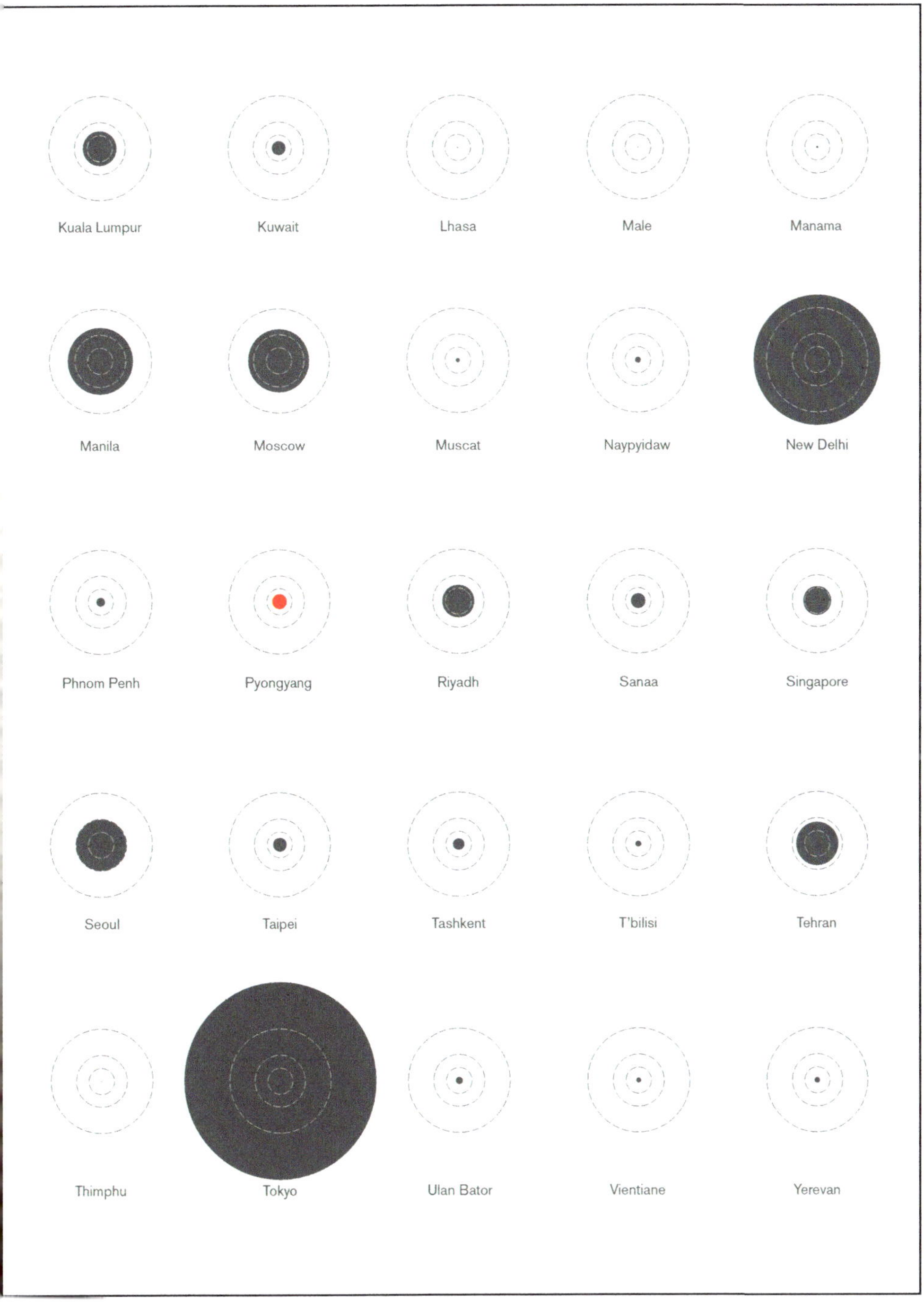
Kuala Lumpur
Kuwait
Lhasa
Male
Manama
Manila
Moscow
Muscat
Naypyidaw
New Delhi
Phnom Penh
Pyongyang
Riyadh
Sanaa
Singapore
Seoul
Taipei
Tashkent
T'bilisi
Tehran
Thimphu
Tokyo
Ulan Bator
Vientiane
Yerevan

DENSITY DATA

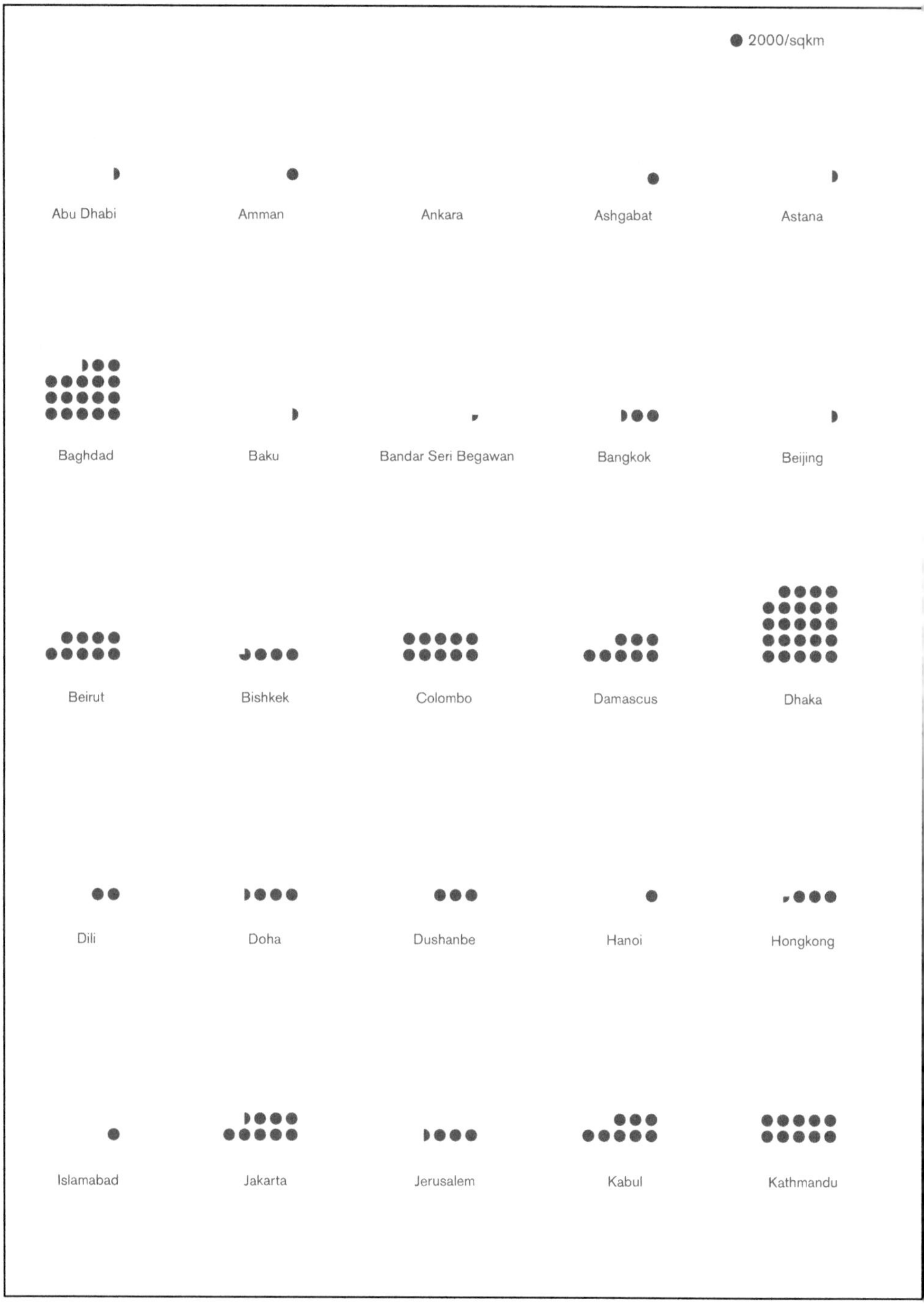

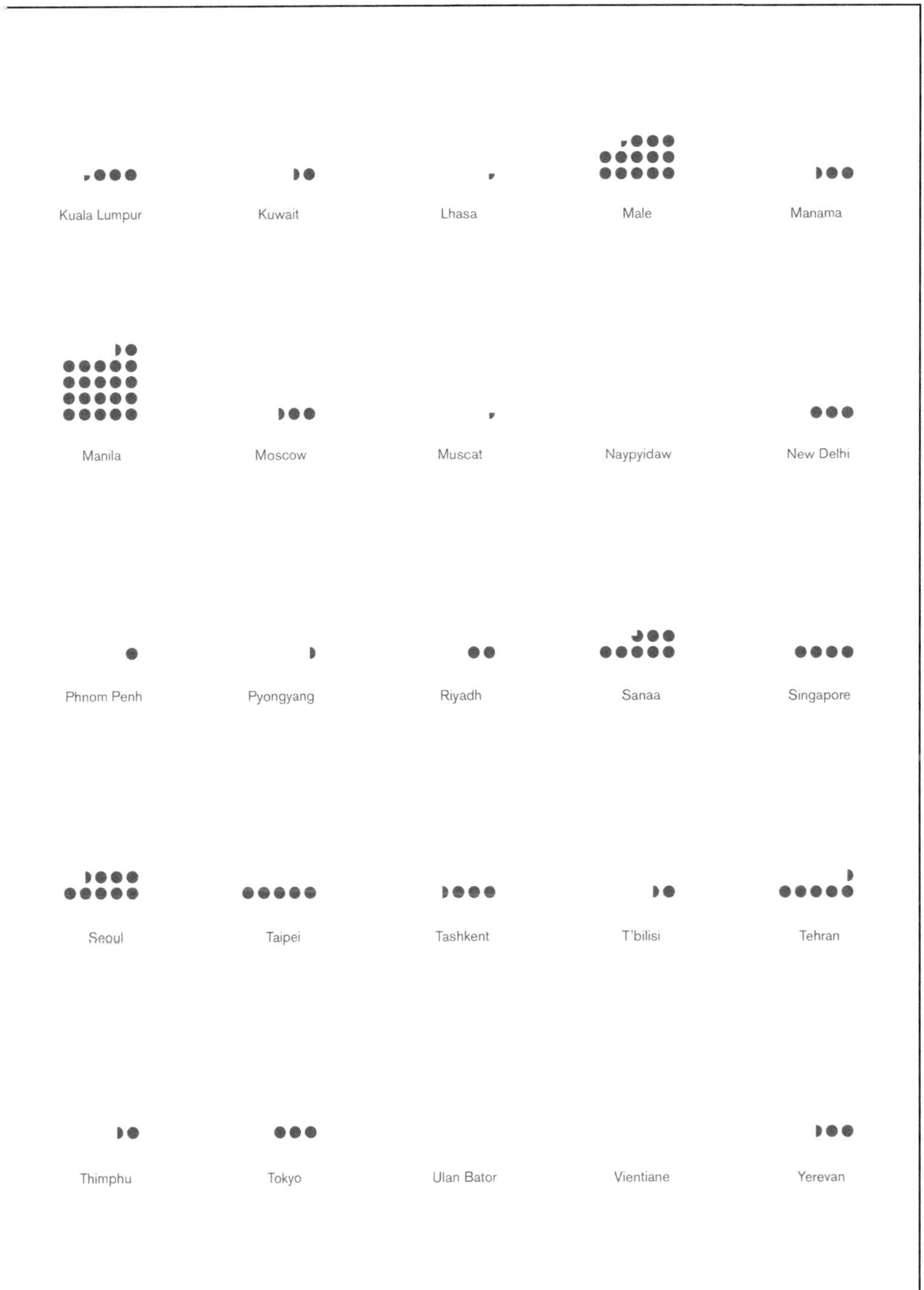
Kuala Lumpur
Kuwait
Lhasa
Male
Manama
Manila
Moscow
Muscat
Naypyidaw
New Delhi
Phnom Penh
Pyongyang
Riyadh
Sanaa
Singapore
Seoul
Taipei
Tashkent
T'bilisi
Tehran
Thimphu
Tokyo
Ulan Bator
Vientiane
Yerevan

CAPITALS OF EAST ASIA

Population

Density

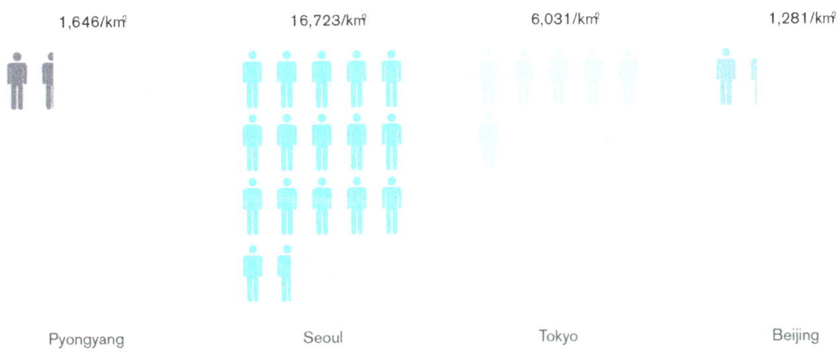

% of National Pop.

CAPITALS OF EAST ASIA

Area(km^2)

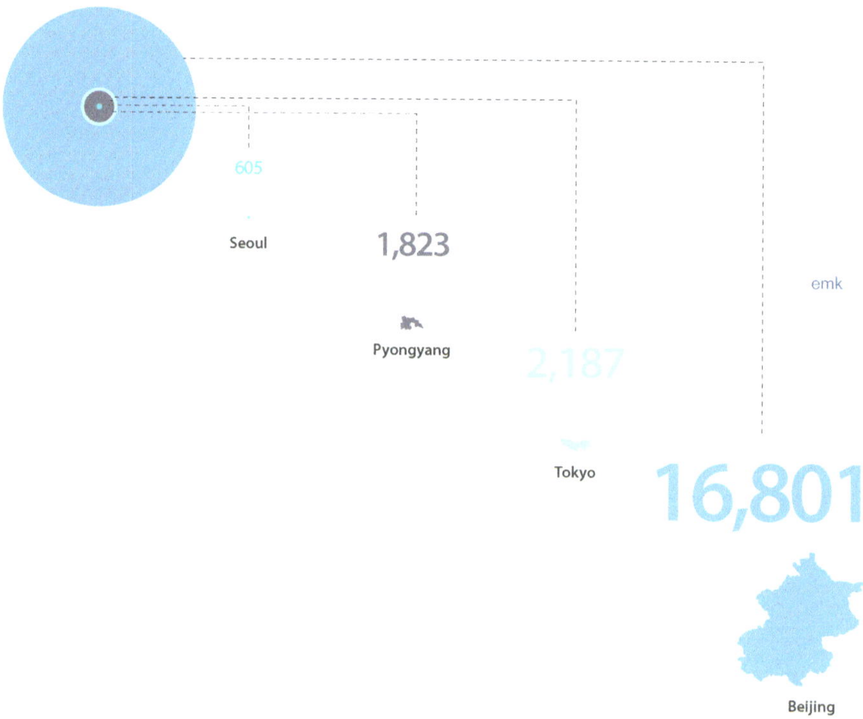

Geography

	Pyongyang	Seoul	Tokyo	Beijing
latitude	39°1'N	37° 33' N	35° 69' N	39°55'N
longitude	125°44'E	126° 58' E	139° 75' E	116°16'E
temp. high	29	30	31	31
temp. low	-11	-6	1	-8
annual rainfall	919mm	1370mm	1530mm	570mm

0

Elevation

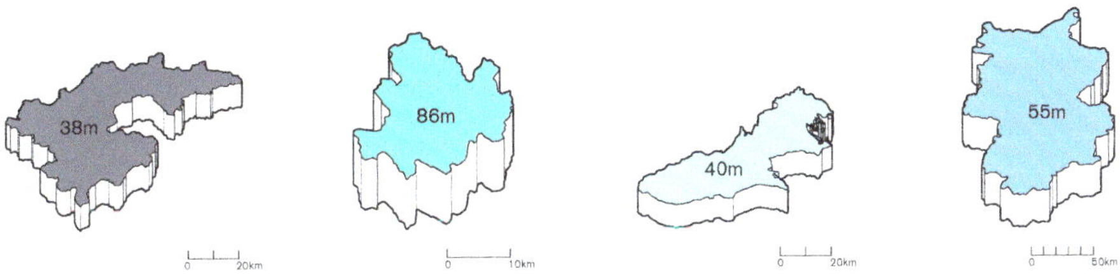

Pyongyang | Seoul | Tokyo | Beijing

Water Body

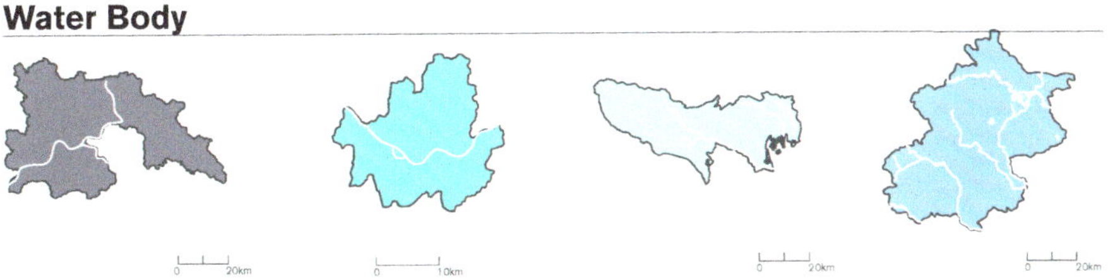

Pyongyang | Seoul | Tokyo | Beijing

International Airports

distance to cities

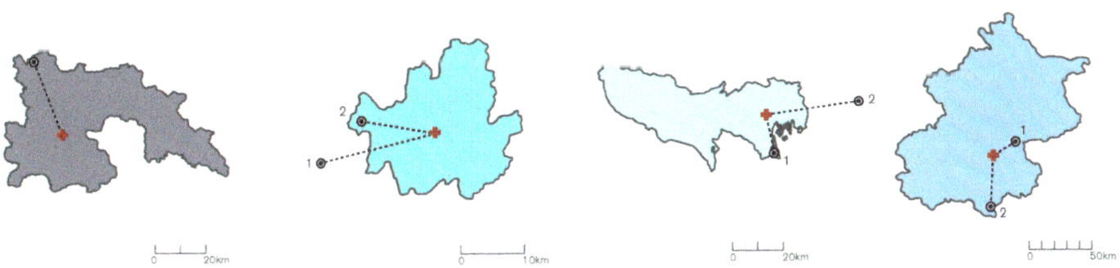

Pyongyang
Sunan int'l airport 22km

Seoul
1. Incheon int'l airport 48km
2. Gimpo int'l airport 16km

Tokyo
1. Haneda int'l airport 17km
2. Narita int'l airport 40km

Beijing
1. Beijing Capital int'l airport 25km
2. Daxing int'l airport(2019) 43km

Cost of Living

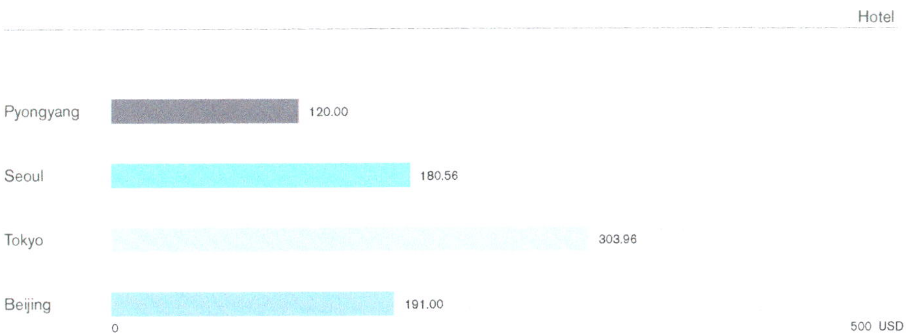
Hotel
Pyongyang
120.00
Seoul
180.56
Tokyo
303.96
Beijing
191.00
0
500 USD

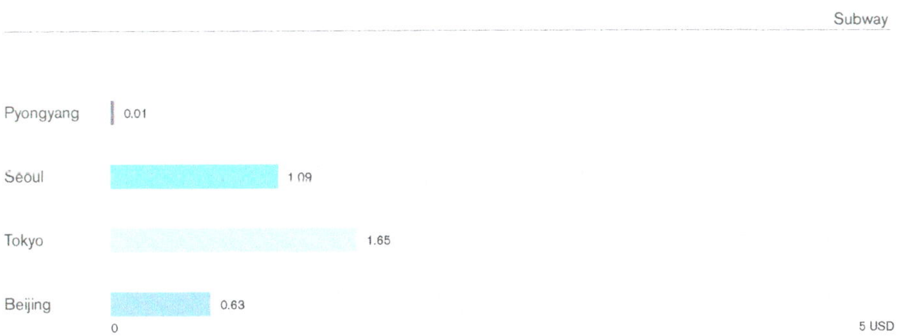
Subway
Pyongyang
0.01
Seoul
1.09
Tokyo
1.65
Beijing
0.63
0
5 USD

THE KOREAN PENINSULA

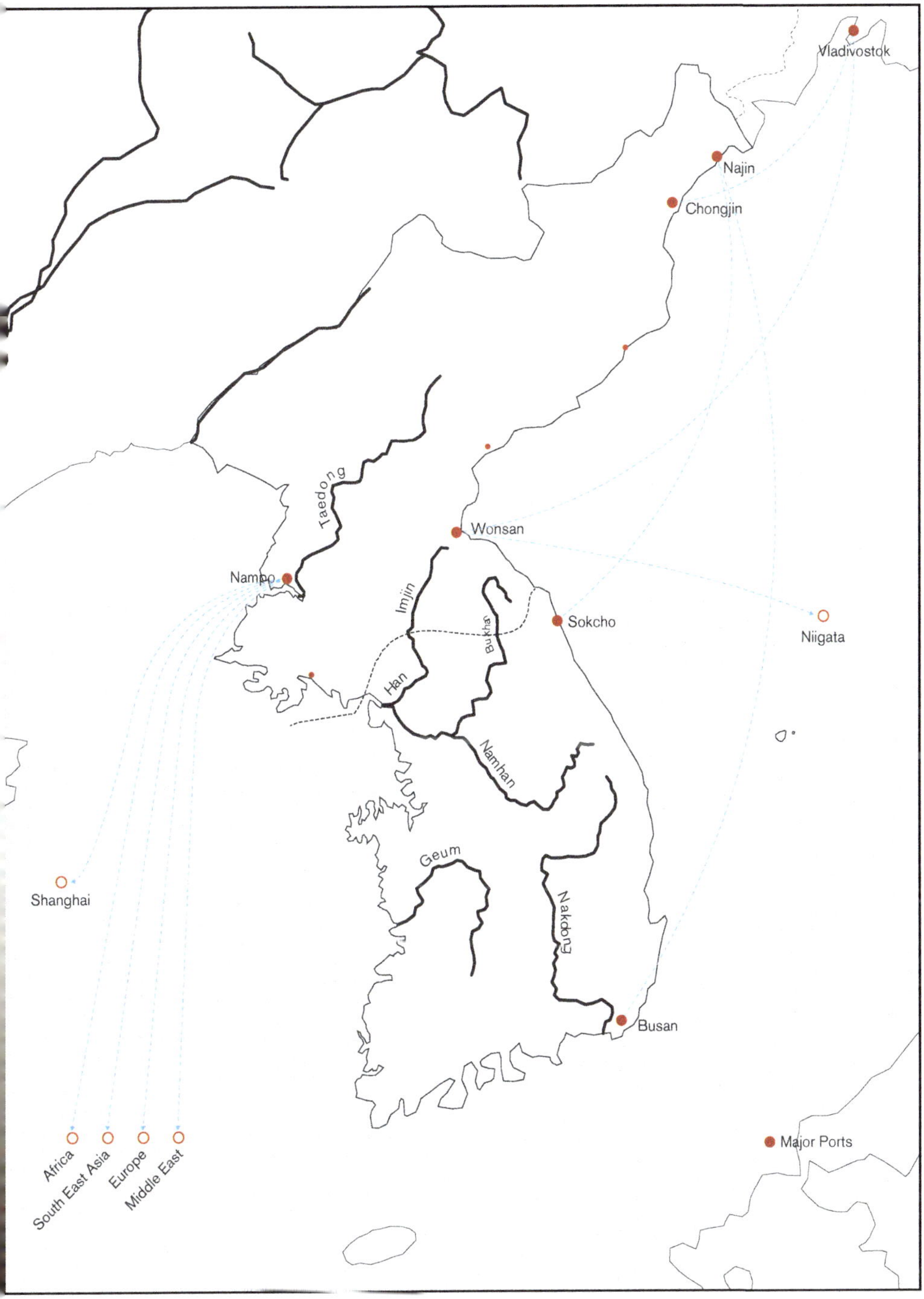
Vladivostok
Najin
Chongjin
Taedong
Wonsan
Nampo
Imjin
Bukhan
Sokcho
Niigata
Han
Namhan
Geum
Nakdong
Shanghai
Busan
Africa
South East Asia
Europe
Middle East
Major Ports

RAILWAY NETWORKS
Beijing
Pyongyang
Seoul
Shanghai

Vladivostok
Tumen
Namyang
Khasan
Rason
Chongjin
Shenyang
Ji'an
Manpo
Dandong
Sinuiju
Hamhung
Pyongyang
Wonsan
Nampho
Kaesong

AIRWAY NETWORKS

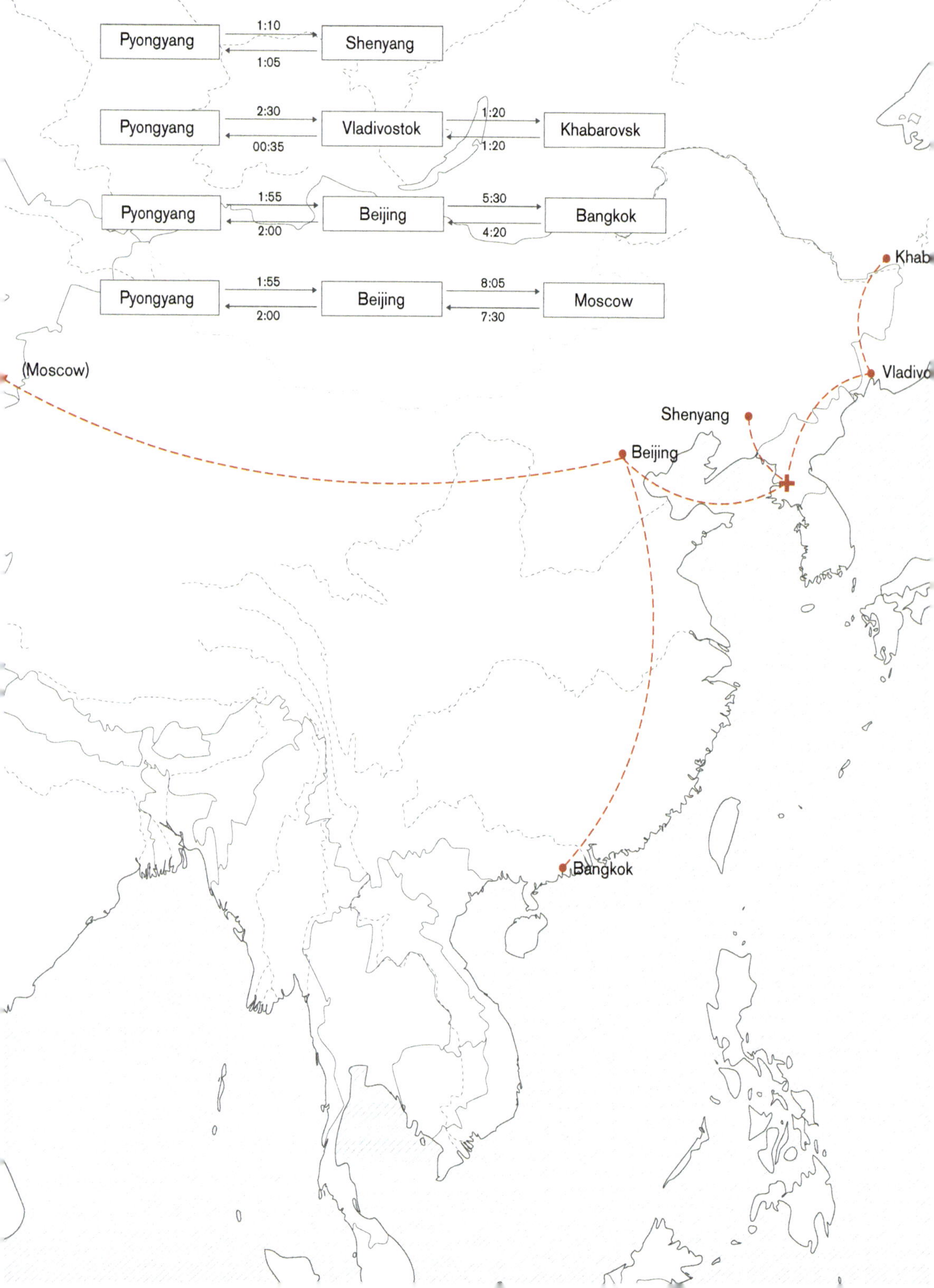

Shenyang
Samjiyeon Airport
Chongjin
Orang
Chongpyong
Sunan Int. Airport
Wonsan
Gimpo Airport
Incheon Int. Airport
Cheongju
Daegu
Ulsan
Busan
Gwangju
Mokpo
Jeju

ADMINISTRATIVE BOUNDARIES

AREA

120,538km²

POPULATION

24,052,231

DENSITY

200ppl/km²

PYONGYANG GEOGRAPHY

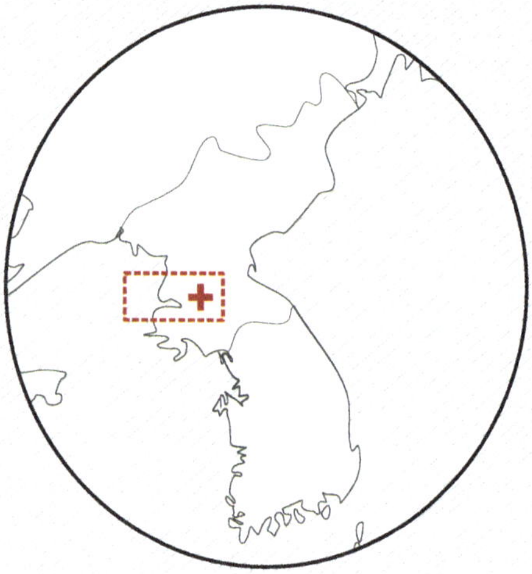

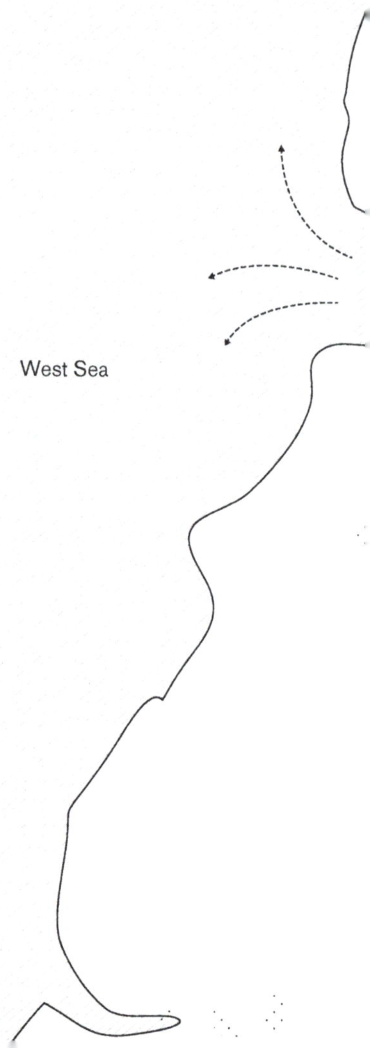

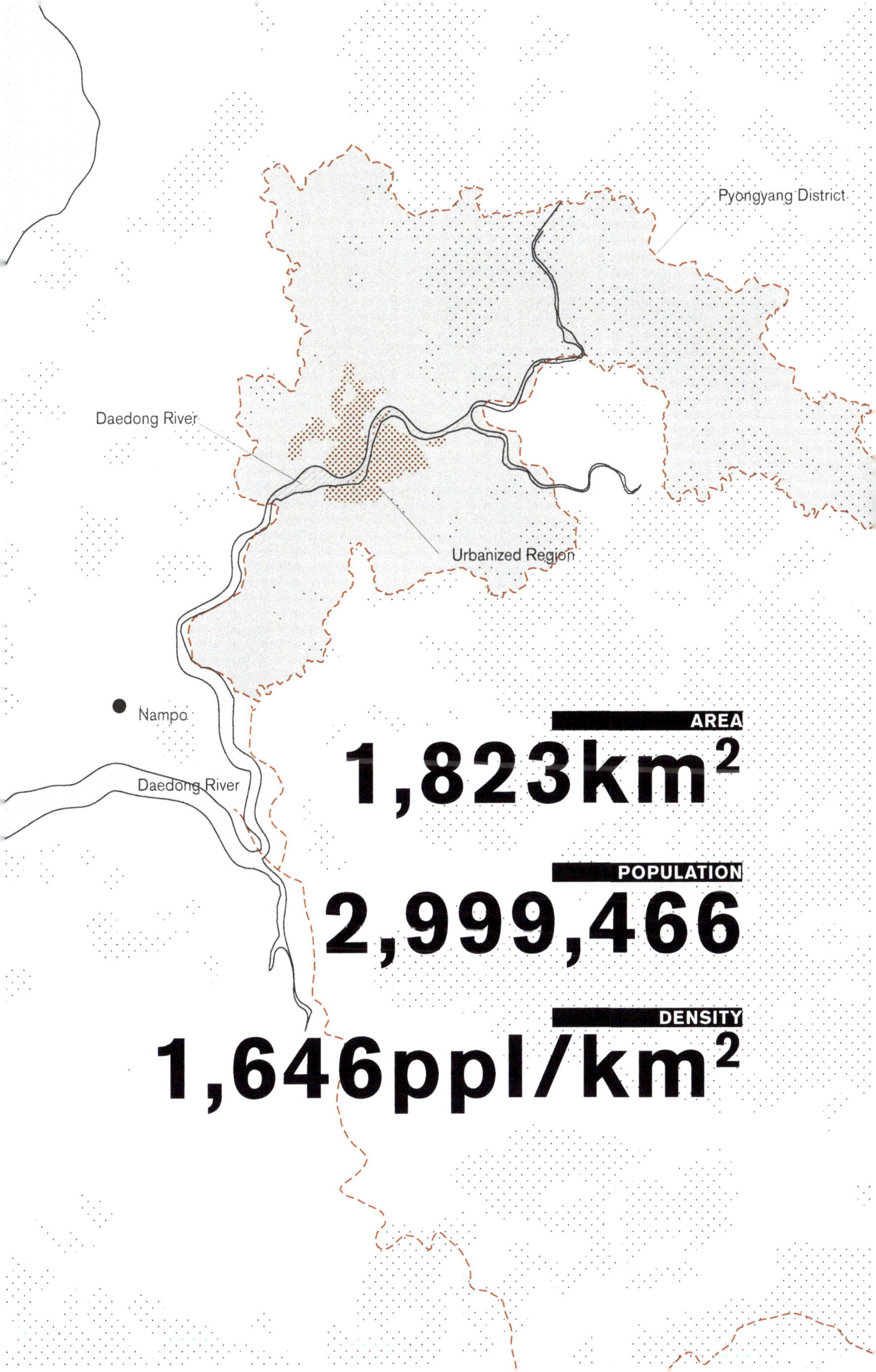

AREA

1,823km²

POPULATION

2,999,466

DENSITY

1,646ppl/km²

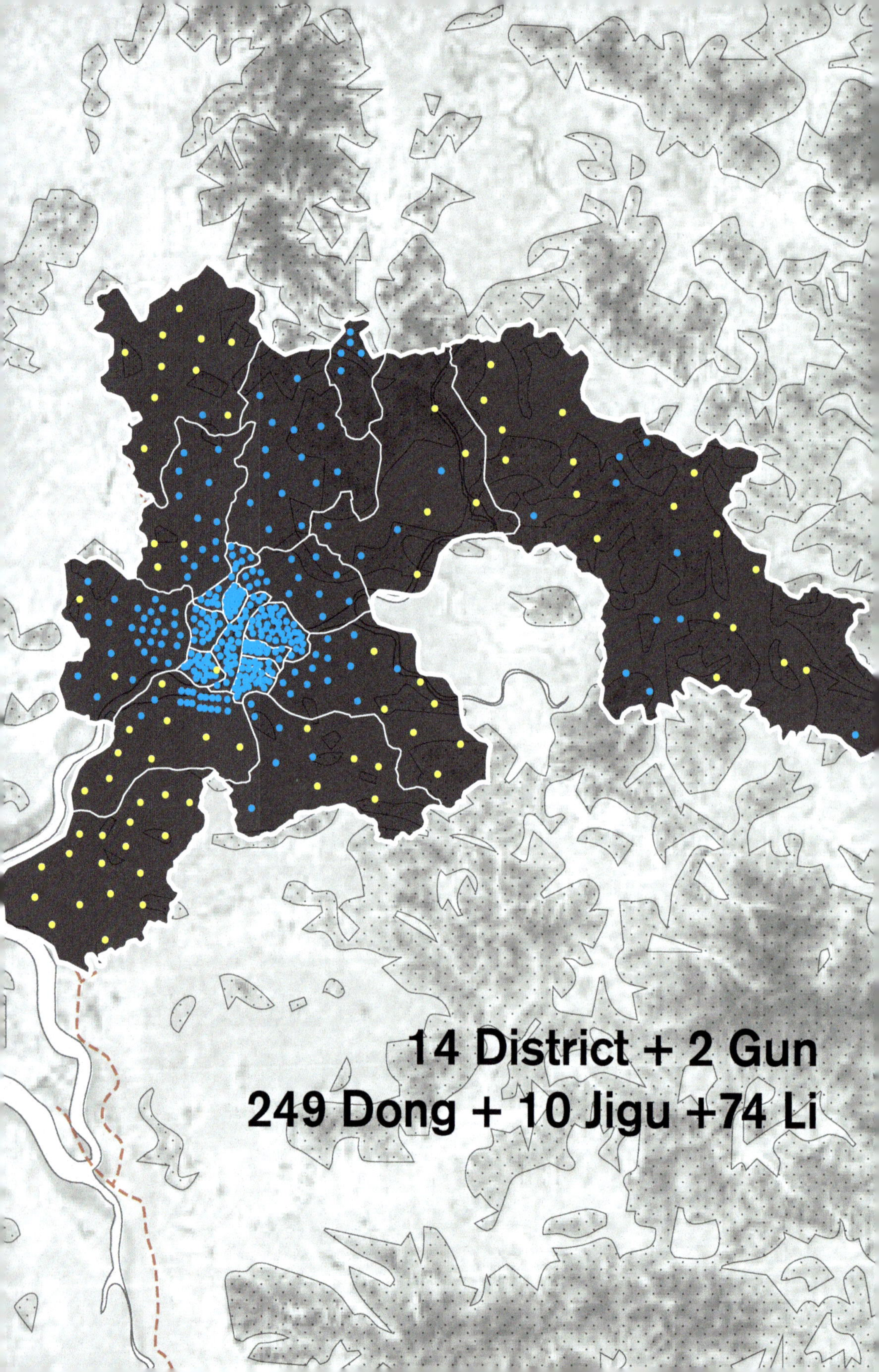
14 District + 2 Gun
249 Dong + 10 Jigu +74 Li

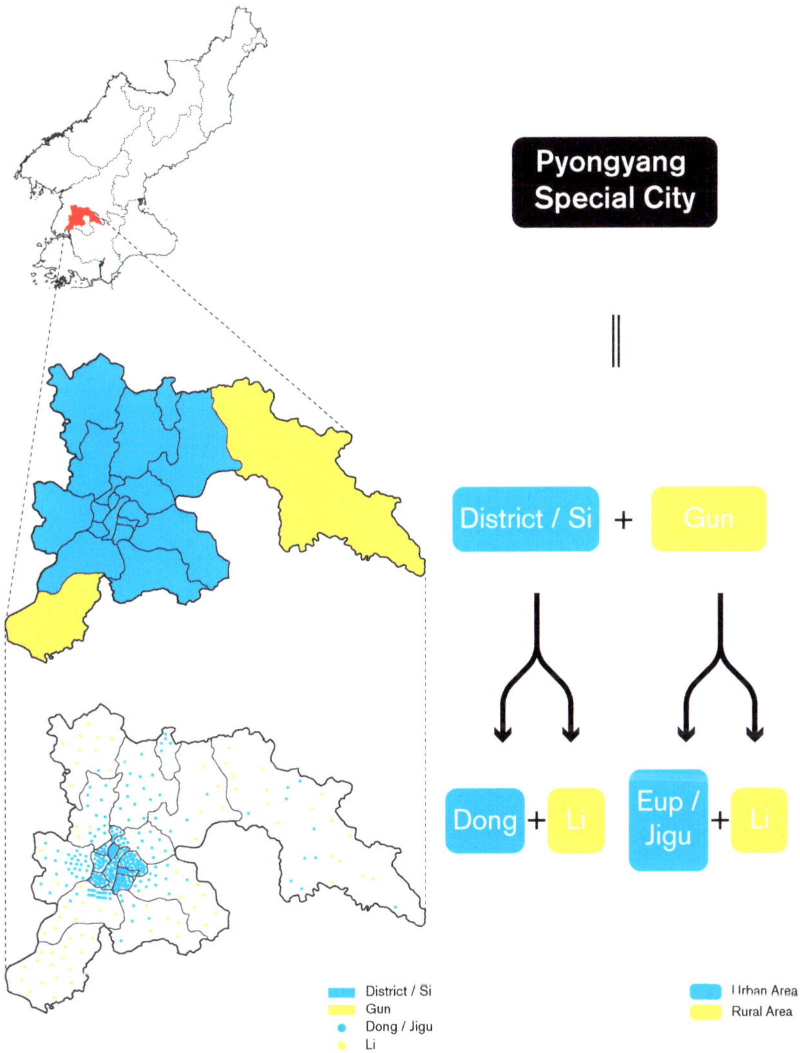

To reduce the difference between urban and rural areas, North Korean cities include rural area to urban boundaries. Therefore, a city is composed with both urban and rural areas, and even within an urban area, there are another level of rural areas, and within rural area, there are sub level of urban areas. In theory, this is the way how North Korean cities tried to structure its cities in more sustainable way.

ADMINISTRATIVE DISTRICTS

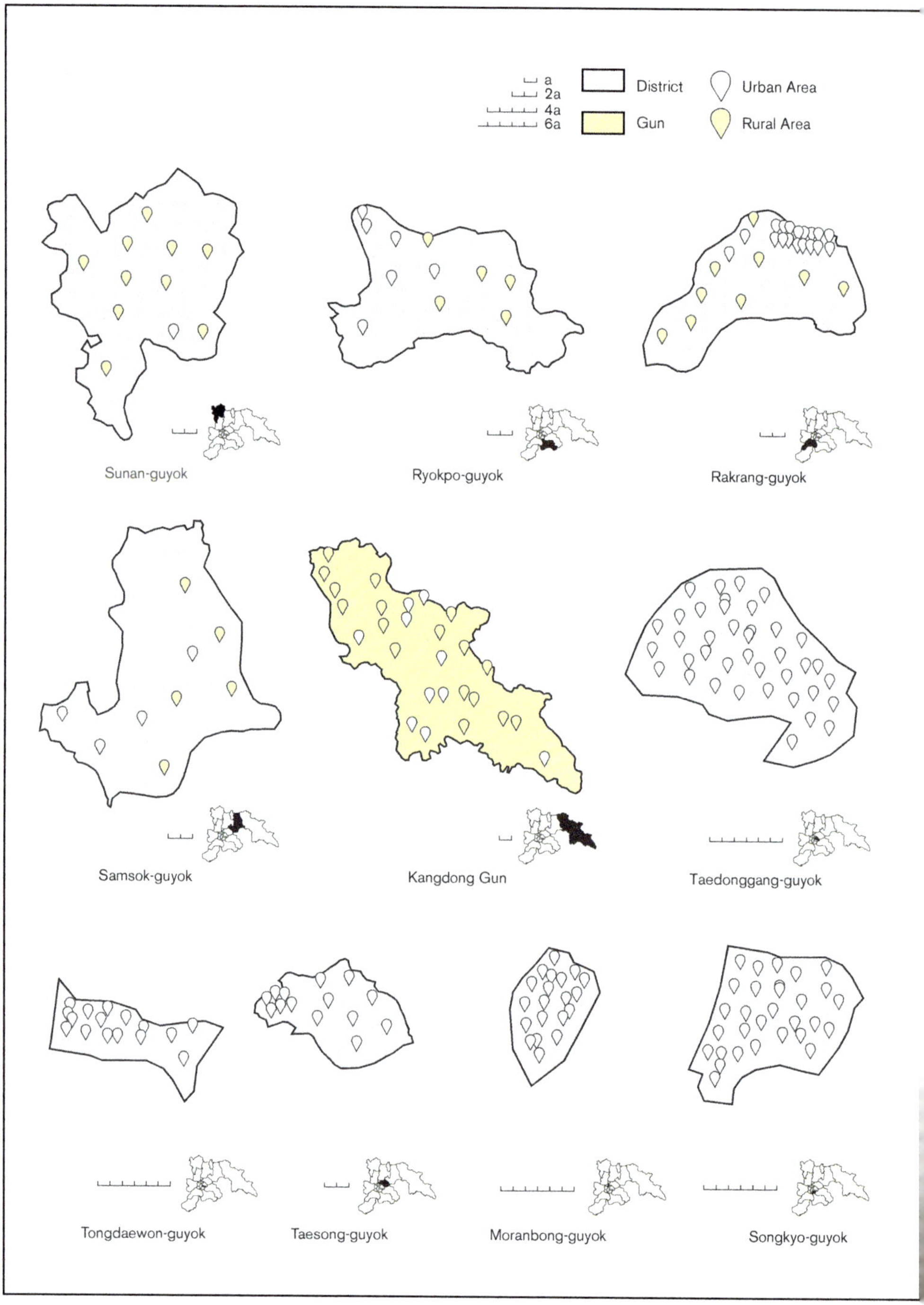

Ryongsong-guyok
Unjong-guyok
Sosong-guyok
Kangnam Gun
Jung-guyok
Sadong-guyok
Hyongjesan-guyok
Mangyongdae-guyok
Pyongchon-guyok
pothonggang-guyok

View of Eastern Pyongyang

INFRASTRUCTURE: TRAIN

INFRASTRUCTURE: LIGHT RAIL

1192

INFRASTRUCTURE: SUBWAY

INFRASTRUCTURE: BUS

강성대국을 향하여!

INFRASTRUCTURE: AIRPORT
Sunan International Airport
Youth Hero Motorway
Pyongyang- Nampo Highway
Pyongyang - Kaesong Highway
Pyongyang - Wonsan Highway

평양
PYONGYANG

위대한령도자김정일동지만세

Since 2011, number of taxi has been increased dramatically which reached to about 500, including second hand taxis imported from China, and recently, Hong Kong joint venture company threw 500 more taxis in the city. It means that there is a new competition in service field and market-economy mechanism is being settled in Pyongyang, and new middle class people who have ability to choose between services is emerging.

Masayuki Aramaki,
interview with Jiji Press

위대한 수령 김일성동지는 영원히 우리와 함께 계신다

LIVING CENSUS

POPULATION

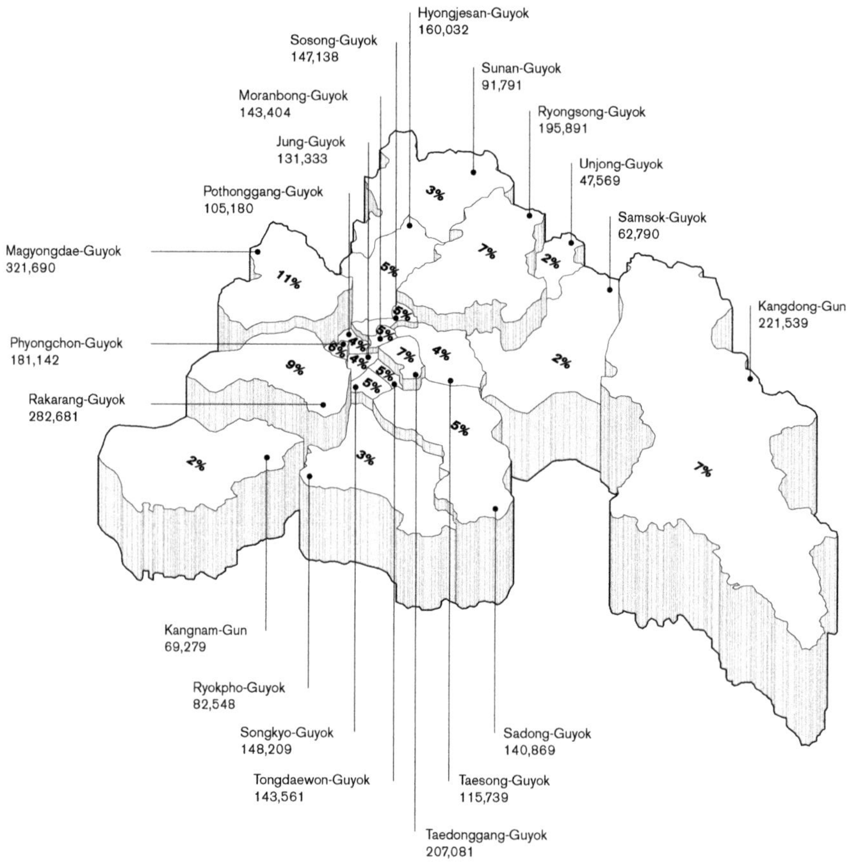

Total 2,999,466

DENSITY

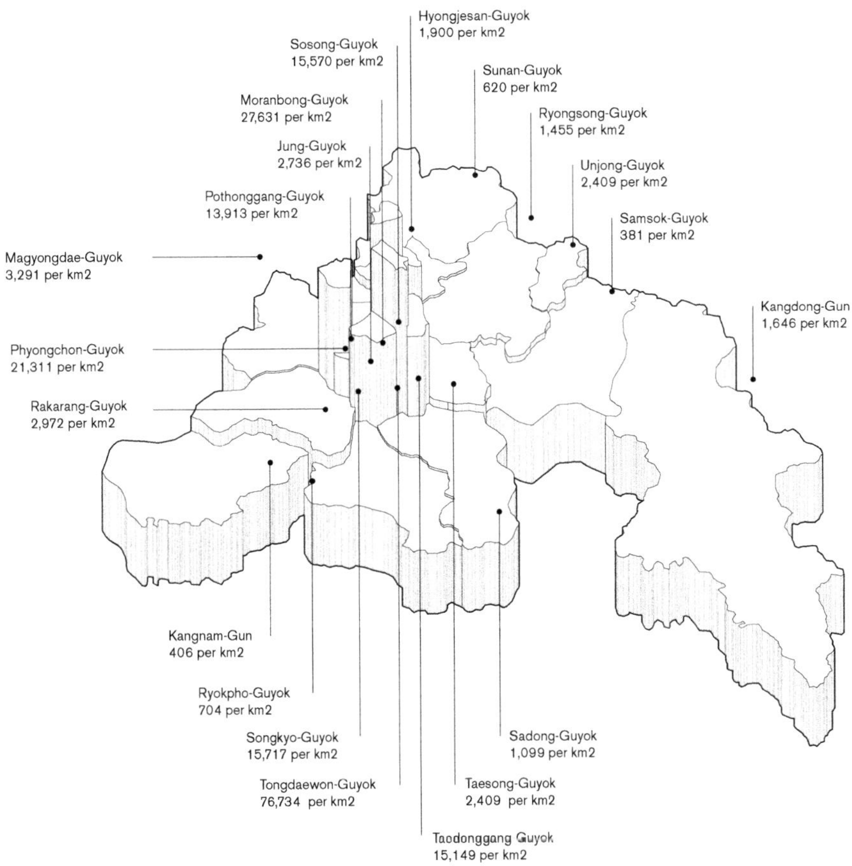

Average 1,823 ppl/Km²

DEMOGRAPHICS

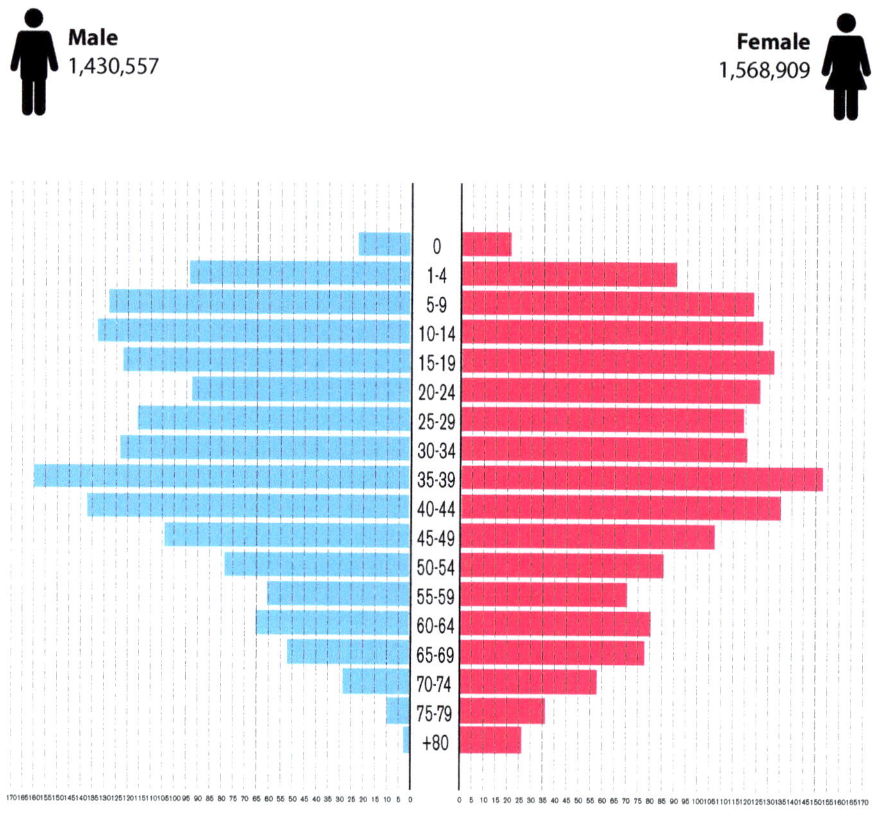

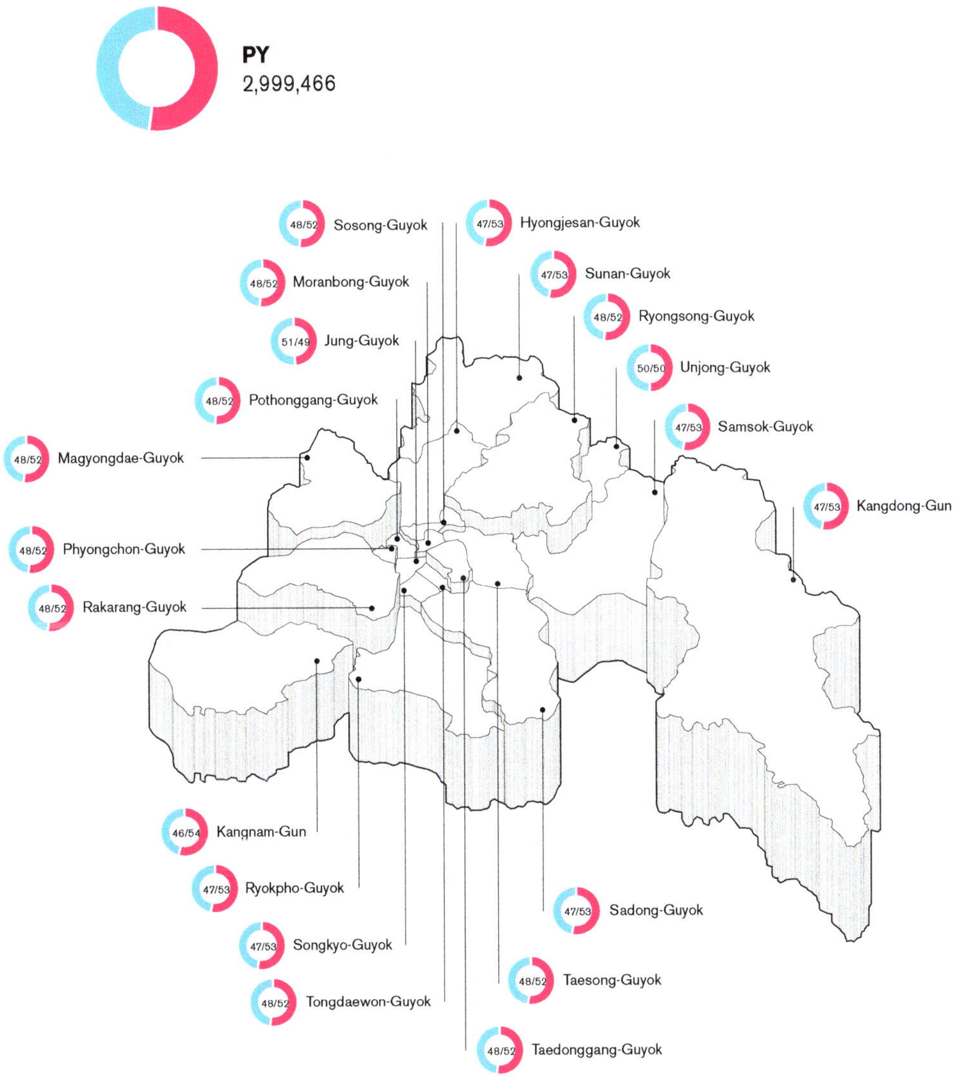
PY
2,999,466
48/52
Sosong-Guyok
47/53
Hyongjesan-Guyok
48/52
Moranbong-Guyok
47/53
Sunan-Guyok
48/52
Ryongsong-Guyok
51/49
Jung-Guyok
50/50
Unjong-Guyok
48/52
Pothonggang-Guyok
47/53
Samsok-Guyok
48/52
Magyongdae-Guyok
47/53
Kangdong-Gun
48/52
Phyongchon-Guyok
48/52
Rakarang-Guyok
46/54
Kangnam-Gun
47/53
Ryokpho-Guyok
47/53
Sadong-Guyok
47/53
Songkyo-Guyok
48/52
Taesong-Guyok
48/52
Tongdaewon-Guyok
48/52
Taedonggang-Guyok

Place of Registration

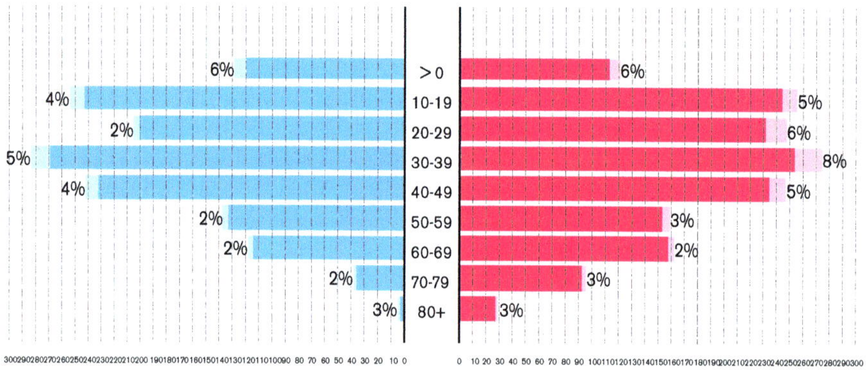

Education Attainment

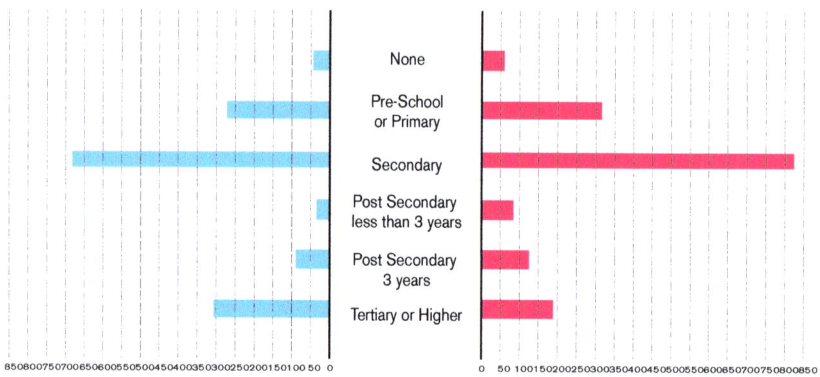

Percentage of Major Industry

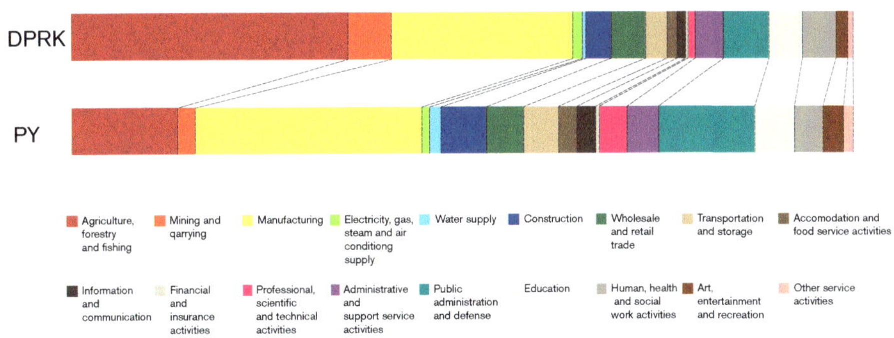

Percentage of Major Occupation

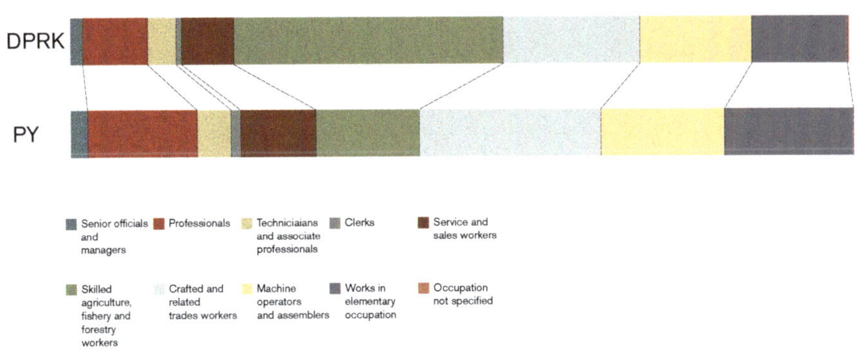

MIGRATION POPULATION

Number of Population in 13 Districts and 2 Guns

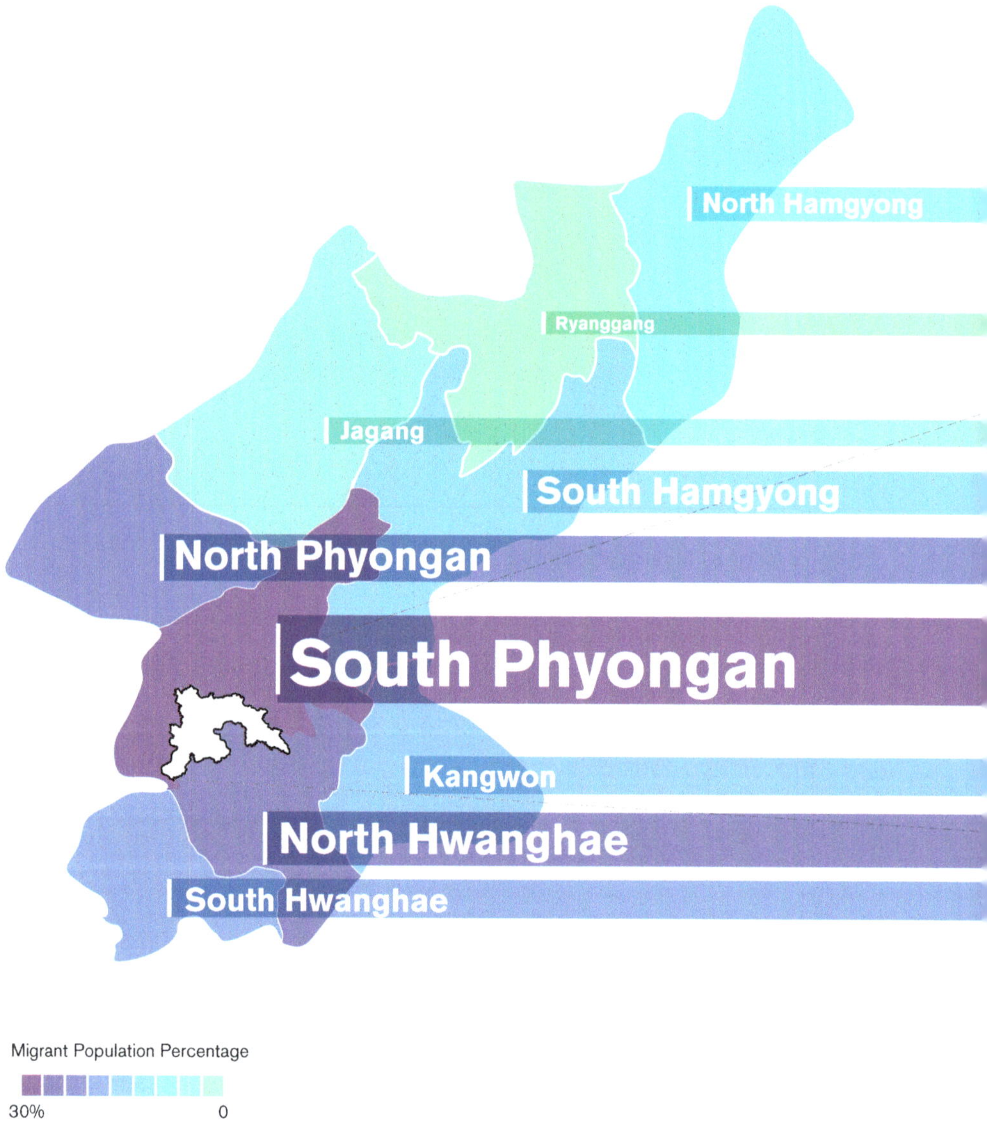

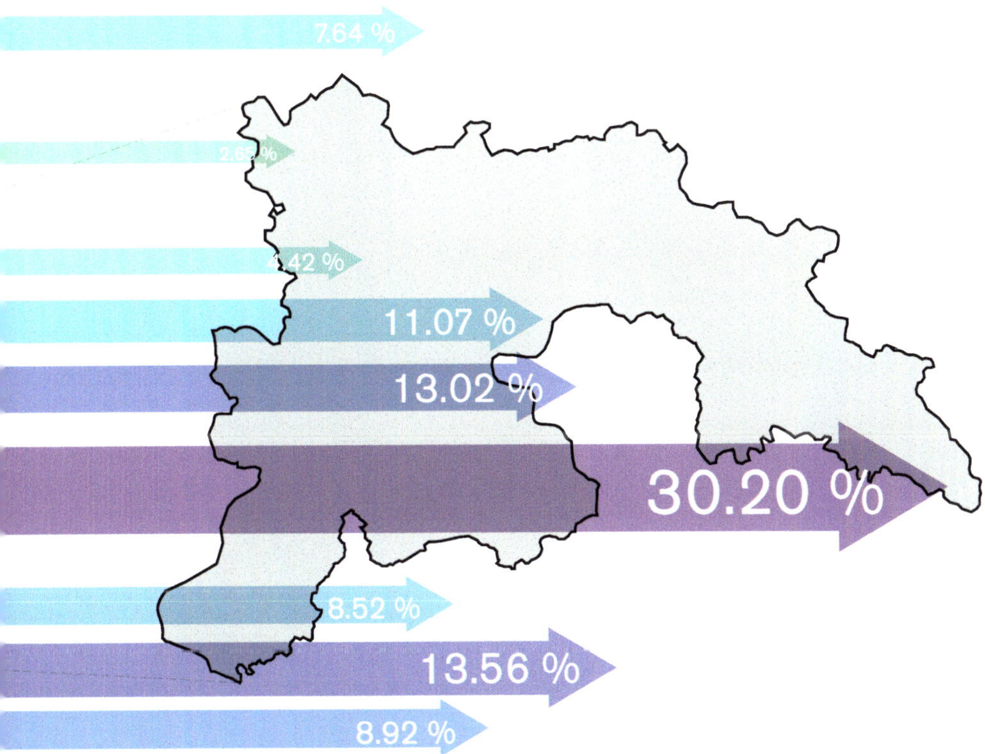
7.64 %
2.65 %
4.42 %
11.07 %
13.02 %
30.20 %
8.52 %
13.56 %
8.92 %

HOUSEHOLDS CONDITION

Households by Type of Dwelling Unit

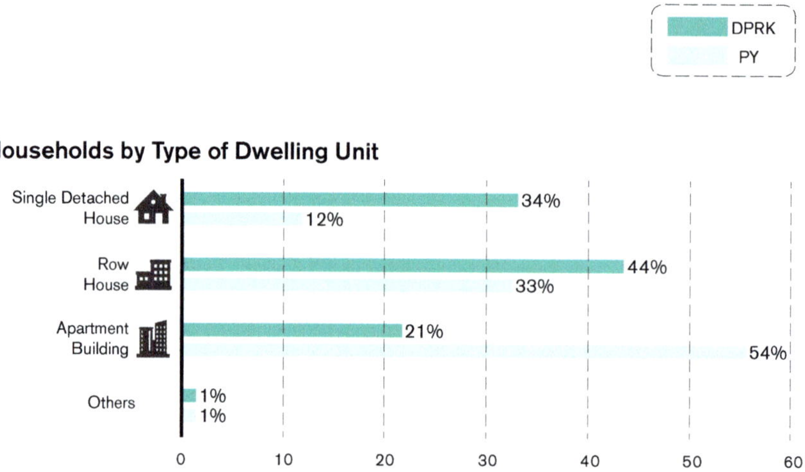

Households by Floor Area of Occupied Dwelling Unit

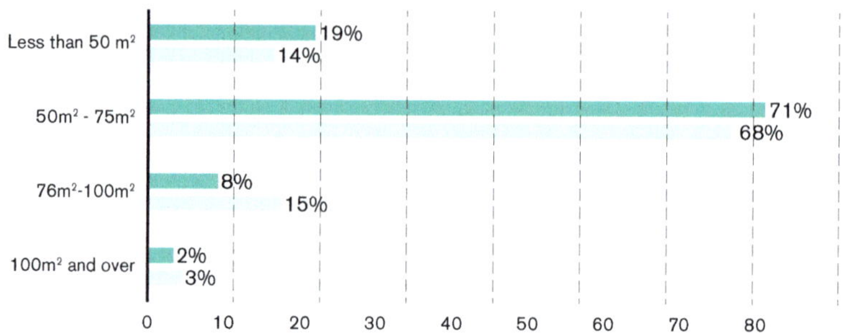

Households by Number of Rooms

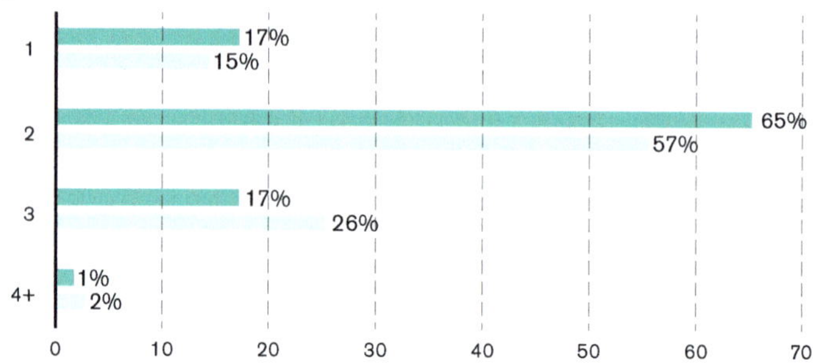

Households by Type of Toilet Facility

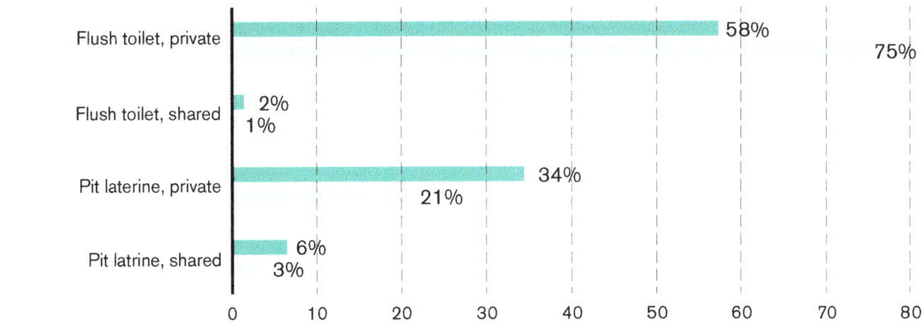

Households by Type of Heating System Used

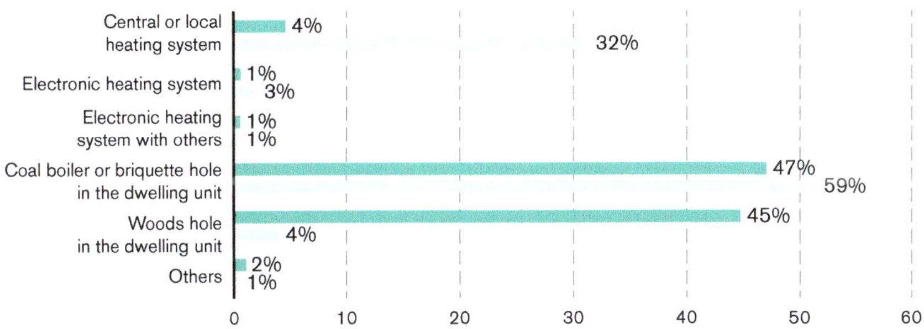

Households by Cooking Fuel Used

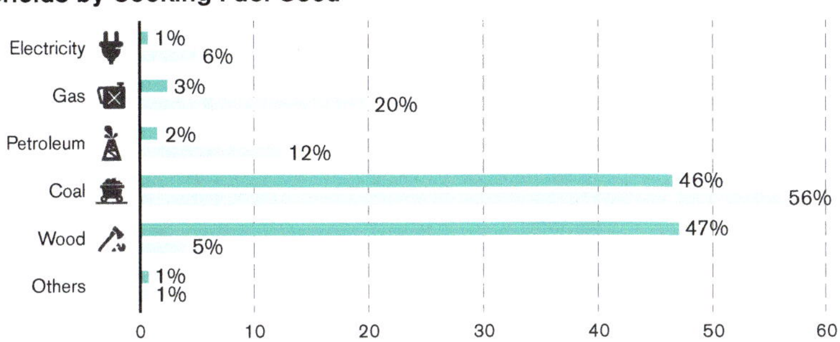

04
PYONGYANG AS A SOCIALIST CITY

One of the few faint glimmers on this benighted landscape is Pyongyang. As the capital, it is one of the few places even marginally accessible to outsiders. Yet even when seen firsthand, Pyongyang defies expectations and resists easy analysis. The first puzzle lies in the grandeur of the cityscape, with its extravagant public buildings and monuments. Despite an economy in shambles, the infrastructure appears modern and, above all, well-maintained. The same effort has gone into ordering human affairs: indeed, Pyongyang is so obsessively regimented that it feels artificial. The untidy business of daily life, from picking up groceries to taking out the garbage, is hidden from sight (no simple feat in a city of 2 million).[1]

Pyongyang, the capital city of North Korea, has taken an important role in the history of the Korean peninsula since it was first built in 427 A.D. In the ancient period, it served as the capital city for hundreds of years. In contemporary times, it remains one of the most important and largest cities in Korean peninsula. Located close to another capital city such as Kaesung (Seoul) and the Chinese territory, it has been a strategic city for politics, economics, and transportations. Currently, as one of few remaining socialist cities in the world, it displays numerous socialist urban structures that integrate its modern architecture. It was rebuilt after the Korean War (1950-1953) and was considered to be an exemplary city amongst other socialist nations.

Pyongyang is located at 39 degrees, 01 minutes North latitude and 125 degrees, 45 minutes East longitude, on the northwest of the Korean peninsula. Four major North Korean cities are distributed to each direction: Wonsan to the east, Nampo to the west, Kaesong to the south, and Sinuiju to the north. Two key elements describe the city's in topography: flat land and the Taedong River. As the actual meaning of "Pyongyang" implies, the city sits on a cozy land in open field surrounded by Mounts Taesong and Jang. Although there is a hill called "Moran Hill" in the center of the city, most in the Pyongyang lands are relatively flat. The Taedong River, one of the longest on Korean Peninsula, flows through the center of the city, which is well developed and balanced on both sides of the river.

HISTORY OF PYONGYANG

Ancient Pyongyang; 427-1897

Pyongyang was first founded in the mid-3rd century as the second capital of Goguryeo (B.C.37-668), an ancient dynasty in the Korean Peninsula. After being designated as capital city in 427, Pyongyang-seong (the fortress of Pyongyang) was built in the sixth century with 23 kilometers long walls and with total surface of 11.85 km^2. Covering most of the area of the modern

Goguryeo Dynasty (BC 37 - 668)
고구려 시대

220_The Han Dynasty comes to an end with establishment of the Three Kingdoms in ancient China.
395_Roman Emperor Theodosius I dies, causing the Roman Empire to split permanently.
570_Birth of Mohammad, founder of Islam.
618_Tang Dynasty of China initiated by Li Yuan.

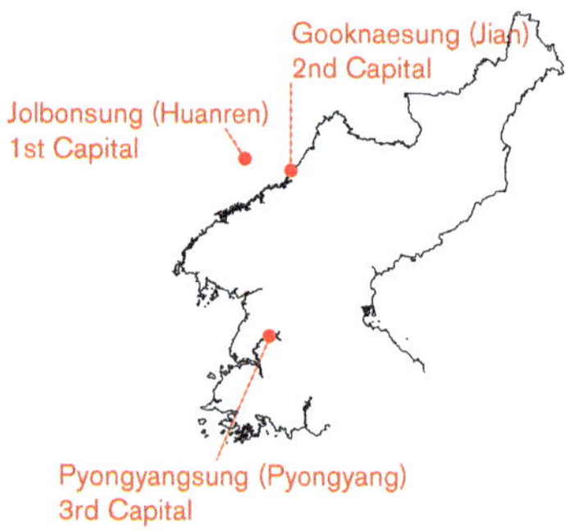

Major Cities

Unifeid Silla Dynasty (668 - 935)
통일신라 시대

726_Byzantine Emperor Leo III the Isaurian destroys the icon of Christ above the Chalke Gate in the capital city of Constantinople, beginning the first phase of the Byzantine Iconoclasm.
805 to 820_Tang Dynasty was under the rule of Emperor Xianzong of Tang.

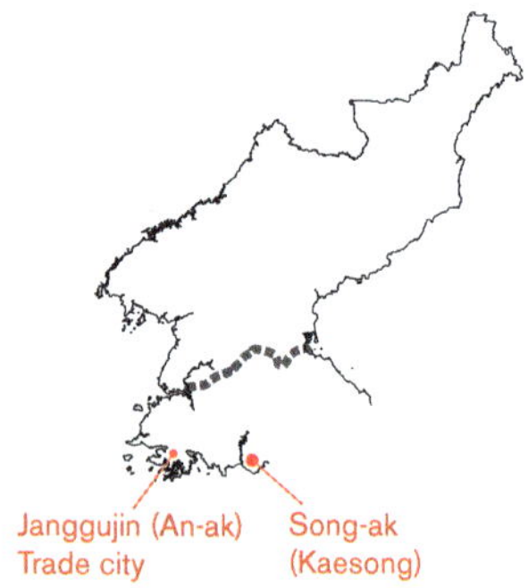

Major Cities

Goryeo Dynasty (918 - 1392)
고려 시대

927_Kingdom of England becomes a unified state.
1099_The Siege of Jerusalem by European Crusaders.
1347_The Black Death, on its march across Asia to Europe, reaches Constantinople.

Major Cities

Joseon Dynasty (1392 - 1897)
조선 시대

1453_Constantinople falls to the Ottoman Turks, ending the Byzantine Empire and beginning the Ottoman Empire.
1492_Christopher Columbus landed in the Americas from Spain.
1804_Napoleon crowns himself Emperor of the French.

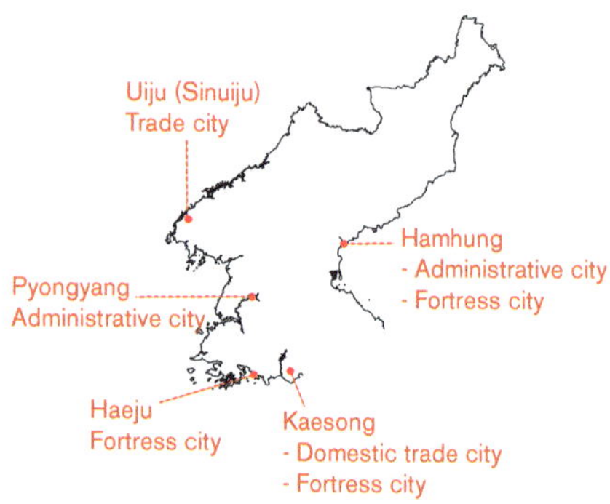

Major Cities

Feast for the Pyongyang Governor, Kim Hong-do1593

Pyongyang, 1593

city the fortress became a major infrastructure that influenced the morphology of Pyongyang,. Like other fortified cities of Goguryeo, Pyongyang-seong also used its surrounding topography to define the boundary of the city: Daedong River, Botong River, and Kumsu Mountain. It was composed of four different forts; Nae-sung (inner fort), Woe-sung (outer fort), Buk-sung (north fort), and Joong-sung (middle fort).

The space between these four forts, Woe-sung, where most of the populace resided, displays a clear trace of the 'Li-Bang' system based on the grid structure.[2] It is an urban planning logic composed with 'Bang,' the basic unit size of the grid, and 'Li', which is an aggregation of different 'Bang'. In those periods, 'Bang' basically had a size of 175x175 m^2, and 'Li' was composed of 4x4 'Bang' (700x700 m^2). This grid structure served as the basic layout system of the city until the end of Chosun Dynasty in 1910.

Joong-sung –the middle fort- was the area for administrations, and also had grid system extended from the outer fort structure of Woe-sung. This central area, surrounded by two rivers, Botong and Daedong, and two other forts, Woe-sung, and Nae-sung was the location of most administration facilities of North Korea. Next to Joong-sung, Nae-sung –the inner fort- is located on a hilly site that shared location with the palace. Buk-sung was constructed as a mountain fortress north of this zone in order to protect the palace from invasion.

Until Goguryeo Dynasty collapsed in 668, Pyongyang took a major role as a city of political, economic and cultural hub of the country, and almost three centuries later, it had its second prosperous period in Goryeo Dynasty. During the Goryeo dynasty (918-1392), Pyongyang was called Seokyung, meaning West Capital and was one of four major cities in the country with Kyungju, Kaesung, and Seoul, which were capital cities of the Silla Dynasty, the Goryeo Dynasty, the Chosun Dynasty and South Korea. The twelfth-century witnessed major renovations and new constructions for palaces based on the master plan to move the capital city from Kaesung to Pyongyang, but ultimately the plan was not realized.[3] However, Pyongyang still played a most important role amongst other cities as a large administrative district and it continued to do so in the Chosun Dynasty (1392-1910) as well. During this period, the city's population increased almost fourfold from 40,000 to 150,000, and Pyongyang became the second largest city in the peninsula, next to Seoul, which was the capital city by then.[4] Despite the increase of population, the basic structure of Pyongyang has not been changed significantly until it opened its Daedong river port to foreign countries in 1897.

In the end of the Chosun dynasty, and before the colonial era, two important histories explain us the strategic position of Pyongyang . The first one is General Sherman incident in 1866, before the city opened the port, and the second is Pyongyang Revival Movement in 1907. After signing a successful treaty agreement with Japan in 1858, the United States Navy reached out to the Korean peninsula to ask for access and cooperation.

Once it opened the port, Pyongyang underwent vibrant economic and cultural changes. The most critical and influential event of this period for the whole peninsula was the Pyongyang Revival Movement in 1907. During the transition period from the dynasty to the colonial era, Korean peninsula started to get exposed to Western culture, including religions and Pyongyang was the first city with an important Christian movement in Korean. The movement started from Jangdaehyun Church in 1907 and influenced the whole nation to fourfold the Christian community. As an unexpected and powerful movement, it soon got attention from the Western media which called Pyongyang the "Jerusalem of the East."

Jangdaehyun Church, 1900s

Site of Jangdaehyun Church now

Botong Mun

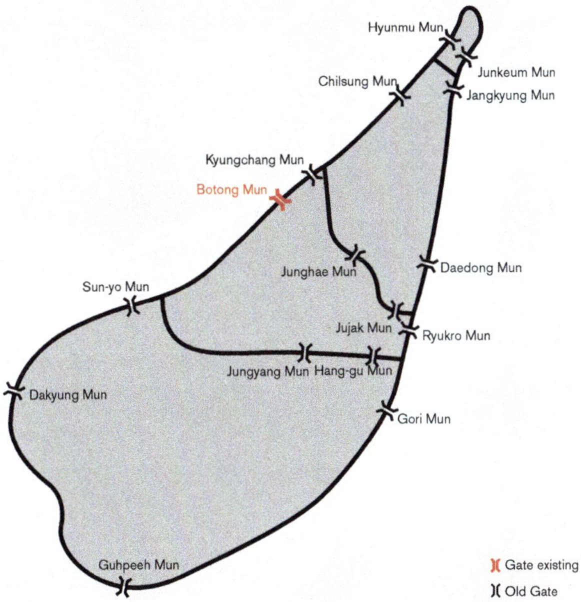

Botong Mun (Gate)

Pyongyang during the Colonial Period

Pyongyang Tram during the Colonial Period

Colonial Era; 1910-1945

After the war between China (Cheng Dynasty) and Japan in 1894, the Japanese military began to occupy several cities in Korean Peninsula including Pyongyang, forcing Chosun to open its ports in 1897. The colonial era started in 1910, and over the period, numbers of cities in the northern part were developed for two major reasons. First, they had more natural resources than similar southern cities, a feature that made them easier to develop them as industrial cities. Secondly, cities in north became strategic points for the war against China; especially from the 1930s, Japanese Empire set up numbers of military cities in the north so that it could easily expand the

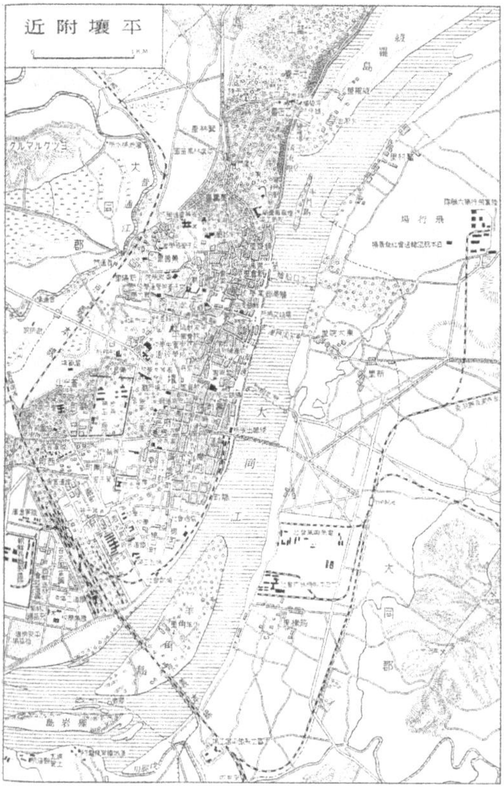

Pyongyang Map, 1930

territory to China. Pyongyang, in northern part of the peninsula, was also designated as a strategic city for its military as well as economic importance.

At the beginning of the colonial period, Koreans mostly resided in one of four forts in Pyongyang while Japanese residents occupied several important zones around the administration facilities. However, ever since the Japanese constructed a railroad station south of the old town and built armory around it, developed nowadays as industrial area, the overall structure of Pyongyang changed dramatically. This area used to be the inner area of Woe-sung where the trace of 'Li Bang' grid structure from the Goguryeo Dynasty remained, although the old city fabric had been removed by the new developments.[5] Japanese authorities started to build a new town in the area corresponding to today's city centre while most Koreans stayed in the old town, initiating an unequal development of Pyongyang as if it were two towns and marking the beginning of the modern urban structure expansion of Pyongyang.

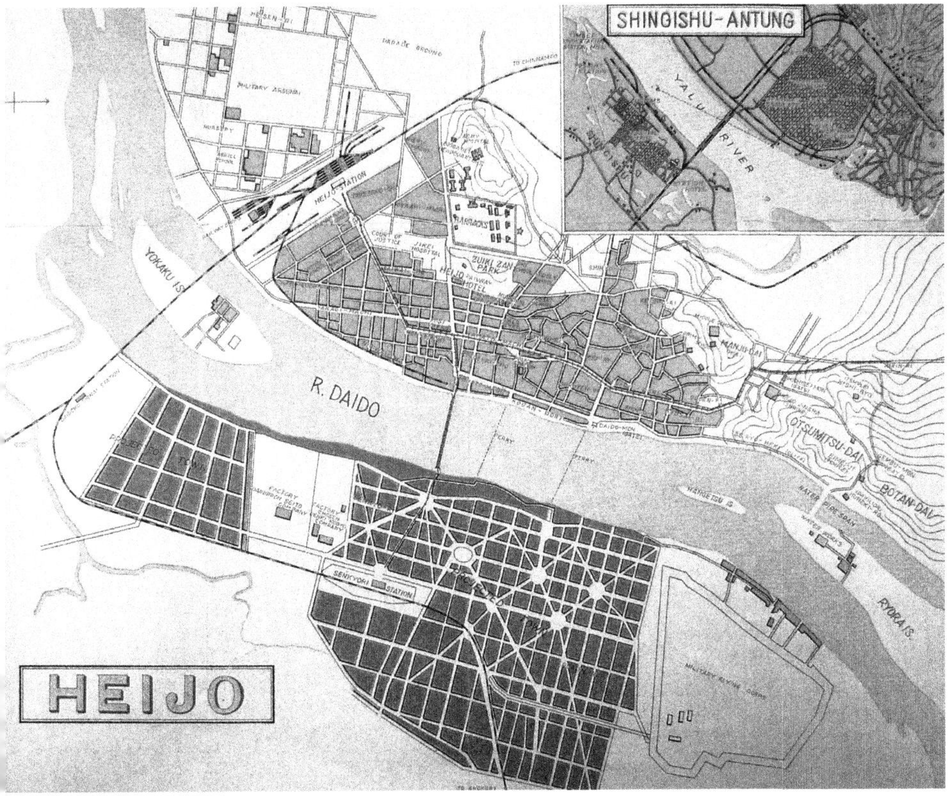

Pyongyang Master Plan by Japan in 1930s

In 1930, the Japanese government announced a long-term master plan for Pyongyang that aimed to design the urban growth to a population of five hundred thousand and an area of 110 km^2 over the next 15 to 20 years. The plan designated industrial, residential, and a green zone after restructuring the existing infrastructure, categorizing the streets in six different scales from 12m to 34m, and using the urban squares as communication nodes.[6] Moreover, an outstanding feature of this master plan lay in the fact that it tried to expand the city to the east of the Daedong River. For the first time in the developmental history of Pyongyang this side of the river was included, introducing an interesting expansion axis with east-west orientation that contraposed the existing north-south axis marked by the river. Although the master plan had not been realized sufficiently during the colonial period, it gave a bigger picture of the city boundaries for the later master plans.

Beginning of Socialist Era

Three years of war between North Korea and South Korea from 1950 to 1953 left little intact and transformed the entire image of every city on the peninsula. Like Seoul, the capital city of South Korea, Pyongyang was also a major battle field during the war. The amount of bombs that the U.S army dropped on Pyongyang was as much as it had used during all five years of the Pacific War. According to North Korean reports, more than three hundred and fifty thousand bombs were used to attack a city with three hundred thousands population. As a result, Pyongyang was completely wiped out during the war, with no existing structures nor remaining buildings in the city. North Korea claims that Daedongmun (South Gate of the old fortress) was the only artifact that was kept by the U.S army in order to use it as a standard point on a blank slate. It was a tragic period for both North and South Korea in many ways. At the same time, however, for North Korea, which had to build a city with its new ideology, it provided a rare opportunity to construct an ideal socialist city from scratch. Unlike other socialist cities in the Soviet Union, Eastern Europe, or China, Pyongyang did not have to contend with existing urban fabric which most orthodox socialist planners considered as problematic vestiges of capitalism or imperialism. The inherited historical cities already functioned within the existing fabric and organization logic and all the inhabited infrastructure was an obstacle for its transformation into a new socialist city on an ad-hoc site. Hence, in spite of ideal plans for the socialist city, socialist planners and their parties actually had to deal with the existing cities and inject social-

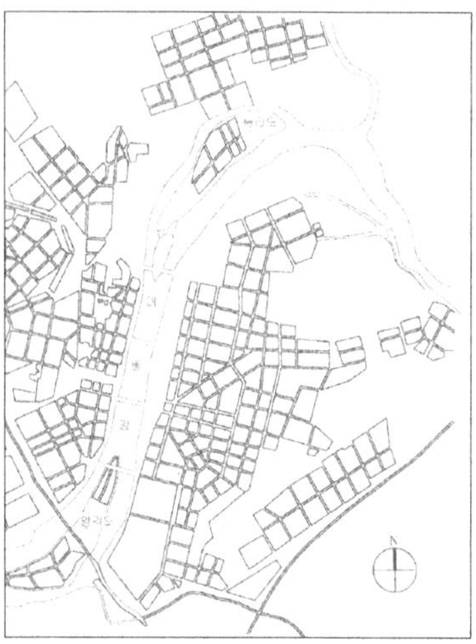

1950 Master Plan

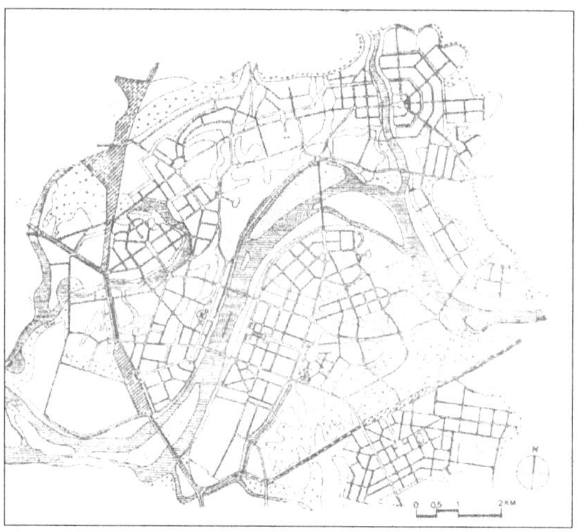

1953 Master Plan

ist features into them as much as possible, instead of replacing the whole structure of the city. However, this obstacle did not exist in Pyongyang after the Korean War.

As the capital of North Korea and one of the biggest battle fields during the war, Pyongyang had the worst condition after the war amongst many other cities in the North to be reconstructed as the capital city again. For instance, Kaeseong, which used to belong to South Korea before the war and to North after, received far less bombs than Pyongyang, and therefore could keep some infrastructures important for the reconstruction. Although other communist states insisted that North Korea rebuilt its capital city elsewhere, Kim Il Sung decided to reconstruct Pyongyang as the capital city of North Korea as well as an ideal socialist city to represent the victory of socialism in the war.[7] He saw it as a great chance to build an entirely new ideal socialist city on the ashes of the old capitalist and Japanese vestiges. In fact, since the first post-colonial years, Kim already had a plan to reconstruct Pyongyang as an ideal socialist city, so he ordered urban planners to design a master plan for it during the course of the war. The reconstruction proceeded quickly after the end of the conflict based on the master plan that Kim Jung Hee provided in 1953, which was a revised version of 1951 master plan that he had initially proposed during the war.

PYONGYANG, AN IDEAL SOCIALIST CITY

> ... Final goal of master plan of Pyongyang is to make the city as internationally standardized city, ideal socialist city, and symbolic city that propagates the revolution of Kim Il Sung. Based on those three goals, Pyongyang focused on five development strategies; improving infrastructures, developing high-rise residential buildings along the major boulevards, building large cultural facilities, creating symbolic structures, and expanding convenient facilities for foreign visitors. (Kim Won, A study on the urban development policy in North Korea, 1990)[8]

After three years of war, North Korea started to reconstruct the entire country, focusing on major cities, based on socialist urban planning strategies. The first three-year reconstruction plan was adopted from 1954 to 1956. During this period, each North Korean city received support from different socialist countries. For example, Pyongyang received support from Hungary and Bulgaria. Therefore, in the early period of the socialist era, the architectural style and urban design of Pyongyang were strongly influenced by those two countries.[9] During this period, the reconstruction was focused on the original city center area, which layed on the western side of the Daedong River.

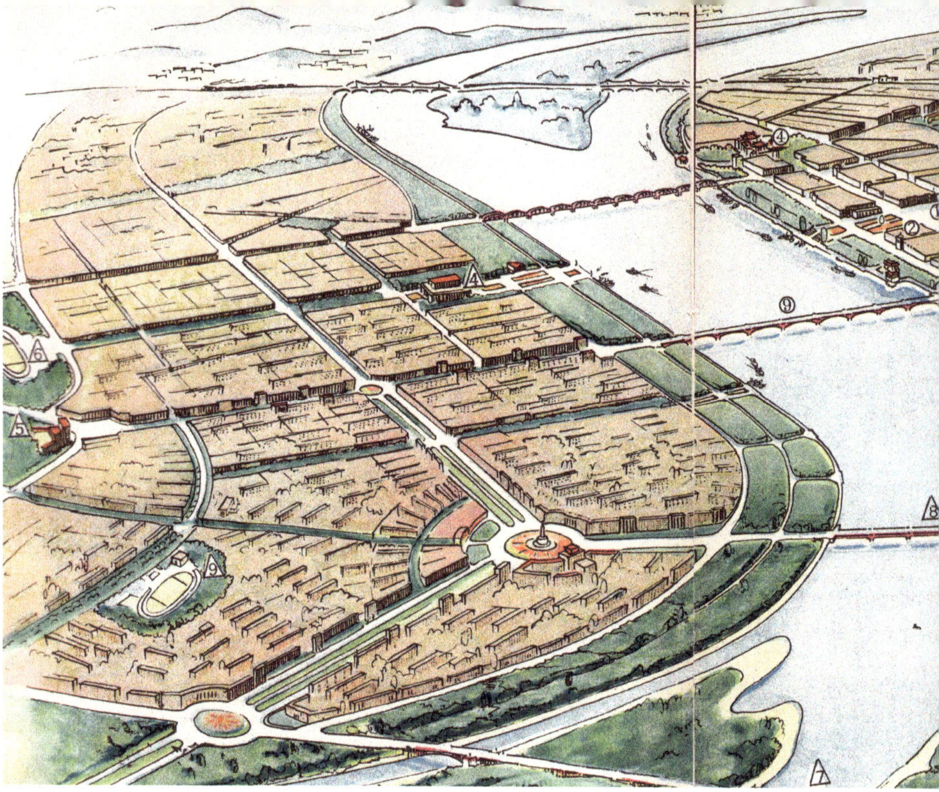

> Pyongyang, and buildings should be developed along the river based on topographical condition. Also, Kim Il Sung Square should be located the east side of Namsan hill, and industrial and business facilities should be planned in southern area parallel to the river. Distribution of health, institutional, cultural, and convenient facilities should be well organized and balanced, and heavy landscape will be planned both in residential district and periphery of the city.[10]

It was not until the five-year development plan started in 1957 that Pyongyang started to inject socialist urban features into the city.[7] The five-year plan was based on the master plan in 1953. On the contrary, the original master plan that Kim Jung Hee provided in 1951 did not include many socialist urban structures and was more influenced by the master plan proposed by the Japanese administration in 1930s. It conceived the east side of the Daedong River as a major developmental area of Pyongyang, and proposed a grid system overlaid with radial streets. However, the reviewed plan from 1953 followed general rules of socialist urban planning. Although the first revision had similarities with original master plan in terms of the city limits and balanced development of the two sides of the river, the key

View of Pyongyang, Sketch, 1950s

structures of the plan were responding to the strategies of socialist urban planning. It distributed several districts in the city and used green spaces as buffer zones between them, as a typical element of socialist urban planning intended to limit the size of the city and eliminate the difference between urban and rural area as much as possible. On the intermediate level, each district was planned around a central square that was used for public or political manifestations and parades of socialist parties which is a very important urban space in socialist urban planning.

PYONGYANG; CITY OF PRODUCTION

> From the 1960s, Kim Il Sung started to direct the whole master plan of Pyongyang, and through series of development strategies, Pyongyang began to have socialist urban features. It adopted the concept of micro-district, which is a socialist residential typology, and structured hierarchical logic in the urban space based on the concept. It organized self-sustainable district so that it can improve the convenience for the residents and efficiency of commuting.[12]

Pyongyang was one of the major cities of the Japanese colonial era that served as a location for heavy industry (especially munitions industries) and as a result infrastructures such as railroads were well developed. After the war, Pyongyang focused on reconstructing those infrastructures as well as the industrial facilities. Once the reconstruction conclude, Pyongyang had a higher industry ratio than other capitalist cities; With the 19% industry in the city, Pyongyang was way ahead from Seoul with only a 2.8% industrial area within the city. In general, South Korean cities today have about a 6% dedicated to industrial area. This result is owed not only to the fact that it had previously been an industrial city, but also to the effort to conceive a productive city, industrially independent and conceptually closer to the rural models of organization and production.

Developing light industries and working units inside the city boundaries, together with reconstructing heavy industries on its limits, helped making Pyongyang a city of production. These facilities are well integrated with the micro-district plan, called 'ju-taek so-gu-yeok gye-hweok' in North Korea. The basic unit of the district consisted of around 4,000 to 7,500 residents with 2,000~2,400 apartment units, and the size of it is around 15 to 30 hectares.[13] Within the district, small industrial facilities and working units are distributed in order to minimize the commuting distance and assure the production in the whole district. Apart from production facilities, other public services such as schools, day care centres or clinics are included in the micro-district; therefore the district itself becomes a self-sustainable area.

This district plan can be compared to the residential district plan of South Korea. A district called 'dong' is similar conceptually to the micro-district in terms of its components except production facilities, residential, schools, and health care facilities. However, a 'dong' has a larger number of residents, around 20,000, is bigger in size, and well-developed streets. In a micro-district in Pyongyang, there are not enough streets within a block. This is mostly both because the district is planned based on walking distance and people are urged to use public transportation instead of private vehicles.

A micro-district in Pyongyang, which merges residential and working functions in a single area, can be structured within self-sustainable blocks of equal land use. This possibly eliminates social segregation between different functional areas. As C.W.Pannell pointed out, the difference between city zones lies mostly in their land use and is not due to the social class of its residents.[14] Therefore, the varied use of a district, containing both production and consumption, avoids having a specific programmatic zone, such as central business district, which is very common in capitalist cities.

View of Pyongyang, 2000

Pyongyang aimed to keep the idea of mixed-use residential districts in order to realize the socialist idea of palliate the distinction between city and countryside, equilibrate social classes and conceptually create the city of production instead of city of consumption.

This type of districts can mostly be seen on the east side of Daedong River right across the Kim Il Sung Square. Unlike the west bank of the river, where the trace of old city fabric remained unchanged after the war, the east side had not actually been well developed by the Japanese 1930s master plan of this area. Therefore, it was a very good opportunity for the Pyongyang authorities to implement a new type of residential district into the area. This micro-district has around 300m by 300m module, which is considered a mega block, with residential buildings at the periphery, and most of the common facilities, working units, and light industries located inside of the block. Hence, unlike other block-type development cities where most of activities happen on the street, in mega-block micro-district of Pyongyang, major social as well as economic activities occur within the block.

RESIDENTIAL AREAS

Low-rise Residential
Mid-rise Residential
High-rise Residential

PYONGYANG; CITY OF GREEN

> Large areas of greenbelt, fountain parks, pleasure parks and fun fairs... Visitors to Pyongyang say they feel as refreshed as they are when in a park. Therefore, Pyongyang is called a park city. The amount of green space per resident is 58 square metres.... Before the liberation of the country, the riverside was considered as an eyesore because of the flood damage and contamination that occurred every year. It has since been turned into a riverside loved by the people.[15]

We have already explained, the creating green space as one of the major concepts of socialist urban planning. It not only provides the quality leisure space and a healthier environment but also limits the expansion of the city. In fact, it is the most important factor that confines and structures the city on the large scale. The importance of "green infrastructure" is also well shown in 1953 Master Plan for Pyongyang by Kim Jung Hee. In the initial plan drawn in 1951, there was no clear structure of green zones or infrastructure. It only showed the general grid of streets and blocks. However, in the 1953 Master Plan, Kim Jung Hee injected "green infrastructure" into the plan. Pyongyang was structured out of several different satellite districts that were confined and limited by "green infrastructure." This was strongly influenced by the 1935 Moscow Master Plan that was based on Howard's Garden City concept. It took advantages from natural topography and Pyongyang rivers so that all networks of "green infrastructure" could be easily integrated into the large scale urban structure .

"Green infrastructure" that Kim Jung Hee proposed can be compared to the "Green Belt" in Seoul, South Korea. Both of them were proposed to control the radical and uncontrolled urban expansion and development. However, while "green infrastructure" in Pyongyang is based on the ideological concept of making the city green and abolishing the distinction between urban and rural areas, it is, at the same time, organically distributed over the city, the "green belt" in Seoul is based on the concept of drawing boundaries between areas of city and agriculture. Therefore, the "green infrastructure" is one of factors of urban structure that is injected into the city in form of a connecting network, while the "green belt" is more a separating single ring detached from the urban structure. The "green infrastructure" in Pyongyang is more actively and carefully considered from the very start of structuring the city.

In reality, however, the concept of limiting the size of satellite districts was not well applied in Pyongyang except for some parts of the city. Because of Pyongyang's fast growth and increasing population size, the areas

Parks in Pyongyang

Moranbong Park

where "green infrastructure" zones were planned, were already occupied by residential developments even before the detailed landscape plan was applied. And as the people's right of residence was important feature to keep in the nation, the area could not be cleared out and left as an informal development-like area. As a result, the balance between residential and other supporting and production facilities that could sustain a micro-district had failed and immigrants into the city started to encroach informally the areas in informal that were supposed to be developed as part of "green infrastructure." However, while areas designated as buffer zone between the districts have been occupied by informal development, other "green infrastructures" for leisure have been well-organized throughout the city.

LANDSCAPE AREAS

Agricultural Lands
Natural Greenspace
Parks and Gardens

Natural elements within Pyongyang are well distributed around the city, including the Daedong River banks, and most of the urban leisure places have been integrated with nature. Since the new master plan focused on the developments on the east side of the river, the Daedong River became a central axis of the city. Therefore, numbers of heavily landscaped parks were located along the river as part of the green infrastructure. From the 1980s onward, to transform the city into a park city, Pyongyang focused on creating parks along the Daedong and Botong River, and developed leisure and convenient facilities around them.[16] There are nearly thirty parks and amusement parks In Pyongyang, with the green area per resident of 40 sqm, which is much higher than in Seoul (16sqm) and cities in the OECD (Organization for Economic Cooperation and Development) countries (average 20sqm).

PYONGYANG; CITY OF SYMBOLISM

> "It is my dream and plan to make Pyongyang as the head of revolution and the capital city for the public. As Pyongyang is the face of North Korea, the central area of Pyongyang is the face of Pyongyang. ... it is very important to create a right axis to make a right central area. Now, I am trying to build Grand People's Study House in front of Kim Il Sung Square, and make the architecture as the Axis of the city".
> Kim, Il Sung[17]

As in other socialist cities, symbolic squares and statues that propagate the victory of socialist revolution are very important elements in creating the urban space of Pyongyang. The central Plaza had always been an important factor in urban planning since Roman period in Europe, and the meaning of the space had been changed based on the paradigm of the society throughout the period. However, the socialist urban planners aimed at redefining the same urban element and using it in different way. The socialist ideology background exalts the importance of an open space that can contain a large number of public for parades, exhibitions and commemorations. Through such events, socialist cities contribute to the strength of social coherence and infuse the public with the ideology of socialism. Most Eastern European cities, not only created new central squares but also transformed existing plazas into public spaces that propagate socialist ideology. For instance, statue and signs in Ban Jelačić Square in Zagreb that existed from the nineteenth century onward were replaced by socialist monuments and symbols under socialism.[18]

Kim Il Sung Square & Grand People's House

Unlike other socialist cities in East European countries, Pyongyang did not have public squares before the socialist period, not only as a consequence of the war but also because of the culture. In traditional East Asian urban planning, zoning and large scale urban structures were more considered than physical factors of urban space, therefore, not only Pyongyang but many other Asian cities were plaza-free till the modern period. In order to fulfil this demand Kim Jung Hee systematically organized new symbolic open spaces in the 1953 Master Plan. Each worked as a central core of a satellite district confined by a green infrastructure. Amongst these symbolic open spaces, Kim Il Sung square is the principal and one of the few remarkable public squares in Pyongyang. Needless to say, the square is the origin point of the central axis of Pyongyang, joining with the ideological monument, "Juche Tower" across the river with the immense public library called The Grand People's Study House with the presidential tribune for parades in front. The directionality of maxi-grid area on the east side of Daedong River is also based on this axis.

With those symbolic squares, monumental artefacts are the other elements that socialist cities, including Pyongyang, emphasize. The reason of it, similar to creating squares is to propagate the victory of socialism and the greatness of the ideology. So, according to North Korean urban theory, depending on how tall, big, or long these artefacts are, the country rates higher in the scale of successful implementation of socialist standards. Also not only artefacts but also monumental statues, towers, and symbols work as urban elements that represent the character of socialist city. As Kevin Lynch pointed out, these elements can be perceived as nodes and landmarks in the city. Approximately, there are 140,000 symbolic buildings and monuments in North Korea –and especially in Pyongyang as its representative city- destined to propagate and symbolize the idea of socialism and the nation. These elements, unlike major open spaces, do not influence the urban structure in large scale, but strongly affect the overarching image of the city.

Monument of Foundation of the Worker's Party

Endnotes

1 Springer, Chris. Pyongyang: The Hidden History of *the North Korean Capital. Budapest: Entente Bt., 2003.*

2 Yi, Wang-gi. *Pukhan Esŏ Ŭi Kŏnch'uksa Yŏn'gu (Research on Architectural History in North Korea).* Seoul: Parŏn, 1994.

3 Yi, Hwa-sŏn. *Chosŏn Kŏnch'uksa (North Korean Architectural History).* Seoul: Parŏn, 1993.

4 Kang, Kŭn-jo, Kyŏng-hye Yi, and Ch'un-hŭi Yi. *P'yŏngyang Ŭi Oje Wa Onŭl.* Chosŏn, P'yŏngyang: Sahoe Kwahak Ch'ulp'ansa, 1986.

5 Son, Chŏng-mok. *Han'guk Kaehanggi Tosi Pyŏnhwa Kwajŏng Yŏn'gu: Kaehangjang, Kaesijang, Chogye, Kŏryuji.* Seoul: Ilchisa, 1982.

6 Yi, Wang-gi. *Pukhan Kŏnch'uk, Tto Hana Ŭi Uri Mosŭp (North Korean Architecture).* Seoul: Seoul Forum, 2000.

7 Springer, Chris. *Pyongyang: The Hidden History of the North Korean Capital.* Budapest: Entente Bt., 2003.

8 Kim, Wŏn. "A Study on the Urban Development Policy in North Korea." The Korea Local Administrat*ion Review 4 (1990): 4123 - 4142*

9 Kim, Wŏn. *Sahoejuŭi Tosi Kyehoek (Socialist Urban Planning).* Seoul: Posŏnggak, 1998.

10 Yi, Hwa-sŏn. Chosŏn Kŏnch'uksa (No*rth Korean Architecture History). Seoul: Parŏn, 1993.*

11 Yi, Wang-gi. *Pukhan Kŏnch'uk, Tto Hana Ŭi Uri Mosŭp.* Sŏul T'ŭkpyŏlsi: Sŏul P'orŏm, 2000.

12 Kim, Hyun-soo, Kim, Kyung-suk. "Nam-Pukhan Tosi Kyehoek ŭi Pigyowa Chŏnmang." Korea Planning Association 1 (1998): 3-12.

13 Yi, Wang-gi. *Pukhan Kŏnch'uk, Tto Hana Ŭi Uri Mosŭp.* Sŏul T'ŭkpyŏlsi: Sŏul P'orŏm, 2000.

14 Leung, Chi-Keung, and Norton Sydney. Ginsburg. *China: Urbanization and National Development.* Chicago: University of Chicago, Dept. of Geography, 1980.

15 Han, Pon-jo. Pyongyang, a Park City. Pyongyang: Ko*rea Pictorial, 2002.*

16 Kim, Wŏn. "A Study on the Urban Development Policy in North Korea." *The Korea Local Administration Review* 4 (1990): 4123 - 4142

17 Kim, Il Sung. In Glorious 50 Years. Pyongyang: Korea P*ictorial., 1995.*

18 Blau, Eve, Ivan Rupnik, and Ivan Rogić Nehajev. *Project Zagreb: Transition as Condition, Strategy, Practice.* Barcelona: Actar D, 2007.

SYMBOLIC AREAS

Sports Facility
Monumental Architecture
Squares and Monuments

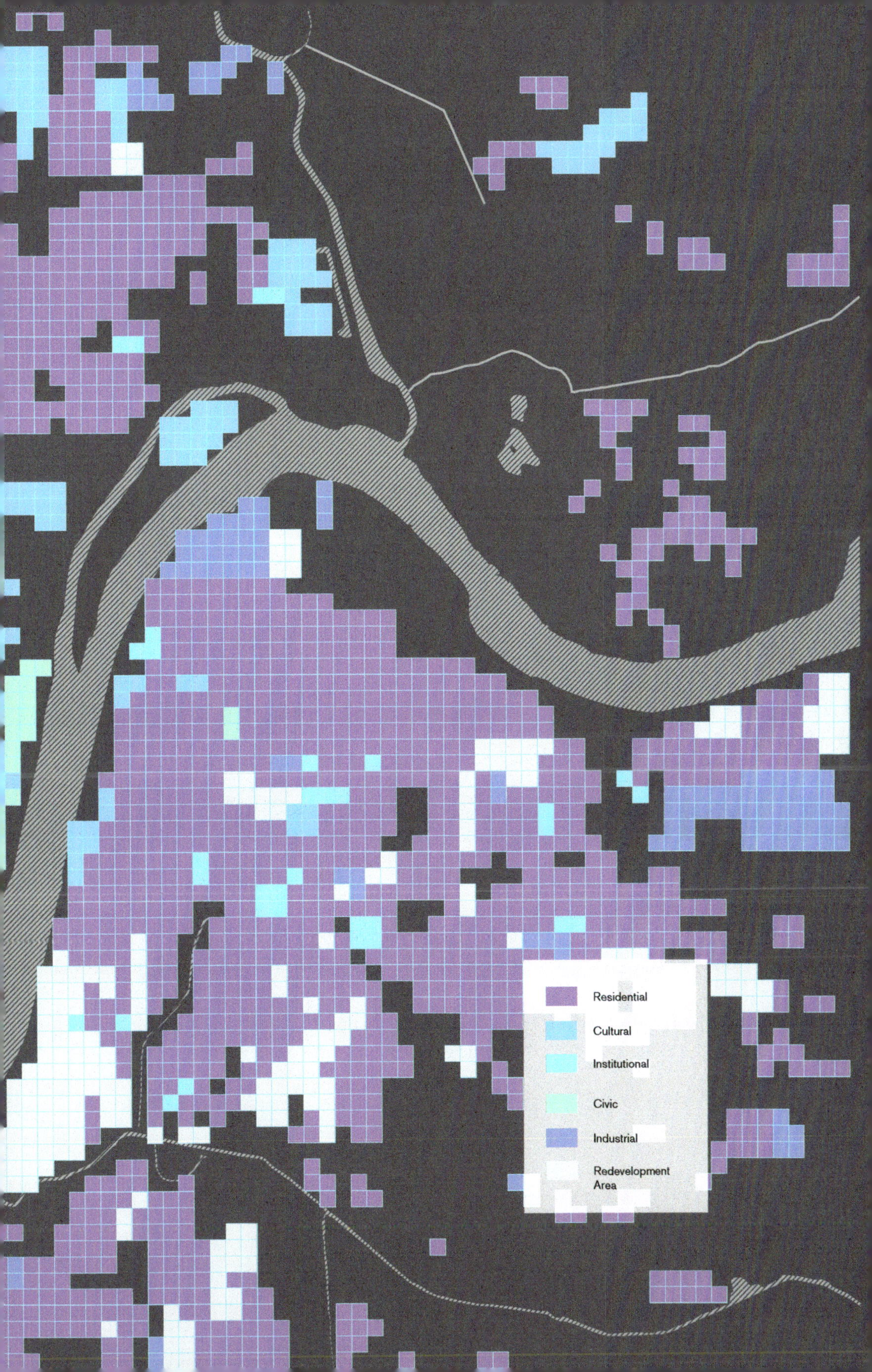
Residential
Cultural
Institutional
Civic
Industrial
Redevelopment Area

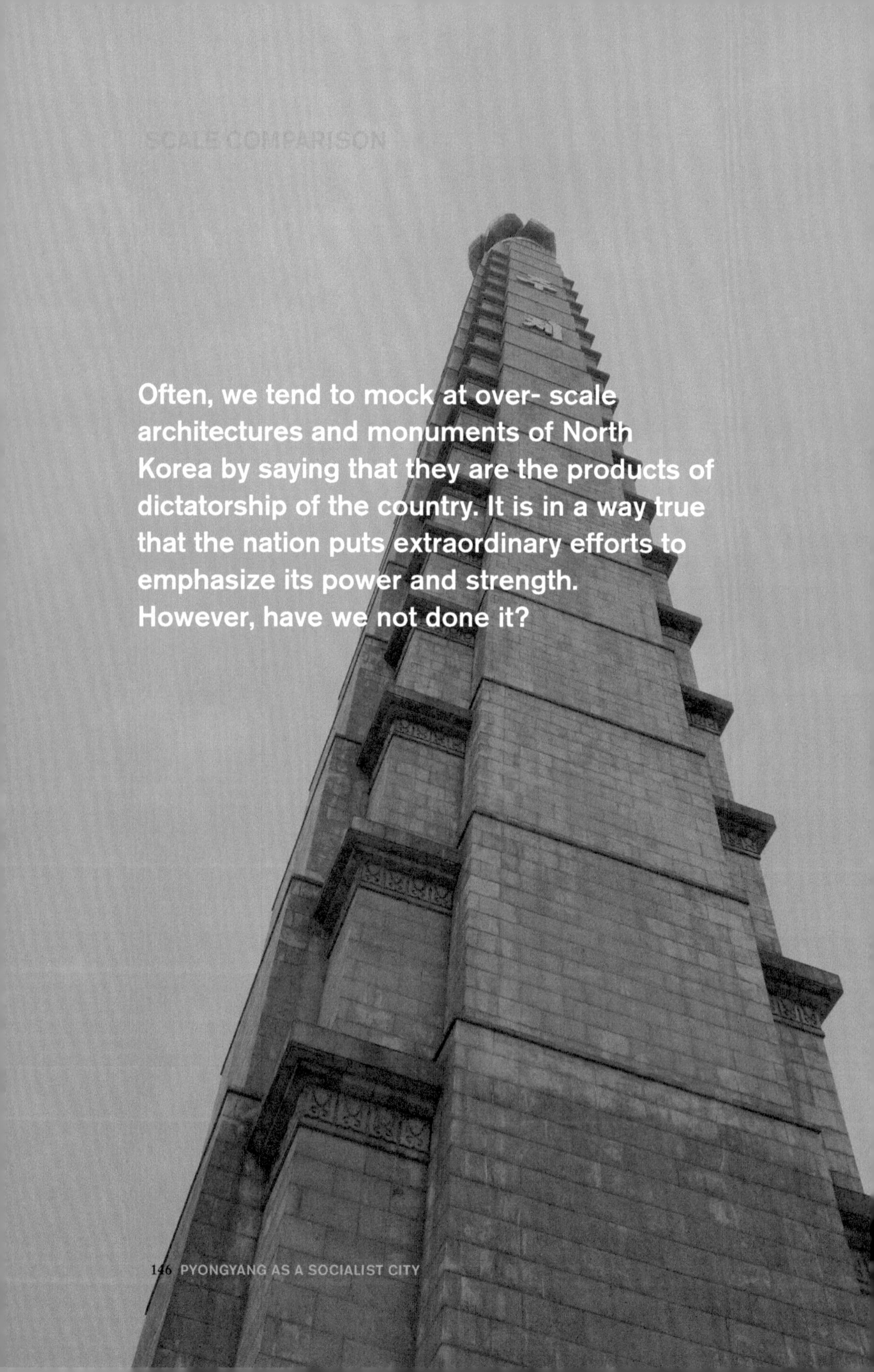

SCALE COMPARISON

Often, we tend to mock at over- scale architectures and monuments of North Korea by saying that they are the products of dictatorship of the country. It is in a way true that the nation puts extraordinary efforts to emphasize its power and strength. However, have we not done it?

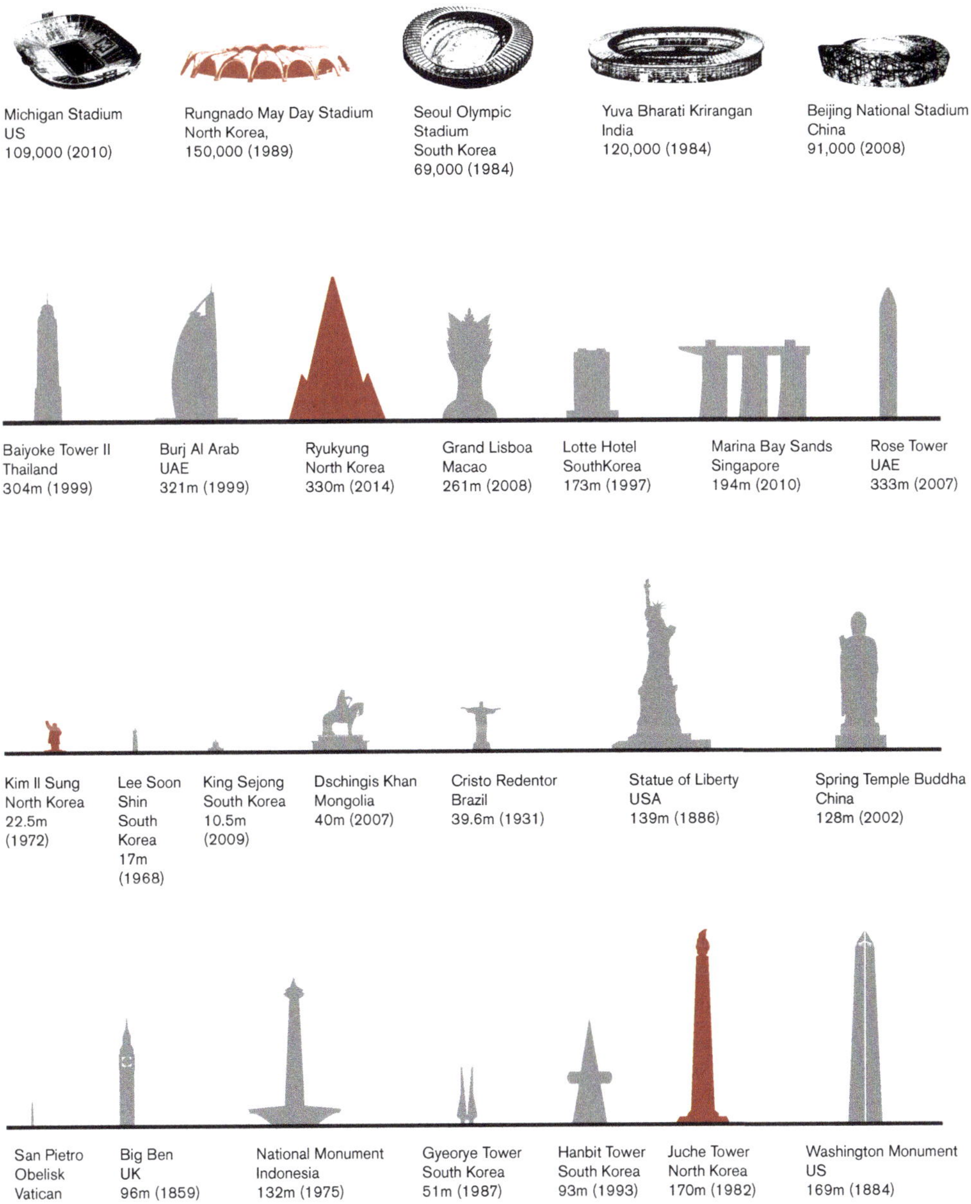

* source from *Pyongyang, And Pyongyang After* (2011), Dongwoo Yim

05
URBAN TRANSFORMATION OF PYONGYANG

After the Korean War, Pyongyang was reconstructed in several stages. the first stage, focused on reconstructing basic infrastructures and government facilities in order to enable the function as the capital city. Starting from the mid-1950s, Pyongyang begun to inject socialist urban features into the city. The 1953 Master Plan by Kim Jung Hee was the background structure of it. Like the 1935 Reconstruction Plan for Moscow, it was the general master plan that structured Pyongyang on a large scale and strongly influenced it's whole future development. It reflected most of the key socialist urban planning guidelines, such as the limited size of city, green infrastructures, and symbolic urban spaces, and it became the back bone of Pyongyang urban structure .

However, aside from the master plan, Pyongyang set up several different development strategies to be developed over time. Since they could be realized more easily on smaller scale than the master plan, they dominated the developmental path of Pyongyang. As a result, with the master plan proposed in the 1950s, these strategies became major factors of transformation of Pyongyang, and the city's current structure and appearance display a mixture of the 1953 Master Plan and several other development strategies.

1953 MASTER PLAN

In order to understand the general structure of Pyongyang, it is essential to understand the 1953 Master Plan first. This is because it was not only the first, but a unique, master plan for Pyongyang that was used as a blue print for the ideal Pyongyang. The revised version of the master plan in 1951 indicated general layouts of the city and development area. Since the master plan in 1951 reviewed the master plan of the 1930s, the 1953 Master Plan logically has similarities with the master plan from the colonial period. The development areas and main infrastructure layouts exhibited similarities between the two master plans. As the 1930s master plan included the eastern part of Daedong River, the 1953 Master Plan also designated it as a major development area and tried to create a balance between the western

1953 MASTER PLAN

River

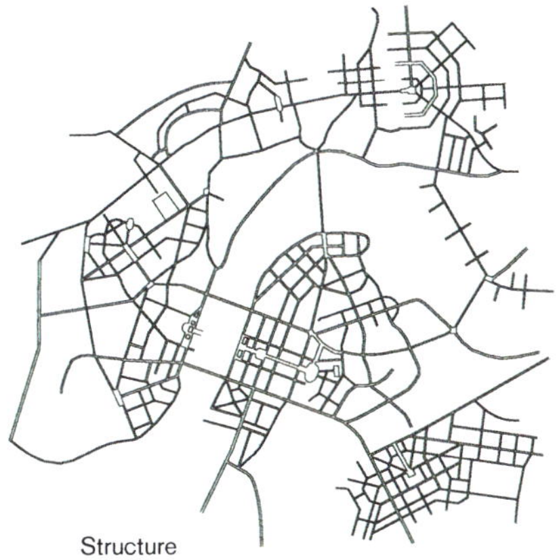

Structure

Green Zone

Nature

Blocks

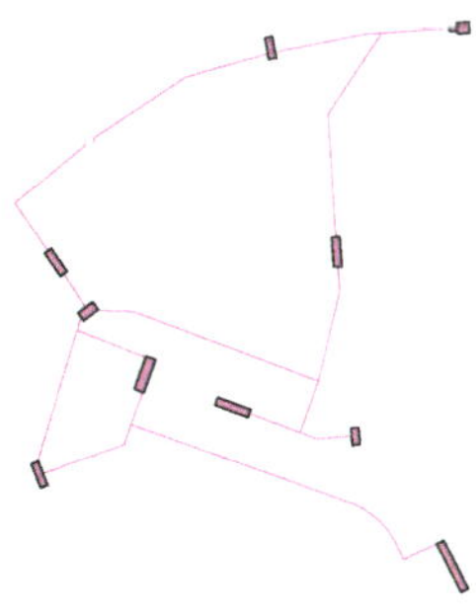

Squares

and the eastern part of the river. Also, in both plans, two major bridges connected the two parts and continued as axis of development.

However, the 1953 Master Plan, includes a couple of strong socialist urban features that neither of the previous master plans has. Since Kim Jung Hee, the master plan's author, had studied architecture in Moscow before he was placed in charge of a new master plan for North Korea's capital by Kim Il Sung, it is apparent that the 1953 Master Plan was strongly influenced by Soviet urban planning strategies and especially the 1935 Moscow Plan, also influenced by Howard's Garden City diagram. Therefore, diagrammatic plans of the three, the 1953 Master Plan for Pyongyang, the 1935 Moscow Plan, and the Garden City diagram, are all conceptually very similar. This suggests that the large-scale urban structure of Pyongyang strictly follows the basic socialist urban planning guidelines. Although the general development area overlaps with the master plan from the 1930s, the 1953 Master Plan divides the area into several separated districts with the green infrastructure functioning as a buffer zone between them. Throughout the distribution of districts, the master plan tries to implement the socialist idea of preventing social and class segregation between the areas. By limiting the size and expansion of each district through green infrastructure, it allows the structure to abolish the differences between urban and rural areas.

In the 1953 Master Plan, not only the large-scale infrastructure but also medium-size urban spaces are carefully designed. Each block is proposed as a 300m x 300m block similar to the North Korean micro-district, the smallest self-sustainable unit in Pyongyang. In order to be more efficient in using infrastructures and public facilities, dozens of blocks are gathered together to make a single district and tied together with a major open square in the centre, with major city infrastructures connecting these central squares. These squares are proposed as symbolic urban spaces to propagate socialist ideology and the victory of the revolution and the war in North Korea.

The district in the old downtown area is designated as the administrative centre amongst several satellite districts. Besides the fact that, like other socialist cities, it tried to eliminate social and class segregation on spatial basis, Pyongyang also had to create a 'central district' so that it could be the representative core that shows the greatness and superiority of socialism. Nevertheless, this central district is quite different from central districts in capitalist cities. In capitalist cities, a central district is mostly occupied by business programs that have the strongest capital power, and it becomes the most competitive zone for development. However, in Pyongyang, in spite of its centrality, the development in the central district is restricted by the plan, and like other satellite districts, it is also confined by green infrastructure.

The interesting feature of the central district of Pyongyang is that it is composed of two physically separated parts: the west side of the Daedong River where Kim Il Sung Square is, and east side of the river where Juche Tower is located. This speaks of the 1953 Master Plan's intention of developing the east part of Daedong River. This region was first considered as a new development district during the colonial era but was never fully developed. However, in the 1953 Master Plan, this area is considered as part of the central district and has had higher priority in the development process, an idea that has been well realized since then.

DEVELOPMENT PATHS: FROM THE 1950S TO THE 1990S

The 1950s

> After the Korean War, the Workers' Party of Korea vigorously pushed forward the work of building the foundation of socialism, while rehabilitating the national economy. The WPK's general task for building the foundation of socialism was to establish the undivided sway of relations of socialist production by transforming small-commodity and capitalist economic forms along socialist lines, abolish the colonial lop-sideness and technical backwards of industry and build the basis of socialist industrialization.[1]

After the Korean War, the Worker's Party of Korea (WPK) focused on the reconstruction of the national economy in parallel with building the foundation of socialism. The WPK discussed the Three-Year Plan (1954-1956) of

Pyongyang during the reconstruction, 1960s

postwar rehabilitation and development of the national economy, and its goal was to build a concrete-strong foundation of socialism in North Korea. After the Three-Year Plan, the Five-Year Plan, also known as the Chollima Movement, which led to the Chongsan-ri Method and the Taean Work System, was set forth at the Third Congress of the WPK in 1956.[2] It focused on reconstruction of heavy industry, such as the Kangson Steel Plant, the Kim Chae Iron Works, and the Chongjin Fishery Station, to ensure political independence from both the Soviet Union and China. As a result, the colonial lop-sideness of industry disappeared, and tangible bases for both heavy and light industry were built.

The 1960s

> The Taean work system is a system of economic management admirably suited to the nature of a socialist system, for it stipulates that the factories and enterprises conduct all their management activities under the collective leadership of Party committees and carry out their economic tasks by giving precedence to political work, infusing the producing masses with an enthusiasm for work; that superiors do everything they can to help their subordinates and that the economy is managed and operated in a scientific and rational way. - Kim Il Sung -[3]

After the reconstruction in the 1950s, setting solid foundations and construction of socialism in all social and economic spheres became the major issue in North Korea in the 1960s. This was especially true in Pyongyang, considered to be the representative of an ideal socialist city. In 1961, the Fourth Congress of the WPK was convened. The congress adopted the First Seven-Year Plan (1961-1967) for further development of socialism. The important goals of the plan were to make the country into a socialist industrial country with modern industries and advanced agriculture, and to improve the people's living conditions. To realize these goals, the WPK focused on improving the economic management system by establishing the Taean work system as a management model. It also established new guidelines for the organization of agriculture, a crucial field for socialist economy, so that the general development could be accelerated.

Under the slogan "A rifle in one hand and a hammer or sickle in the other!", the WPK proposed to strengthen both economy and defense. A strong economy could be realized, it argued, through the expansion of heavy industry on a large scale as well as through the reinforced if its branches. Therefore, the independent light industry and transport systems to connect the industrial network began to be structured in the 1960s.

Pyongyang Station, 1960s

Another task that the WPK tried to resolve in the 1960s was the question of socialist rural area. In 1964, Kim Il Sung published the "Theses on the Socialist Rural Question in Our Country" and argued about the essence and contents of the rural issues under socialism. The theses became the back bone of the WPK's program, and the WPK insisted that only through these tenets the country could succeed in changing the entire appearance of the rural area. After all, North Korean cities, including Pyongyang, became modernized industrial cities in parallel with advanced agriculture.

In addition to the overall construction plan for North Korean cities, Pyongyang, as the capital city, had specified strategies to convert itself into an ideal socialist city. The development of Pyongyang focused on five strategies that would propagate the ideology of socialism: expansion of major boulevards, construction of high-rise buildings along the boulevards, building large scale civic and cultural facilities, creating symbolic and sculptured squares, and expanding leisure, sports and tourism facilities.[4]

EXPANSION OF THE CITY

During the colonial period in the early 20th century, development of Pyongyang was mostly confined in former Pyongyang Fortress, and new development just started to happen across the Daedong River in 1930s. The 1953 Master Plan to reconstruct the city included the Eastern part of the city actively, which later became one of the major development areas in the 1960s. Current city has grown even bigger than the master plan, and in many areas, the unexpected expansion did not necessarily follow the master plan.

In the original master plan, Pyongyang was planed as 200,000 population city, which now has almost 3,000,000 people. Although North Korea has a strict rule to regulate migration between cities, it really could not restrict the radical growth of the city. Later, this resulted the need of high-rise type apartment developments as well.

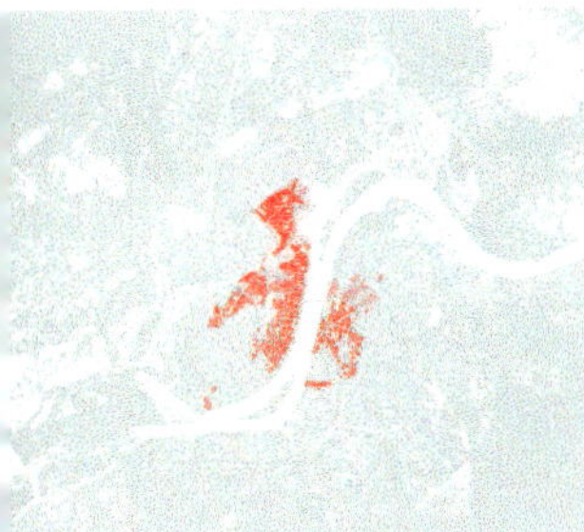

945

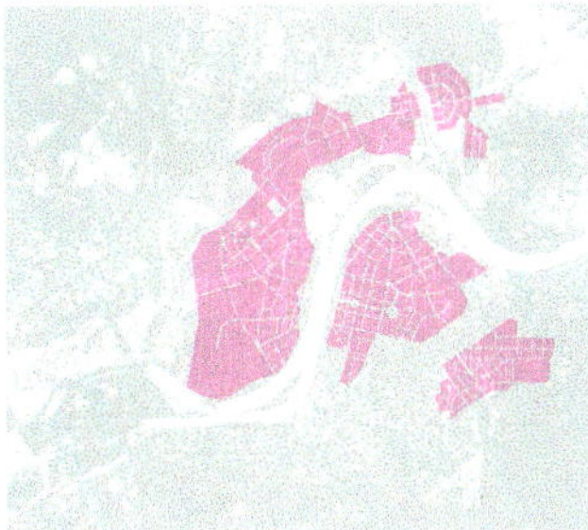

Master Plan

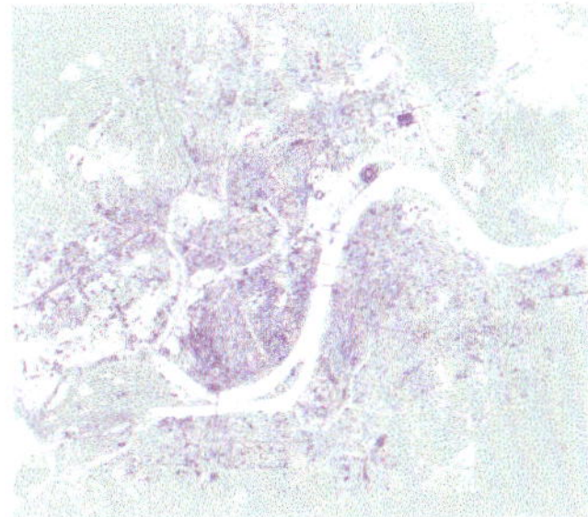

2000s

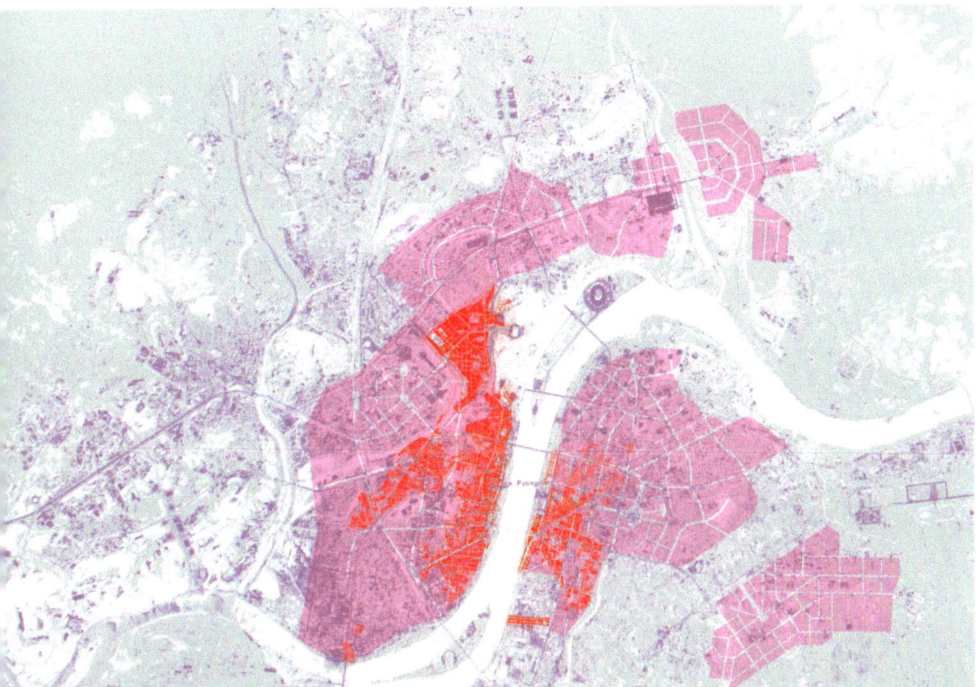

DEVELOPMENTS OF MAJOR STREETS

In the original 1953 Master Plan, the city was planned in two ways: district and connection. Several districts were planned in Pyongyang, that were buffered by green zone, and each district was connected to others with major boulevards. Although this was the basic rule of the original master plan, few areas followed this rule as the city expanded radically within thirty years.

Couple of districts that were reconstructed and developed before the city expansion had chance to follow the original master plan, whereas, some other parts totally ignored the original master plan. For instance, the Gwangbok Street Development and Tongil Street Development, the two most known high-rise apartment developments, are developed outside of the master plan zone with the introduction of major streets, Gwangbok and Tongil.

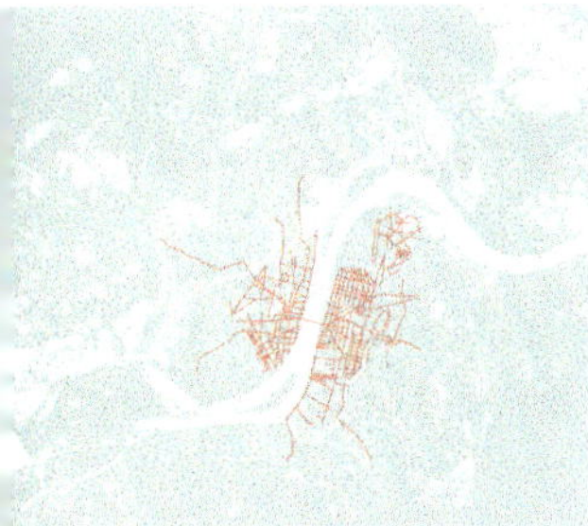

1945

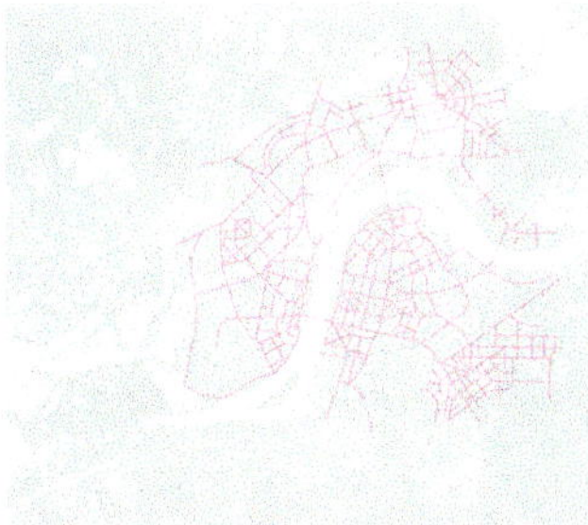

Master Plan

2000s

TRANSFORMATION OF LANDSCAPE AREA

In the 1953 Master Plan, Green Infrastructure, landscape area, was introduced to control the expansion of the city. This idea was borrowed from the Garden City idea, which influenced socialist urban planning strategy very much. However, as explained, as Pyongyang grew more than what was planned in the beginning, this landscape structure changed dramatically. Many areas that were planned as landscape area were converted to low-rise housing developments. This low-rise development pattern shows that it was not carefully planned from the beginning but rather emerged in the city with less control.

At the same time, Pyongyang also gained "Green Zone" with having agricultural areas within the city. Garden City and the 1953 Master Plan suggested leisure and park for the buffer zone. However, Pyongyang adopted the idea of having agriculture area to keep the rural aspect within the city, and this resulted the city to have zones that function as buffering area.

Master Plan

Hills

Landscaped Area

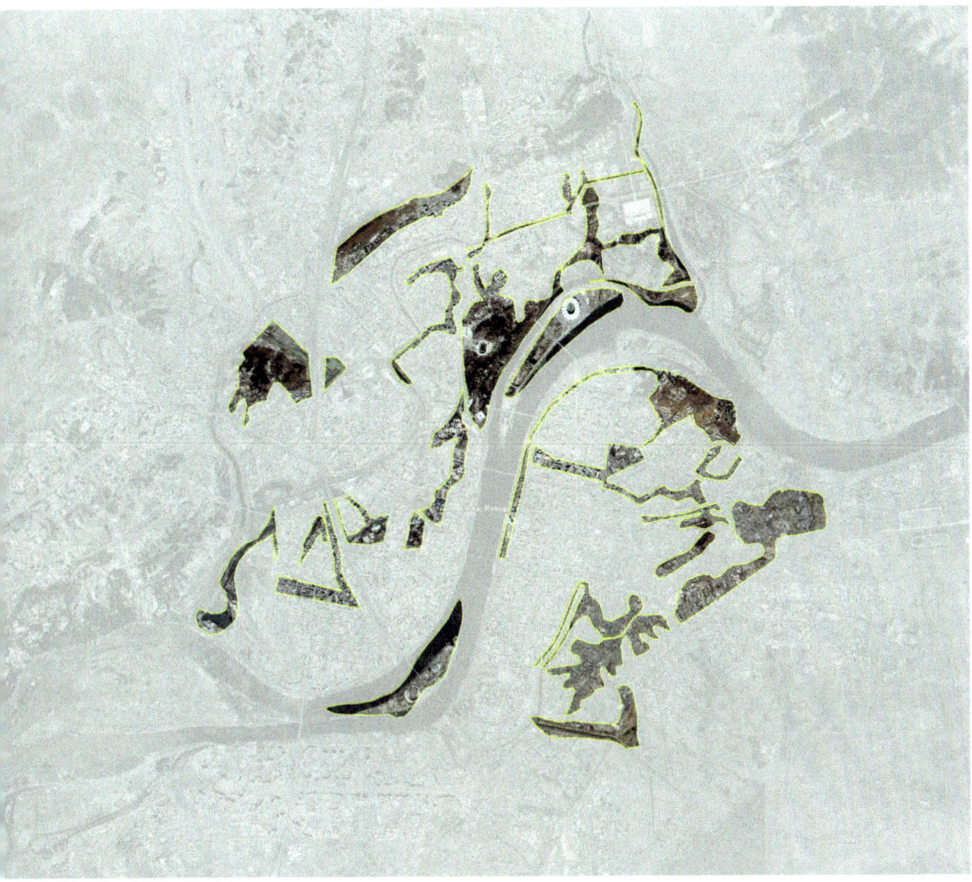

The 1960s was the first period that Pyongyang started to construct and imprint socialist features in the city, and by realizing those strategies, it could achieve both the appearance of the socialist capital city.

The 1970s

During the 1970s, North Korea replaced Marxism-Leninism with its unique Juche ideology, first pronounced by Kim Il Sung in the 1950s as an ideology independent from the Soviet Union. Most of posterior constructions and developments reflected Kim's definitive ideas. At the Fifth Congress, the WPK made plans to complete the socialist transformation by generating three revolutions: ideological, technological, and cultural. The congress adopted the Six-Year Plan (1971-1976) that focused on developing the technical foundations of socialism. Under the slogan "Let us meet the requirements of Juche in ideology, technology and culture!, the WPK sent three-revolutionary team members to factories, enterprises and cooperative farms in order to lead the revolution within these organizations.

Construction Site in Botong Plain

Concrete Block Factory

The 1970s was the most stable period in North Korea's contemporary history both politically and economically and numerous architectural monuments – around twenty only in Pyongyang- symbolizing the propagation of socialism were built during this period.[5] Also, following the Juche Idea, which hinged on ideological independence from the Soviet Union, Pyongyang reconstructed most of boulevards with the support of the Soviet Union and erected a series of high rise residential buildings along those boulevards. In the 1970s, the first high-rise residential typology was introduced, not only because the population of the city had grown quickly, but also because it was an effective way to modernize the image of major city boulevards. Therefore, the development pattern, situating high-rise residentials at the periphery of the block, and low-rise residentials and working facilities in the centre, became an archetypical development type in North Korean cities.

STREET TRANSFORMATION

Districts that were developed in the earlier period of the reconstruction mostly followed the rule of the 1953 Master Plan, and therefore, the street structure was also well inbeded into the city. However, as the city grew, wider and longer highway type streets were introduced in the city.

[illegible] Masterplan

Streets developed as planned

Additional Streets

Current Street Condition

SQUARE TRANSFORMATION

In the 1953 Master Plan, several districts were introduced in the city along with main squares. Each square searved as main public space of the district, and major boulevards connected one to another. However, the current square structure does not function as public space within a district but rather works as symbolic gestures with less rule of displacement.

Main Square Structure in the Original Master Plan, 1953

Current Main Square Structure

SQUARE TRANSFORMATION

1953 Master Plan

2000s

Pyongyang, 1975

The 1980s

> The Sixth Congress of the Workers' Party of Korea in October 1980 defined modeling of society on the Juche Idea as the general task of the Korean revolution. It raised the achievement of the complete victory of socialism as the immediate task.[6]

The 1980s was a turning point of North Korean development, showing a visible sped up in this period. The WPK proposed the Third Seven-Year Plan (1987-1995) that established material and technical foundations to consolidate the socialist society of North Korea. It carried out large-scale capital construction successfully and built numbers of great monuments in Pyongyang.

The plan also focused on improving people's living standards and brought a revolution in both light industry and housing, planning to provide 150,000-200,000 houses per year in the country over the period.

There were four major development patterns in Pyongyang during the 1980s.[7] First, the large-scale high-rise residential development was carried out. The first high-rise apartment was introduced to Pyongyang in the 1970s, but still, most newly built residential apartments were mid-rise. However, to meet the goal of the Third Seven-Year Plan, which was to provide 150,000-200,000 houses, the development concentrated on construction of denser and higher residential apartments. The high-rise apartments ranged from 10 to 40 stories and the unit size was around 65 sqm, which was almost twice as big as residential units from the 1960s.[8]

Second, the development of Pyongyang started to expand to the periphery of the city. Although it was planned as a new development area in both colonial era and the 1953 Mater Plan, it was not until the 1980s that the east side of Dacdong River started to be highly developed. Similar to the developing of the other side with Kim Il Sung Square, Pyongyang could create a strong axis with two major symbolic spaces, Kim Il Sung Square and Juche Idea Tower. Both were proposed in the 1953 Master Plan. Also, with high-rise development the western side of Botong River and southern part of Daedong River were developed in the 1980s as new residential districts.

Third, Pyongyang started to expand green spaces throughout the city in order to convert itself into an international city. It tried to create a city in the park instead of park in the city. The development pattern of expanding green spaces also met socialist urban planning strategies that accentuated the importance of parks to provide the people with leisure and resting spaces. Both sides of riverfront along the Daedong River were developed as parks and major leisure parks in Pyongyang, including Mangyungdae Leisure Park, opened in the 1980s.

Lastly, in the 1980s, numbers of convenient facilities, cultural buildings, sports centres and international hotels were developed in Pyongyang. Like expanding green spaces in the city, this was a move towards the approximation to international standards and promotion of Pyongyang. In this period, Ryukyung hotel, which might have been the tallest hotel in the world at the time if completed, underwent construction. The largest sports complex in Pyongyang was developed along Chongchun Street, and May-Day Stadium, the largest stadium in the world seating 150,000, was built.

The 1990s

The whole national economy of North Korea began to collapse during the 1990s. After the fall of Berlin War, economic supports from the fellow communist bloc had reduced dramatically, and the great recession and famine, notoriously known as Arduous March, had started in the mid-1990s. Therefore, most of large-scale developments that were to evidence the superiority of socialism were cancelled or postponed. For instance, Ryukyung Hotel had to stop its construction after the structural part was finished because of financial difficulties, and it was suspended until recently when middle eastern company Orascom invested on it and resumed the construction in 2008. Until the great famine started, meanwhile, Pyongyang continued developing large residential districts in the early 1990s to solve the housing shortage

Pyongyang, 1980s

Pyongyang, 1980s

problem. Following one of the largest housing developments in the city, Gwangbok Street development which provided about 100,000 units in 1989, Tongil Street development had happened on the other side of the Daedong River from Gwangbok Street, providing around 30,000 new units.[9]

URBAN TRANSFORMATION

1953 Master Plan vs. Development Paths

Beside the central district of Pyongyang, there are only few satellite districts built according to the master plan. The development path during the 1960s differed from the 1953 Master Plan not only because of the city's fast growth, but also because of new development strategies that Kim Il Sung adopted. As mentioned before, once proposed, the development guidelines of the 1960s followed five strategies. However, some of these strategies conflicted with the larger master plan scheme. For instance, the development strategy of focusing on major boulevards and constructions along them could not be reconciled with the scheme of a multi-core system. While development patterns of multi-core systems from the 1953 Master Plan were

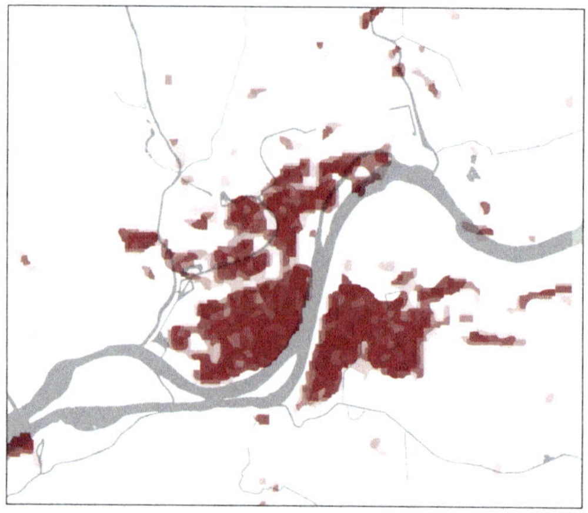

1962

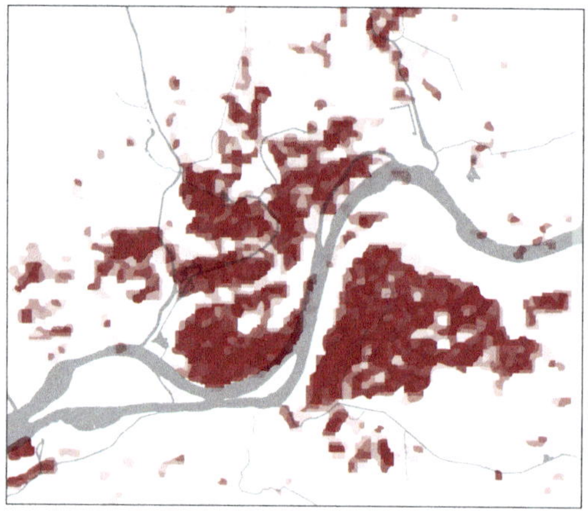

1985

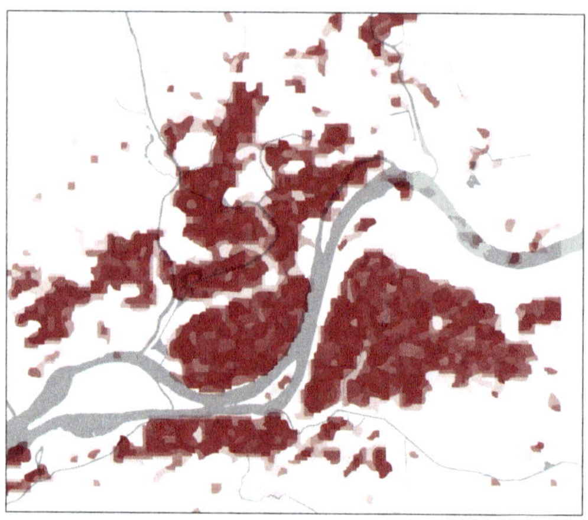

2004

focused on central squares in each satellite district, developments along the boulevards followed a more linear pattern, instead.

New urban strategies developed throughout the periods corresponding with national economic plans made the central district more 'central' than initially proposed. The 1953 Master Plan, envisioned major urban spaces distributed evenly in each satellite district in order to prevent the social segregation between districts. As Kim Il Sung insisted, the district should appear and function as the face of Pyongyang, and thus, both major symbolic spaces and monumental buildings were to be concentrated in it. This monumental saturation of urban spaces makes them more effective in terms of state propaganda.

Also, the fast growth of population, made necessary to focus on large-scale residential construction in Pyongyang in order to resolve the continuous problem of housing shortage. This development was fast and dense, causing a residential oriented districts. In a socialist city, as previously discussed, the micro-district with well-balanced development between residence, industry, or workshops, is the basic form of development. Hence, because of its high immigration rate, Pyongyang focused its efforts on

Ryukyung Hotel During the Reconstruction

expanding housing rather than on developing production facilities. High-rise developments started in the 1970s and became the major development pattern of the 1980s.

Although North Korea had a strict control of migration through of system of residence permit linked to the occupation place, this unexpected immigration flow into Pyongyang kept increasing throughout the periods. This resulted in an increased informal residential development. Although the government still held its grip on several different low-rise housing typologies, it could not control all the development growing informally throughout the city, fulfilling the area where planned construction was missing or in process. As a result, informal development encroached areas planned as parks and landscape areas in the 1953 Master Plan. Therefore, green infrastructures that were proposed as buffer zones between satellite districts to limit the size of the city were never fully implemented.

These development patterns that conflicted with the master plan perspective continued throughout the period of fast construction. However during the 1980s, some development also tried to follow the 1953 Master Plan. For instance, new areas across Daedong River (on the east side) were carefully realized according to the original plan. The most important city axis was established by creating Juche Idea Tower and a major monumental space around it, and by structuring the housing blocks based on the concept of the micro-district. Not only thir size, but also the distribution of micro-district programs, is well displayed in this area. Ten to fifteen storey residential buildings are located at the periphery of the block, and common facilities as well as working centres are distributed in the block interior. With the development of the eastern part of Daedong River, Pyongyang finally achieved the central district proposed in the 1953 Master Plan, and moreover, the district was acknowledged as an ideal socialist urban structure.

Additionally, the 1980s was the period in which Pyongyang successfully implemented the 1953 Master Plan proposals for green spaces . Although all proposed green infrastructures not realized well, other planned green spaces were realized in this period. Numbers of parks proposed in the master plan together with green infrastructure were mostly related to natural topography or rivers of Pyongyang. And in the 1980, to make the city in the park, Pyongyang focused on improving the landscape and expanding leisure parks. For instance, Mangyungdae Leisure Park, which opened in 1982, was built in Mangyungdae area on a natural hill at the downstream of Daedong River. The total area of the park is 56,000 sqm and the capacity is 100,000 guests per day. Also, river front parks were developed along Daedong River in the 1980s, which were also drawn in the master plan. They are used as urban parks to create another city axis perpendicular to major axis of Kim Il Sung Square and Juche Idea Tower.

Like any other city, Pyongyang was not fully built based only on its master plan from 1953. The central area, which was first reconstructed right after the war, has been well structured based on the master plan. It has Kim Il Sung Square as a major monumental space of the district as well as of the city, and major administrative facilities that make this urban centrality. However, as the city grew rapidly and socialist propaganda became a priority, Pyongyang began to adopt several different development strategies in order to fulfil those changes from the 1960s. And this is the moment when the development pattern of Pyongyang began to diverge from the master plan. Although most strategies were chosen to strengthen the representation of the socialist ideology, they differed from the master plan that was also trying to envision an ideal socialist city. Since they had to deal with fast growth, most of the new strategies worked on a smaller scale (instead of the large scale urban structure) so that they could react directly to the specific change. Therefore, in spite of the numerous socialist features in the city, the larger scale urban structure of Pyongyang has not been well developed in comparison with the model of an ideal socialist city. Nevertheless, thanks to its well-structured master plan, Pyongyang has had a back bone for its development path throughout the period, and the central district in particular has been well-structured and created as an ideal socialist city based on the 1953 Master Plan.

Endnotes

1 Kim, Pok Rok. *Glorious 50 Years.* Pyongyang: Korea Pictorial, 1995.

2 *Ibid.*

3 *Ibid.*

4 Kim, Wŏn. *Sahoejuŭi Tosi Kyehoek (Socialist Urban Planning).* Seoul: Posŏnggak, 1998.

5 *Ibid.*

6 Kim, Pok Rok. *Glorious 50 Years.* Pyongyang: Korea Pictorial, 1995.

7 Kim, Hyun-soo. *Pukhan Ŭi Tosi Kyehoek E Kwanhan Yŏn'gu (A Research on North Korean Urban Planning).* Master's thesis, Seoul National University. 1994.

8 Kim, Wŏn. *Sahoejuŭi Tosi Kyehoek (Socialist Urban Planning).* Seoul: Posŏnggak, 1998.

9 *Ibid.*

AGE OF BOULEVARDS

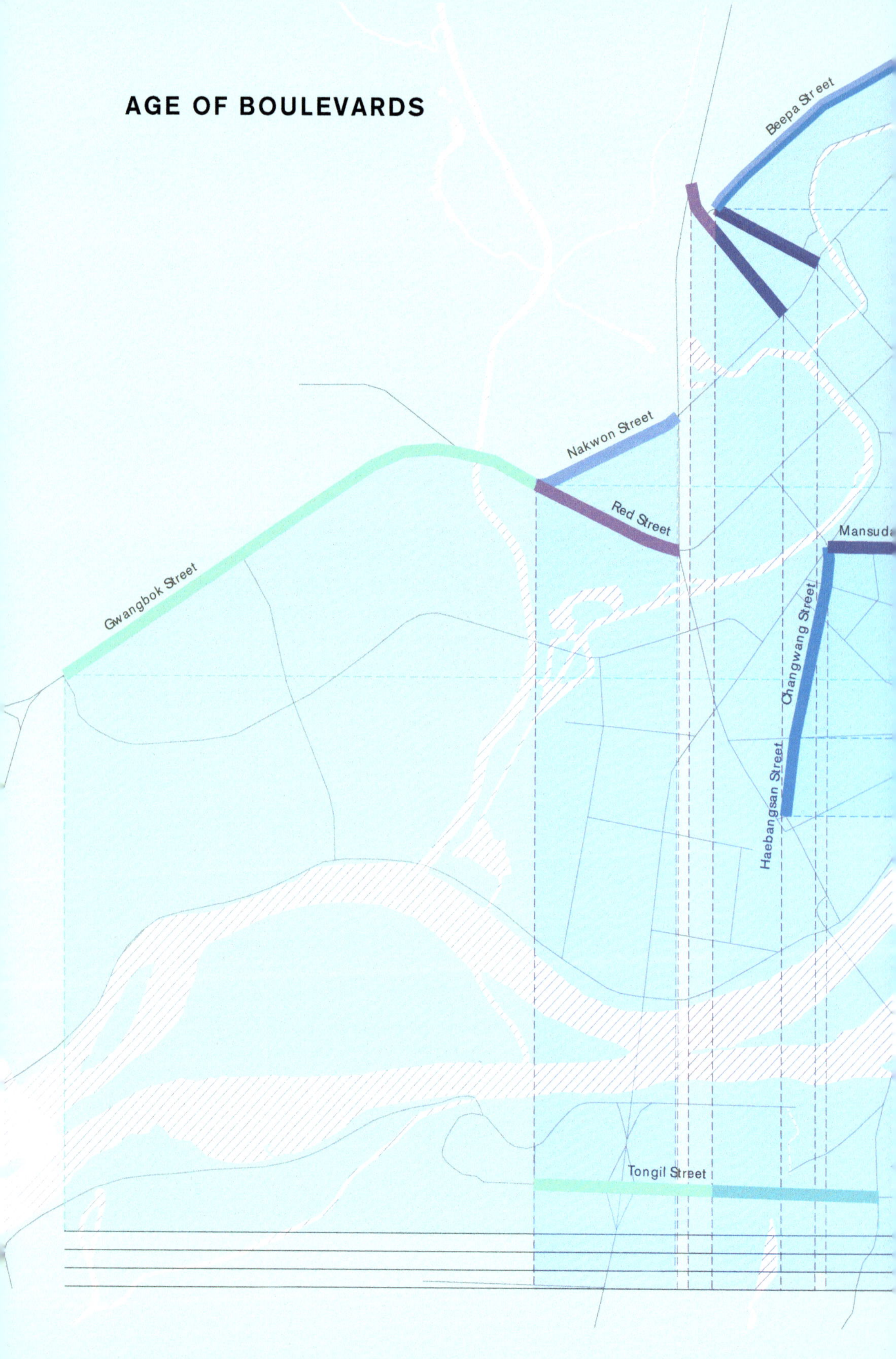

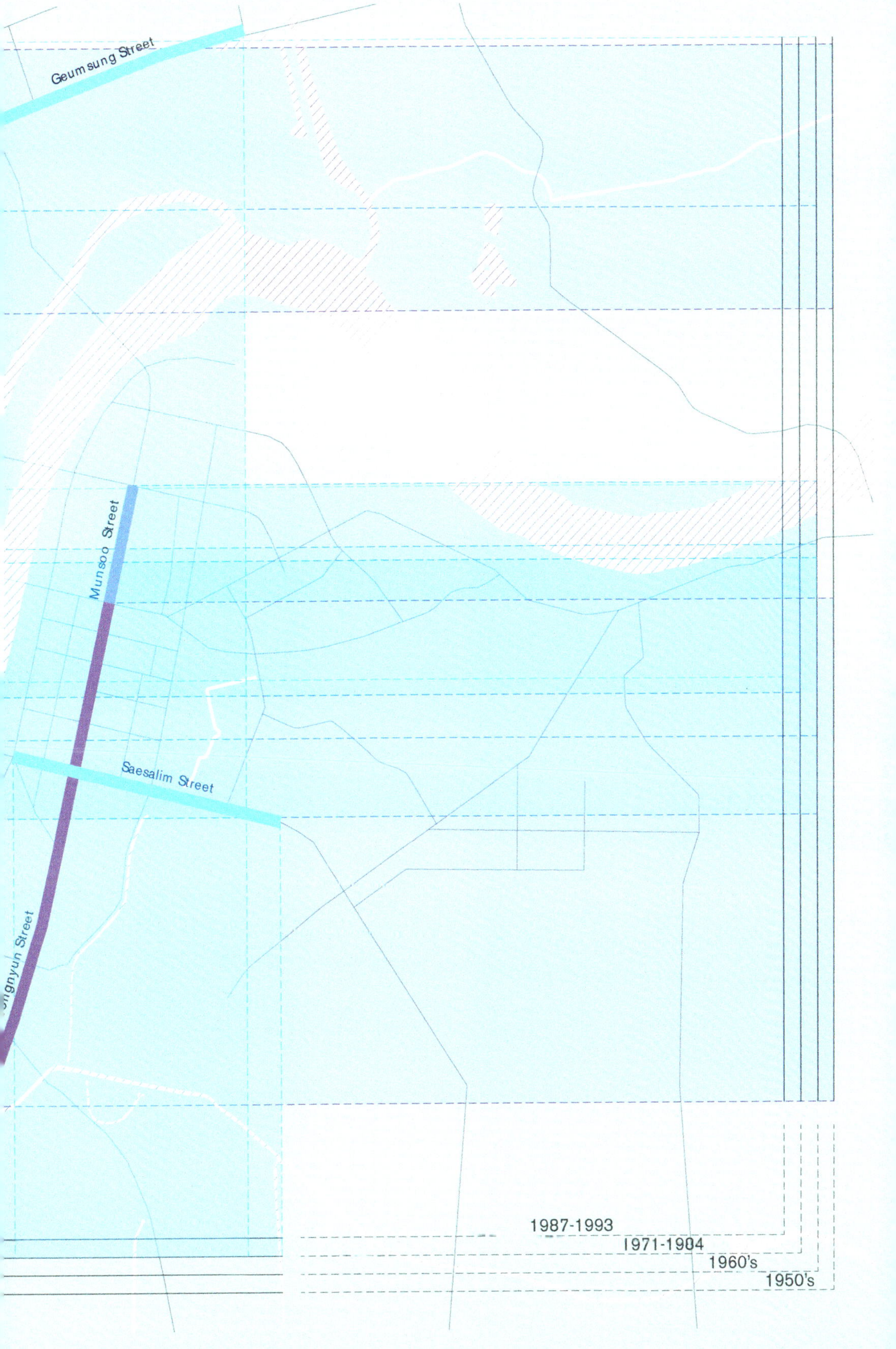
Geumsung Street
Munsoo Street
Saesalim Street
Sngnyun Street
1987-1993
1971-1984
1960's
1950's

AGE OF MAIN BUILDINGS

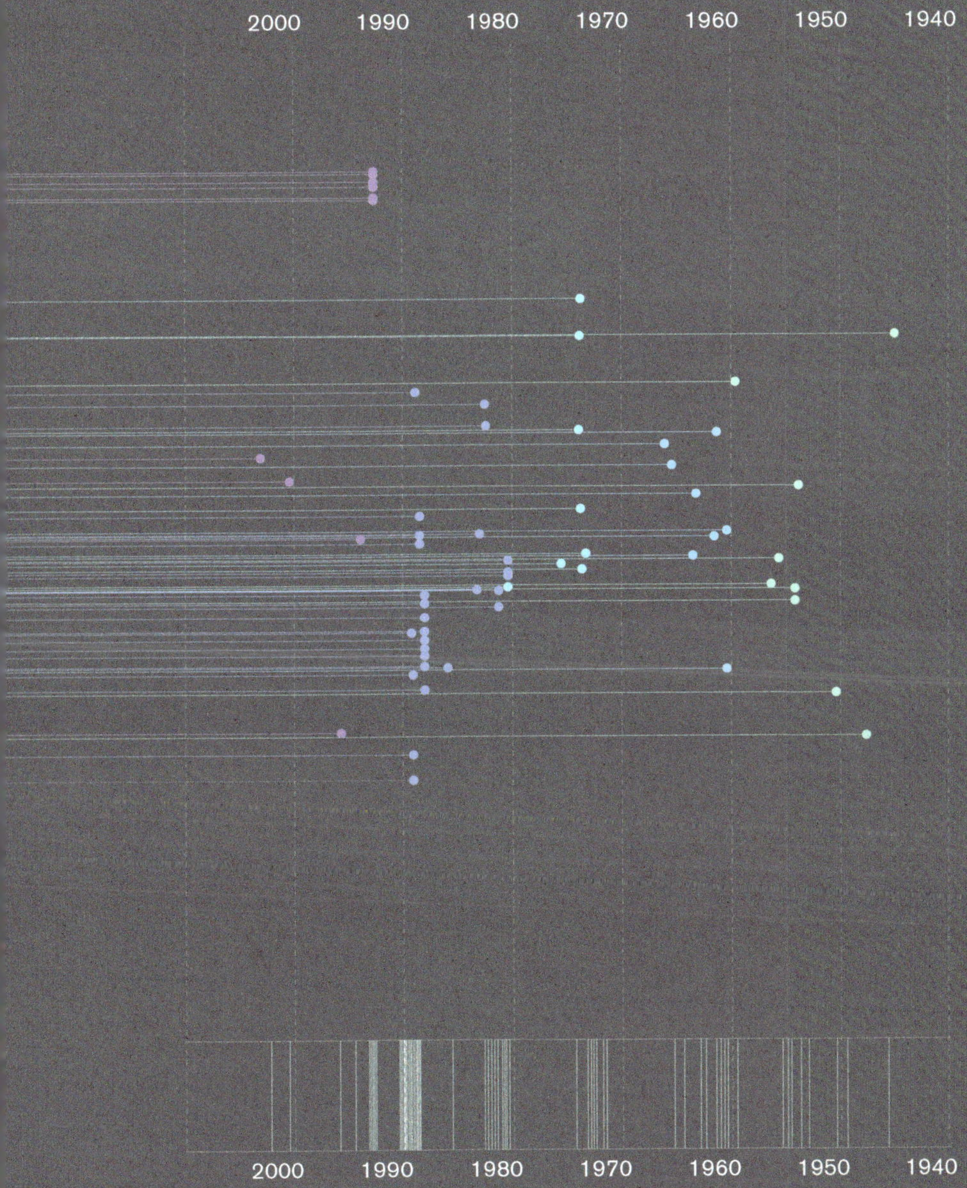
2000 1990 1980 1970 1960 1950 1940
2000 1990 1980 1970 1960 1950 1940

4 DISTRICTS COMPARISON

Four areas are picked to compare morphology of different spots of the city based on the 1953 Master Plan. It shows different development pattern depending on how it was planned in the original master plan.

A. Realized Master Plan Area
B. Planned as Landscape Area in the Master Plan
C. Developed Area in different way from the Master Plan
D. Developed Area that was not part of the Master Plan

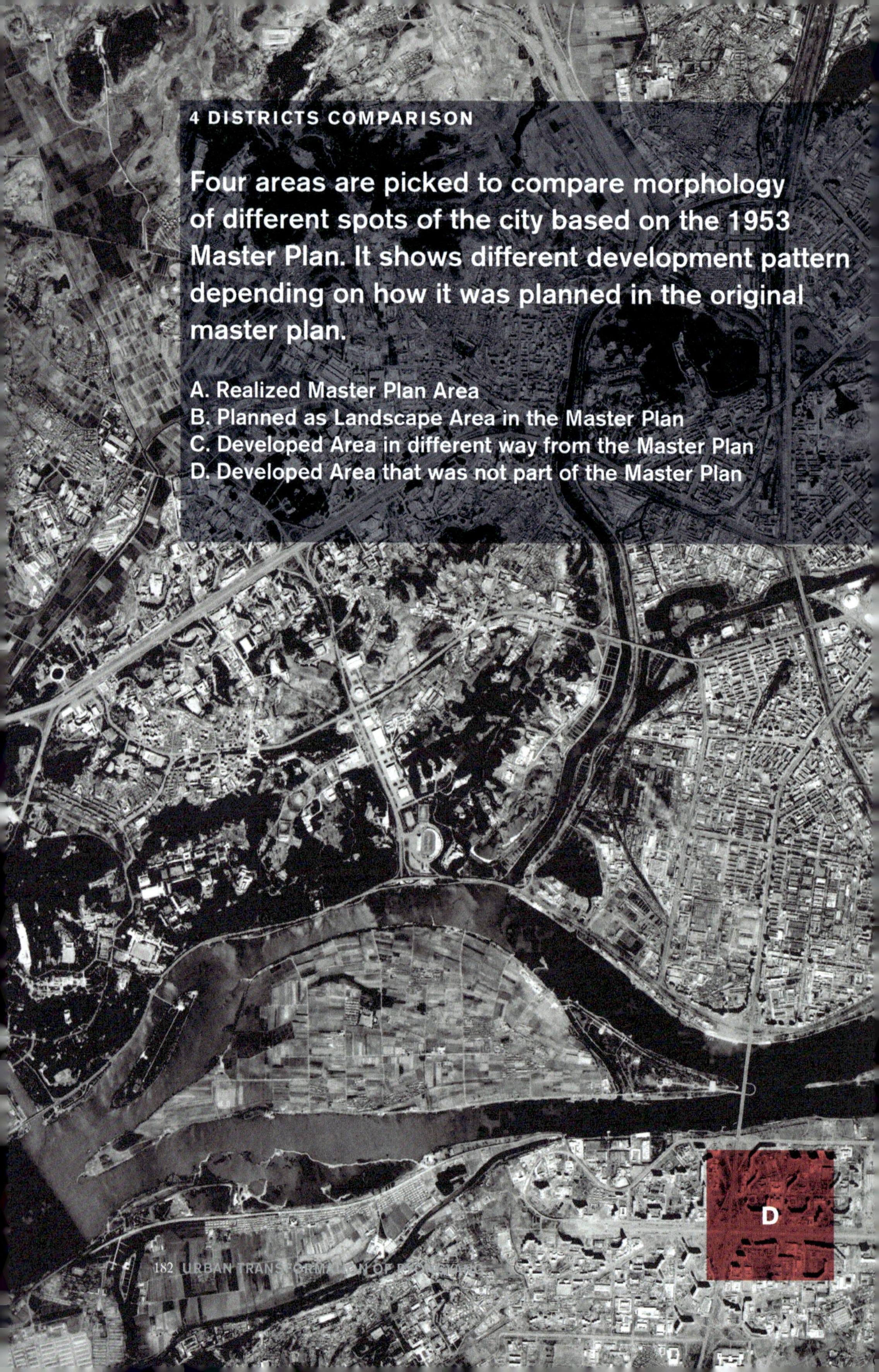

Pyongyang
North Korea, Pyongyang
A
B
C

A. Realized Master Plan Area
B. Planned as Landscape Area in the Master Plan
C. Developed Area in different way from the Master Plan
D. Developed Area that was not part of the Master Plan

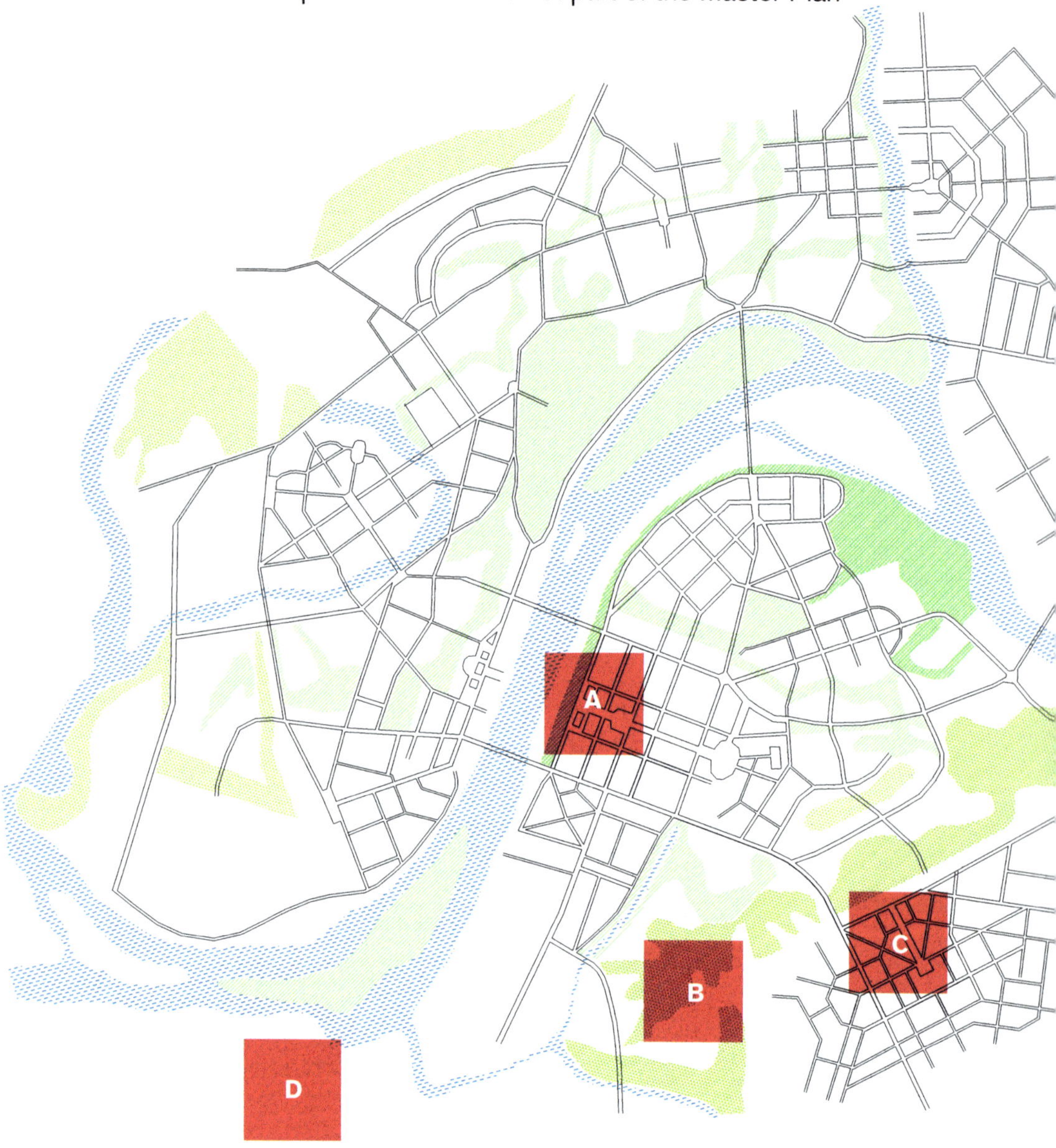

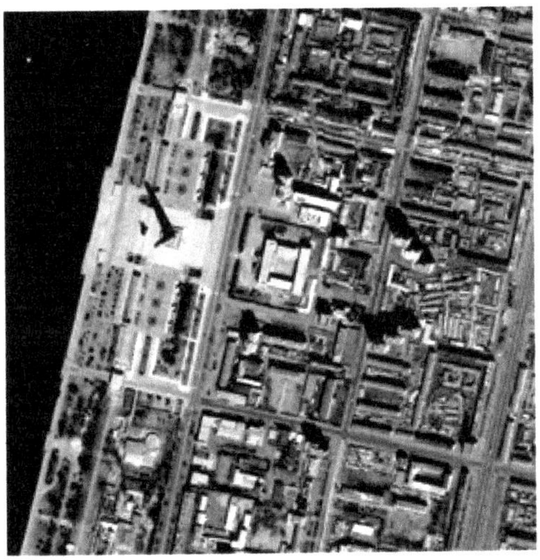

A

B

C

D

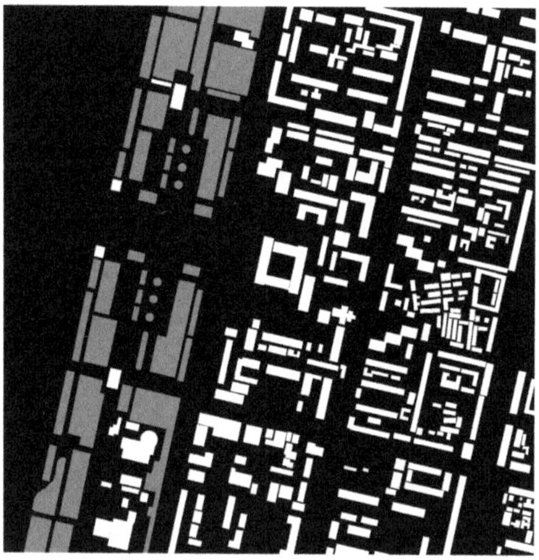

A

B

C

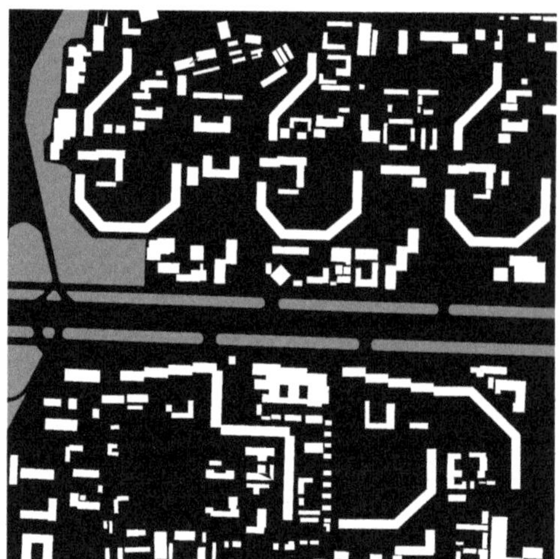

D

A

B

C

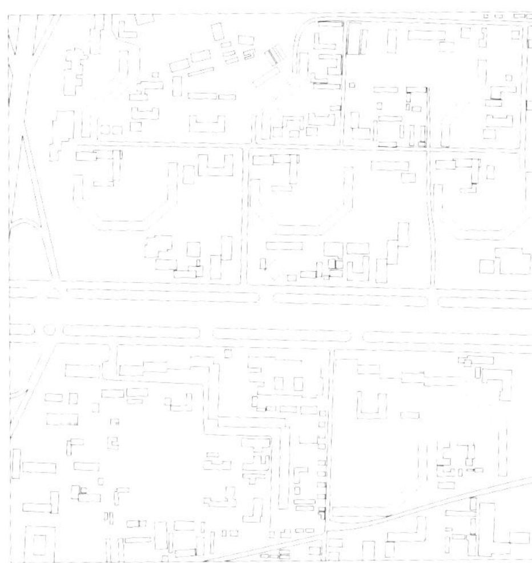

D

4 DISTRICTS COMPARISON

Central development area of Pyongyang is less than 5% of the over all area of the city. And the centre area of this city center is conceived as the face of the nation that reflects the greatness of the regime. Therefore, the area is reconstructed in the first phase of the reconstruction from the war, and it follows the original 1953 Master Plan rule most strictly.

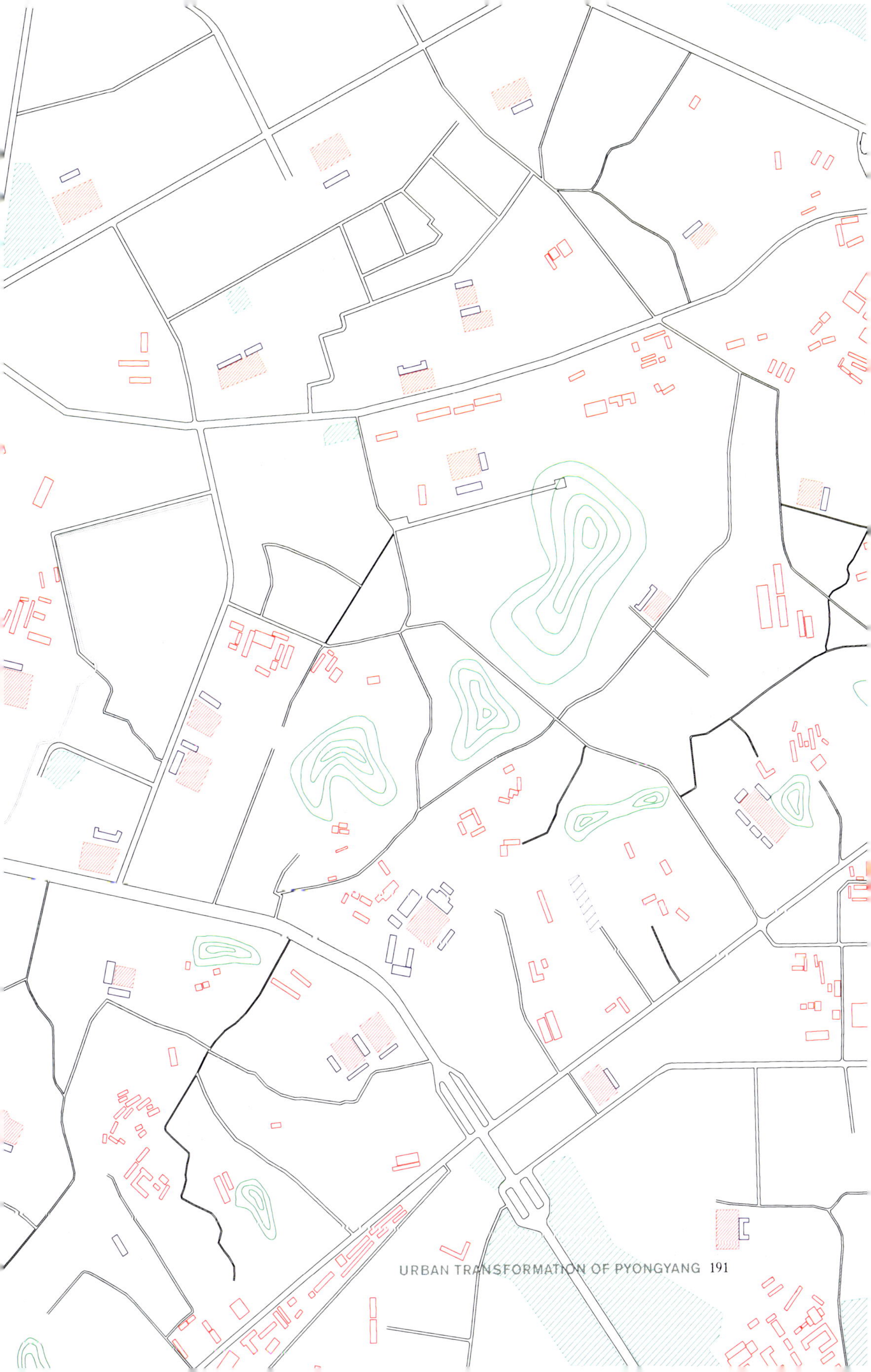

FIGURE GROUNDS

Street

Topogaphy

River

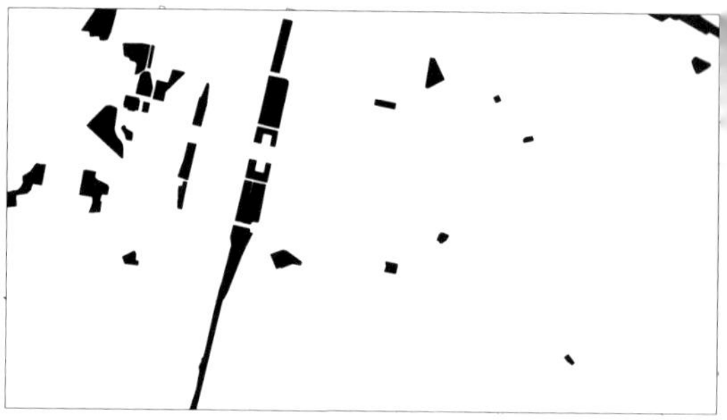

Landscape

Railway

Agriculture

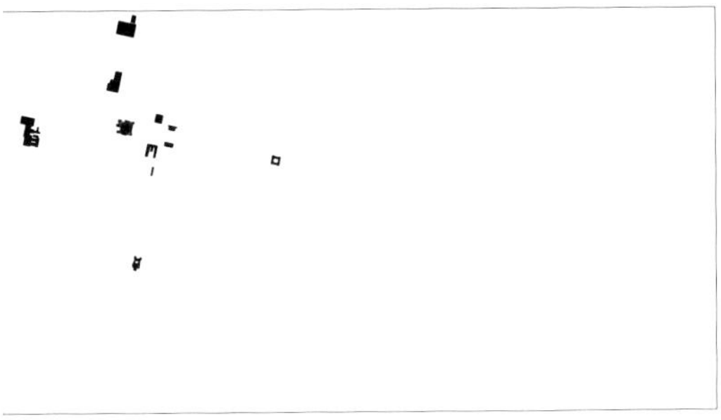

Civic

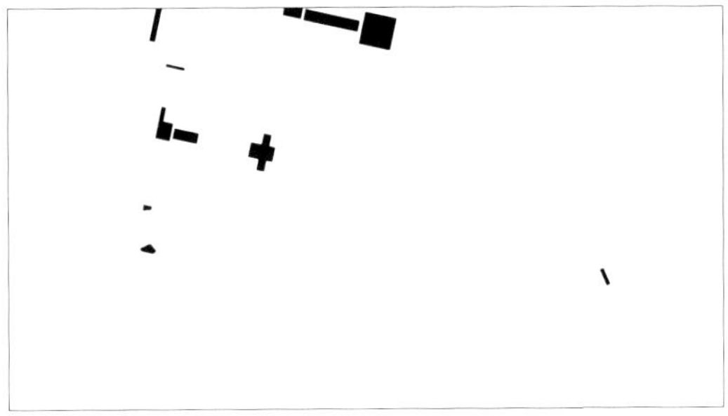

Square/Plaza

Institution

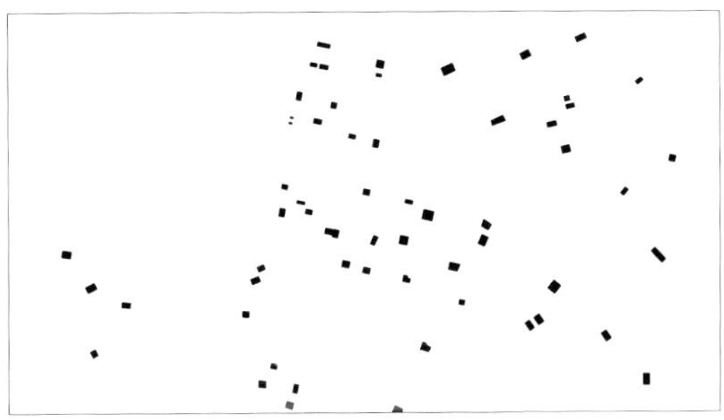

Playground

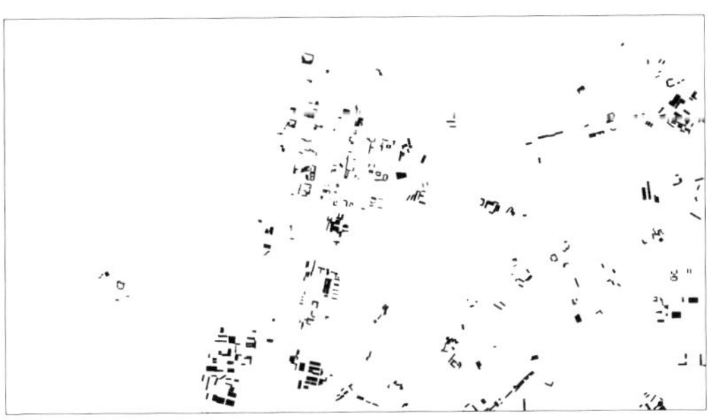

Industry

Vacant Lot

MAJOR STREETS

Four major streets are jextaposed to show the different morphologies along the streets. B. Chung-nyun Street is developed in the 1950s, D. Sae-sal-lim Street in the 1970s, and the two other streets were developed in the late 1980s.

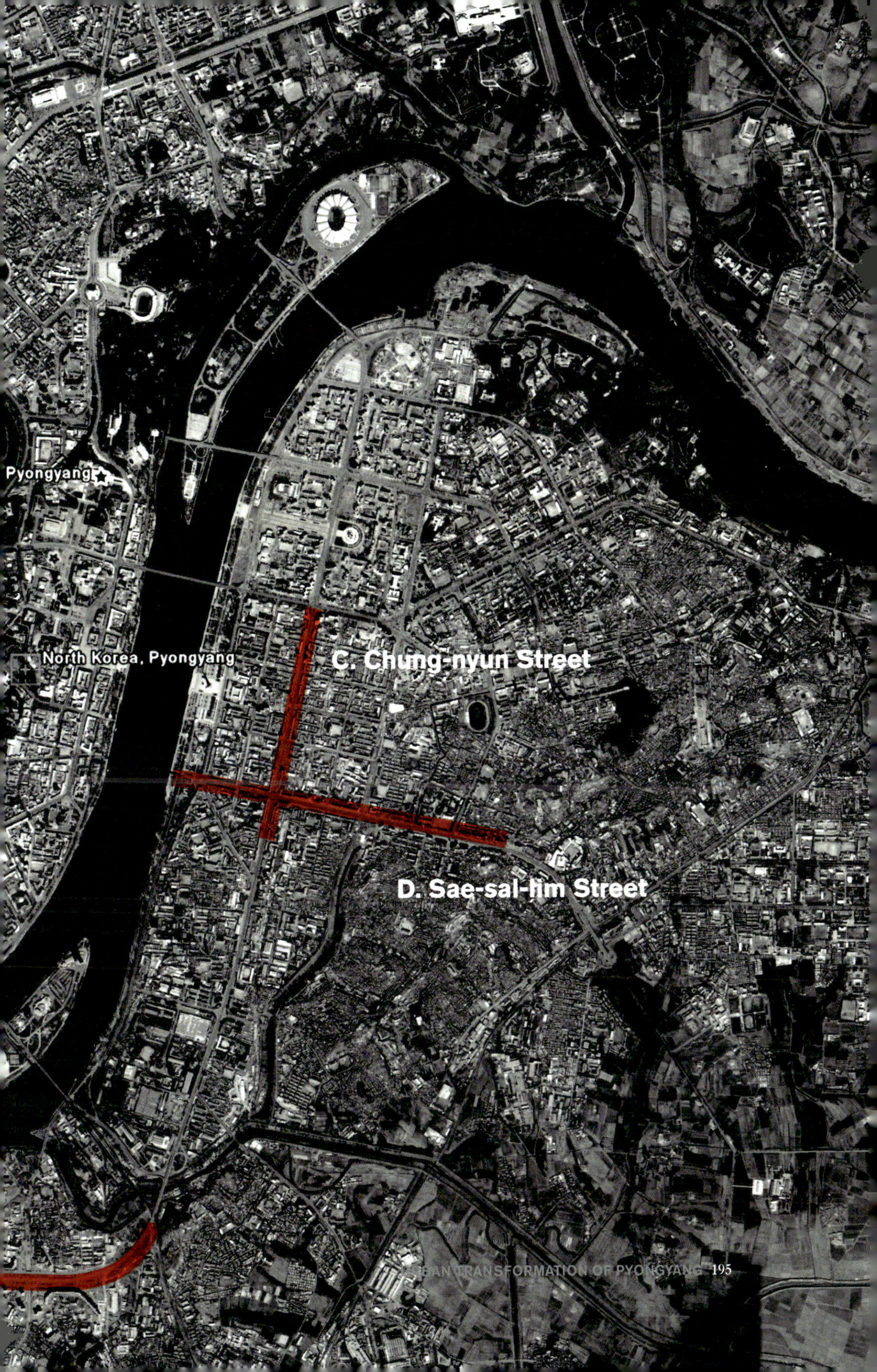
Pyongyang
North Korea, Pyongyang
C. Chung-nyun Street
D. Sae-sal-lim Street

A. Gwang-bok Street

B. Tong-il Street

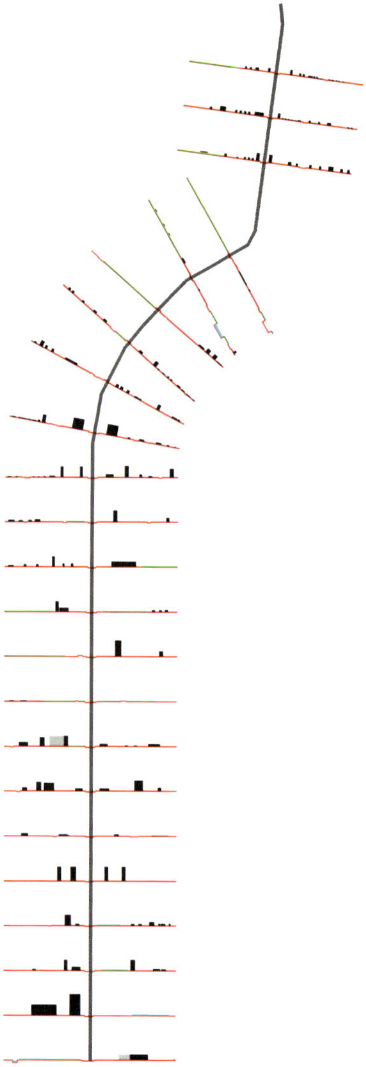

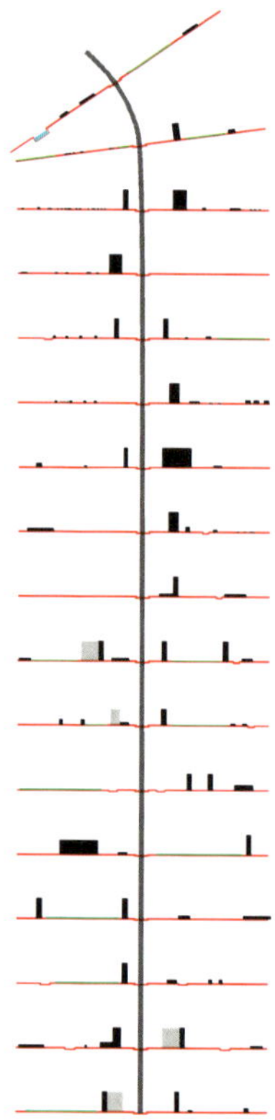

C. Chung-nyun Street

D. Sae-sal-lim Street

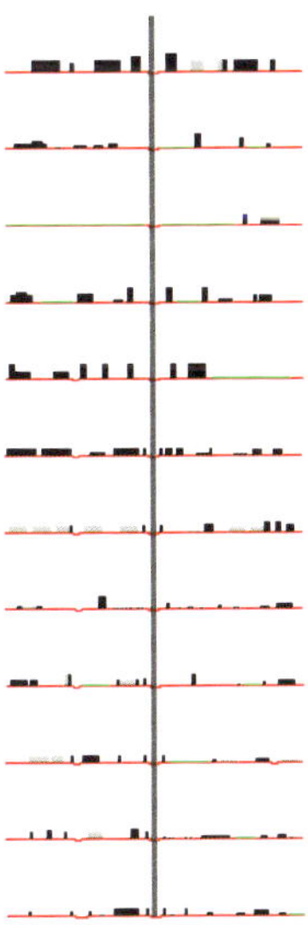

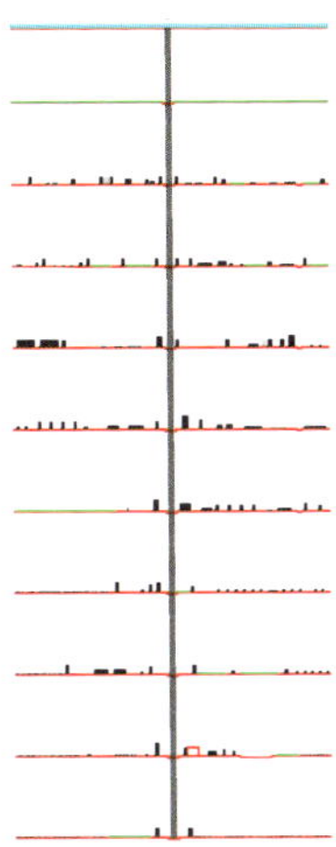

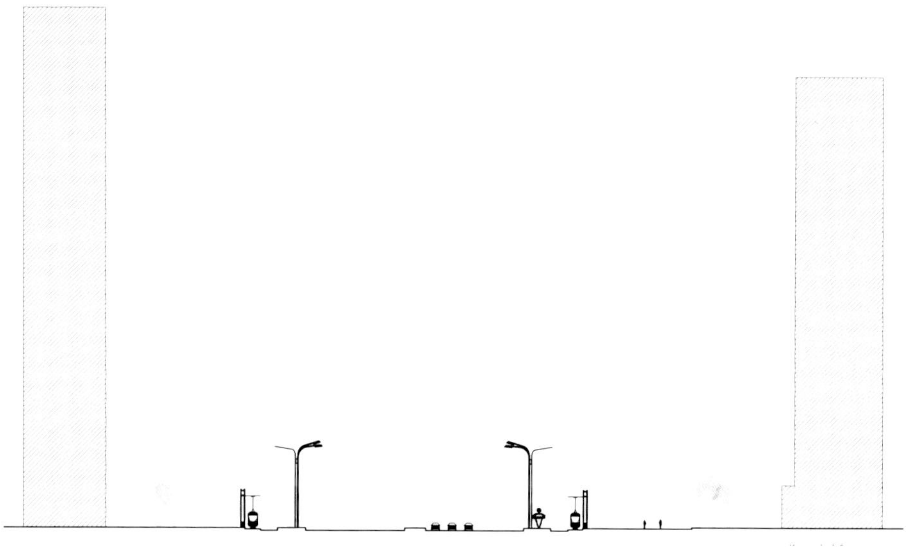

A. Gwang-bok Street

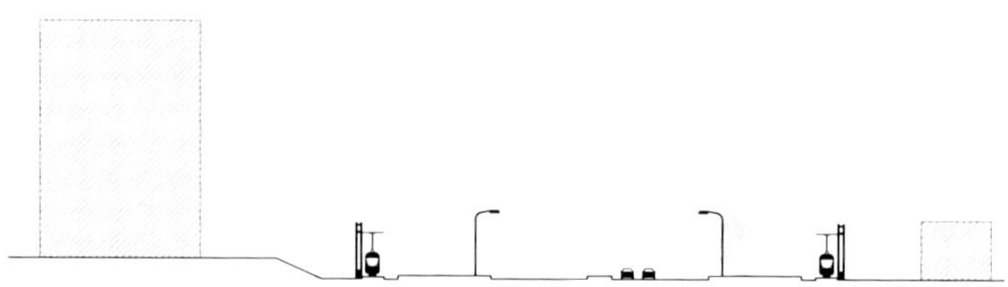

B. Tong-il Street

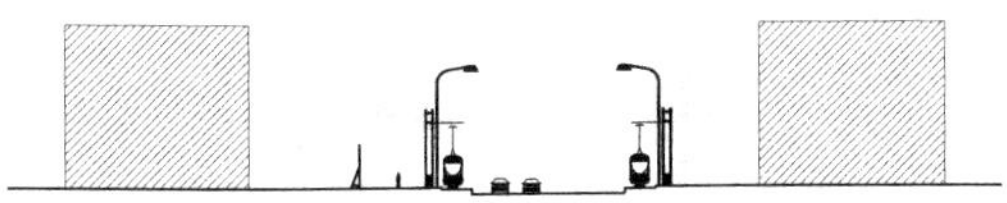

C. Chung-nyun Street

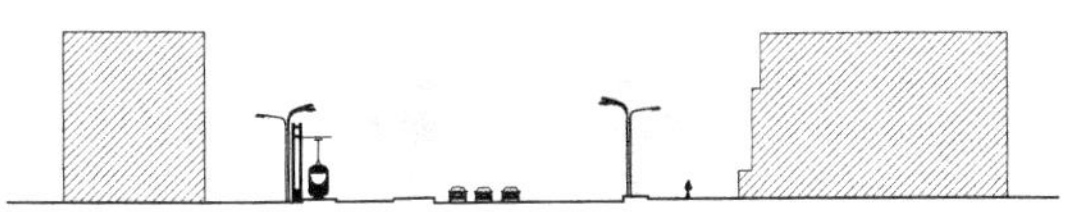

D. Sae-sal-lim Street

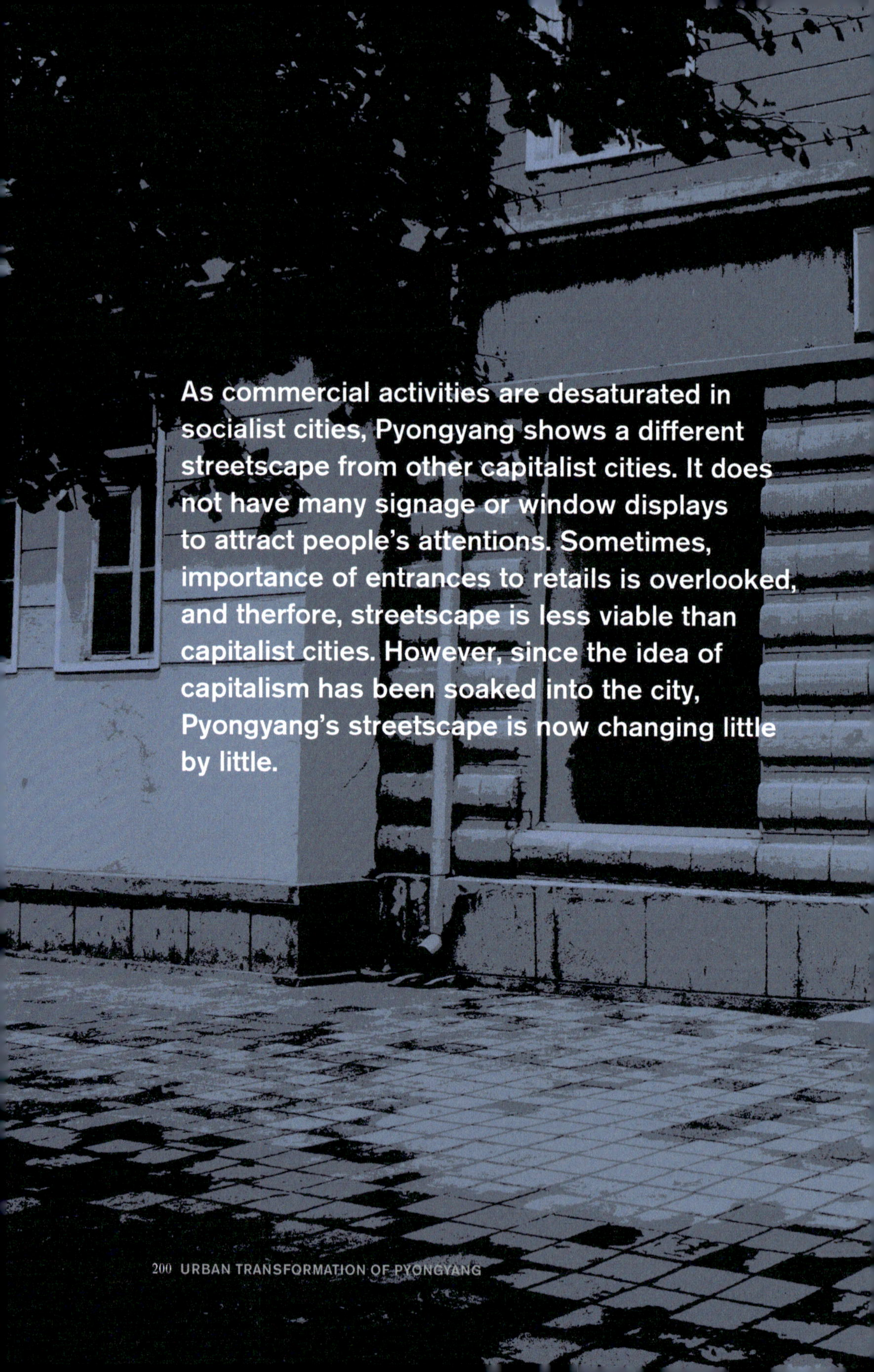

As commercial activities are desaturated in socialist cities, Pyongyang shows a different streetscape from other capitalist cities. It does not have many signage or window displays to attract people's attentions. Sometimes, importance of entrances to retails is overlooked, and therfore, streetscape is less viable than capitalist cities. However, since the idea of capitalism has been soaked into the city, Pyongyang's streetscape is now changing little by little.

BOOKSTORE: CAMBRIDGE, USA

DISPLAY

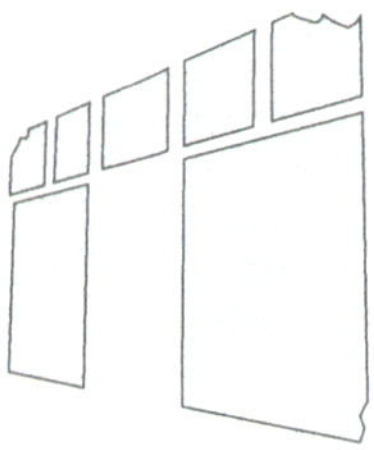

SIGNAGE

ENTRANCE

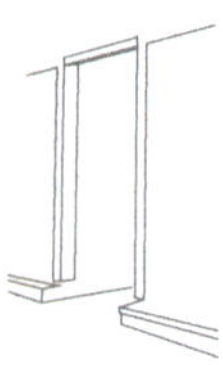

MISC.

BOOKSTORE: PYONGYANG, NK

DISPLAY

SIGNAGE

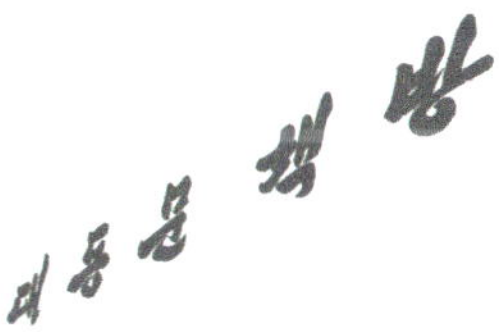

ENTRANCE

MISC.

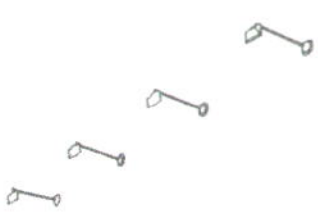

GROCERY: CAMBRIDGE,USA

DISPLAY

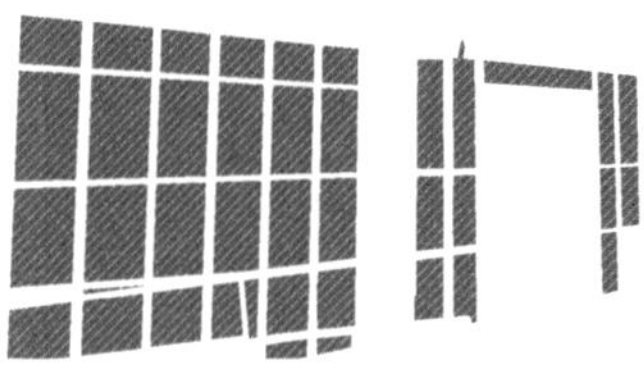

SIGNAGE

ENTRANCE

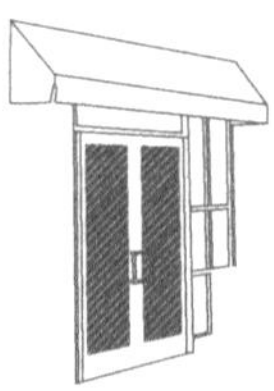

MISC.

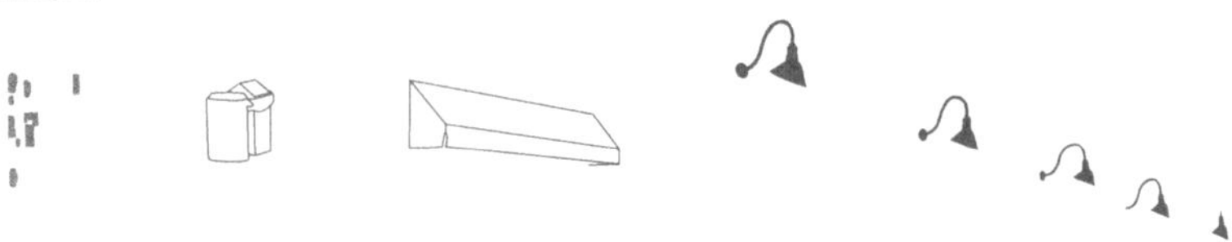

GROCERY: PYONGYANG, NK

DISPLAY

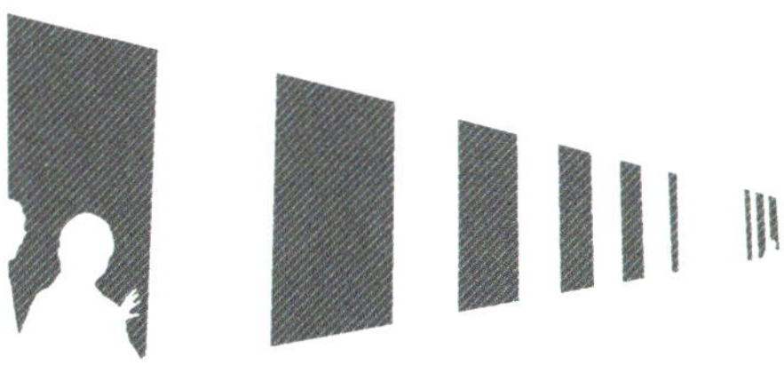

SIGNAGE

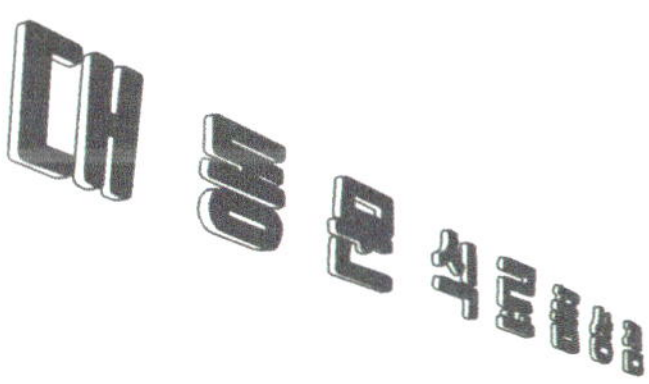

ENTRANCE

MISC.

RESTAURANT: CAMBRIDGE, USA

DISPLAY

SIGNAGE

ENTRANCE

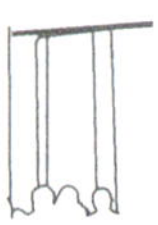

MISC.

RESTAURANT: PYONGYANG, NK

DISPLAY

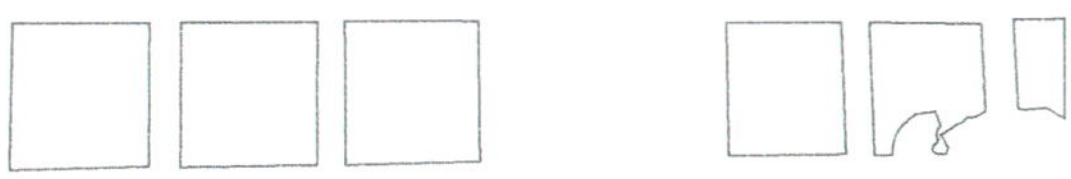

SIGNAGE

ENTRANCE

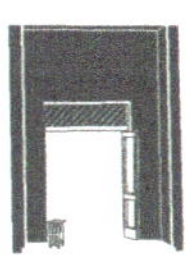

MISC.

HAIR SALON: CAMBRIDGE, USA

DISPLAY

SIGNAGE

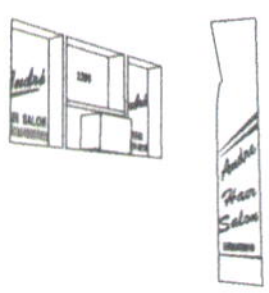

ENTRANCE

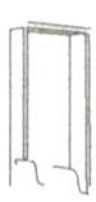

MISC.

HAIR SALON: PYONGYANG, NK

DISPLAY

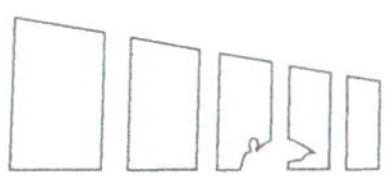

SIGNAGE

ENTRANCE

MISC.

SPORTS SHOP: CAMBRIDGE,USA

DISPLAY

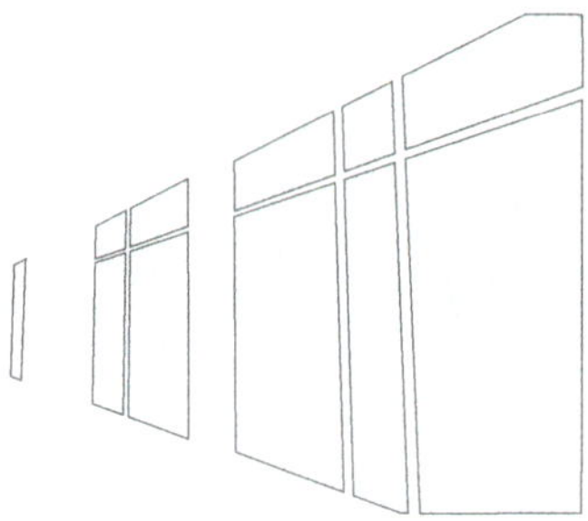

SIGNAGE

ENTRANCE

MISC.

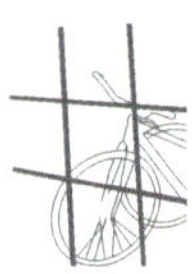

SPORTS SHOP: PYONGYANG,NK

DISPLAY

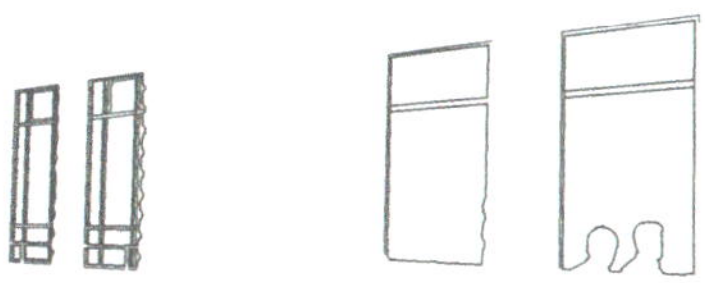

SIGNAGE

ENTRANCE

MISC.

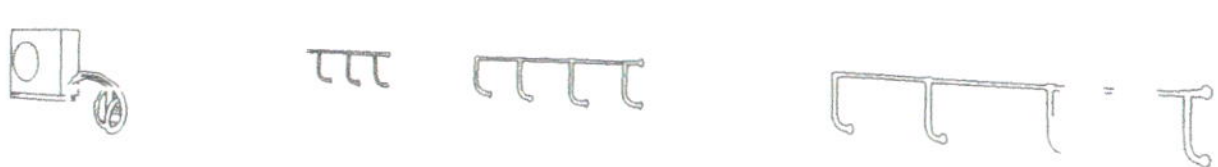

Apartments near Monument
to the Foundation of the Worker's Party

Apartments along the Gwangbok Street

06
MICRO-DISTRICT & HOUSING TYPOLOGY

INTRODUCTION

Similar to Perry's neighborhood unit concept, *micro-district* is socialist planning strategy to structure residential district along with various amenities such as, service facilities, schools, civic programs, and so on. They both define certain scale and size of residential district so that it becomes the basic scale unit that forms the city and the society. Despite of similar idea of looking at residential districts, there is a fundamental difference between the two: the production facility in micro-district. To address spatial equality and to keep close distance between the working and living place, micro-district implemented light-industry factories and workshops along with housing. North Korea also adopted this idea to develop a self-sustainable unit so that each district, in theory, can sustain itself without relying on the others. As part of efforts to structure a micro-district, there are different types of housing developed in Pyongyang, the capital city of North Korea; high-rise, mid-rise and village type.

High-rise typology is mainly seen in Pyongyang and not much in other cities in North Korea and it has strong formal architectural gesture. It was first introduced to the city in 1980s to accommodate new residents, recently readdressed to the city, during a period of fast population growth in Pyongyang and has higher quality interiors. Linear type mid-rise apartments are often used to construct perspectival effect along the major boulevards. Many of them were developed in the 1960s and the 1970s, and in many cases, this typology is used to form housing bloc that follows the organization of micro-district and therefore, it is easy to find production facilities, schools and service amenities along with this type. Lastly, townhouse and single family types are developed as village type in rural area with one or two stories. Recently, many environmentally friendly elements, such as solar panel, wind mill, or greenhouse, are implemented to these rural types, though not realized yet, as idea of future typology.

THE IDEA OF MICRO DISTRICT IN NORTH KOREA

In socialist urban planning, the micro-district concept was used as basic logic for organizing the residential area. As the idea of socialism emerged from experiencing low quality living conditions of working class, it was crucial for socialist urban planners to develop more sustainable living environment. While the Industrial Revolution was pushing the urbanization of many cities throughout the nineteenth century, living conditions of working class were getting worse because of the lack of sewer system, not sufficient windows for ventilation and insulation and narrow streets for infrastructures. Therefore, the idea of micro-district emerged to improve these conditions. It provides specific quantitative guidelines for housing, streets and service facilities. For instance, each residential district has 75-125 acre, which is about 300-400 meters radius boundary, and four to five of residential districts form a residential complex with a population of 5,000 to 15,000.[1]

It has similarities to Clarence Perry's neighbourhood unit concept in a way that they both have schools, internal streets with minimum through traffic, and designated park area. Perry's neighbourhood unit concept is often applied in the Western cities in building more self-sustainable residential areas and mostly implemented in suburban areas. It is not surprising to see the similarities between the two ideas because they both were developed to resolve existing problems caused by fast nineteenth century urbanization. Unlike the neighbourhood unit concept, however, which was mostly developed through suburban planning, the micro-district concept was implemented to both urban and rural context with multi-story residential buildings.

Mid-rise Microdistrict Area in Eastern Pyongyang

Microdistrict as basic structure of a city

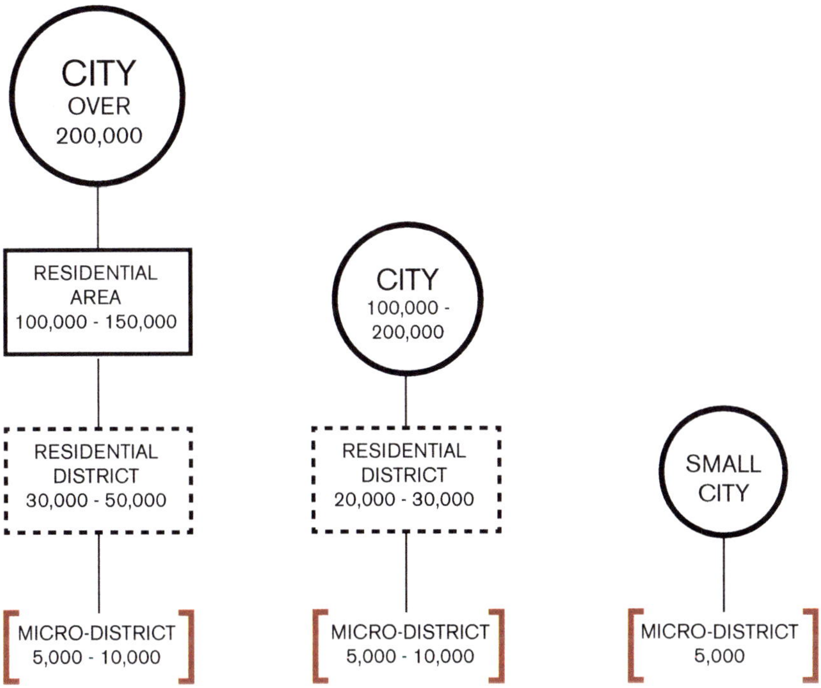

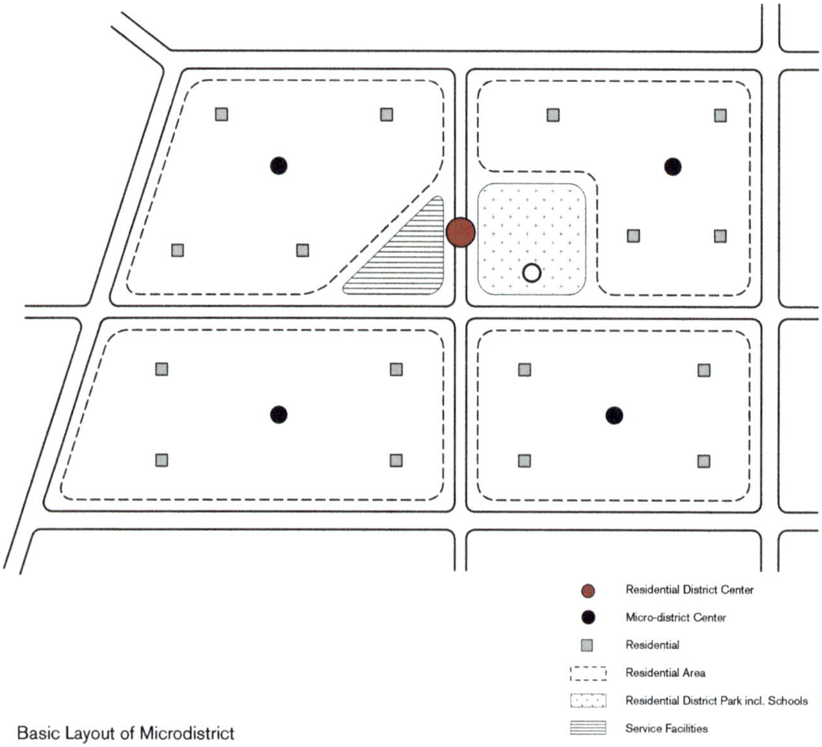

Basic Layout of Microdistrict

NORTH KOREA MICRO-DISTRICT

North Korea adopts this socialist micro-district concept into its own version; *Chut'aek soguyŏk kyehoek. Chut'aek soguyŏk* can be translated into micro-district, and basic unit of each micro-district has four to five residential groups containing 1,000~1,500 or 2,000~2,500 inhabitants. The Basic logic of structuring a micro-district follows these guidelines: 1) it must be planned to have the most convenient environment for residents, 2) it must be planned efficiently in both construction and economic management, and 3) it must be neat and aesthetically achieving.[2] In terms of size micro-district varies depending on the street structure, administrative level and size of city, and its geographic condition. For instance, while micro-district in Pyongyang is around 15 to 20 hectare with 5,000 to 6,000 residents, the one in Shinuiju, the border city between China and North Korea, has the size of 12 to 16 hectare with 3,000 to 4,000 residents. In short, micro-district has flexibility to adjust its size and capacity depending on geographic and

Pyongyang Microdistrict

demographic conditions. Although, in general, its size is mostly limited to an average of 15 to 30 hectare in order to maintain the walking distances to services and amenities.

As previously mentioned, service amenities are integrated into micro-district and since the scheme limits through traffic in favour of pedestrian walk, the distance between housing and service amenities is the crucial factor that determines the size of micro-district. Therefore, service amenities tend to be located in the center of a district and include, school, kindergarten, child care center, grocery, distribution center, laundromat, civic facilities, and clinic. In the micro district plann, about 4 hectare (7 ~ 8 m^2 per person) is designated to the service amenities, including parks, for 5,000 residents. For 5,000 to 7,000 residents district, the school has capacity of about 880 to 1,200 and kindergarten of 350 children. This size micro-district, of about 7,000 people in 20 hectare area, has the density of 360 people per hectare and about 20% building coverage ratio. Since the high density condition is considered as the main cause of slum environment in the industrial

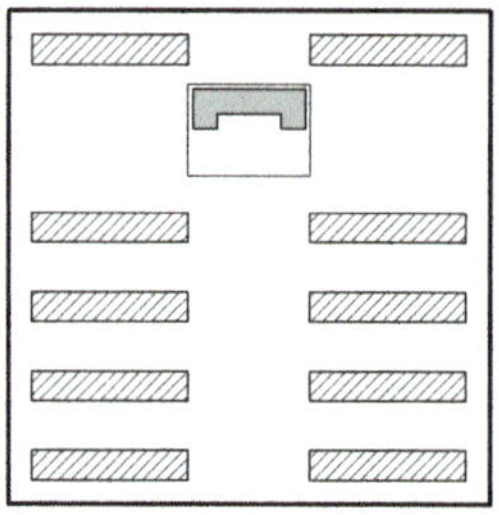
Juxtapose Type

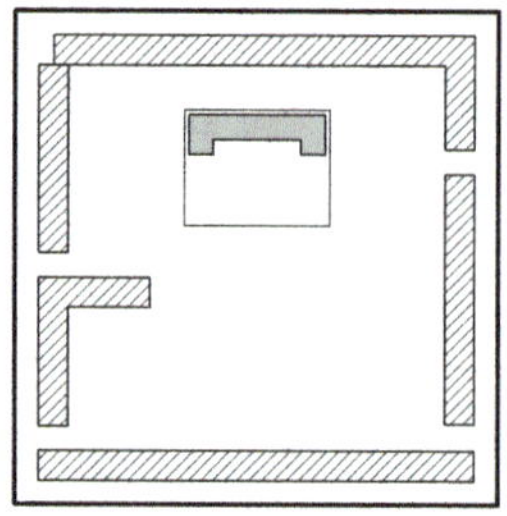
Periphery Type

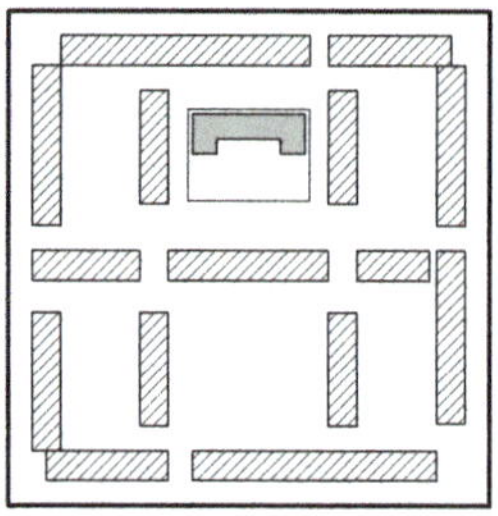
Mixed Type

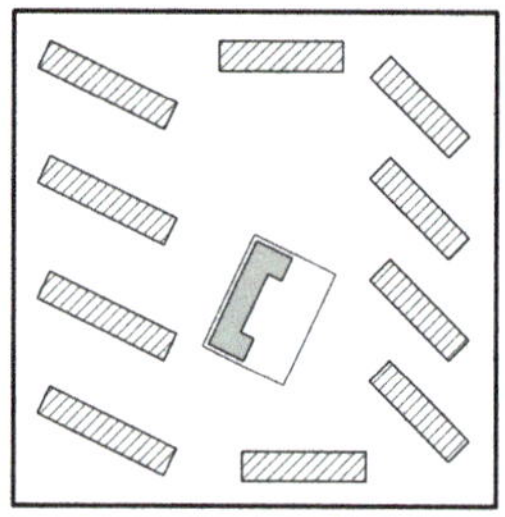
Free Type

era, micro-district kept its density low by limiting the buildings height to four or five stories and building coverage ratio to 20%. Nonetheless, these theoretical numbers were ignored when the city was growing, and therefore, in the current fabric of Pyongyang, it is hard to see a micro-district that has 20% building coverage. And when a district has low building coverage ratio, it has high-rise apartments as tall as thirty stories.

LAYOUT OF MICRO-DISTRICT

There are four different types of layout of a micro-district, depending on how residential buildings are located: juxtapose type, periphery type, mixed type and free type.

The juxtapose type can provide the best orientation for most of units, especially for single loaded corridor type apartments. However, it does not have enough public space within the block and has disadvantage in increasing density and height. The periphery type has an advantage of forming a linear streetscape with a least amount of construction. As periphery buildings of micro-district block already form a border between streets and blocks, there is less need for an additional effort of creating the streetscape.

Also, periphery blocks create community open spaces protected from big streets. Mixed type is a mixture between periphery and juxtapose type. In the periphery-type block, buildings wrap around the micro-district and the block interior is divided into multiple spaces depending on different uses and programs. This is the most used micro-district layout type in North Korea. Lastly, the free type layout is often used when micro-district is in a difficult topographic condition. Although more rationalized and geometric shapes are preferred in North Korea for economic and security purposes, following geometry in a radical topography would require higher budget for construction, and therefore, free way of laying out buildings is encouraged to accommodate topography and orientation.

Many lines were developed to enhance the micro-district concept, but nonetheless, the theoretical concept has to be rephrased to accommodate the actual conditions of the city. Restrictions on building heights and footprints had to be loosened, size of micro-district had to be adjusted, and the regulations of district layout had to be rearranged. At the same time, some of the outlines, such as eliminating through traffic, providing schools and children daycares, implementing production facilities within a micro-district, are relatively well kept throughout the city of Pyongyang. One of the most recent developments by the government, Eunha Scientist Street Development, still shows how it tries to keep some elements of micro-district concept in the development.

HOUSING TYPOLOGY IN PYONGYANG

Low-rise Village Type

Similar to China, North Korea also emphasized the importance of building strong villages in order to strengthen the nation's socialist idea, and therefore, it always emphasized developing housing typologies for village areas to provide modern type of living. Kim Il Sung, the first leader of North Korea, also insisted that village housing construction should continuously be developed so that all the farmers in rural areas can live in neat and convenient houses.[3] And because of the unique administrative structure of North Korea, these low-rise village houses emerge in Pyongyang as well.

Unlike clear separation between rural and urban area in South Korea, North Korea structures its administrative boundary based on the idea of having both urban and rural function in a city. For instance, a city is composed with both urban area and rural areas and the urban area is again consisted of different level of urban and rural areas. The same structure happens in rural areas as well. This is to reduce the distinction between rural and urban areas, which the socialists saw as the biggest problem of industrial

Low-rise Prefabricated Houses

Low-rise Prefabricated Houses

cities, and to keep production function, such as agriculture, in the city. As a result, Pyongyang has a city boundary almost twenty times bigger than urbanized area that also includes villages even within urbanized area.

Starting in the early 1960s, village types were provided, with the name of *culture house (mun-hwa-ju-taek)*, the term first used in Japan in the 1920s to name houses that adopted western style and typology , as part of seven years strategic plan to supply about 600,000 units around the nation. And to meet this number, North Korea organized *village construction units* in each administrative area called "*gun*".[4] Kim Il Sung strongly emphasized modernizing village area in his book[5] about North Korean socialist village program, and Kim Jung Il also wrote his thesis in 1964 about the role of admiral area "*gun*" as an important part of constructing socialist nation. Because it was part of nation's propaganda, village development was not left behind during the reconstruction and urbanization of the country in 1960s.

Like other socialist housing types, village typologies also encouraged standardized design in order to achieve more efficient way of construction. Each lot for village type house was limited to 250~350 m^2, and the single story type was favoured in the beginning of the strategic plan. Although both single detached house and attached two family houses were introduced in the beginning, people preferred single detached house, and therefore, major standard house type in villages. They were able to be mass produced by developing *material base camp*, production facilities for construction materials, in each city and "gun."[6] Most of materials needed for building a standard house, such as reinforced concrete beams, concrete masonry units, light wall masonry units, corrugated metal sheets, were mass produced in these factories. This standardization and mass production of materials helped the nation to provide numbers of village houses in a relatively short time. After the wave of single story village house, multiple story housings, between two and four stories, were developed in rural areas. These types had central heating, each unit had its own bathroom and waterworks, and therefore, it had less distinction from the urban housings, which was one of the most essential elements in socialist planning.

Interestingly enough, some of these village type houses in Pyongyang emerged in the areas planned as landscape areas in the original master plan from the 1950s. Influenced by Garden City Movement, green infrastructure zone was a crucial aspect in the socialist urban planning and in the 1950 Master Plan for Pyongyang, it emphasized areas of green infrastructure intended to control the growth of the city. However, as in most of cities, the master plan was not fully realized as the city grew, and many areas that were planned as green spaces were filled with low-rise houses following an informal pattern. On the other hand, which will be discussed later, the high-rise housings were developed in the areas that were not part of the original master plan. It tells us the growth of Pyongyang was not fully predicted and the city had to address the fast pace of population growth that was not expected in the 1950s master plan.

Recently, many sustainable ideas have started to be implemented into these low-rise village type houses. Although some of them remain proposals, , they indicate the design direction the village type is moving to. Especially houses whose energy necessities are covered by methane gas has already become popular type in North Korea. The lack of a stable energy source is one of the biggest problems in the country, especially in rural areas, so North Korea kept on developing alternative energy sources.

Mid-rise Urban Type

In Pyongyang, mid-rise apartment was the dominant residential type massively provided in the 1960s and the 1970s.[7] After the first wave of reconstruction from the Korean War in the 1950s, the city had its basic structure defined in those periods. In the 1960s, North Korean version of micro-district was established, focused on providing mostly mid-rise apartment buildings. Until the high-rise typology was introduced in the 1980s, the mid-rise was the dominant typology that formed streetscape along the major boulevards in Pyongyang. Also because it was developed before the rapid population increase, mid-rise typology was able to follow certain rules of micro-district, unlike high-rise typology that had to deal with larger population that contradicted several logics of original micro-district concept.[8]

In general, there are two types of mid-rise residential buildings; linear type and tower type. Linear type mid-rise apartments are used to structure the limits of each block of micro-district and form streetscapes. It was somewhat influenced by Eastern European countries that supported North Korea during the reconstruction after the war. In his book "*Chut'aek soguyŏk kyehoek (Planning Microdistrict),*" Yi argues that the periphery site planning type for a micro-district is more efficient way to structure streetscape, and it can protect the inner neighbourhood space from the visual and sound impact of outer boulevards.[9] Although the periphery type had a partial disadvantage as it did not allow all housing units to have southern orientation, it was often used especially in the East side of Pyongyang in the 1960s. As a consequence, in many Pyongyang streets , when you drive or walk along streets, it is hard to find out what is happening inside of the block, and most of communal activities are oriented inwards instead of towards the streets.

Along with the linear type, ten to fifteen story tall tower type mid-rise apartments are often used to emphasize perspectival view on the street.

Mid-rise Linear Type Housing

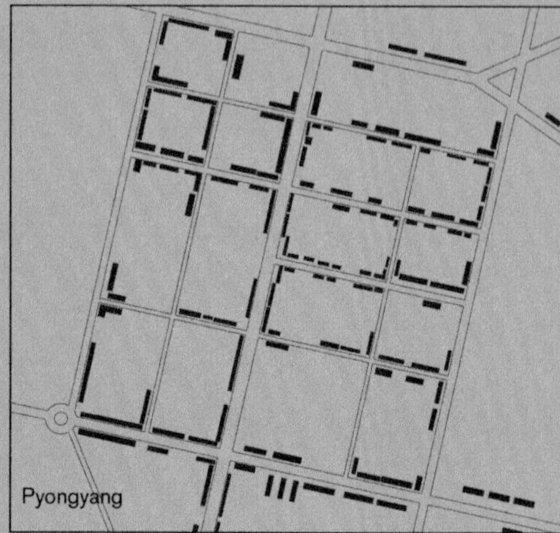
Pyongyang

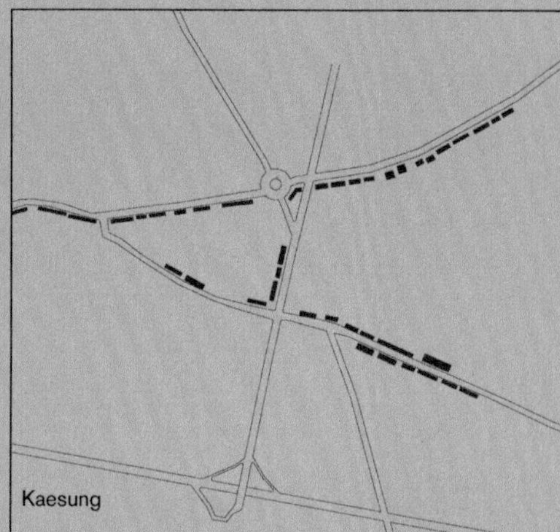
Kaesung

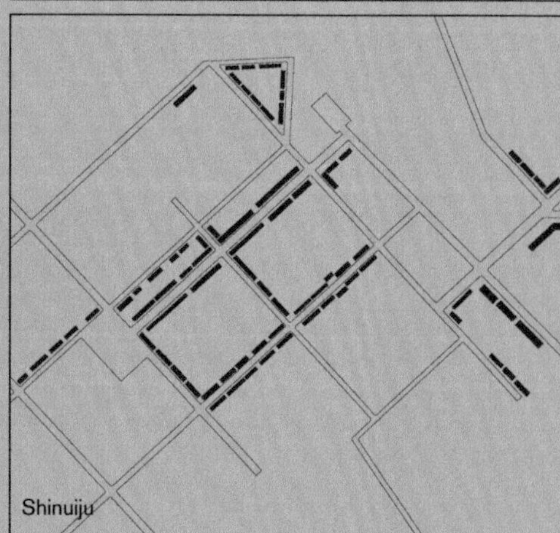
Shinuiju

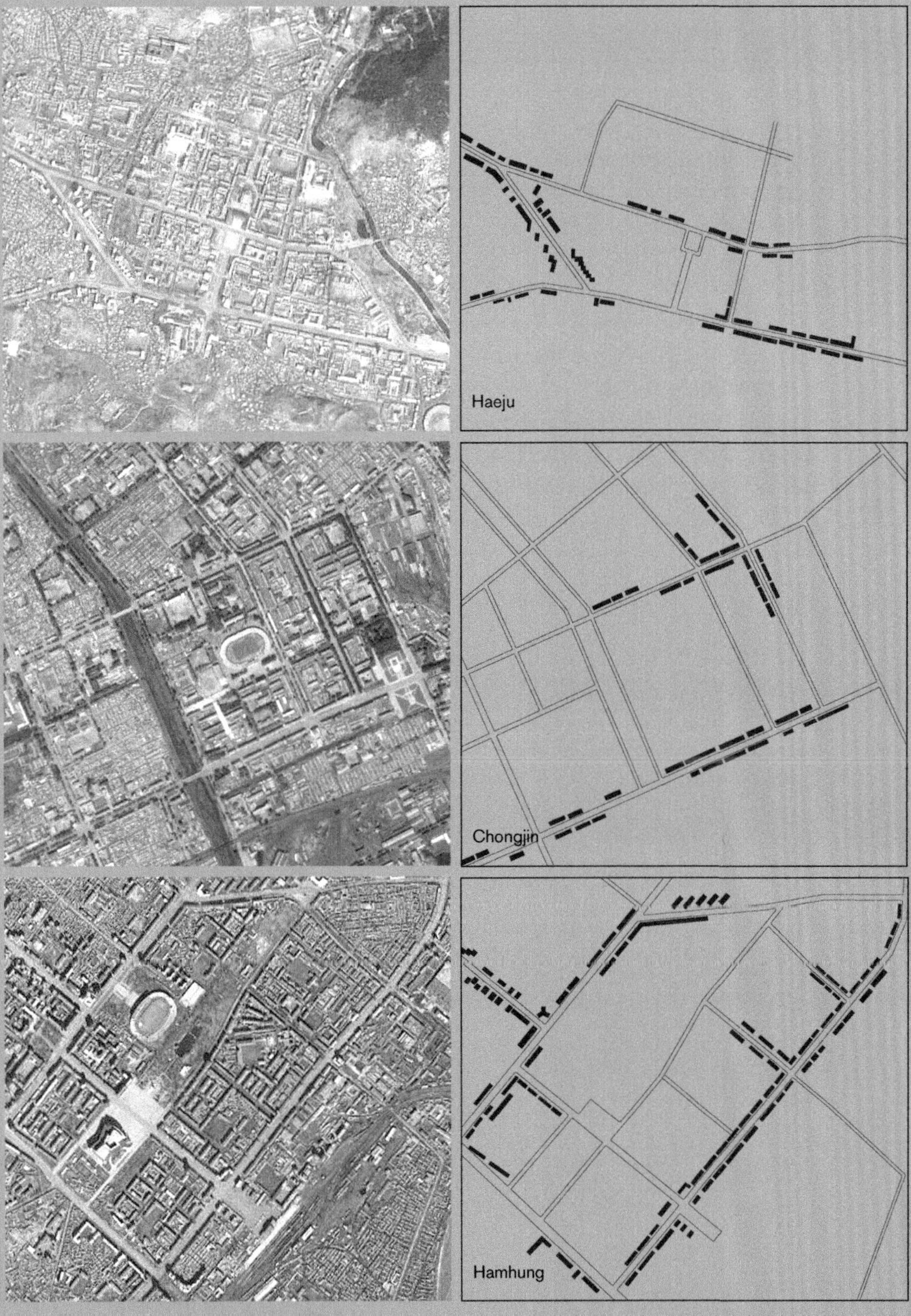
Haeju
Chongjin
Hamhung

Although the linear type apartment buildings give strong horizontal effect in streetscape, it may cause fatigue without any vertical gestures. Therefore, tower type apartments, which are higher than the linear type yet lower than the high-rise apartments, are inserted into the streetscape to provide three dimensional experiences in the city. Still this tower type mid-rise apartments are rarely erected isolated but emerge along with linear type to form a certain perspectival view.

Perspectival view is very much emphasized by Kim Jung Il, the second leader of the nation and the father of the current leader, and in his book *"Kŏnch'uk Yesullon(On Architecture)"* where he requested architects to consider perspective views of the project from the beginning.[10] He insisted that putting straight buildings along the streets is an old fashion and streets have to be formed in three-dimensional way. Therefore, many tower type mid-rise apartments were inserted into existing linear type residential blocks, not only at the periphery but also inside of the block.

Two clear examples show the way how tower type apartments are used to emphasize perspectival view from streets. First one is at the Victorious Fatherland Liberation War Monument gate. Unlike many other tower type apartments, these two tower buildings are not positioned along with linear type apartments but with the gate of the monument park whose style emphasizes horizontality. As the city does not have either real estate value or zoning regulation, it is possible to build an architecture solely based on the perspectival effect, and these two mid-rise towers were built to emphasize the effect of the gate.

Photo with existing two towers

Photoshoped image without two towers

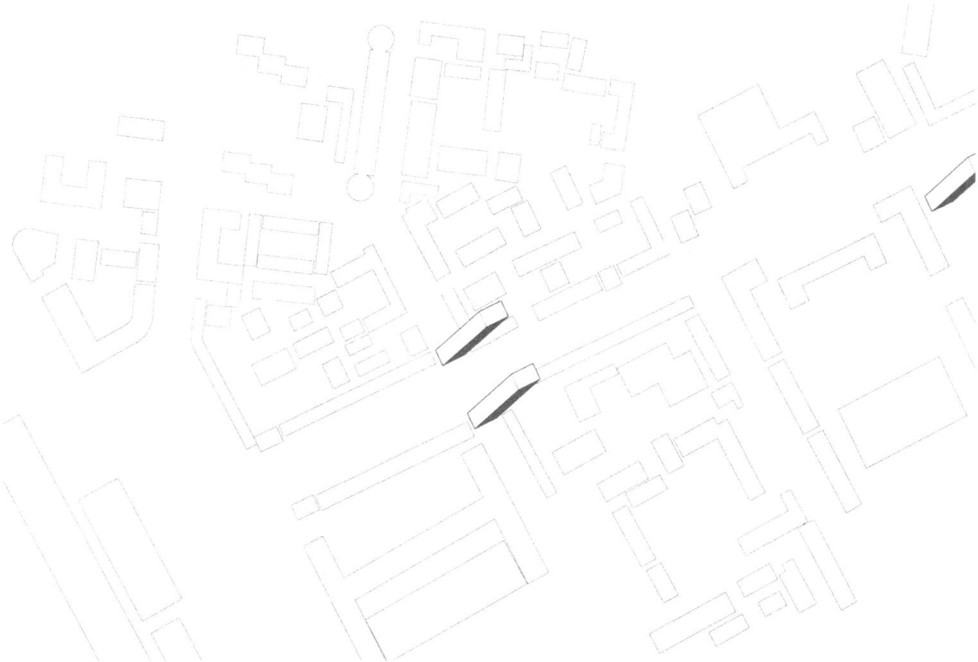

Yonggwang Street Case

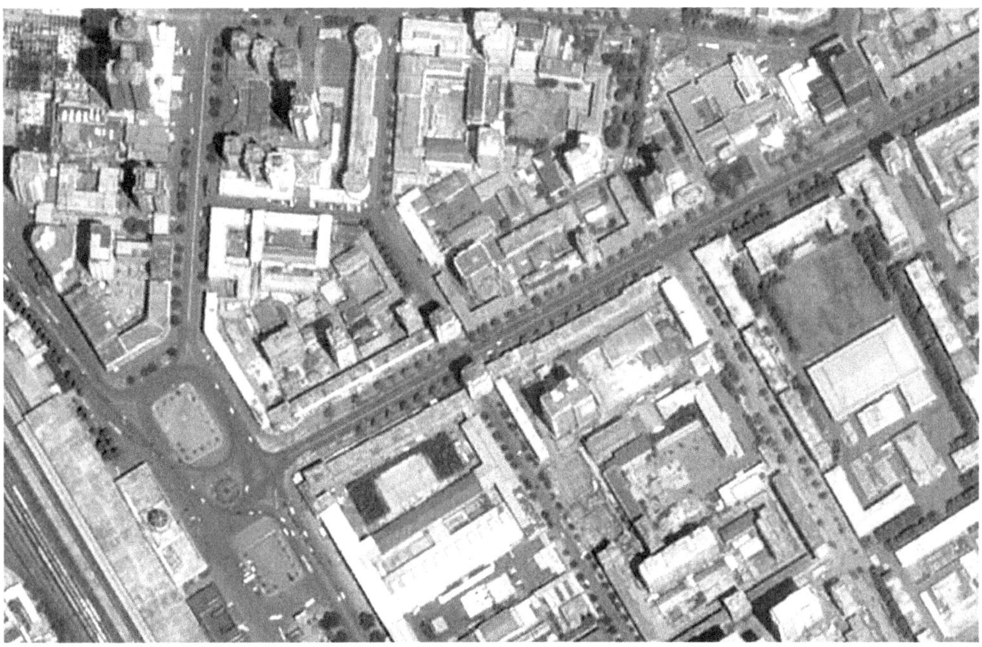

The second example is near the Pyongyang train Station along the Young-gwang Street. Two mid-rise towers were built on either side of the street along with the long linear type apartment blocks that run more than 1km straight. An interesting fact of these two buildings is that they block intersecting street to acquire enough lots to build towers. That way the street structure is destroyed and intersection exists only as the crossing. These two examples show the importance of creating a "perfect" perspectival view along the street and how Pyongyang takes advantage of having no real estate value and no private domain.

Recently, many apartment buildings provided by private sector are filling in existing residential blocks or redeveloping low-rise village type housings. Because their developable land area is limited , they are mostly developed in mid-rise tower type. Although housings must (theoretically) be provided by the government, many private developments are filling the gap between government controlled housing supply and emerging new public demand by increasing middle class. Pyongyang is somewhat accepting these developments under certain control by the government officials; as they emerge spontaneously, private construction is one of the main factors that breaks the rule of micro district.

Gate to the inner part of the district

High-rise Urban Type

As mentioned before, most of the high-rise type apartments can only be seen in Pyongyang. High-rise type apartments were introduced durig the construction boom of the 1980s. In the beginning, it was for the accommodation of the increasing population of the city, but also to show the prosperous era of the country. As said, micro-district concept pursues a low density development, and therefore, high-rise type was not introduced in the original plan. However, despite of restrictions of migrations between cities, population of Pyongyang continuously increased throughout the period, and it started to implement high-rise type apartments in the city as its solution.[11]

Interestingly enough, most of these high-rise type apartments emerged in the areas where they were not part of the original 1953 master plan of Pyongyang. Although not all of features of this plan were realized, residential blocks until the 1970s followed its general idea and developments were mostly limited to areas designated by the master plan. However, the general city boundary of the master plan began to break in the 1980, mostly because the population of the city went beyond the targeted number in the 1950s, and new housing typology had to be introduced in new areas in order to accommodate this increasing number of population.

Especially in the late 1980s, through the Third 7-year Strategic Planning between 1987 and 1993, the government planned to provide 150,000 to 200,000 housing units every year. The population of Pyongyang jumped almost double in twenty years, from 1.5 million in 1967 to with 2.8 million people in 1986. Therefore, the city expanded in both ways: vertically and horizontally. This trend extended in the 1990s when Gwangbok Street and Tongil Street were developed in the fringe of urbanized area of Pyongyang.

Interestingly, high-rise apartments in those districts, which go beyond thirty stories, have strong formal gesture. As the city does not need to deal with real estate value, it has freedom to develop formal gestures in the high-rise typology. Most of times in capitalist cities, as high-rise typology emerge to accommodate high density and high real estate value, it has little room to wiggle, and therefore, it is mostly about how much floor area you can accommodate within the regulation rather than formal gesture. However, in Pyongyang, where there is no push on real estate profit return, high rise buildings are not just to house more residential units but also to show the greatness of the regime or the economic prosperity. Therefore, these high-rise apartments become another type of propaganda monument along with spectacular cultural or sport facilities.

The formal gesture of the high-rise apartment buildings is also shown in their names. Unlike mid-rise or low-rise housings, which are mostly

High-rise Apartments in Pyongyang

Pyongyang High-rise Apartment District

named after their neighbourhood, many high-rise apartments are named after their forms, such as hexagon type, Y-type, windmill-type, curved type or screen type. And most of high-rise apartments in Pyongyang emphasize horizontality in their elevation. They use deep balconies so that effect of horizontal language can be strengthened with their shadows, and balance between horizontal gesture and vertical gesture became general language of the high-rise type apartments.

Similar to streetscape in mid-rise districts, the high-rise district, also lays out low-horizontal buildings at the block periphery in a form of a plinth for the high-rise buildings so that the streetscape can be conceived more three-dimensionally. And not only low-rise service amenity buildings but also symbolic cultural buildings are used to provide variations along the street. Even colour code are implemented differently depending on the location and type of the building. Along the Gwangbok Street, high-rise apartments along the street are painted in white, whereas apartments in the back are painted in light grey and low rise service amenity buildings are in accent colours.[12] It is to strengthen unity of the street with colour code and, at the same time, give extravagancy with highlighted colours.

Recent Housing Trend in Pyongyang

Unlike mass production of housing by the government in the past years, recent researches show that there are increasing number of privately developed apartments in the real estate market in North Korea, especially in border cities and Pyongyang. In some years, like 2011 and 2013, statistics show that more than 50% of people who have recently bought apartments, had purchased them through the private market.[13] Some of "luxury" apartment's prices in Pyongyang went up to $200,000 USD in early 2015 according to Joung, which is almost double the price of 2014.[14] This new trend does not necessarily show the collapse of government-controlled housing market, yet it shows the potential changes in housing typology. Pyongyang is currently undertaking two real estate development strategies simultaneously: the government controlled supply and private development. Not surprisingly, private developments have to involve, at some degree the intervention of government officials so that they can be developed smoothly. Meanwhile, as we witness in recent development of Mansudae apartments, which went up to $200,000 UDS, people still need to pay for the apartments that are supplied by the government.

Although the real estate market has not adopted to the market economy system fully yet, it shows that both private and public development respond to market demand to attract emerging middle class for higher return. Surveys show that there are increasing number of people who spend their extra money in renovating interiors of their individual units.[15]

As real estate market focuses more on individual taste and capital, it seems there is less effort on pushing micro-district concept anymore. Although few government developments, such as Eunha Scientist Street complex in 2013, still follows basic idea of micro-district, most of recent developments in Pyongyang, even including government constructions have less things in common with micro-district concept. For instance, although it was projected as a complex, Mirae Scientist Street development along the Daedong River, completed in 2015, does not include any of educational facilities or service amenities except some commercial program. Especially in this development, it shows the government's interest in waterfront development, which means that it is aware of prime real estate areas and more focusing on profit return than on forming a micro-district.

No matter whether developed by public or private capital, recent developments focus on real estate investment value, location and interior quality. It means that housing development is no longer interested in providing public benefits, such as daycare center, schools, service amenities, clinics and so on, and it will be followed by emergence of new housing typology and potential collapse of micro-districts.

In conclusion, various housing typologies have been developed along with the micro district idea in Pyongyang and throughout North Korea. Although the original micro district idea did not predict certain typologies, even new typology such as high-rise housing were accommodated to micro district programs and ideas. However, as the market-oriented economy is being slowly absorbed by the local economy and society in recent years, many social aspects of micro district and housings are being overlooked or put behind.

Endnotes

1 Fedchenko, G. Irina., "Social Accessibility in the Large Post-Industrial City: From Traditional Planning of Microdistrict to Newest Demands", http://www.livablecities.org/downloads/49th-Portland/Fedchenko_Irina.pdf

2 Yi, Sun-gŏn, and Wan-gi Paek. *Chut'aek Soguyŏk Kyehoek.* P'yŏngyang: Kungnip Kŏnsŏl Ch'ulp'ansa, 1963.

3 Kim, Il-sŏng. *Kim Il-sŏng Chŏnjip.* P'yŏngyang: Chosŏn Nodongdang Ch'ulp'ansa, 1992.

4 "*gun*" is administrative district of rural area and Pyongyang now has two "*gun*" within its administrative boundary.

5 Kim Il-sŏng, Uri nara sahoejuŭi nongch'on munje e kwanhan t'eje (Theses on the socialist rural question in our country), P'yŏngyang, Chosŏn Rodongdang Ch'ulp'asa, 1964

6 Yi, Hwa-sŏn.Chosŏn kŏnch'uksa, Kwahak Paekkwa Sajŏn Chonghap Ch'ulp'asa, 1989

7 Although there is no clear definition of mid-rise type, in this essay, it is limited to buildings between five and fifteen story tall buildings. In other cities in North Korea, even fifteen story building can be categorized as high-rise, however, in Pyongyang, residential buildings between five and fifteen story tall buildings show similar gesture in the city that is clearly distinguished from high-rise residential buildings that are over twenty story tall.

8 Yim, Dongwoo. *P'yŏngyang Kŭrigo P'yŏngyang Ihu: P'yŏngyang Tosi Konggan E Taehan Tto Tarŭn Sigak, 1953-2011.* Kyŏnggi-do P'aju-si: Hyohyŏng Ch'ulp'an, 2011.

9 Yi, Hwa-sŏn.Chosŏn kŏnch'uksa, Kwahak Paekkwa Sajŏn Chonghap Ch'ulp'ansa, 1989

10 Kim, Chŏng-il. *Kŏnch'uk Yesullon: 1991-yŏn 5-wŏl 21-il.* P'yŏngyang: Chosŏn Nodongdang Ch'ulp'ansa, 1992.

11 Pyongyang was originally planned for 500,000 people, but now has almost 3 million inhabitants.

12 *Chosŏn Kŏnch'uk*, 2011.

13 Jeong, Eunmee. "Food, Clothing and Housing of North Korea's Residents and Social Changes." *The World Conference on North Korean Studies*, 2014.

14 Joung, Eun-Lee. "An Analysis on the Status of a Real Estate Investment in North Korea." *The World Conference on North Korean Studies*, 2014.

15 Jeong, Eunmee. "Food, Clothing and Housing of North Korea's Residents and Social Changes." *The World Conference on North Korean Studies*, 2014.

MICRO DISTRICT

ngyang
North Korea, Pyongyang

GRID CITY COMPARISON

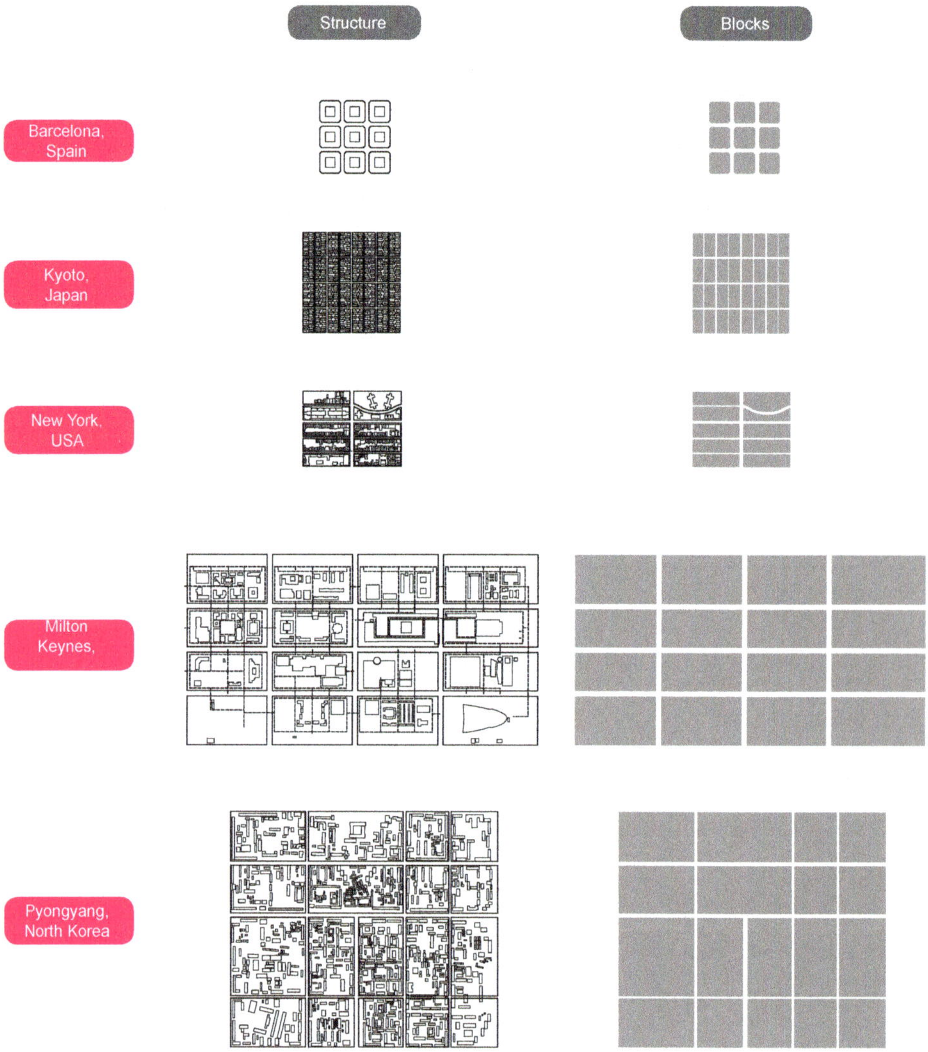

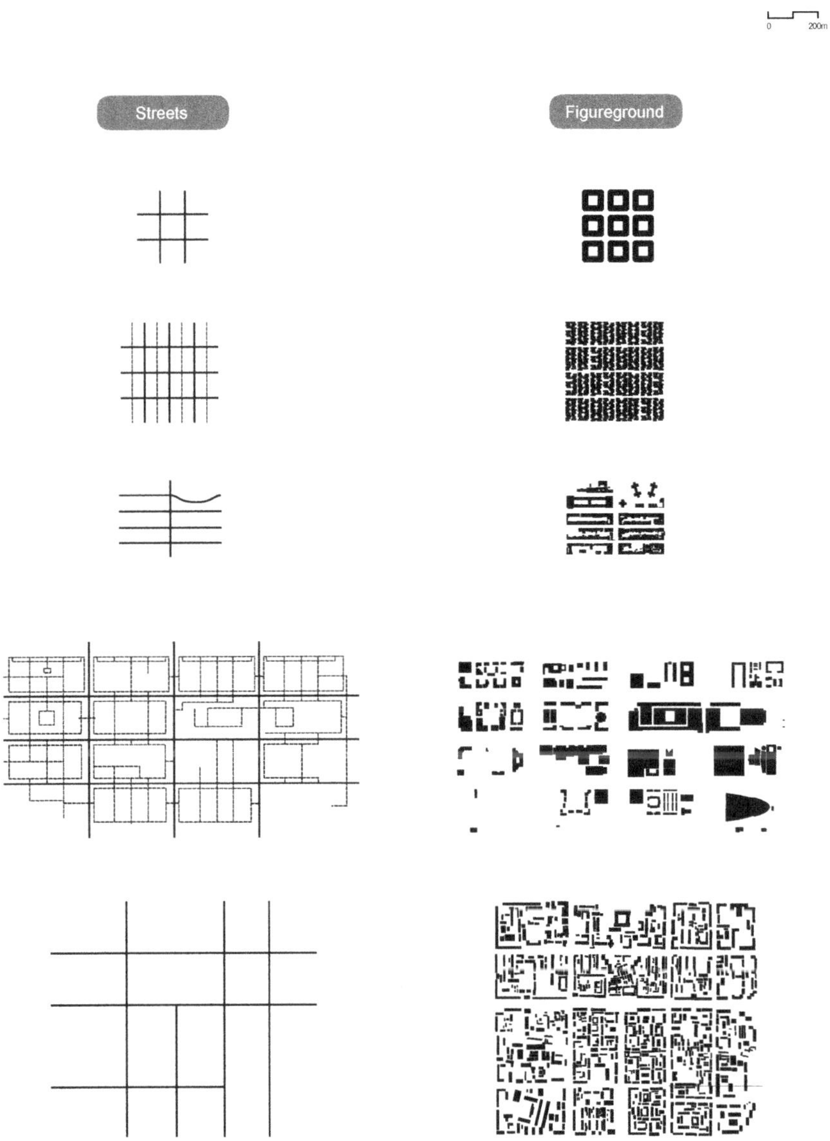

* source from *Pyongyang, And Pyongyang After* (2011), Dongwoo Yim

PRECINCT*

Kwangbok Street, Mangyungdae Guyok

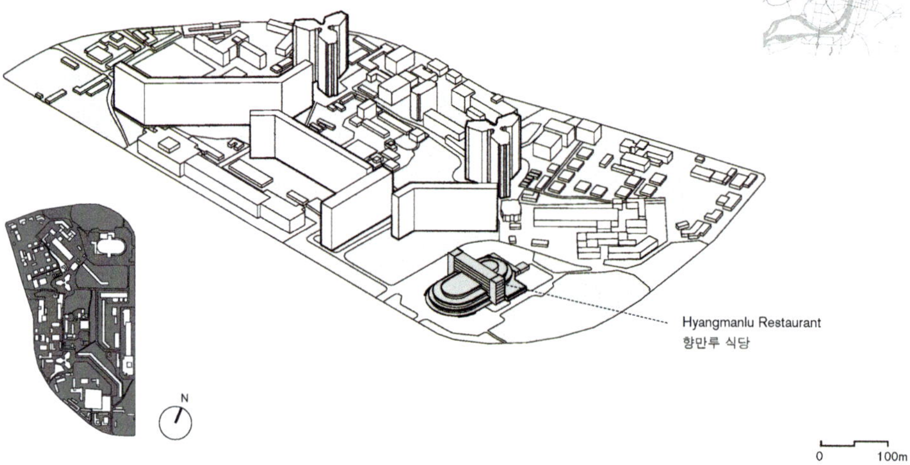

Tongil Street, Rakrang Guyok

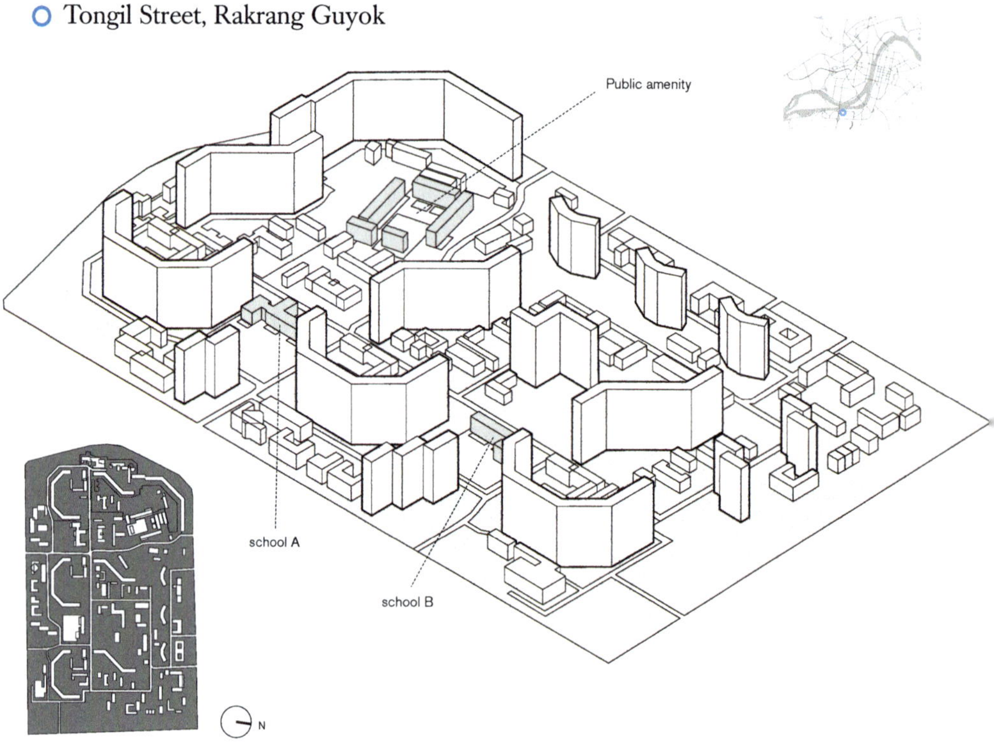

Ponghwa Street, Potonggang Guyok

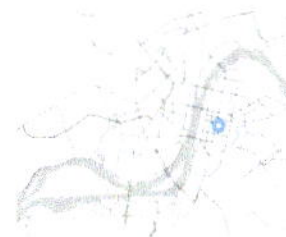

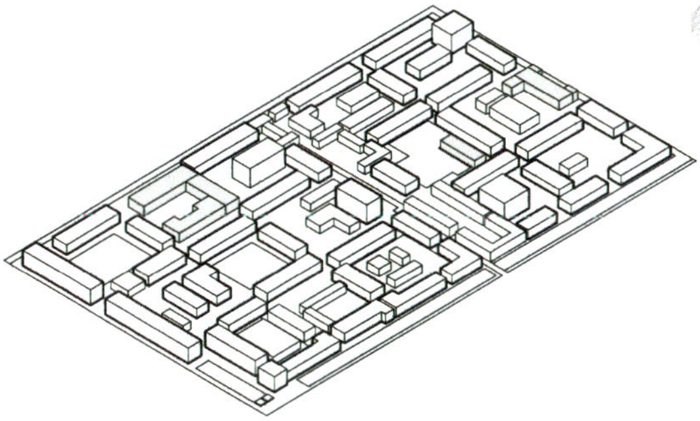

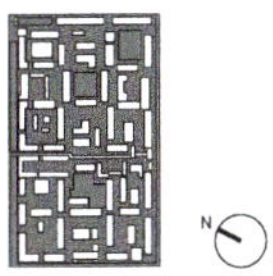

Ponghwa Street, Potonggang Guyok

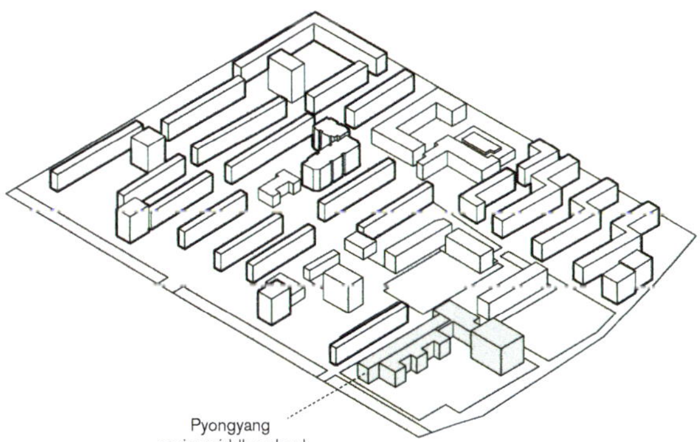

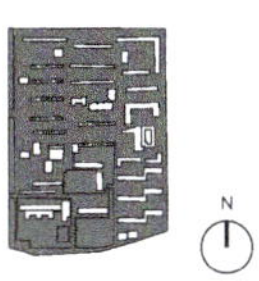

* source from *North Korean Atlas* (2014), ed. Dongwoo Yim, Rafael Luna

PRECINCT

Saesalim Street, Tongdaewon Guyok

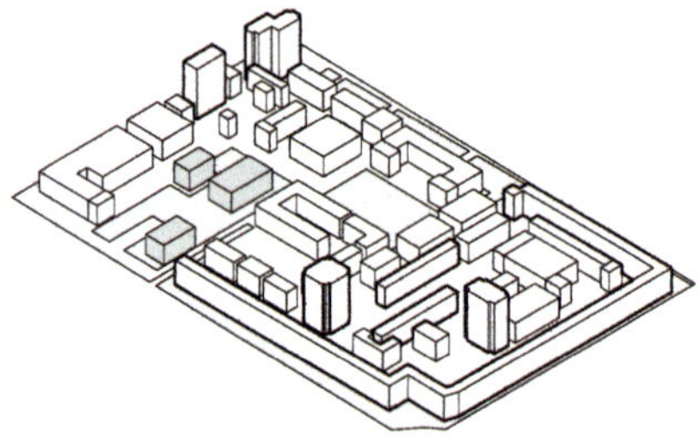

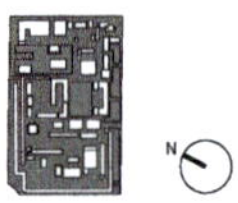

Mansudae Street, Joong Guyok

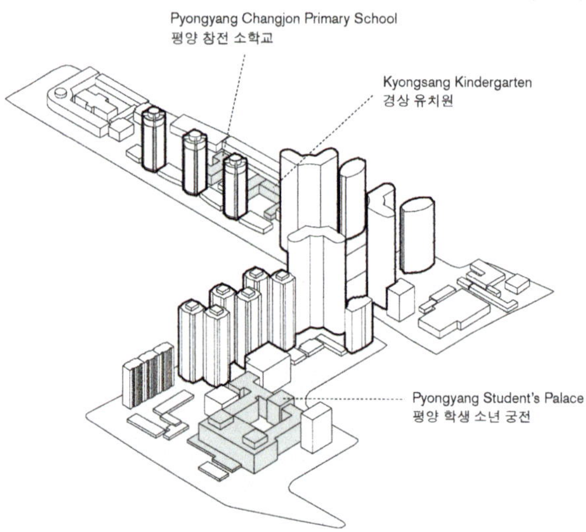

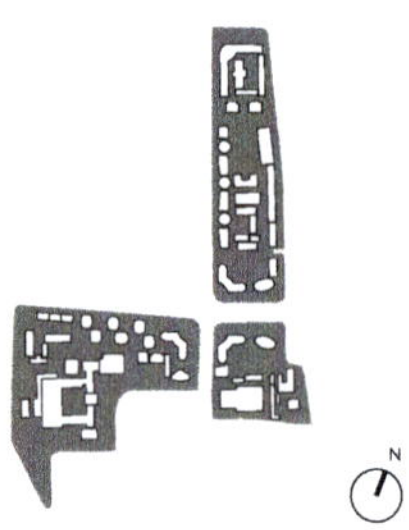

Pangjik Street, Songgyo Guyok

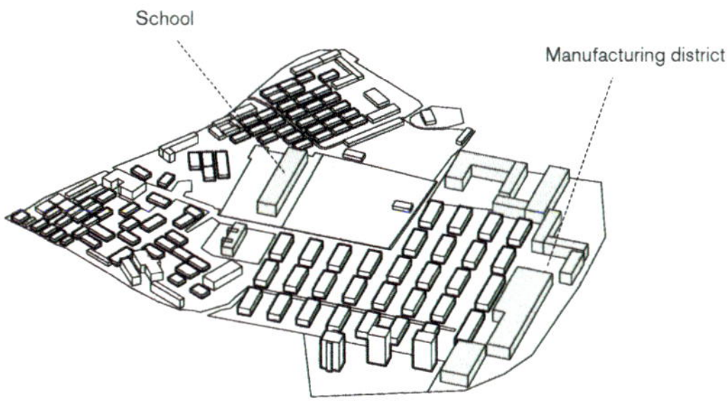

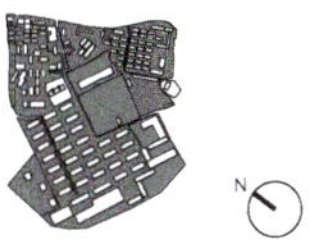

Chollima Street, Phyongchon Guyok

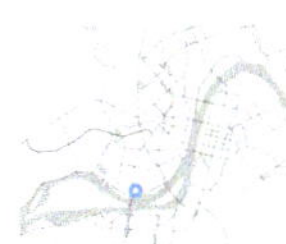

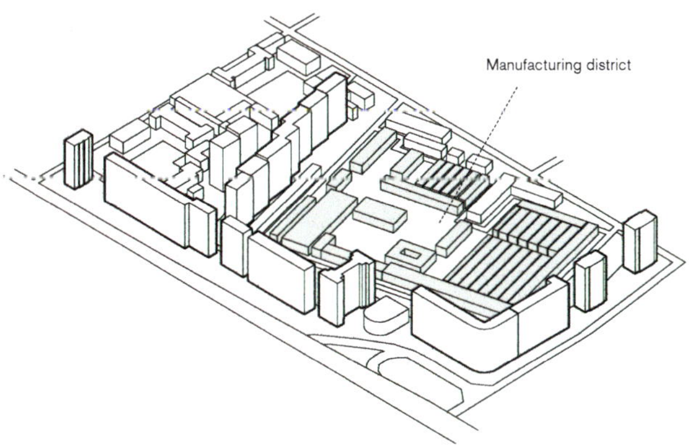

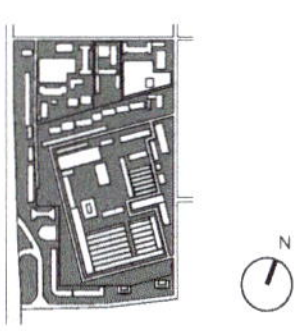

MUNSOO STREET

Munsoo Street, 2000's

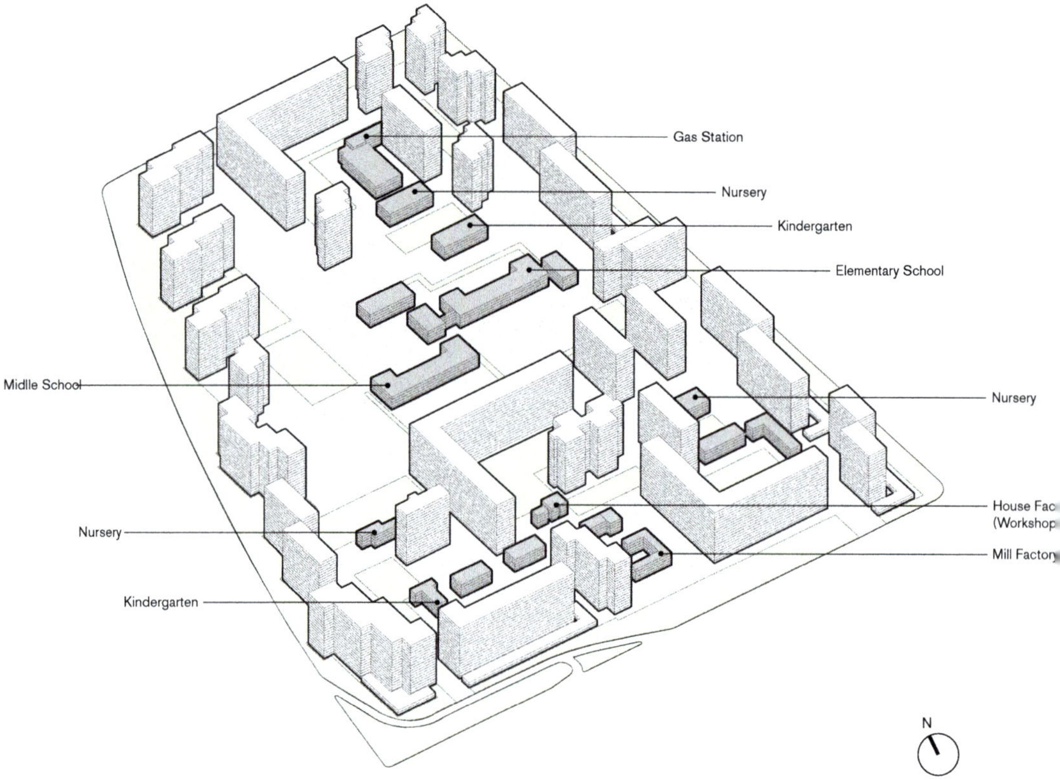

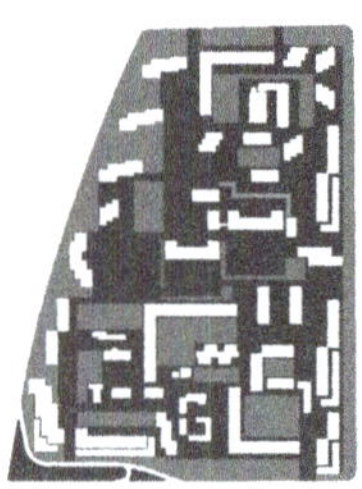

Legend

- Housing Tower
- Social Infrastructur
- Green
- Additional Building

Munsoo Street, 2015

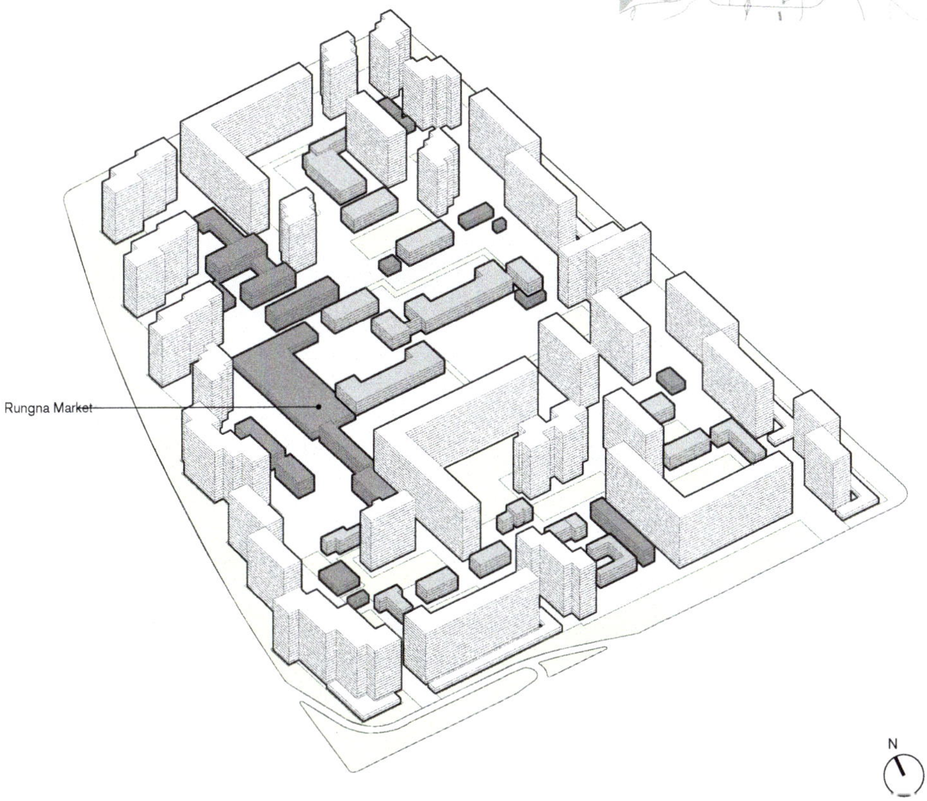

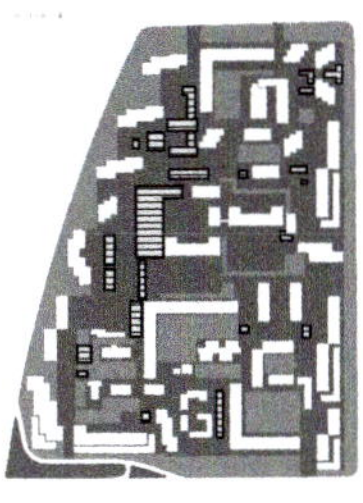

Legend

- Housing Tower
- Social Infrastructure
- Green
- Additional Building

HOUSING TYPOLOGY

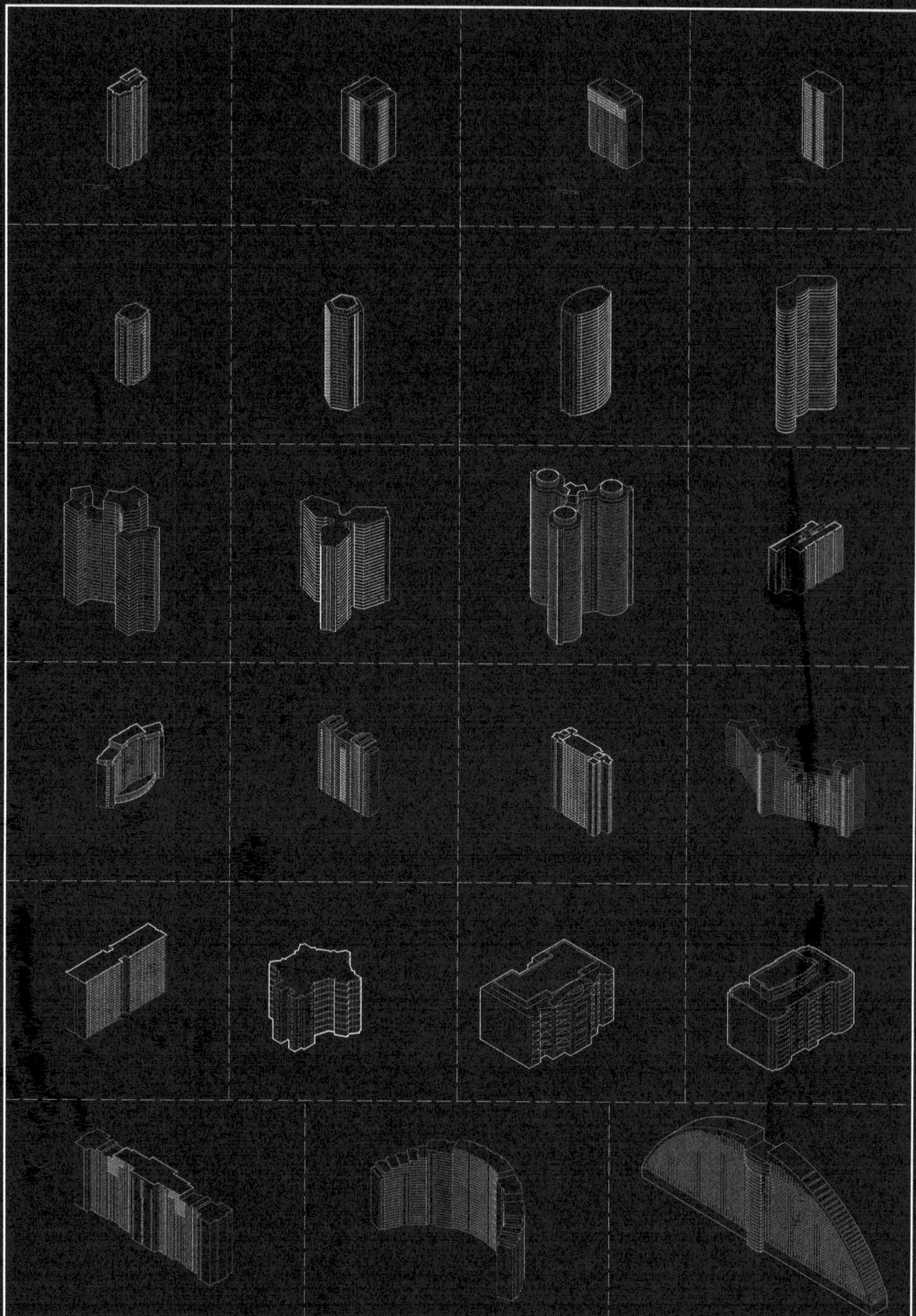

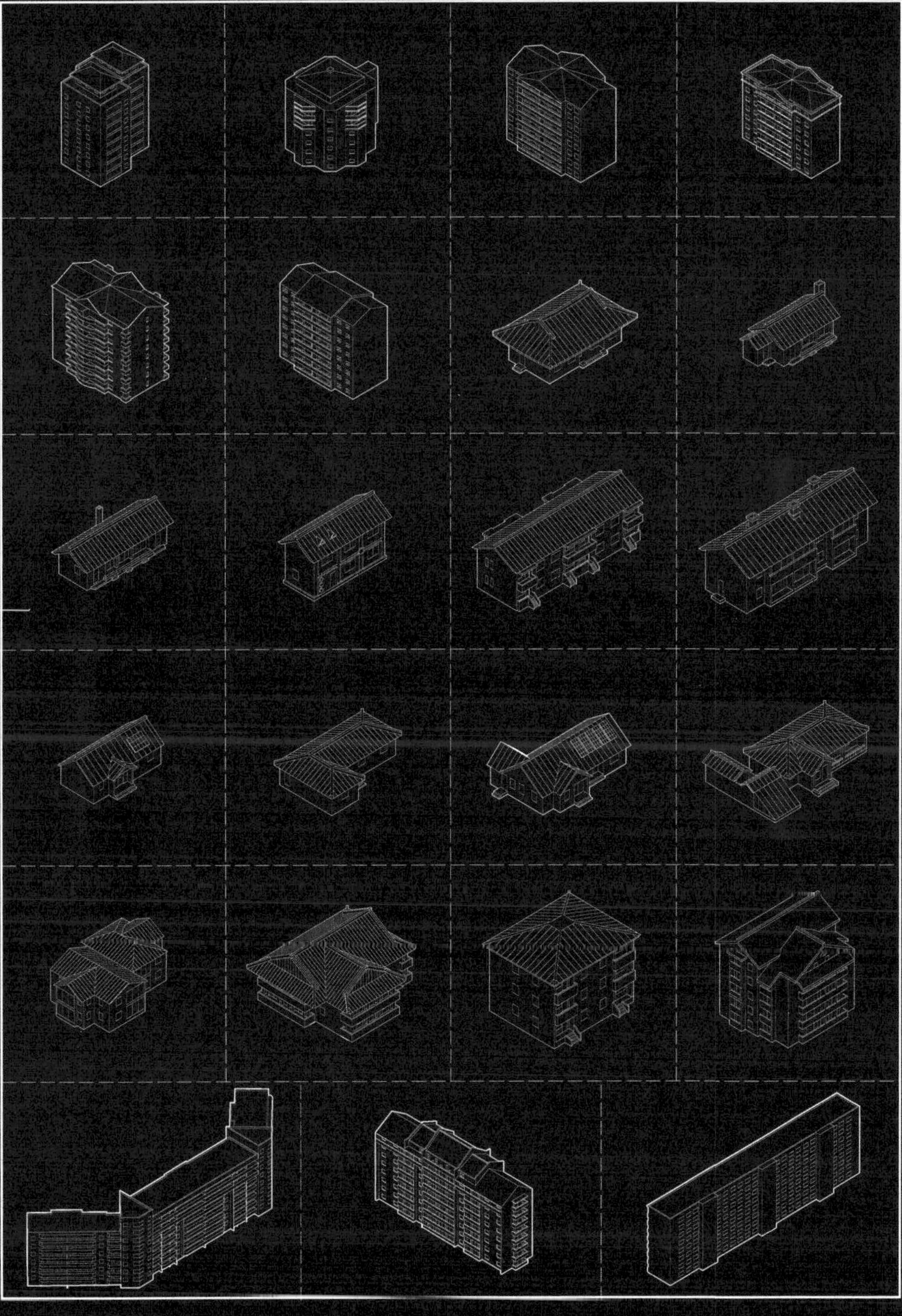

LOW-RISE TYPOLOGIES

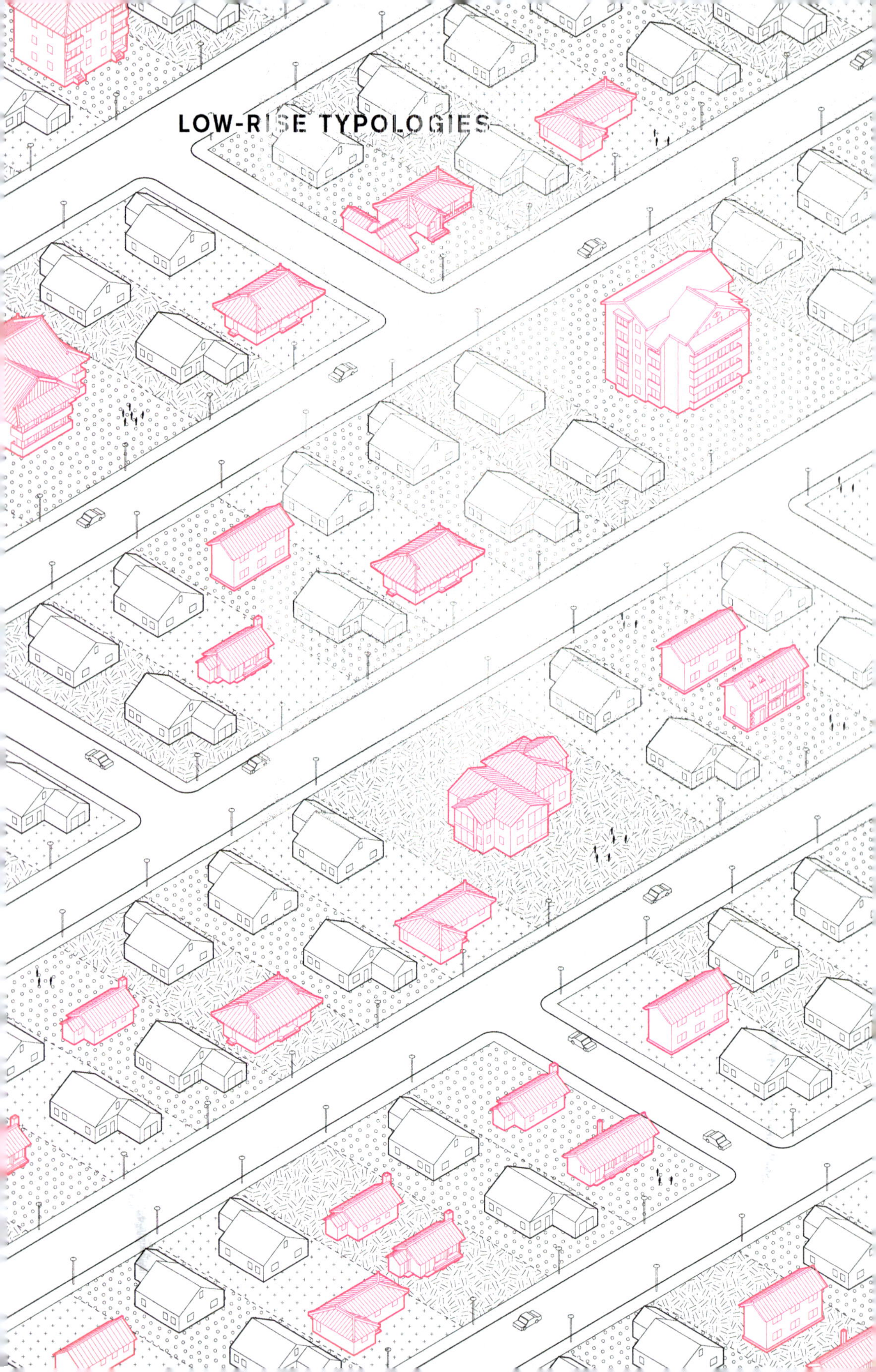

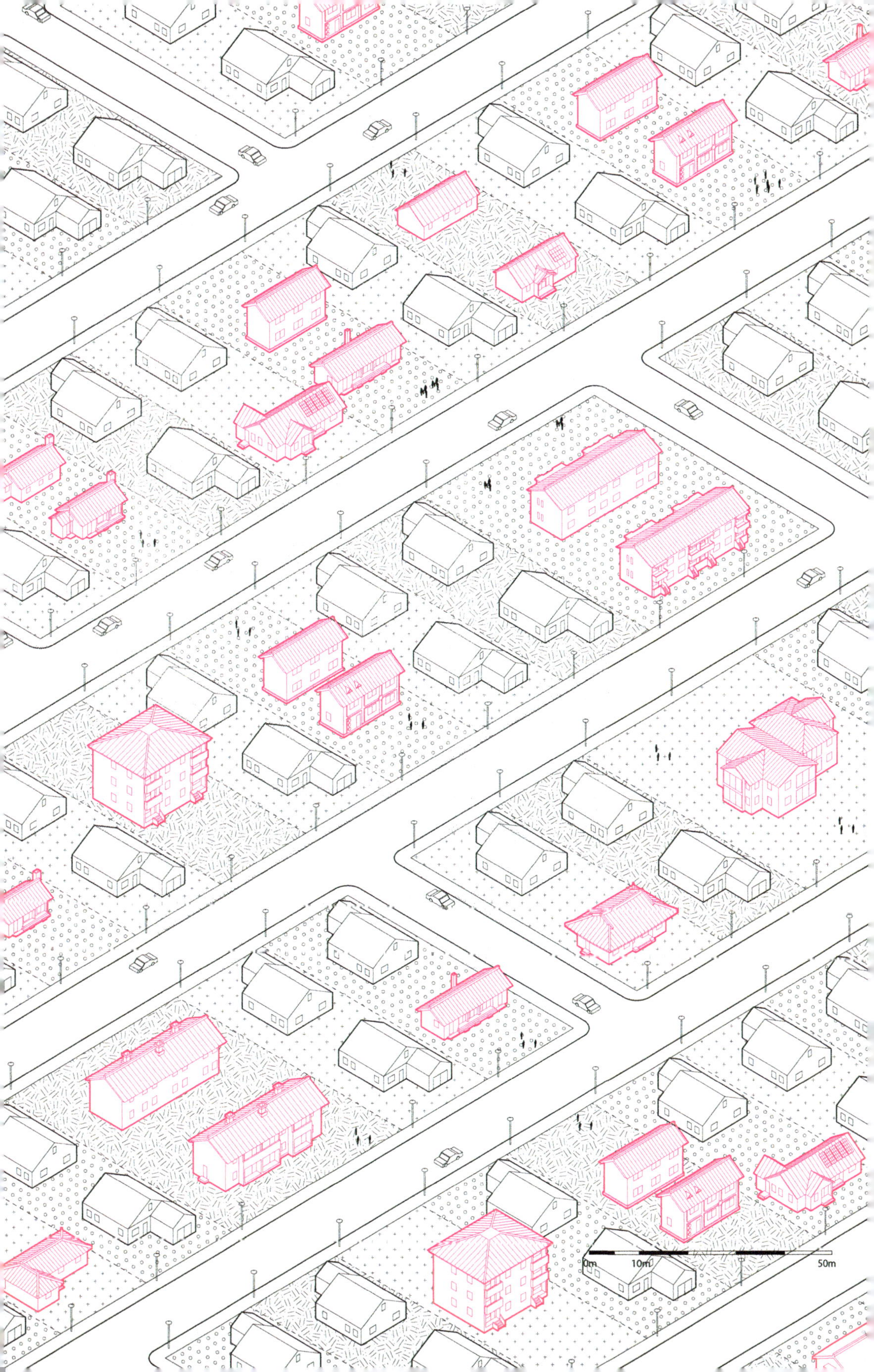
0m
10m
50m

MID-RISE TYPOLOGIES

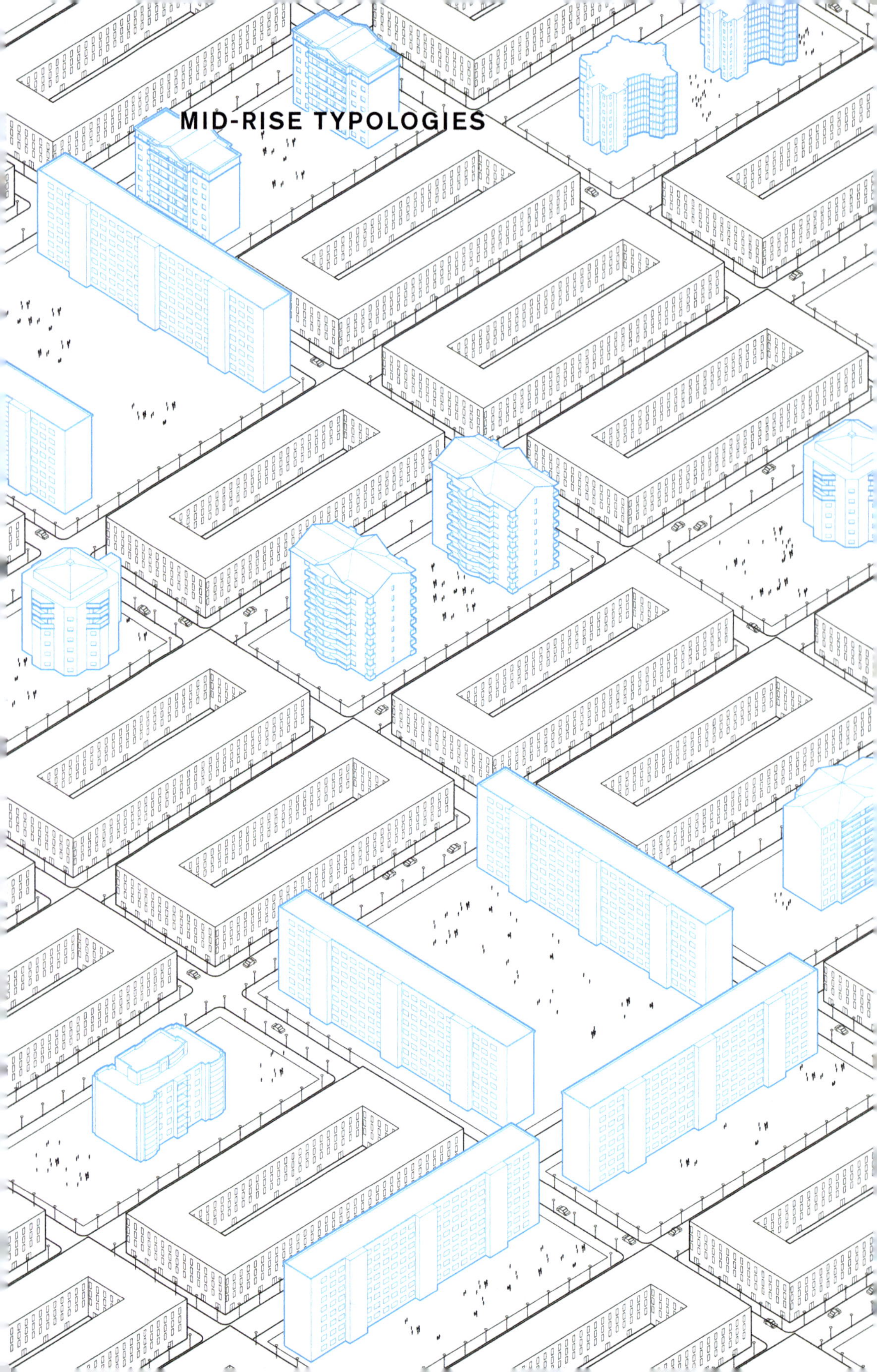

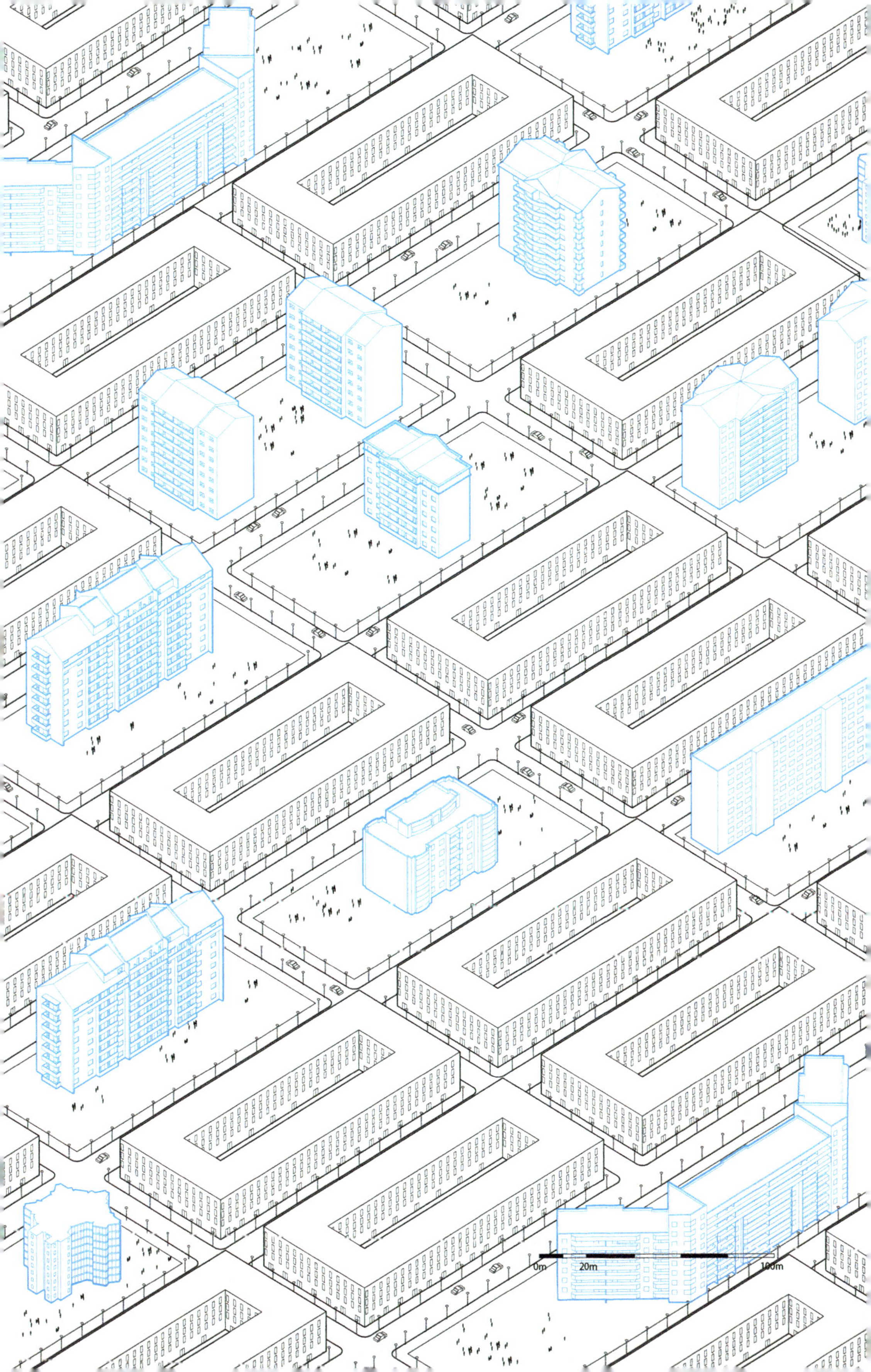
0m
20m
100m

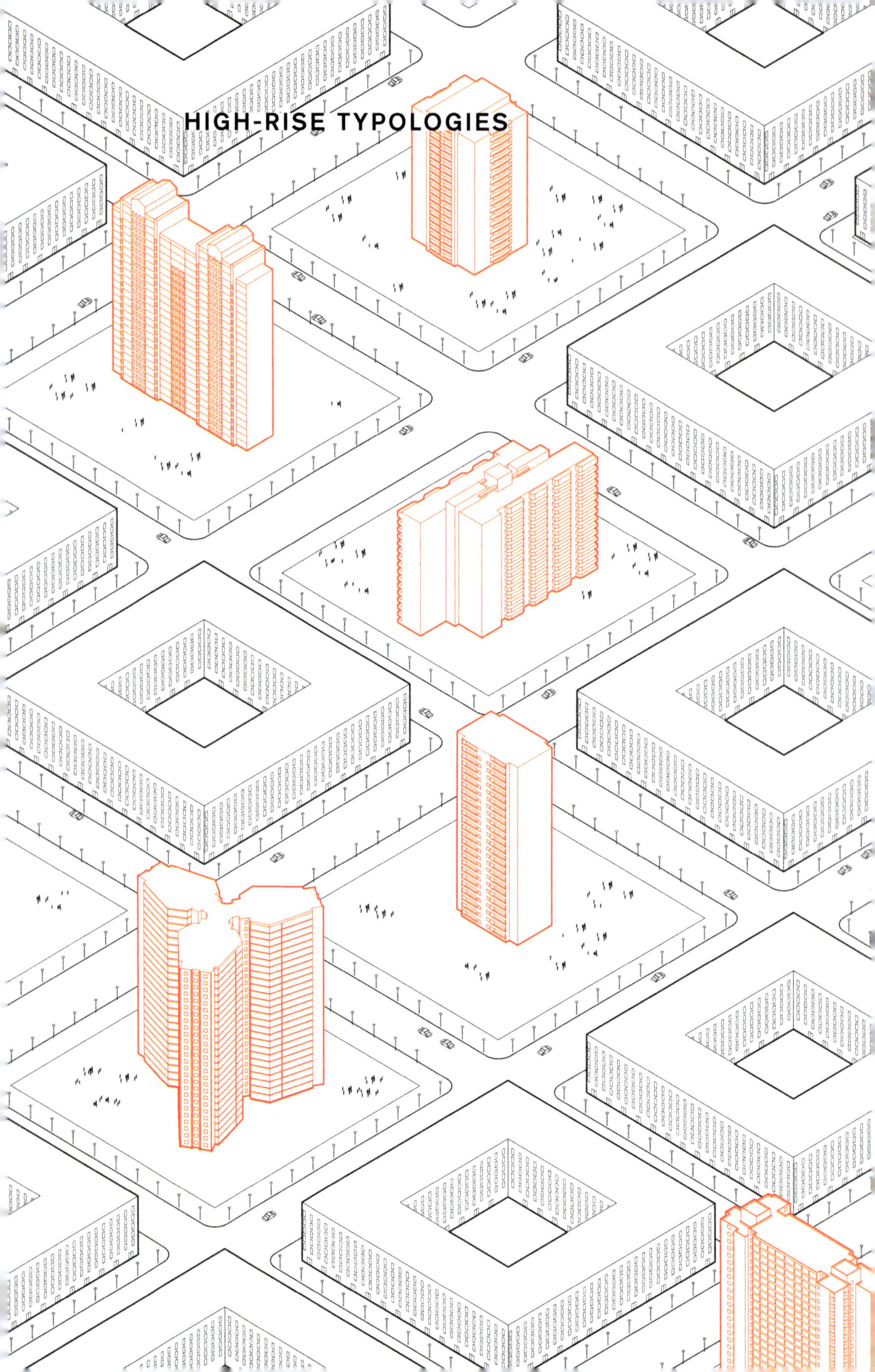
HIGH-RISE TYPOLOGIES

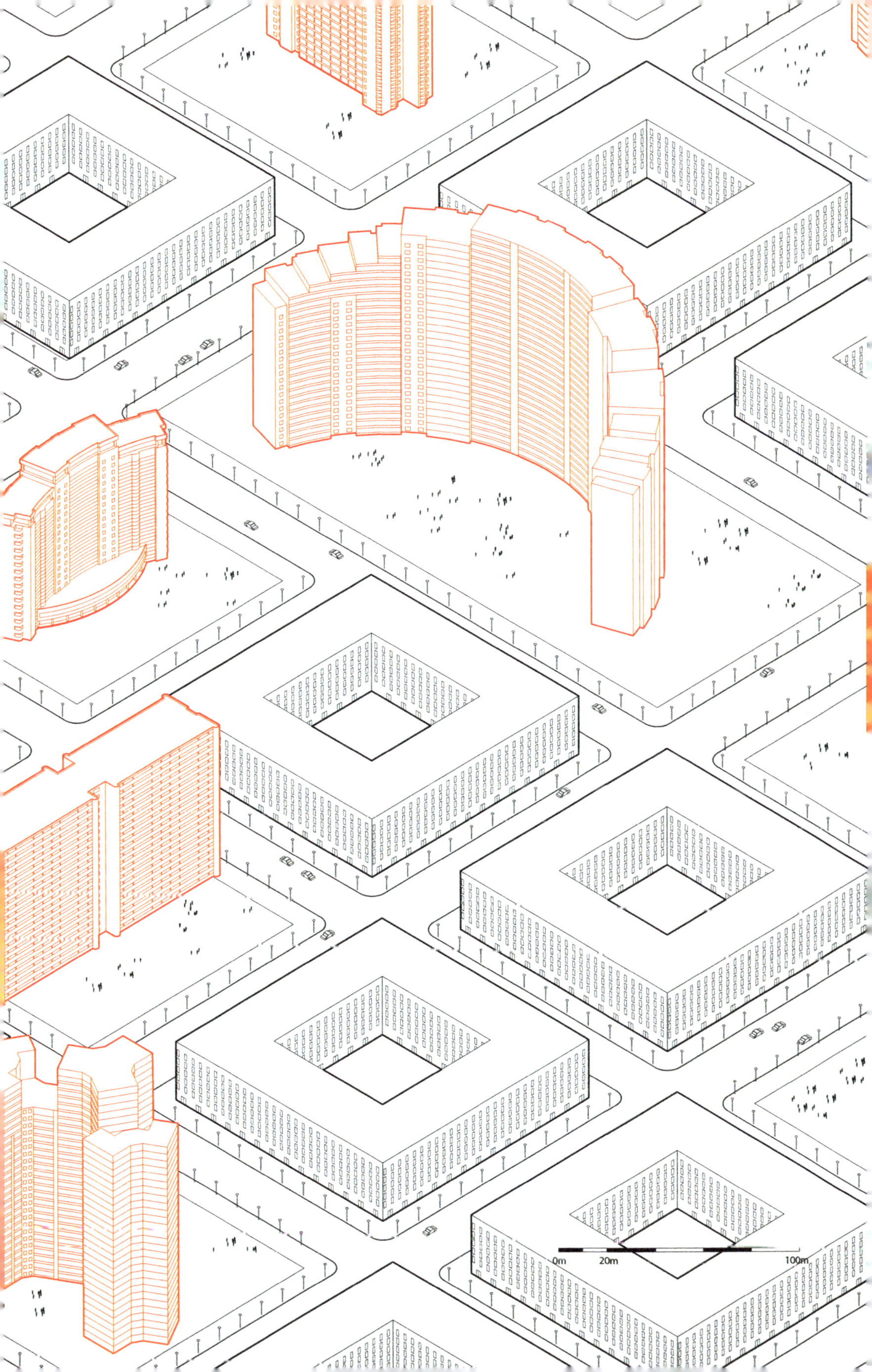
0m
20m
100m

HIGH-RISE TYPOLOGIES

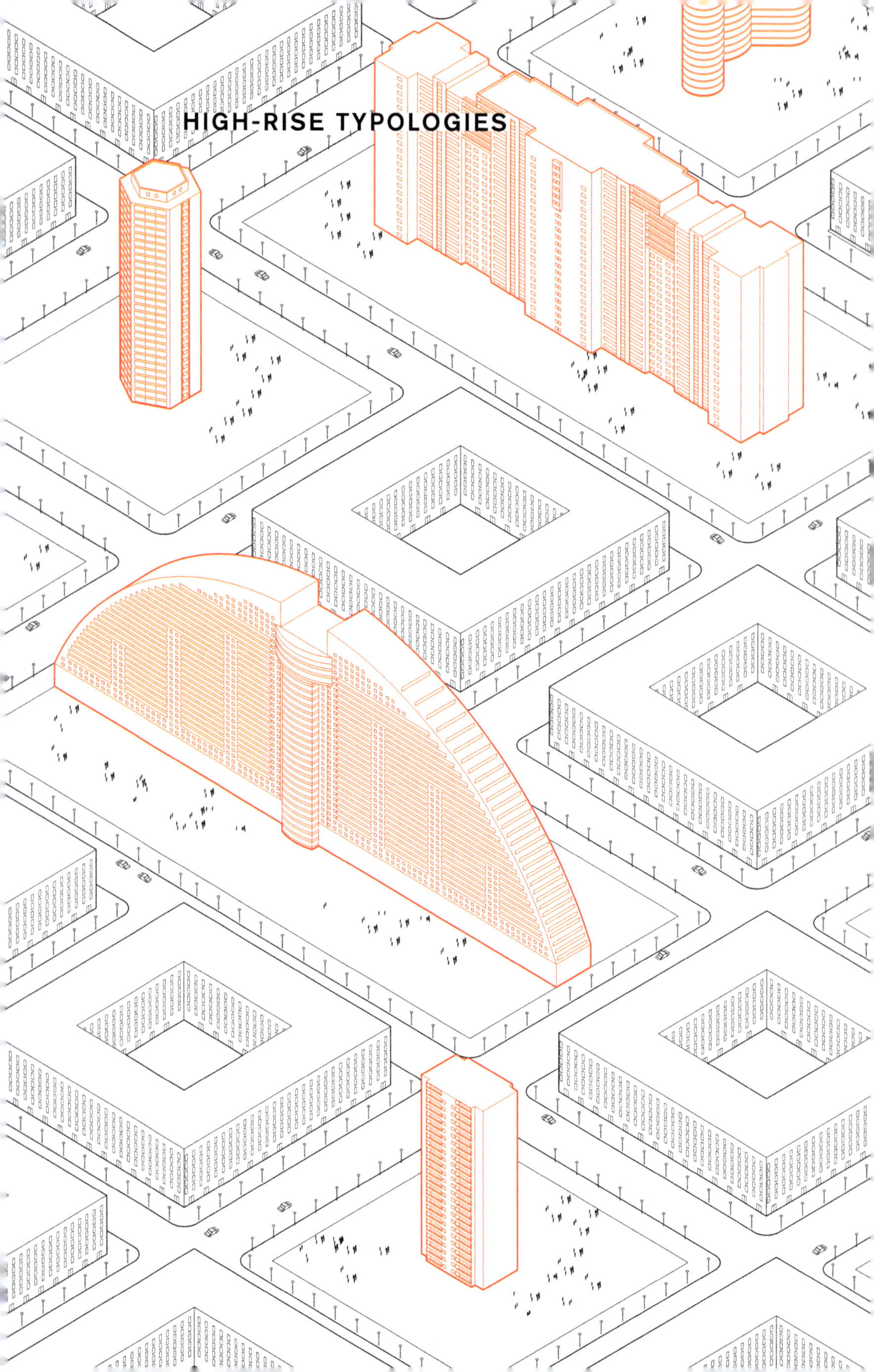

0m
20m
100m

07 RECENT TRANSFORMATIONS 2010-2015

MANSU HILL STATUE

2010

"After the death of the second leader Kim Jong Il in 2011, Pyongyang now has two grand statues on Mansu Hill where the first leader Kim Il Sung's statue has been standing."

2015

RYUKYUNG HOTEL

2010

"The construction of Ryukyung Hotel was ceased in 1992, and after 16 years of wait, the construction restarted again in 2008. Currently, the exterior facade is completed."

2015

SUNAN INTERNATIONAL AIRPORT

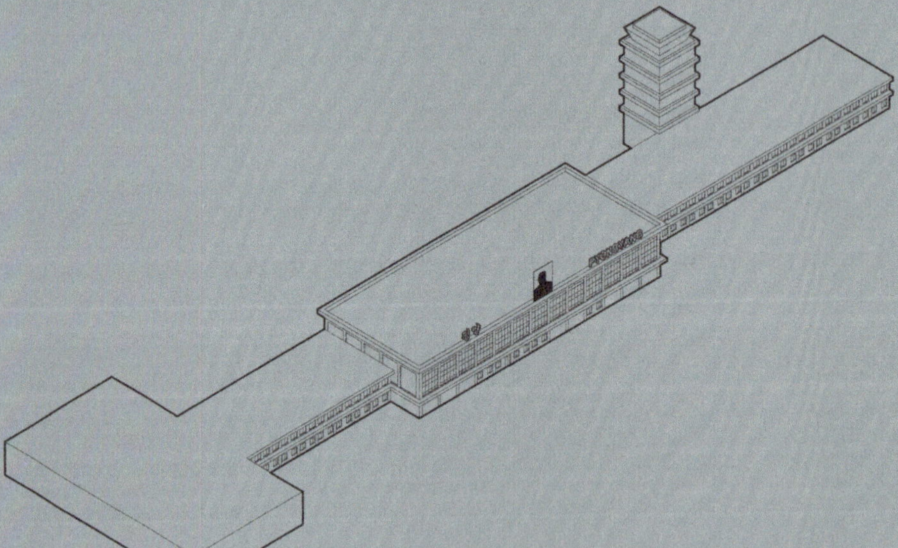

2010

photo by Calvin Chua

" There is no Kim Il Sung portrait in the new renovated airport"

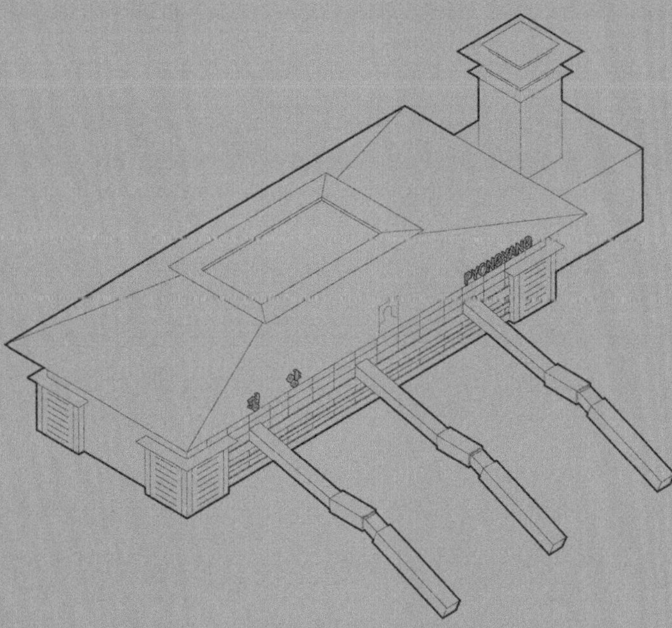

2015

HOUSING DEVELOPMENTS IN CITY CENTER

"Real estate developments by private developers are not secret anymore in North Korea, especially in Pyongyang. Private developers, such as "Don-ju", invests on multiples of housing properties and sell or rent them to individuals, which is not much different from free-economy."

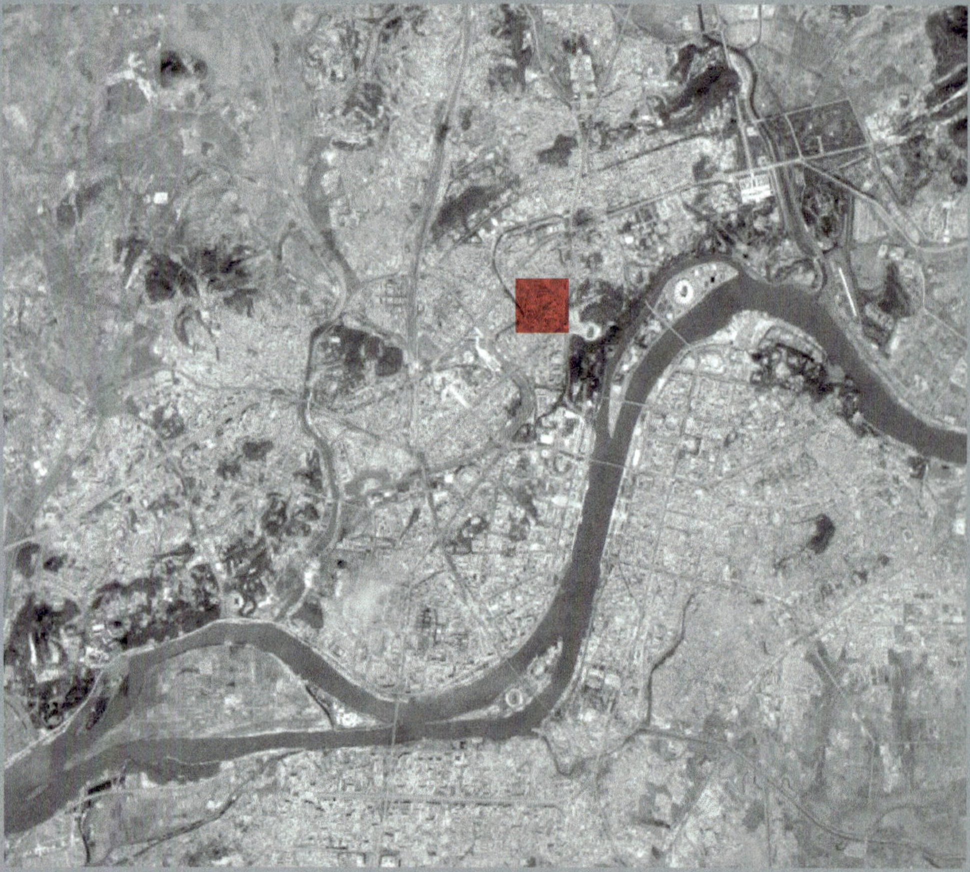

2000

2005

2010

2015

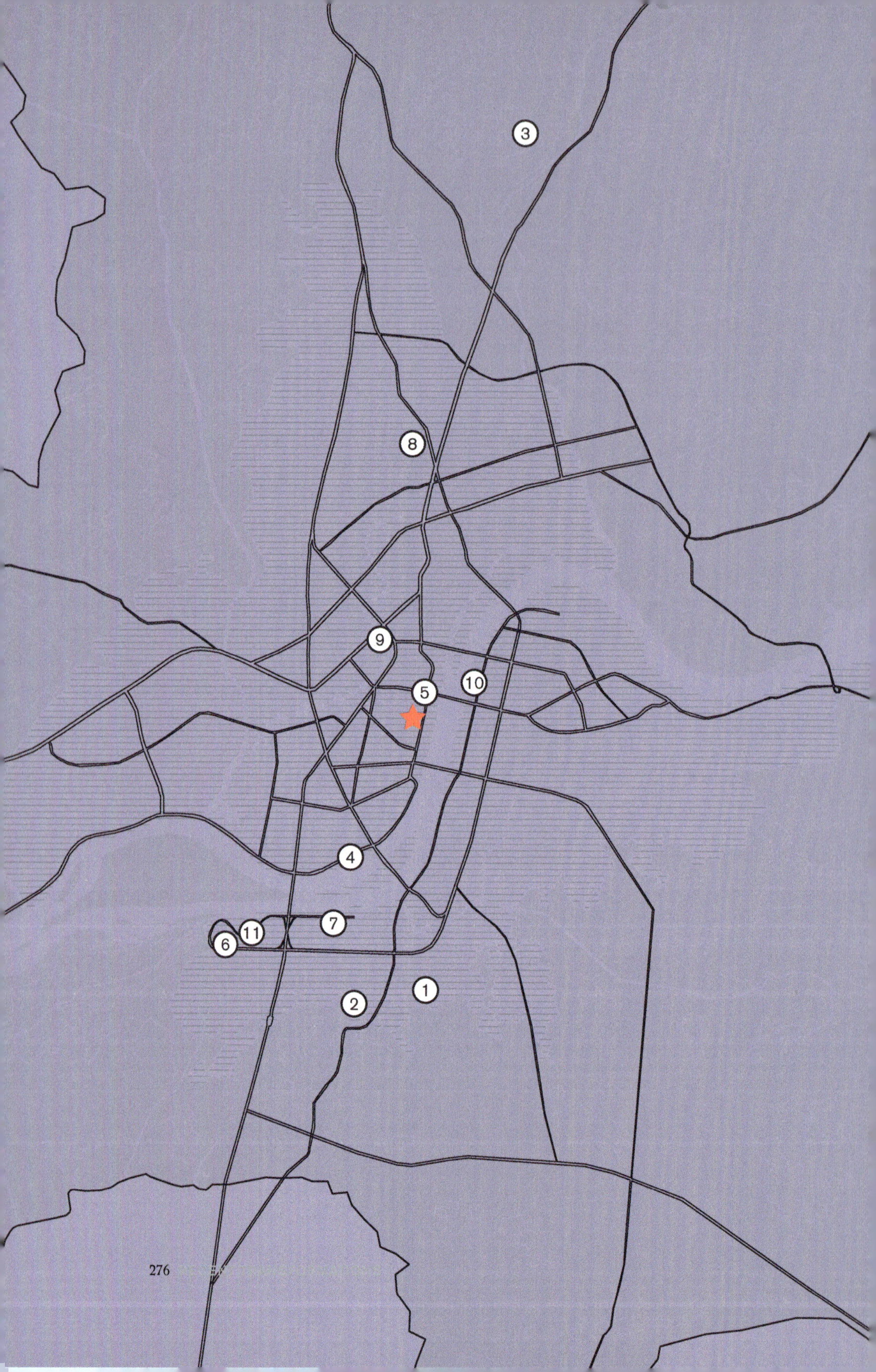
3
8
9
5
10
4
7
11
6
1
2

1 FRINGE I_PRIVATE DEVELOPMENT
2 FRINGE II_PRIVATE DEVELOPMENT
3 FRINGE III_PUBLIC DEVELOPMENT
4 WATERFRONT_PUBLIC DEVELOPMENT
5 CITY CENTER_PUBLIC DEVELOPMENT
6 DENSIFICATION_INFILL DEVELOPMENT
7 SYMBOLISM_ICONIC DEPARTMENT STORE
8 SYMBOLISM_NATIONAL PROPAGANDA
9 SYMBOLISM_ENHANCING PROPAGANDA SPACE
10 LEISURE PROPOSITION I
11 LEISURE PROPOSITION II

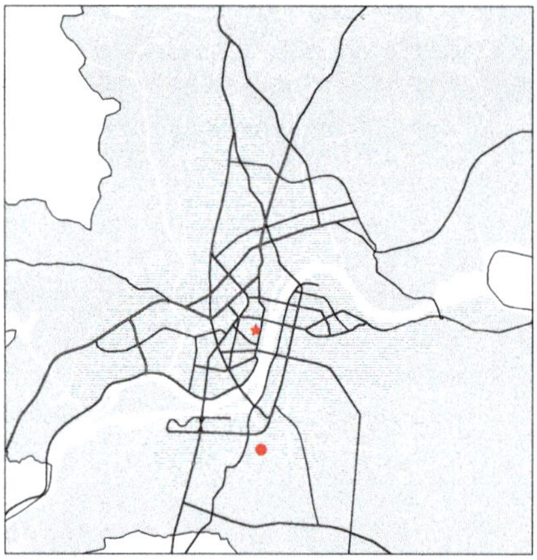

FRINGE I_PRIVATE DEVELOPMENT

In Pyongyang, there is a less clear boundary between urban and rural area. As a socialist city, Pyongyang tried to engage rural agriculture area with urban fabric. However, as the private real estate market grows, these fringe areas, the area between urban fabric and rural agriculture area, become desirable points for the private developer. Because, it is easier to deal with government control yet not much far from the city center. Fringe development is still different from suburban development in a way that it does not require much additional infrastructure work, and therefore, it emerges ahead of large scale suburban development that truly responds to the new demands from emerging middle class people.

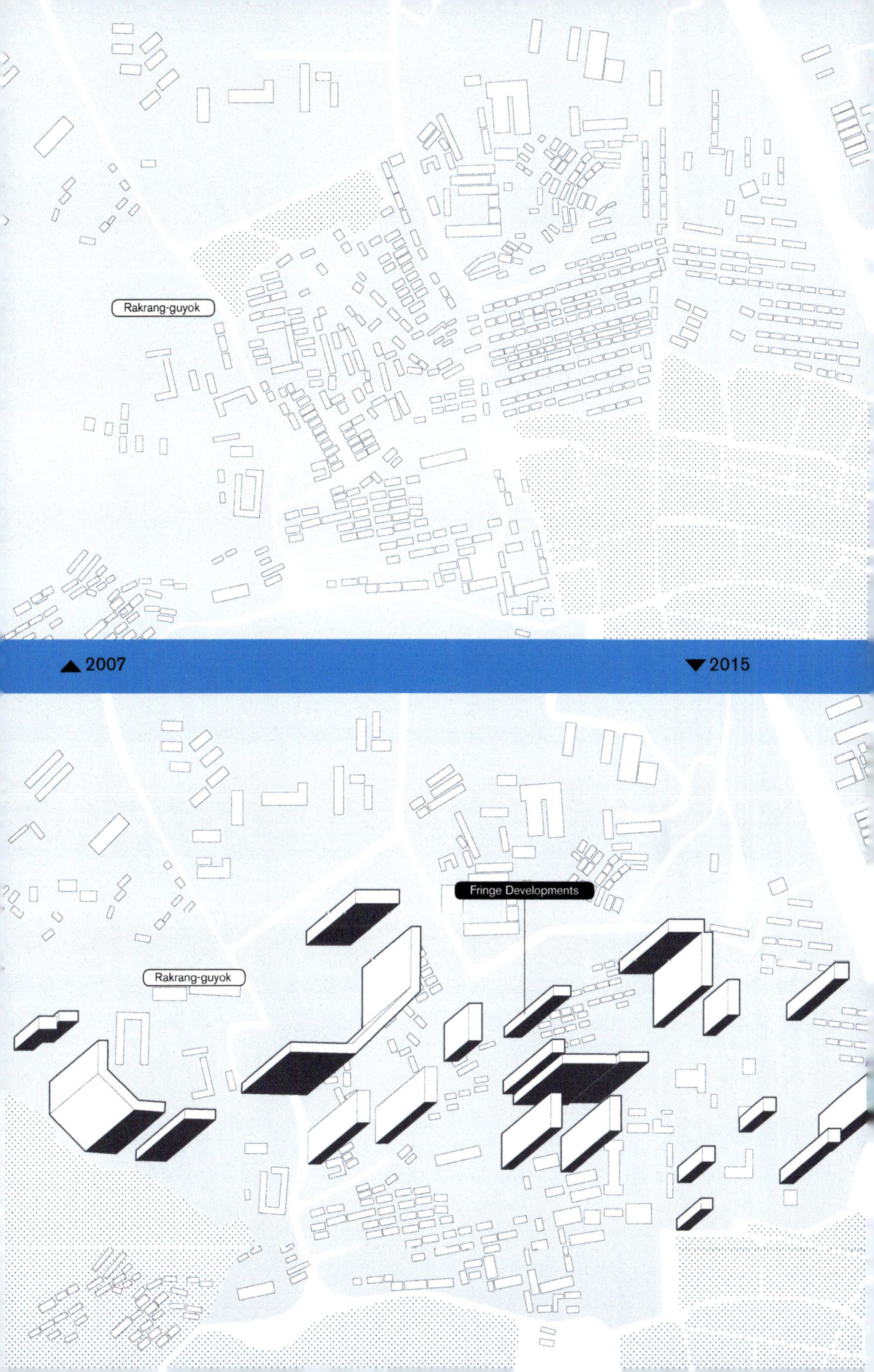
Rakrang-guyok
2007
2015
Fringe Developments
Rakrang-guyok

★ Kim Il Sung Square

● Fringe II_Provate Development

FRINGE II_PRIVATE DEVELOPMENT

Developments in fringe area, the border between urban fabric and rural agriculture, are mostly done by private developers. One of the surveys says that more than 50% of people have bought their houses through private market. This does not necessarily mean that the government control over the housing supply has collapsed, but rather shows a new chain between capitalist developer and communist officer has emerged. Still many parts in city center are developed by the government and public housings are supplied through these developments. Therefore, private developers have less room in the city center and more possibilities in the fringe areas.

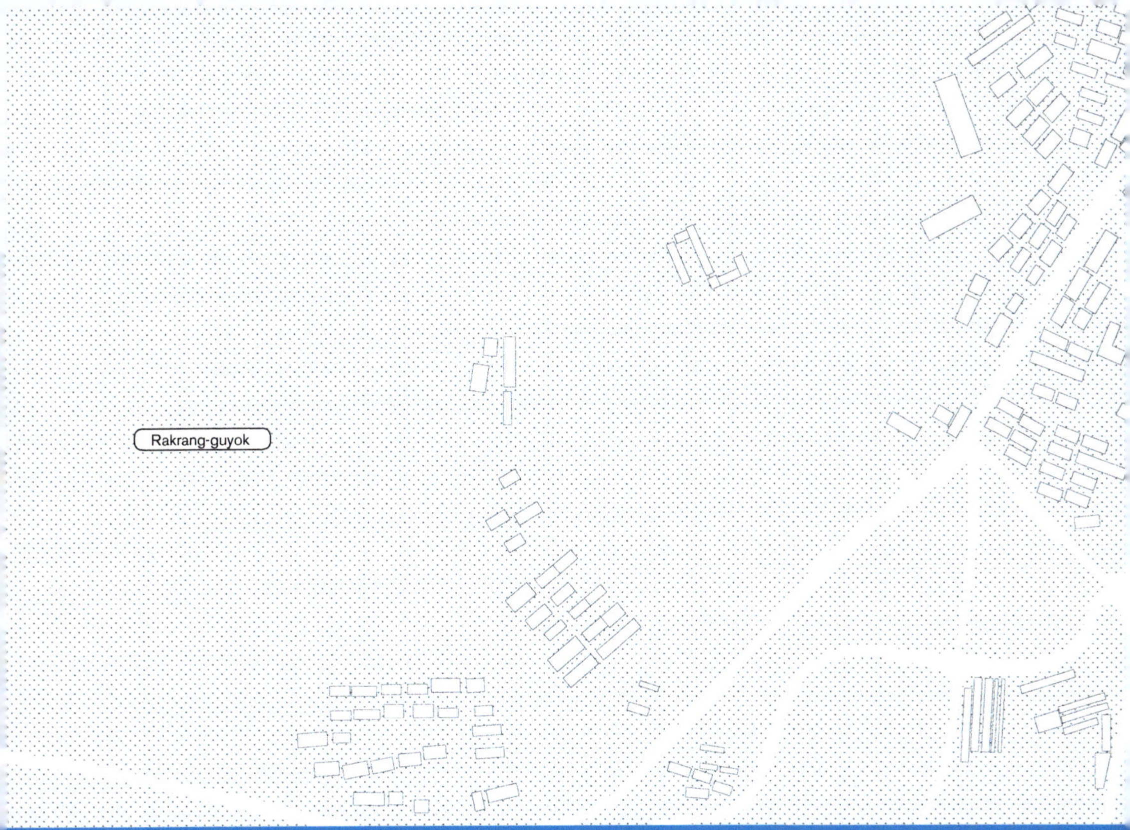

▲2007 ▼2015

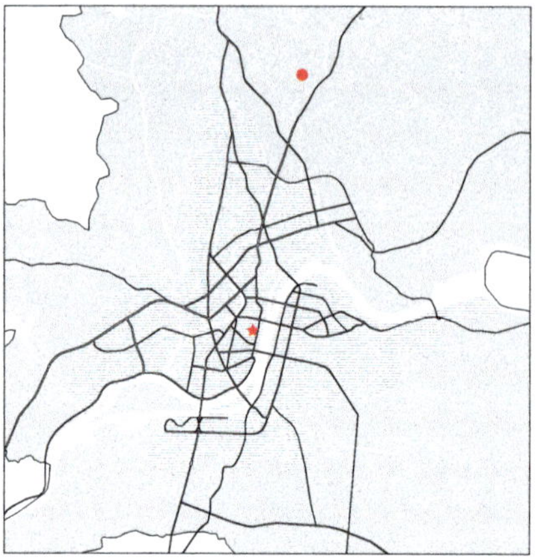

FRINGE III_PUBLIC DEVELOPMENT

Eunha Scientist Street is a residential district development in north of city center, Ryongsung District, completed in 2013. There are total 1,000 units in 21 buildings along the avenue with schools from elementary schools to high schools. As the name tells, it is developed for scientists as part of strategy to emphasize science of the nation. Unlike paint finish in most of residential developments, apartments in this development have tile finish, which is very a rare case in North Korea.
It is located within 1km distance from Ryongsung train station, which is just 11 km away from Kim Il Sung square, the city center. It shows potential fringe development of the future Pyongyang of how and where new residential developments might happen along with public transportation.

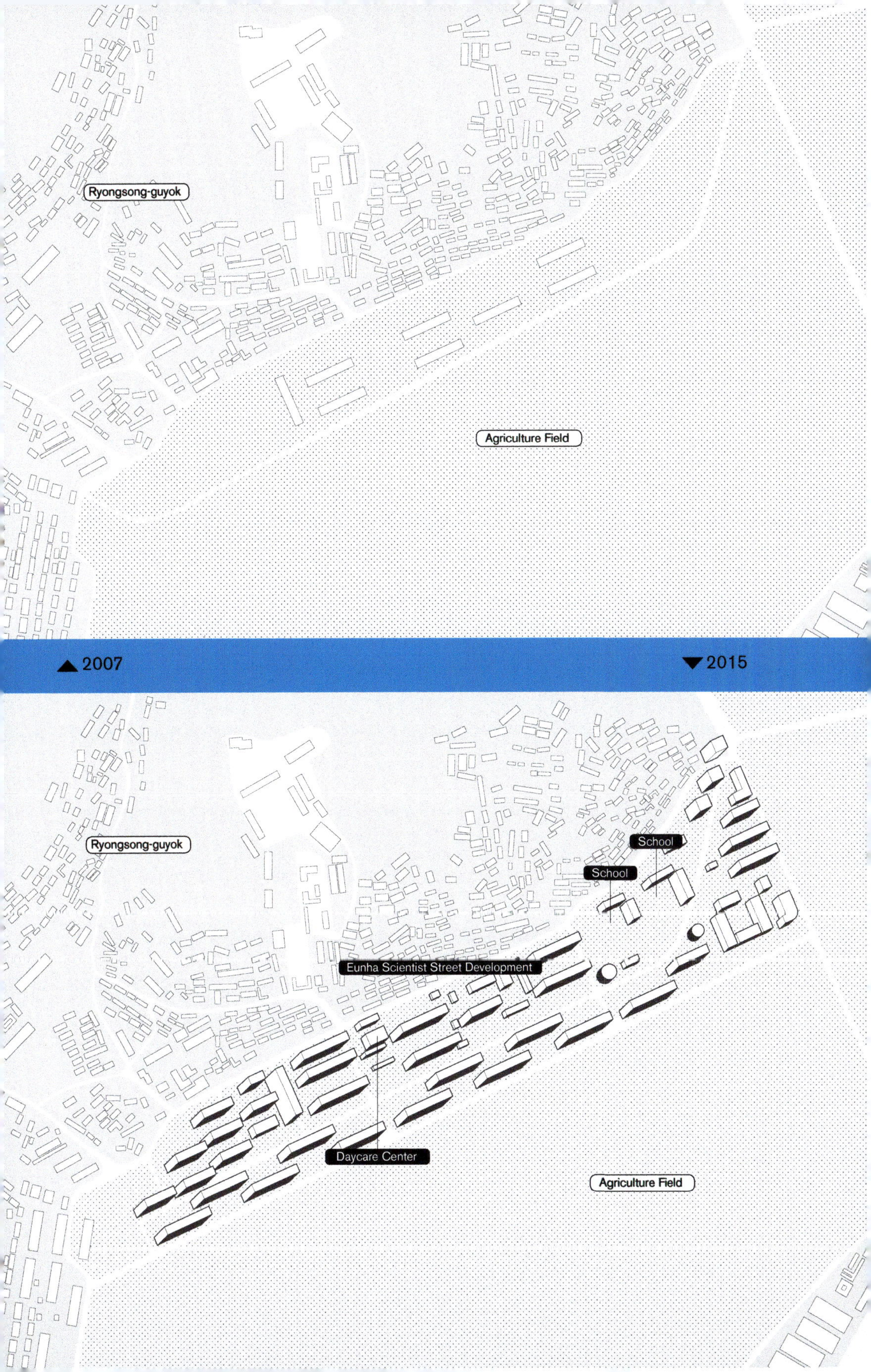

Ryongsong-guyok
Agriculture Field
2007
2015
Ryongsong-guyok
School
School
Eunha Scientist Street Development
Daycare Center
Agriculture Field

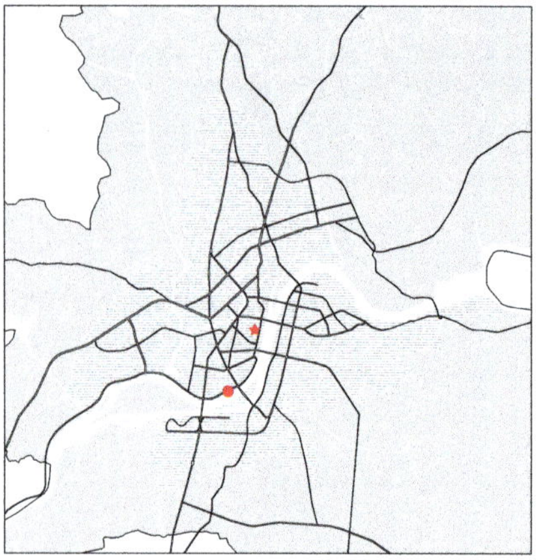

★ Kim Il Sung Square
● Waterfront Development

WATERFRONT_PUBLIC DEVELOPMENT

Mirae Scientist Street is a recent waterfront development completed in 2015. It is located on the waterfront between Ryanggak Island and Pyongyang Station. Similar to Eunha Scientist Street development, it is to encourage scientist and to emphasize the importance of the science of the country.

As there used to be no real estate value in Pyongyang, as a socialist city, there was less demand to develop certain parts of the city that have potentially high real estate value, such as the waterfront in this case. Although it was developed to supply apartments for scientists, the development shows that the government is aware of taking advantage of developing prime real estate spots.

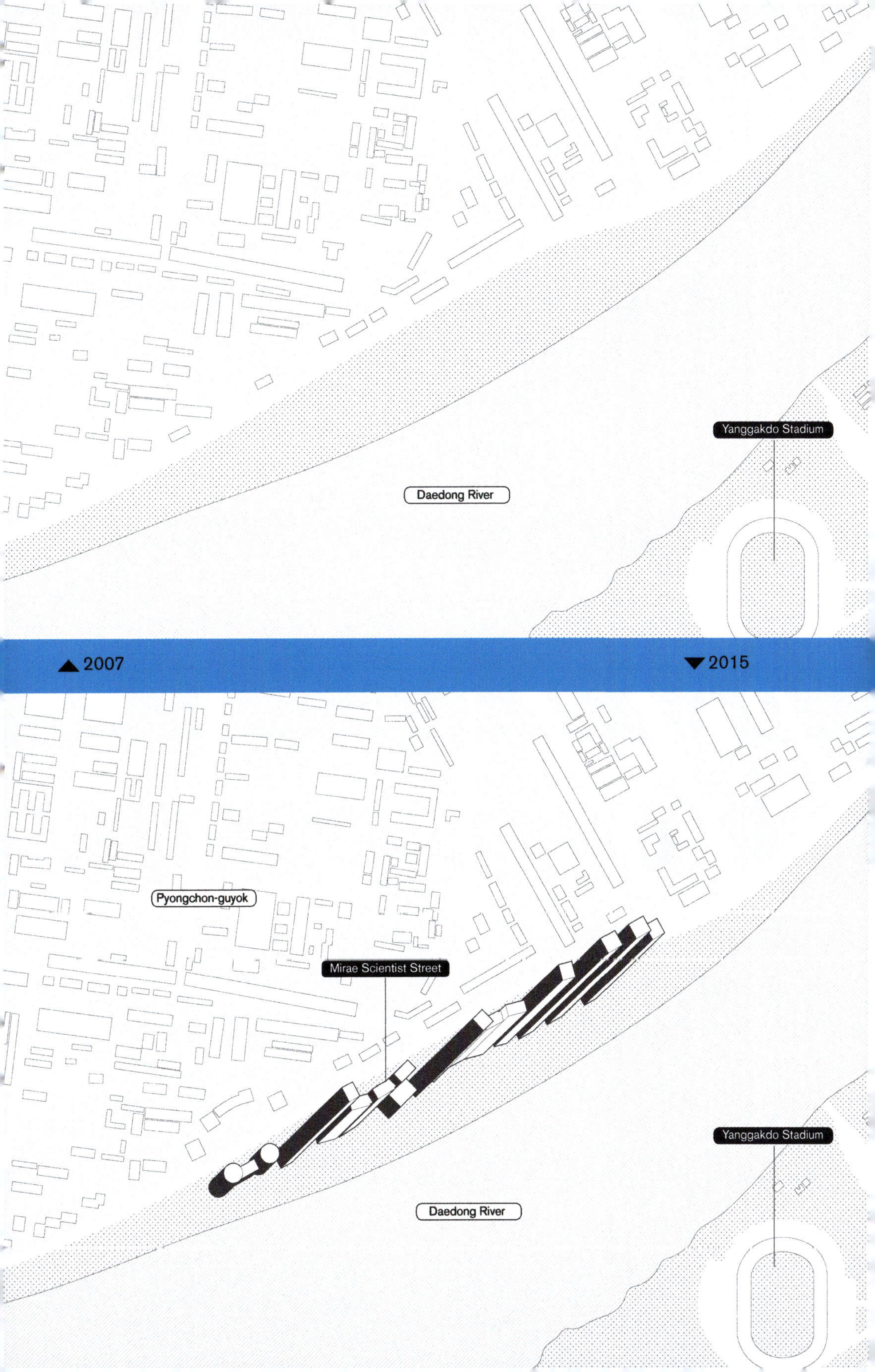

Yanggakdo Stadium
Daedong River
▲2007
▼2015
Pyongchon-guyok
Mirae Scientist Street
Yanggakdo Stadium
Daedong River

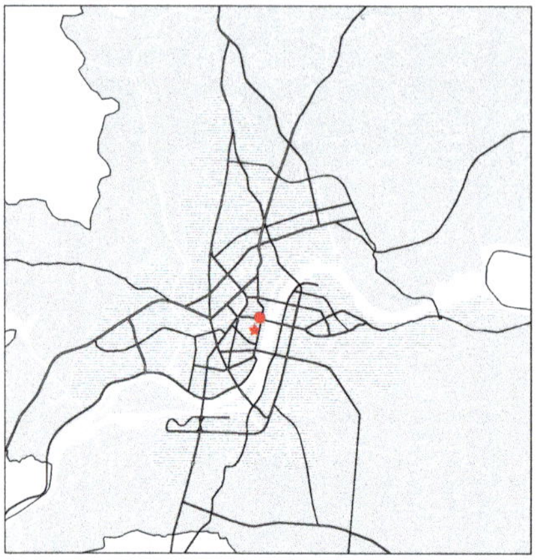

CITY CENTER_PUBLIC DEVELOPMENT

Similar the waterfront, in most of capitalist cities, the city center is also one of the hottest real estate points that gets much development force. It mostly has better transpotation, more ameneties and more cultural facilities. Although Pyongyang tried to reduce discrepancy between districts within the city, it was inevitable to have better quality environment in the city center than other areas. Therefore, the development push in the city center grew along with emerging middle class, and instead of allowing private sector to develop it, the government controlled directly and provided so called 'luxury' apartments in 2012. Mansudae apartment block has total 3,000 units in 14 buildings that are around 40 - 45 story tall. It is located right off of the Kim Il Sung square, less than 800m away to the north. This development is quite well known as luxury apartment in Pyongyang that requires over $100,000 USD to purchase.
Intersting fact about this development is that it demolished existing linear type mid-rise apartment to develop this new high-rise luxury apartment. It shows that the development is not only to reflect new demand of emerging middle class but also to show off the prosperity of the nation.

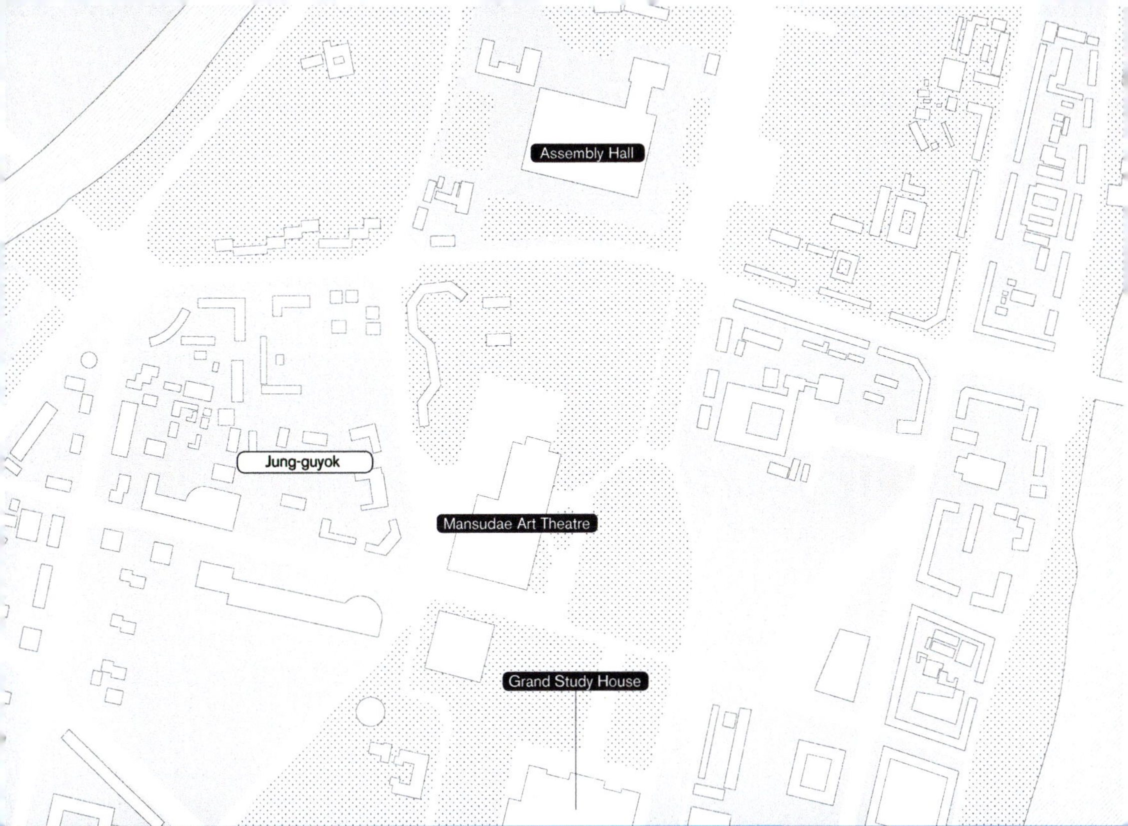
Assembly Hall
Jung-guyok
Mansudae Art Theatre
Grand Study House

▲2007 ▼2015

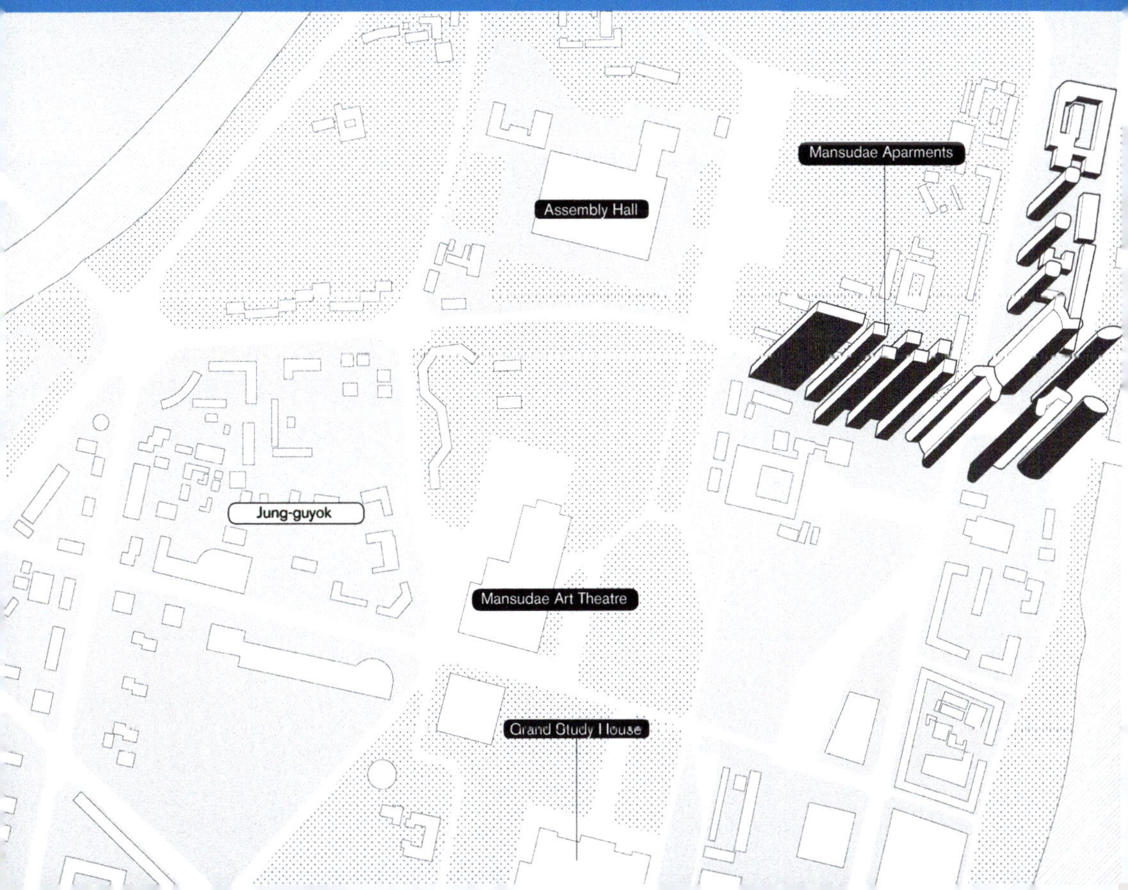
Mansudae Aparments
Assembly Hall
Jung-guyok
Mansudae Art Theatre
Grand Study House

DENSIFICATION_INFILL DEVELOPMENT

Densification is inevitable path when a city is in tranformation. In a micro-district, more apartment buildings and service amenities are built to accommodate increasing demand of emerging middle class people. It seems densifying through infill development happens more easily in high-rise type micro-disctricts, because they have less building coverage area which gives more room to be filled in with new programs. Especially, market facilities, that used to be controlled by the government, are increasing recently along with residential blocks.

The precedent is a pricinct along the Tongil Street, southwest from the city center, that was first developed in early 1990s as part of high-rise development plan.

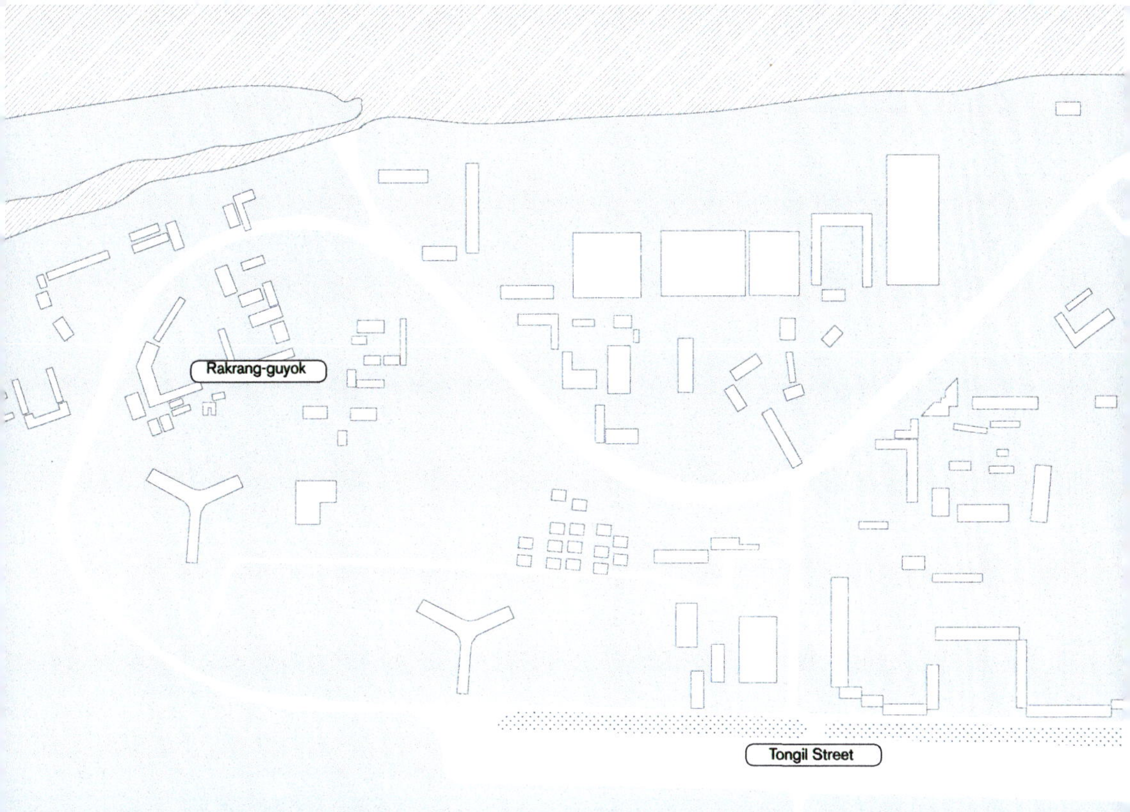
Rakrang-guyok
Tongil Street

▲2007 ▼2015

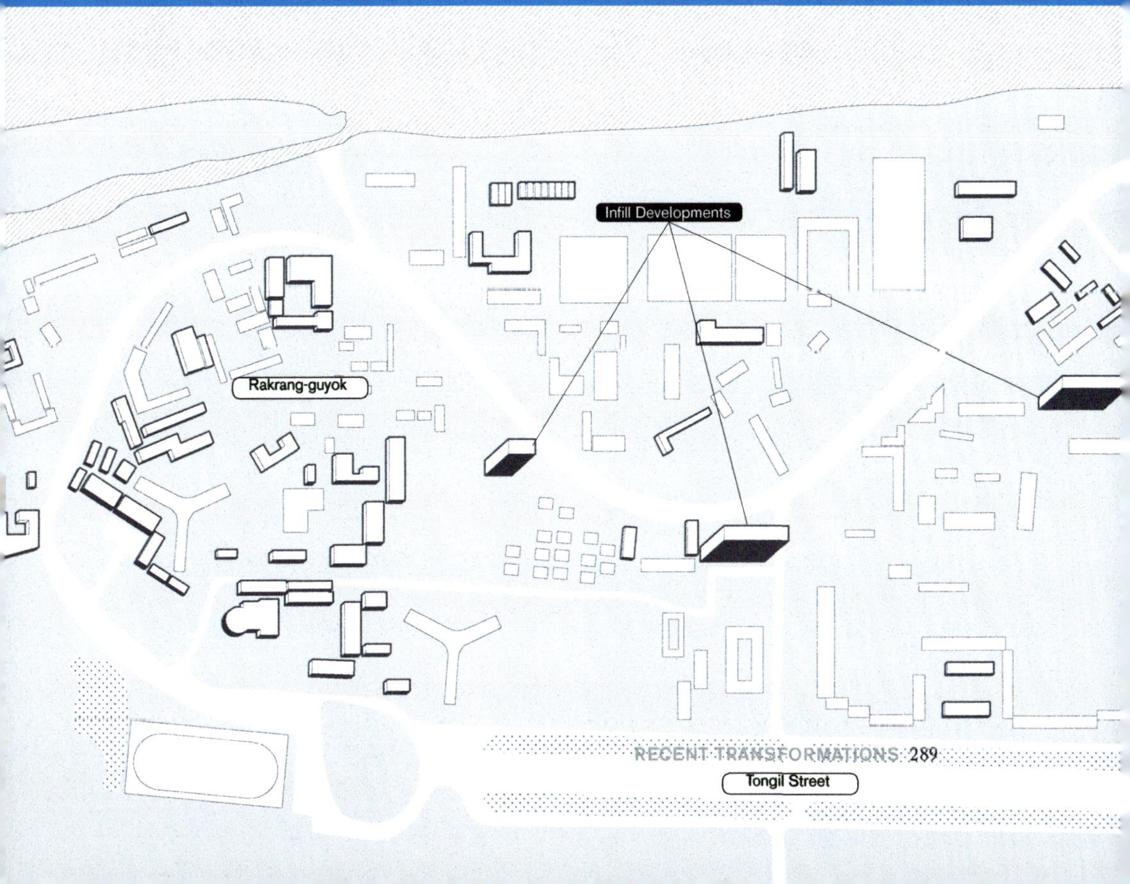
Infill Developments
Rakrang-guyok
Tongil Street

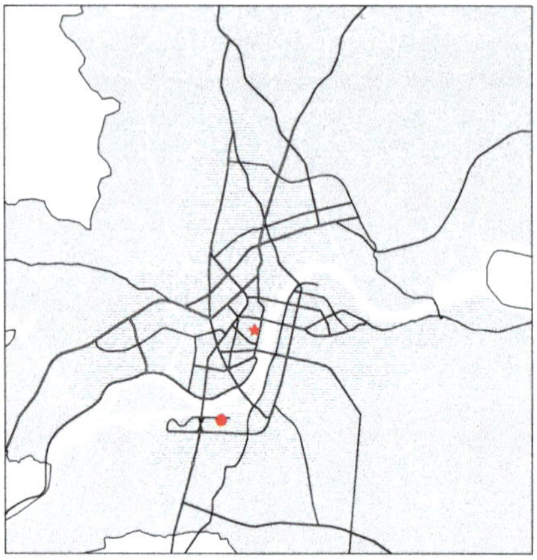

SYMBOLISM_ICONIC DEPARTMENT STORE

Symbolism is still a key element in urban planning and design in Pyongyang, and one of the ways to emphasize the symbolism is putting an iconic building along with urban square/plaza. Grand People's House is the backdrop of Kim Il Sung Square and Korean Revolution Museum is the backdrop of Mansudae plaza, where Kim Il Sung and Kim Jong Il's statues are.

This grandiose urban space sitting perpendicular to Tongil Street was first formed along with Tongil Street development in the 1990s. In 2004, the government put Tongil Street Market in this urban space to accommodate semi-controlled market economy system. Now, there are 100,000 customers a day, and it almost functions as free economy market.

As this urban space is becoming more important and significant, it might have been critical for the city to build an iconic building as a backdrop of this symbolic urban space and the market.

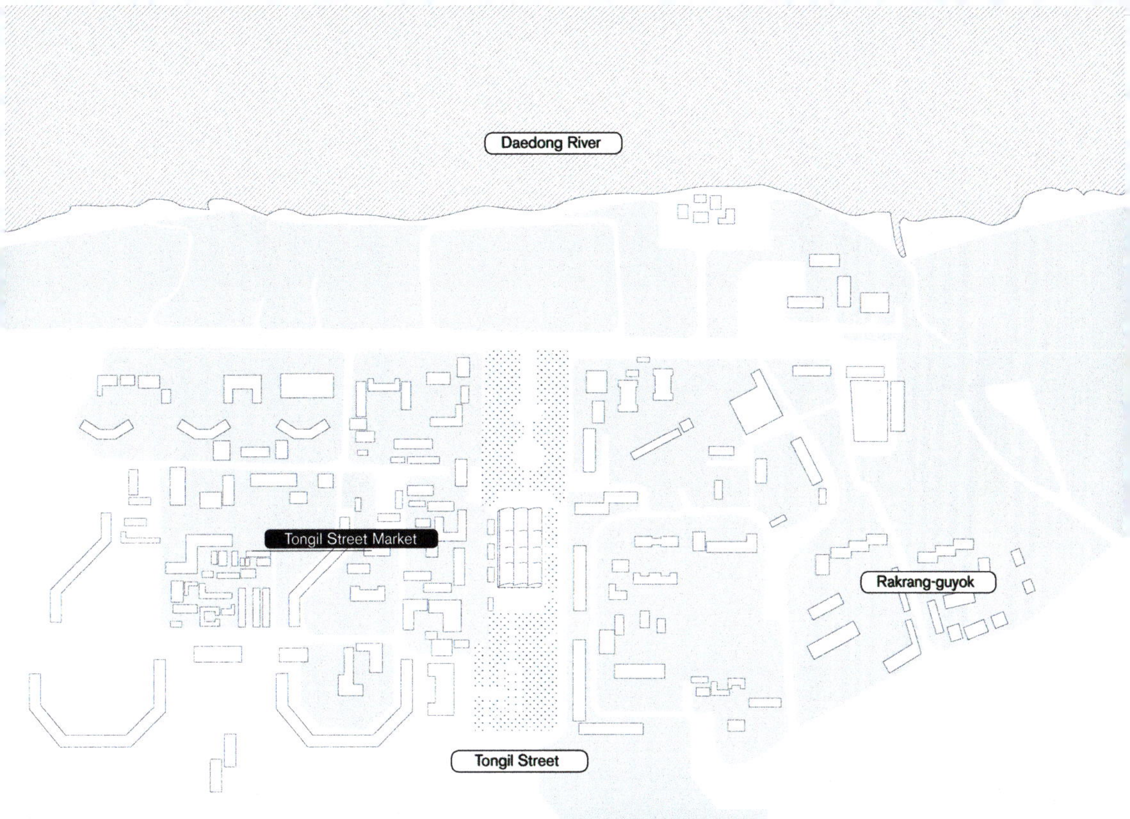

Daedong River
Tongil Street Market
Rakrang-guyok
Tongil Street

▲2007 ▼2015

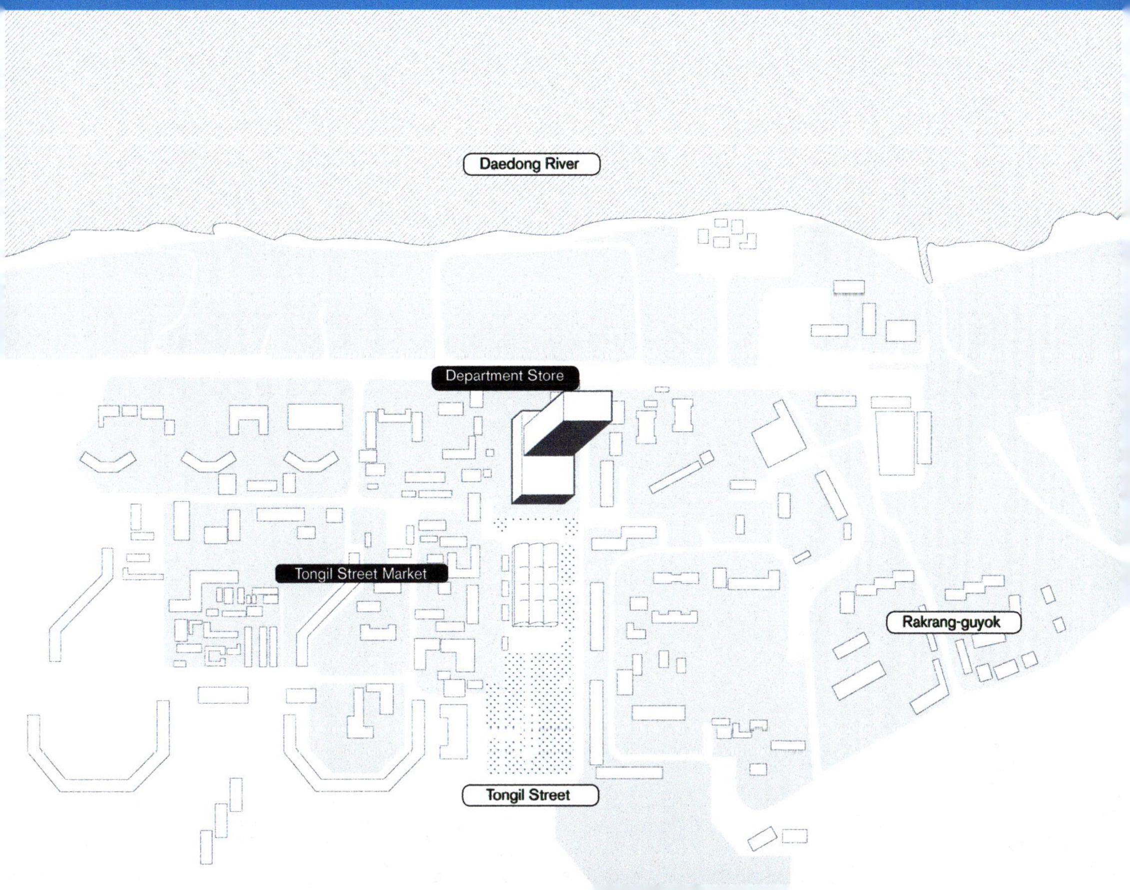

Daedong River
Department Store
Tongil Street Market
Rakrang-guyok
Tongil Street

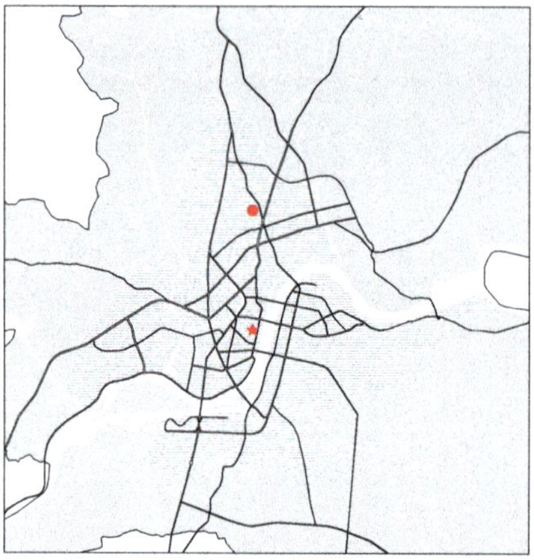

★ Kim Il Sung Square

● Symolism_National Propaganda

SYMBOLISM_NATIONAL PROPAGANDA

Although many recent developments are focused on responding to emerging market economy and demand, national propaganda still acts strongly so that the government can show the strength and make one united society. The Korean War Veteran's Cemetery was built in 2013 to celebrate 60th anniversary of the victory of the Korean War. Even though Pyongyang already has numbers of symbolic buildings, monuments and urban spaces related to the Korean War, it seems the city still keeps the strategy of enhancing its propaganda through constructing artifacts. The cementery is along the highway between Sunan International Airport and Pyongyang city center, and the therefore, it is easily seen by most of visitors to the city.

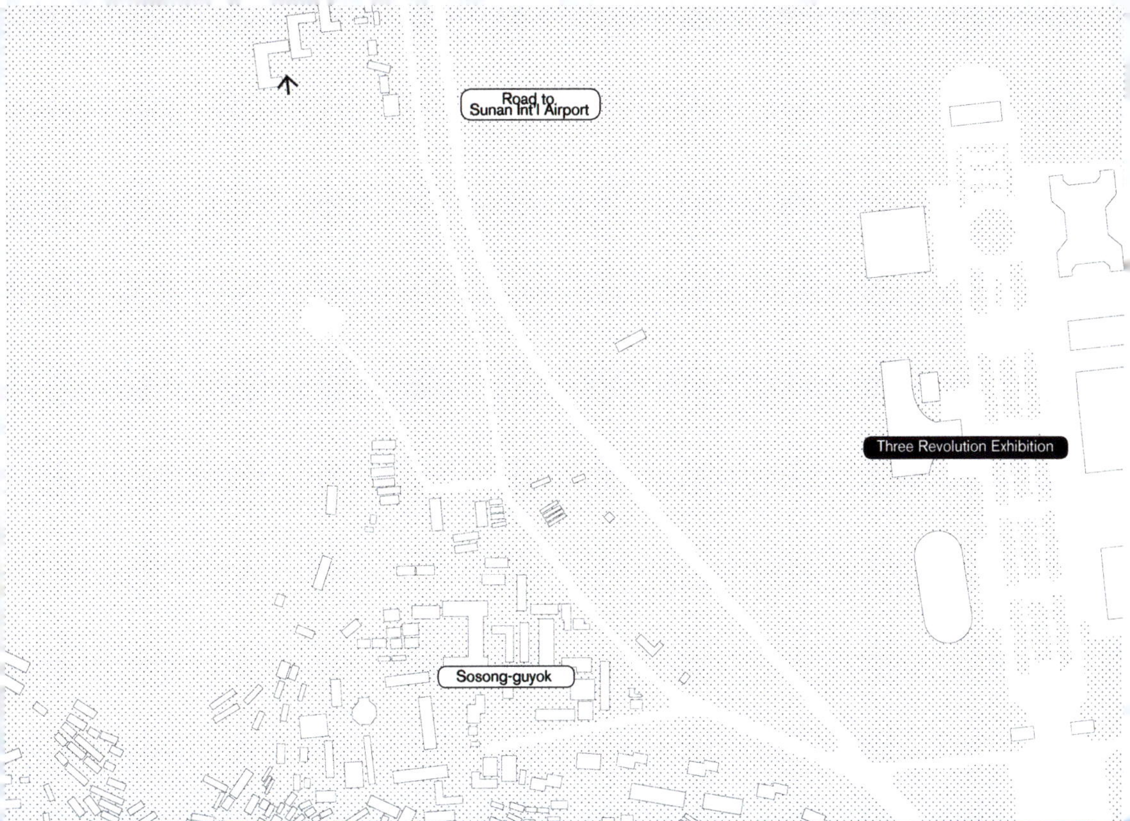
Road to Sunan Int'l Airport
Three Revolution Exhibition
Sosong-guyok

▲2007 ▼2015

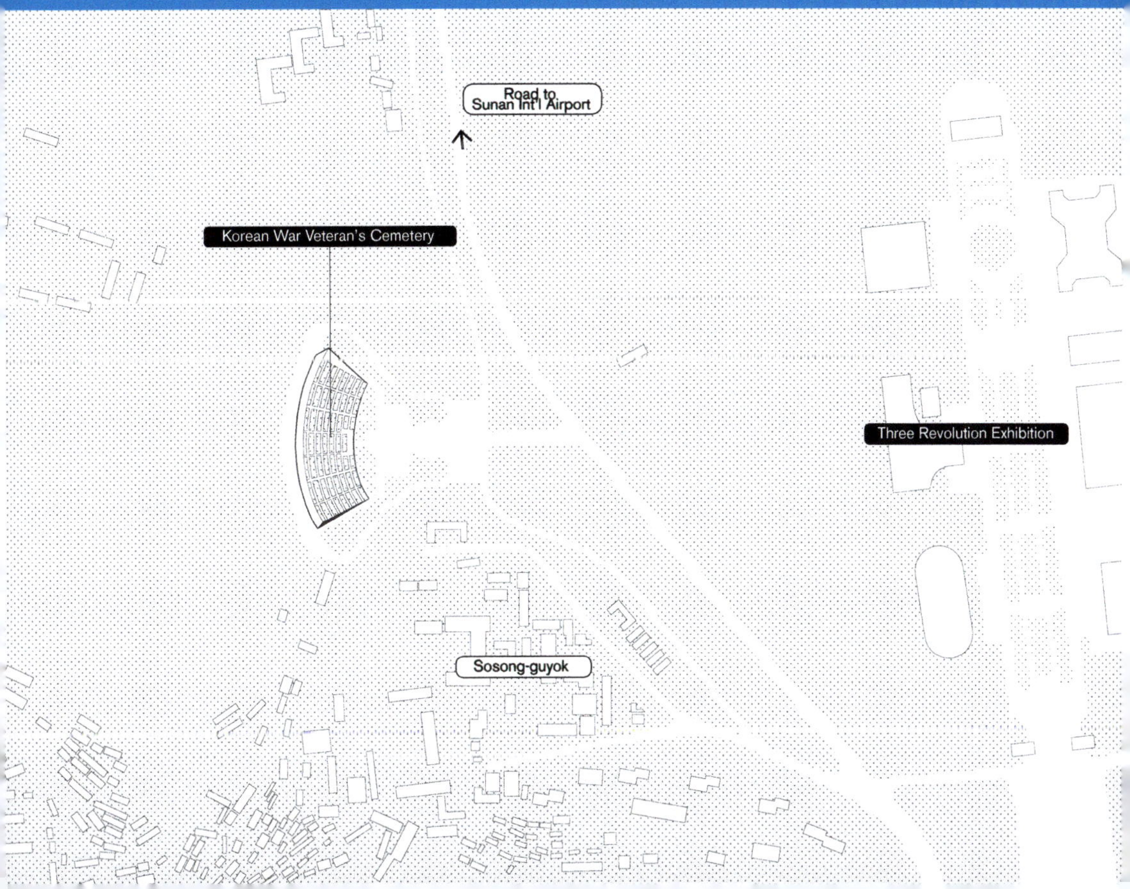
Road to Sunan Int'l Airport
Korean War Veteran's Cemetery
Three Revolution Exhibition
Sosong-guyok

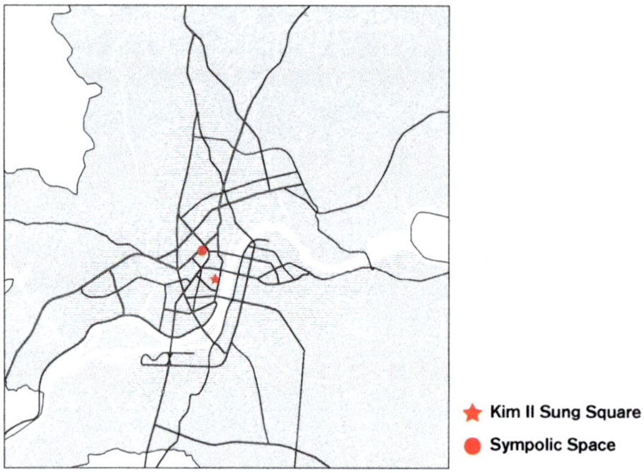

SYMBOLISM_ENHANCING PROPAGANDA SPACE

Fatherland Liberation War Memorial Museum is built in 2013 as addition to the original memorial monument and square. Originally, the square had no symbolic architecture but monuments and sculptures along with the gate at the front. Although many recent developments in Pyongyang focus on responding to new demands from emerging middle class, the government still pushes many aspects to enhance its propaganda and show greatness of the regime. As the face of North Korea, Pyongyang will not easily put aside its efforts on building symbolism, while it transforms itself to accommodate new era.

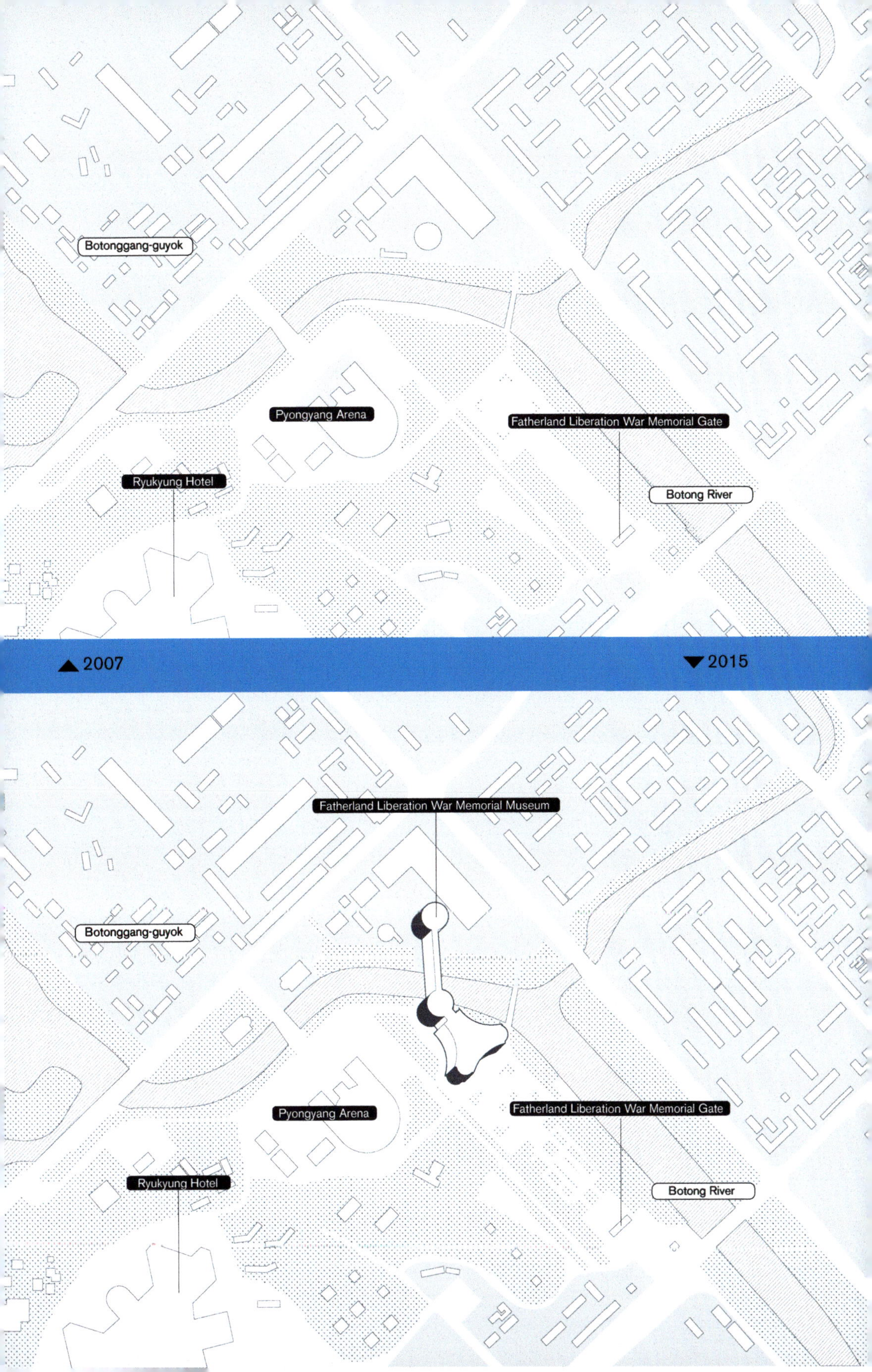

Botonggang-guyok
Pyongyang Arena
Fatherland Liberation War Memorial Gate
Ryukyung Hotel
Botong River
▲ 2007
▼ 2015
Fatherland Liberation War Memorial Museum
Botonggang-guyok
Pyongyang Arena
Fatherland Liberation War Memorial Gate
Ryukyung Hotel
Botong River

LEISURE PROPOSITION I

The importance of sports and leisure facilities always have been emphasized by North Korean leaders. The nation's first leader Kim Il Sung once mentioned that it is important to provide enough leisure places for workers as their resting places. Therefore, Pyongyang has more numbers of public sports and leisure facilities per capita than any South Korean cities. This perspective continues in present, and more sports and leisure facilities are developed within the city boundary.

Ryugyong Health Complex (Ryugyongwon) & Outdoor Ice Rink is located at the waterfront of Daedong River, in front of Central Youth Hall where bowling venue and karaoke are. Completed in 2012 on a vacant lot along the river, it shows another type of waterfront development that the city pursued in recent years along with Mirae Scientist Street development.

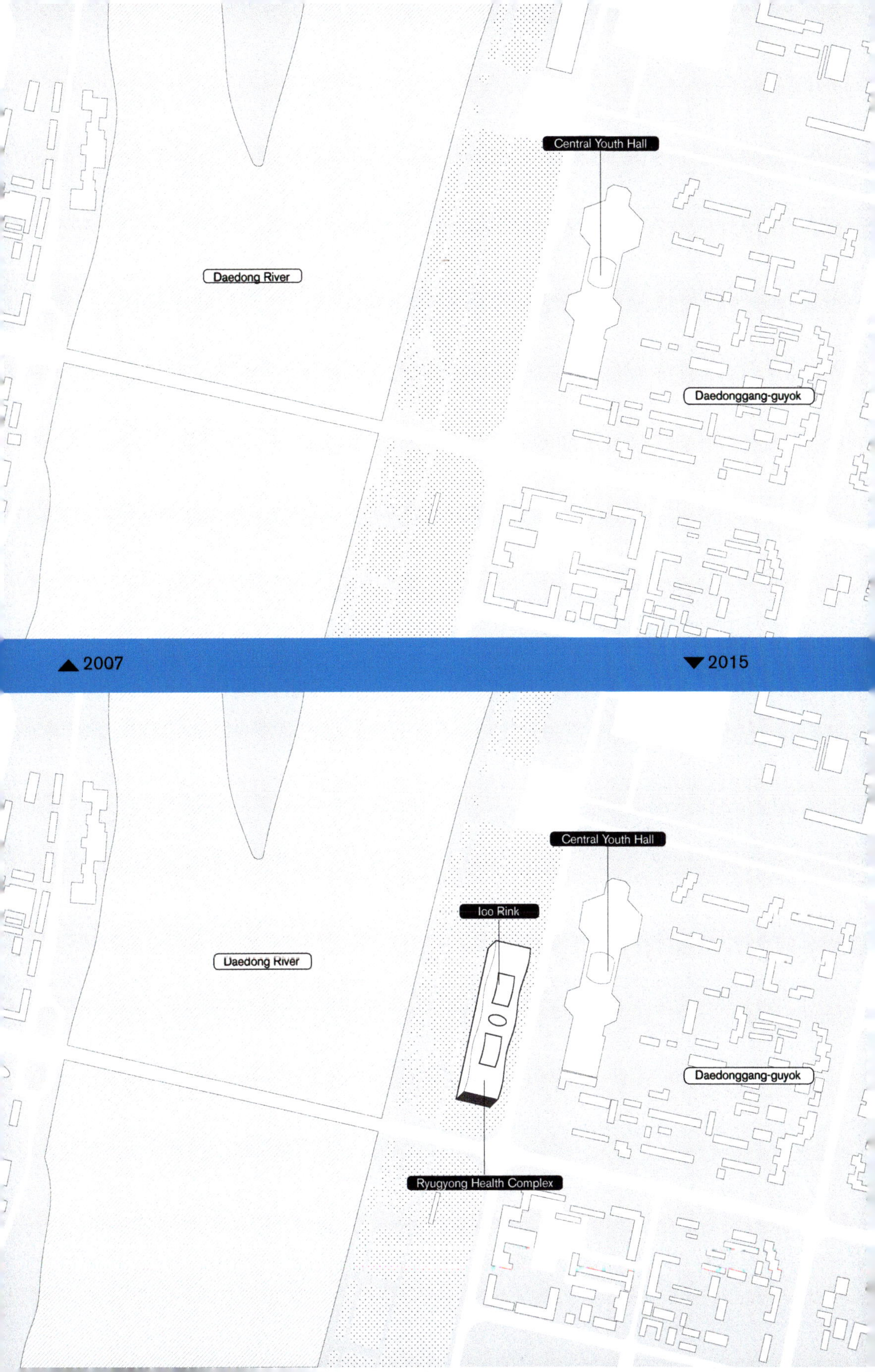

Central Youth Hall
Daedong River
Daedonggang-guyok
2007
2015
Central Youth Hall
Ice Rink
Daedong River
Daedonggang-guyok
Ryugyong Health Complex

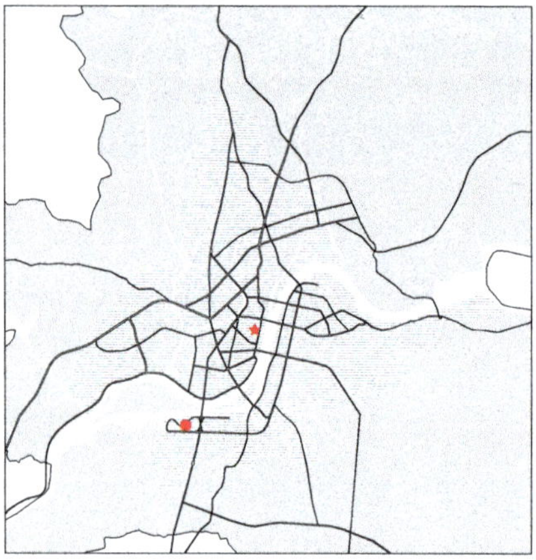

★ Kim Il Sung Square
● Leisure Proposition II

LEISURE PROPOSITION II

Tongil Street Sports Center was first built in 2012 at the end of the Tongil Street with indoor facilities, such as gym, swimming pool and rehab facilities, and later completed outdoor sports field in 2015. The outdoor sports field area is about 15,000 m2 that include football field, basketball courts, skateparks and tennis courts. Because of its location, which is at the west end of the Tongil Street residential district, the sports center and field seem to be developed as neighborhood leisure and sports facility rather than as a city facility. It means that the government's effort in leisure proposition is expanding towards more micro level, instead of staying only in the macro level.

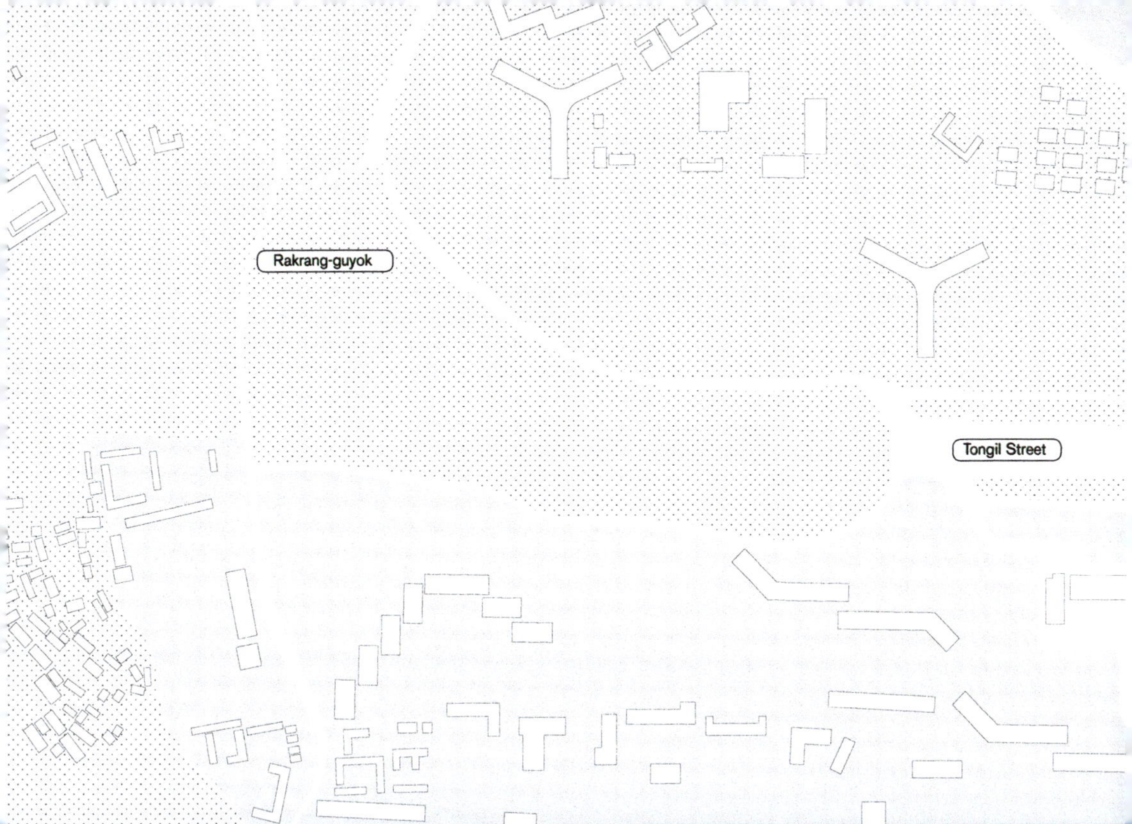
Rakrang-guyok
Tongil Street

▲2007 ▼2015

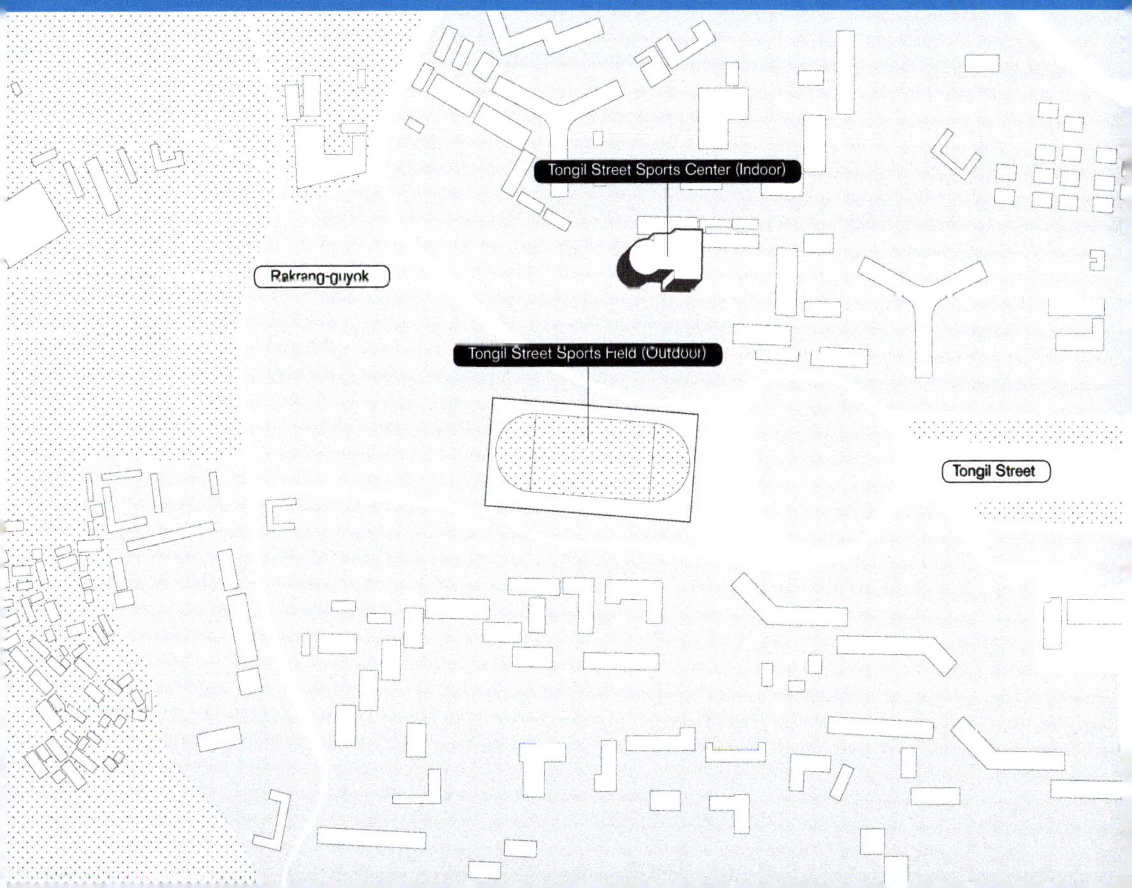
Tongil Street Sports Center (Indoor)
Rakrang-guyok
Tongil Street Sports Field (Outdoor)
Tongil Street

SPECULATIVE EXPANSION : HORIZONTAL

KEEPS THE DENSITY OF URBANIZED AREA

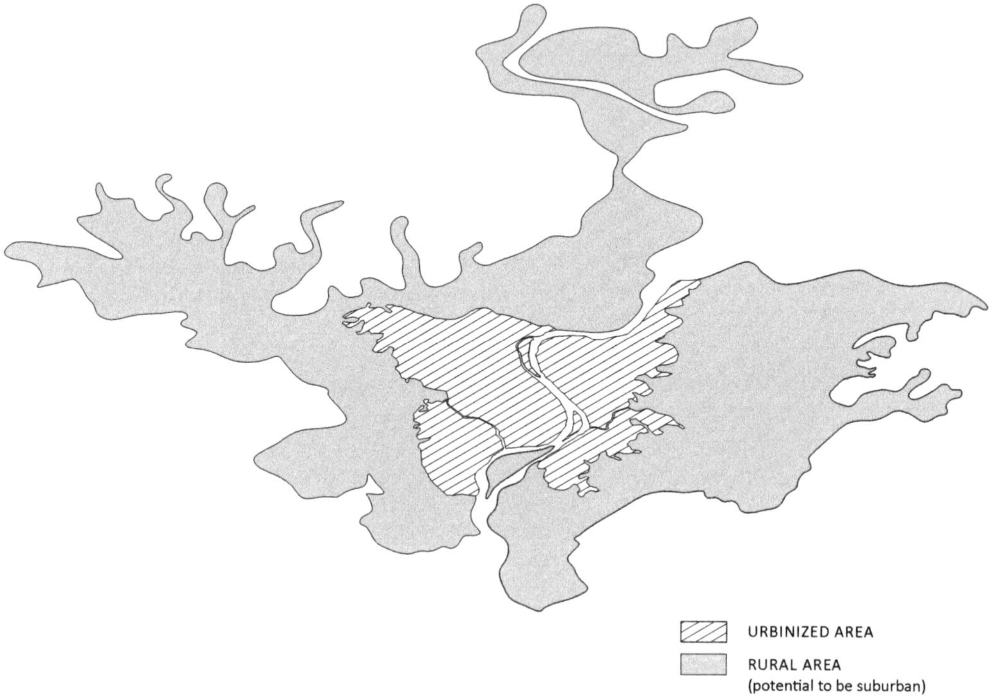

Current Condition of Pyongyang

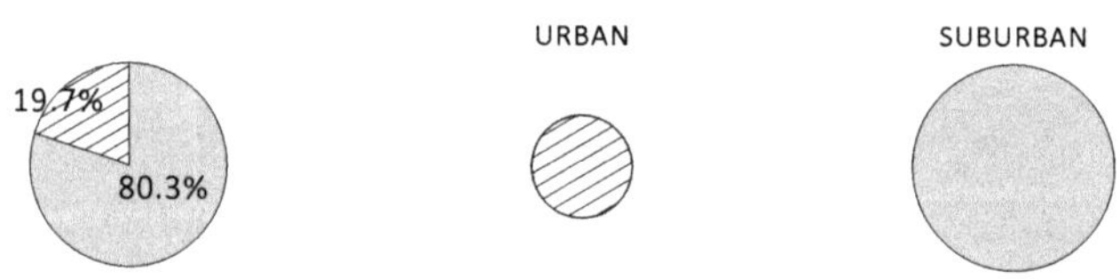

AREA	150 KM2	610 KM2
DENSITY	18,820 PPL/KM2	708 PPL/KM2
POPULATION	2,823,000	432,000
POPULATION	86.7%	13.3%

4,882,500

x 1.5 of Current Population

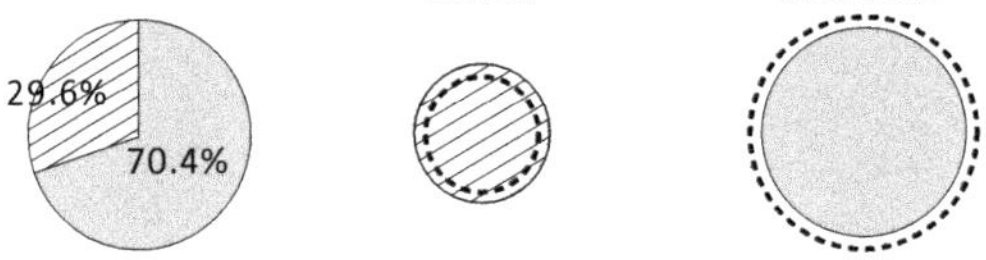

	URBAN	SUBURBAN
AREA	225 KM2	535 KM2
DENSITY	18,820 PPL/KM2	1,211 PPL/KM2
POPULATION	4,234,500	648,000
PERCENTAGE	86.7%	13.3%

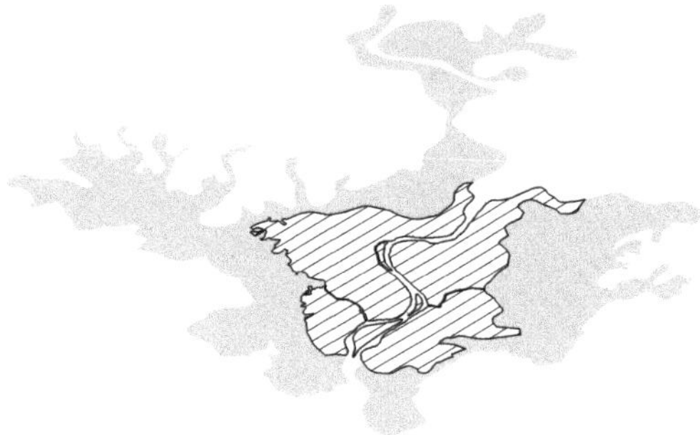

6,510,000

x 2.0 of Current Population

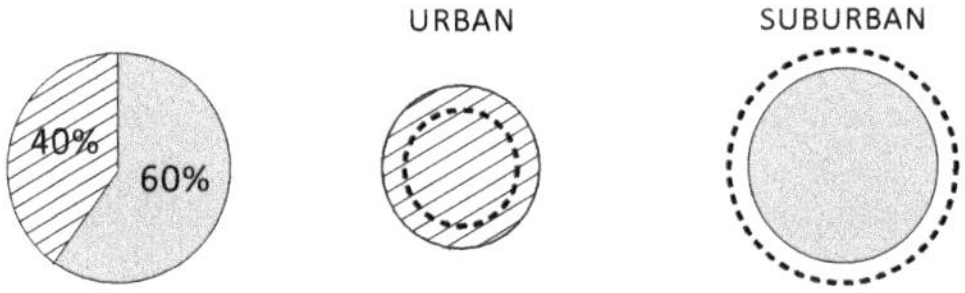

	URBAN	SUBURBAN
AREA	300 KM2	460 KM2
DENSITY	18,820 PPL/KM2	1,878 PPL/KM2
POPULATION	5,646,000	864,000
PERCENTAGE	86.7%	13.3%

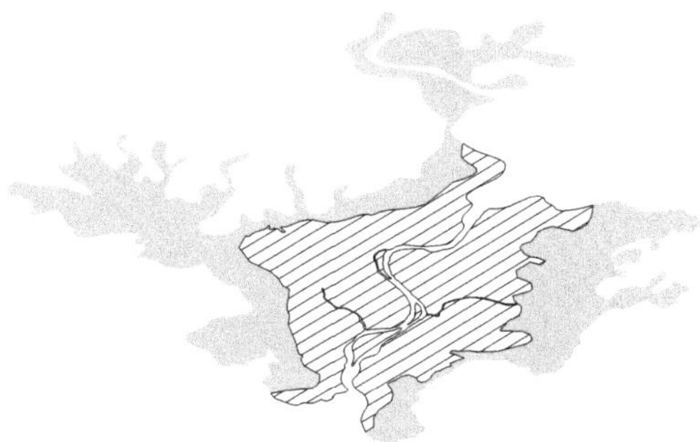

9,765,000

x 3.0 of Current Population

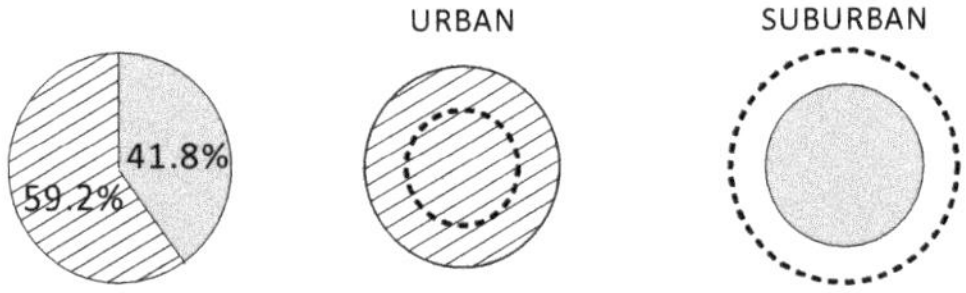

	URBAN	SUBURBAN
AREA	450 KM2	310 KM2
DENSITY	18,820 PPL/KM2	4,180 PPL/KM2
POPULATION	8,469,000	1,296,000
PERCENTAGE	86.7%	13.3%

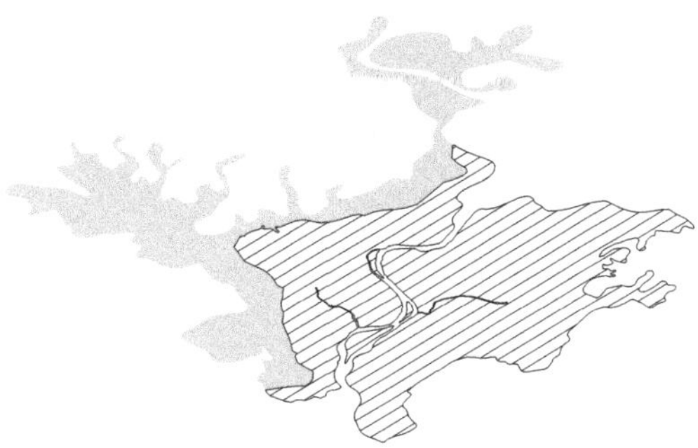

SPECULATIVE EXPANSION : VERTICAL

KEEPS THE AREA OF URBANIZED AREA

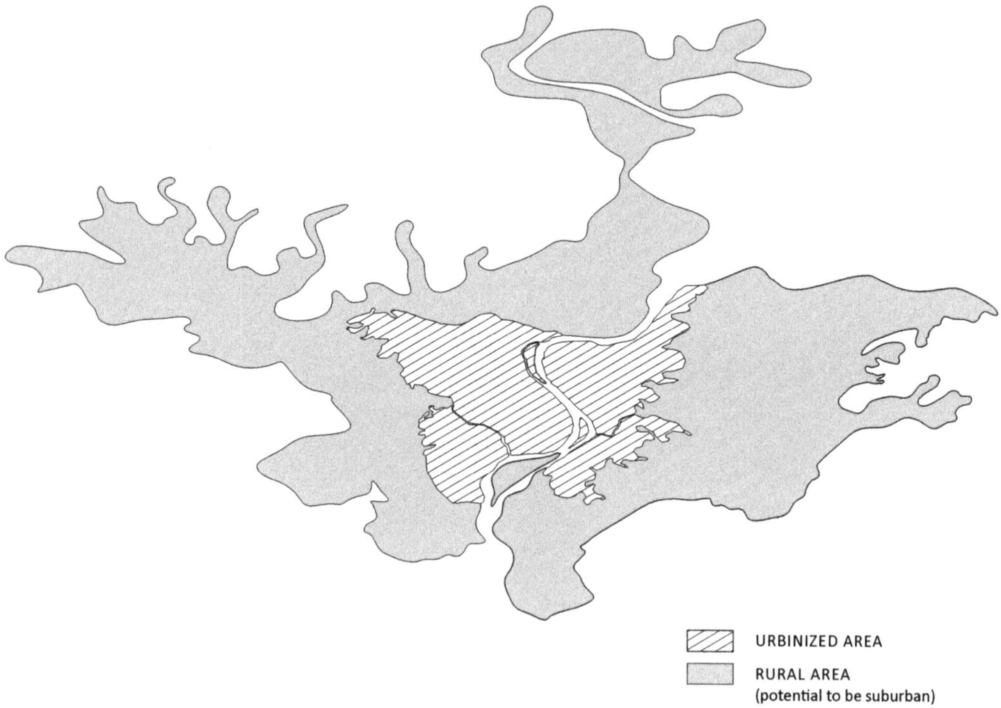

Current Condition of Pyongyang

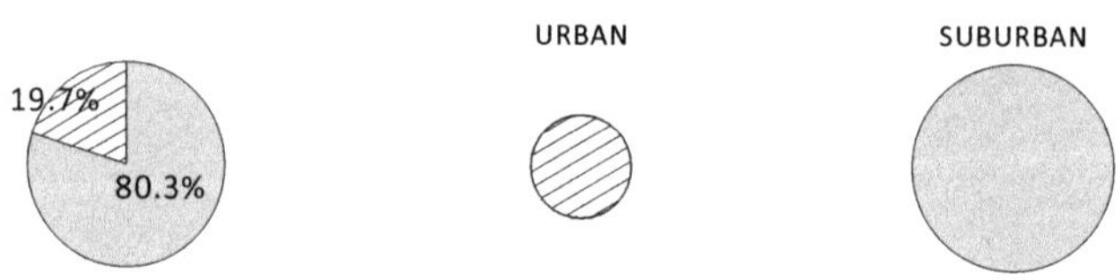

AREA	150 KM2	610 KM2
DENSITY	18,820 PPL/KM2	708 PPL/KM2
POPULATION	2,823,000	432,000
PERCENTAGE	86%	14%

4,882,500

x 1.5 of Current Population

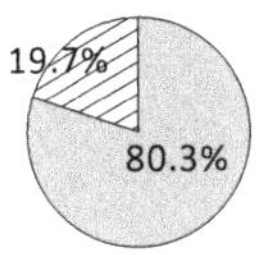

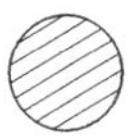

	URBAN	SUBURBAN
AREA	150 KM2	610 KM2
DENSITY	29,670 PPL/KM2	708 PPL/KM2
POPULATION	4,450,500	432,000
PERCENTAGE	91.1%	8.9%

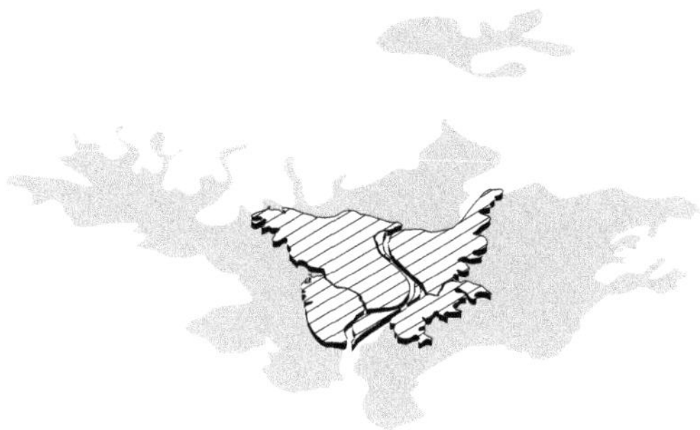

6,510,000

x 2.0 of Current Population

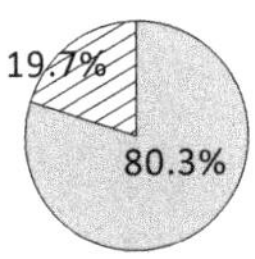

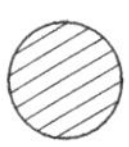

	URBAN	SUBURBAN
AREA	150 KM2	610 KM2
DENSITY	40,520 PPL/KM2	708 PPL/KM2
POPULATION	6,078,000	432,000
PERCENTAGE	93.3%	6.7%

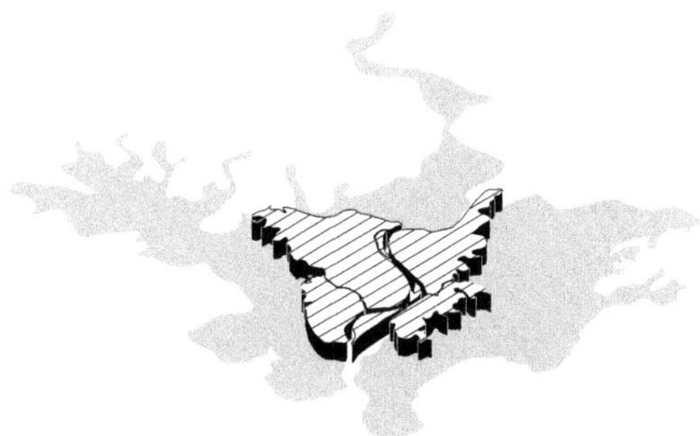

9,765,000

x 3.0 of Current Population

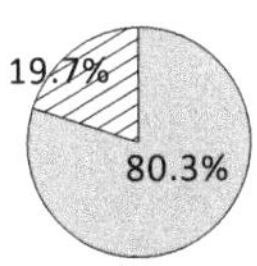

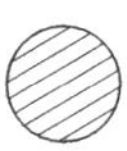

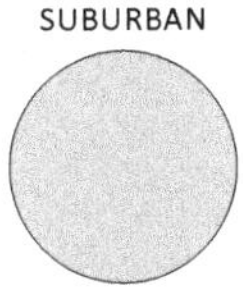

	URBAN	SUBURBAN
AREA	150 KM2	610 KM2
DENSITY	62,220 PPL/KM2	708 PPL/KM2
POPULATION	9,333,000	432,000
PERCENTAGE	95.5%	4.5%

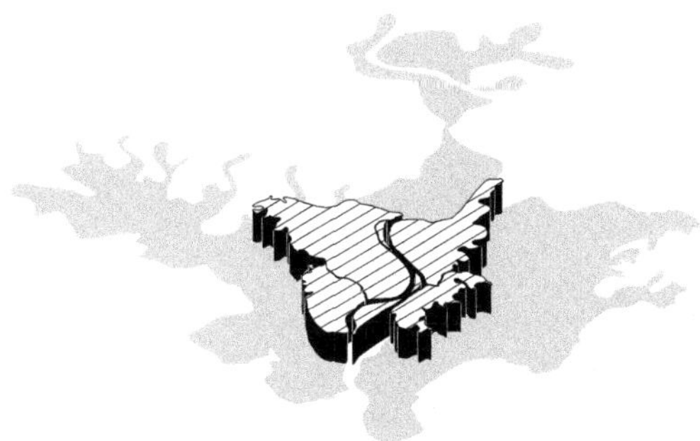

08 PYONGYANG SPECULATION

> The enormous dislocations of the post communist transition are visibly registered in the physical fabric of Central European cities. Everywhere there is evidence of wild "illegal" building, abandoned industrial buildings converted into provisional dwellings, living space turned to commercial uses, new skyscrapers and office towers rising among small suburban houses in semi-urban areas with little or no infrastructure. In recent years a literature of "transitology" has emerged that sensationalizes these phenomena, describing them as "urban mutants," "infections," and "parasitic developments," while celebrating them as the improvised formations of a "fluid," "anarchic," "hybridized," new "culture of urban action." It seems clear that the transitional urban landscapes of post communist cities radically challenge traditional urban concepts - particularly of public and private space, property, and use- as well as current planning practices. [1]

After the Eastern Bloc collapsed in 1991, the former socialist cities underwent enormous transformations after adopting the new economic system, the market-oriented capitalist economy. Not only the society itself but also the physical morphology of the cities started to change. This was mainly due to differing conceptions of land-ownership between the two different economic systems. In a capitalist city, which allows privatization of land, the basic logic of an economic system is a supply-demand structure that inspires the competition between parties interested in a piece of land, and this competition creates the land value. On the other hand, in a socialist city, which does not accept privatization, the land has no capital value. Under the ideal that all the properties should be owned by the state, there is no competition between possible constituents of a property except government's development plan and strategy. Therefore, in a socialist city, the most important factor that determines the usage of a land is the state's overall master plan instead of the flow of capital. For instance, because a certain area does not have any capital value, a Central Business District (CBD) does not exist in socialist city; instead, public facilities, monumental squares, and administrative programs fill the urban centre.

> Enormous changes in urban internal spatial structure have been brought about by emerging transitional institutions under economic reform. Spatial restructuring has transformed the ideal pattern of the 'socialist city', a process witnessed in Chinese cities as well as other post-socialist cities in Central and Eastern Europe. Rebuilding the socialist city has proceeded through reconfiguring the built environment as well as changing political economic institutions.[2]

Following the transition to a market-oriented system, the flow of capital has become the main logic of a society; the large-scale investment has occurred, and most of all, privatization of the land has been allowed in former socialist cities. These changes directly influenced the physical form of the city because of their close relation to urban development projects. For example, in the case of East Germany, especially in Berlin after the collision of Eastern Bloc, the urban transformation happened unevenly in places with the most dynamic economy and are potentially profitable.[3] As a result, East Berlin has now an urban morphology that is a mixture of free market development and controlled master plan structure. Thus to detect the development path of former socialist cities, a key question to consider is: "what areas in a former socialist city are potentially profitable?"

Since realizing and promoting socialist ideology through the physical form of a city, the most important goal in socialist urban planning is that the general urban structure has a strong socialist character. And these spaces that display extreme contrasts to capitalist urban spaces become the most flexible areas for transformation when the transition to a market-oriented economy system begins. Therefore, in this chapter, the argument of urban transformation of Pyongyang will focus on three major socialist urban morphologies that were discussed before: city of symbolism, city of production, and city of green and their transformations at the beginning of the market oriented economy that is slowly getting implemented in North Korea.

Pyongyang in Transition

> With the end of the Cold War, North Korea lost hefty aid from Moscow and Beijing. The funds had propped up the economy, as did trade with other communist countries, and the loss of revenue sparked a financial collapse and bouts of starvation during the 1990s estimated to have killed as many as 2 million people. Bankrupt and desperate, the secretive

> Pyongyang government launched an experiment with the free market in July 2002, deregulating prices and hiking salaries.[4]

> The major issue is Chinese strategy of preoccupancy. The fact that ten thousand Chinese businessmen visited Pyongyang for their future investment and there are more than three thousands of residing business men is not a secret anymore. There were more than ten times of investment fair for Chinese enterprises in 2004. Increase of Chinese investment from last year is strongly related to "7.1 Improvement Strategy for Economic Management" that generated individual enterprise establishments and businesses. Low tax regulation improved investment environment, and low cost of production influenced Chinese businessman to judge that Pyongyang will become a very profitable market within ten years. They say that current situation of Pyongyang can be compared to late 1970s or early 1980s of China. Opening an undeveloped market will generate large investment for light industries and SOC (social overhead capital), and it is clear that preoccupancy strategy will focus on long term plan instead of short term profits.[5]

North Korea, including Pyongyang, has already begun its economic transition. There are numerous scenarios and arguments regarding what kind of economic model it will take on. However, regardless of the specific system that Pyongyang might adopt in the near future, it seems clear that the state authorities have begun to open its market to foreign investment, which may ultimately influence the physical form of the city. As "Pressian" reported, numbers of Chinese businessmen are visiting Pyongyang to test its potential for new investment and development. After Pyongyang carried out the "7.1 Improvement Strategy for Economic Management" in 2002, a new wave of investment emerged in North Korea, starting with the Kaesong Industrial Complex, which collaborated with the South Korean enterprise "Hyundai Asan" and public sector "Korea Land Corporation."

"7.1 Improvement Strategy for Economic Management" is considered as a turning point of conversion of the North Korean economic system into a market-oriented system. There are four major points that the improvement strategy highlights. First, it allows for gradual improvement of payment based on the efficiency of labour or the difficulty of work. It reduces the disadvantage of "equality" and generates motivation for labour. Secondly, it abolishes the controlled price system on the market. It encourages the market to have prices based on supply-and-demand logic. Third, the strategy allows for more independence and freedom for enterprises to generate more efficient and better products. Although the state still controls the general economy, individual enterprises are allowed to set their own outputs and price. Lastly, it encourages direct dealing instead of controlled distribution. People have to buy their needs, which had previously been distributed for free, directly from national retailers.[6]

The "7.1 Improvement Strategy for Economic Management" also influenced small-scale commercial activities. Since the strategy allowed for gradually improved salary and encouraged the freedom of direct dealing, new forms of retail have emerged in Pyongyang. The increasing number of mobile vendors on major streets and squares in Pyongyang is another sign of economic transition. As Axenov noted, mobile trade forms and kiosks emerge first in the earliest transition stages to the market-oriented economic system.[7] This is because these typologies are very flexible and can fill the gap between the actual people's necessities and the capacity of controlled production and distribution.

Besides the government's effort to carry out this new economic strategy, the transition in North Korea gradually happens also because the control over the economic transactions loses. After the economic collapse in the 1990s, the controlled-economy started to lose its power of managing demand and supply in the market oriented system. Some people started to earn and save money, of course illegally, and this circumstance created a certain accumulation of capital and an informal demand and supply system in the city. For instance, there have been several cases of property sales in Pyongyang in recent times. Although it is still illegal to deal out housing units, new apartments are built without getting any government control and they are sold to individuals illegaly. Therefore, with the combination of a new economic strategy and collapse of the controlled economic system, North Korea will face a fast economic transition in the near future that will bring about the physical transformation of Pyongyang as well.

Incremental Growth

> Integral Urbanism offers punctuation marks or reference points to "inflect" the landscape and our experience in it. These interventions activate "dead" or neutral spaces. They acknowledge and care for abandoned and neglected spaces. By increasing density of activity and perhaps building mass, they make connections between places, people, and experiences. There are numerous expressions of this attitude toward intervention. ... Bernard Tschumi's "events" are intended to punctuate space and time, as demonstrated by the "folies" at the Parc de la Villette in Paris. ... Michael Gamble and Jude LeBlanc have described

their method for large-scale suburban strip retrofitting as "incremental urbanism."[8]

As experienced by other former socialist cities in the last ten to fifteen years, Pyongyang also has a strong possibility to be transformed after the adoption of market-oriented economic system. Since economic change is already happening in some way, the issue is not whether Pyongyang will change or not but rather which growth model will Pyongyang follow and how the city will transform. Due to various background situations such as economic scale, political stability, or urban fabric, different former socialist cities had followed distant development and growth patterns from each other. For example, most Chinese cities with strong economic backgrounds, have a large scale investment and development based on a master plan that structures the entire city new. On the other hand, in some Eastern European cities such as Zagreb that have a small scale economy and investment within its historical fabric, transformation is restricted to these parameters and affects only some parts of the city and to some extent. Nevertheless, both cases, experienced morphological transformation according to their scales that exhibited a mixture of market-oriented physical form and socialist urban structure.

The urban structure of Pyongyang has its own unique feature as a socialist city. After it was almost completely demolished during the Korean War in the 1950s, Kim Il Sung planned to convert Pyongyang into an ideal socialist city. Although the whole city was not structured following the 1953 Master Plan, Pyongyang contains numerous socialist urban characteristics. Several development strategies throughout periods -marked by national macro-economic plans- that influenced urban structure of the original master plan provided alternate ways of realizing the idea of socialism, creating numbers of essentially socialist urban spaces. Thus, a new growth model should consider keeping the unique urban structure of Pyongyang as well as reflecting the new wave of economic transition.

Amongst many other growth patterns, the incremental growth model can be suggested for the future development of Pyongyang. Although the radical growth model with the new city master plan can be a possibility for a former socialist city, a consideration of the economic scale and existing idealistic socialist urban structure of Pyongyang suggests that the incremental growth model is more likely to be adopted. As Ellin has observed, this incremental growth model generates new development at "greyfield," defined as an underutilized area, and activates those 'dead' spaces in the city. Unlike master plan types of development, the model focuses on catalytic urban projects that can influence and generate other developments in the city. It is more dynamic and flexible model than the rigid master plan that Michael Speaks defines as "soft urbanism."[9]

The model also has its advantage of keeping the existing structure of the city. Since the incremental growth model focuses on individual catalytic projects instead of a large scale master plan, the transformation happens on smaller scale mostly through maintaining the existing urban fabrics. As Pyongyang is presently identified with its current morphology that is a result of layering both the 1953 Master Plan and several posterior development strategies, it is very important to keep the socialist urban fabric of the city recognizable, letting the new growth model add other layers in the complex construction of the new morphology of Pyongyang. Therefore, by choosing the incremental growth model as its future development strategy, Pyongyang would keep its ideal socialist urban structure as the backbone and adopt a new logic of morphology on top of it.

Potential Urban Space

> It is clear that the processes of political, economic, and social transformation currently underway possess the potential of infusing new energy and ideas for the restructuring of the spatial fabric of the post-socialist cities. One of the great challenges in their future urban development is to create out of the mono-functional, underdeveloped settlements lively and attractive cities, i.e. to create cities that are able to channel the dynamic process of change to their advantage. The repair of public space could play, undoubtedly, a key role here, serving as the backbone of urban reconstruction.[10]

Considering the incremental growth model as the development plan of Pyongyang for the near future, it is interesting to see where and how those new catalytic developments will take place. Learning from studies of other former socialist cities that have been transformed since their transition to the market-oriented economy, several urban spaces in Pyongyang exhibit strong potential to be transformed in the near future. As discussed before, over the course of the transition to the market-oriented economy system, urban spaces that captured the strong character of socialism became potentially the most transformable spaces, sometimes because of their locational and infrastructural advantages and sometimes because of their lack of capitalist logic or land value. Moreover, a number of scales of transformations unfold in these urban spaces. For instance, in areas that have infrastructural advantages as well as potential land value, large scale of investments and developments occur, and the area's structure and program transform. On the other hand, urban spaces that have locational advantage but cannot attract large investments are occupied by public with market-oriented economic activities. These differing scales of transformations are to be expected in the area of Pyongyang that possesses the characteristics of a city of symbolism, production, and greenery.

Developed according to the 1953 master plan and several posterior urban strategies, Pyongyang has now a clear physical urban character of socialist ideology. Major symbolic spaces, such as Kim Il Sung Square and Juche Tower, were created following the master plan, and partial plans and production programs in the city were realized both by the master plan and development strategies. Lastly, although the landscape plan based on the 1953 Master Plan was not well realized, the landscape structure, including the agricultural area is well developed based on landscape improvement strategies throughout different periods. Therefore, we can say that the urban character of Pyongyang is defined with these three major urban morphologies, and it is interesting to see an incremental growth of them after the transition. The new development in those areas will change their existing morphologies, giving us a new perspective of Pyongyang in the new era.

Transformation @ Symbolic Space

> The centre is the heart of the city, it is the political centre for its citizens. The most important political, administrative and cultural establishments are in the city centre. On the central squares, political demonstrations, parades and festivals on public holidays take place. The city centre with squares, main avenues and voluptuous buildings (skyscrapers in the big cities) determines the architectural silhouette of the city. Squares are the structural basis for urban development.
> - Sixteen Principles of Urban Design, German Democratic Republic-[11]

In a socialist city, the center is a showcase of symbolic space and buildings that propagate the ideology of socialism. The city center is one of the areas in which transformation happens in the first stage of economic transition. Though lacking a CBD, a socialist city has its own type of central district where most symbolic buildings, monumental squares, and administrative facilities are located. The city center itself is a symbolic ground in a socialist city. Mostly, it is located in the middle of the city and infrastructure systems, including transportation, are well organized in the area. Given its infrastructural and locational advantages, the land value of the area becomes higher in market-oriented economies than other city districts. Therefore, the new

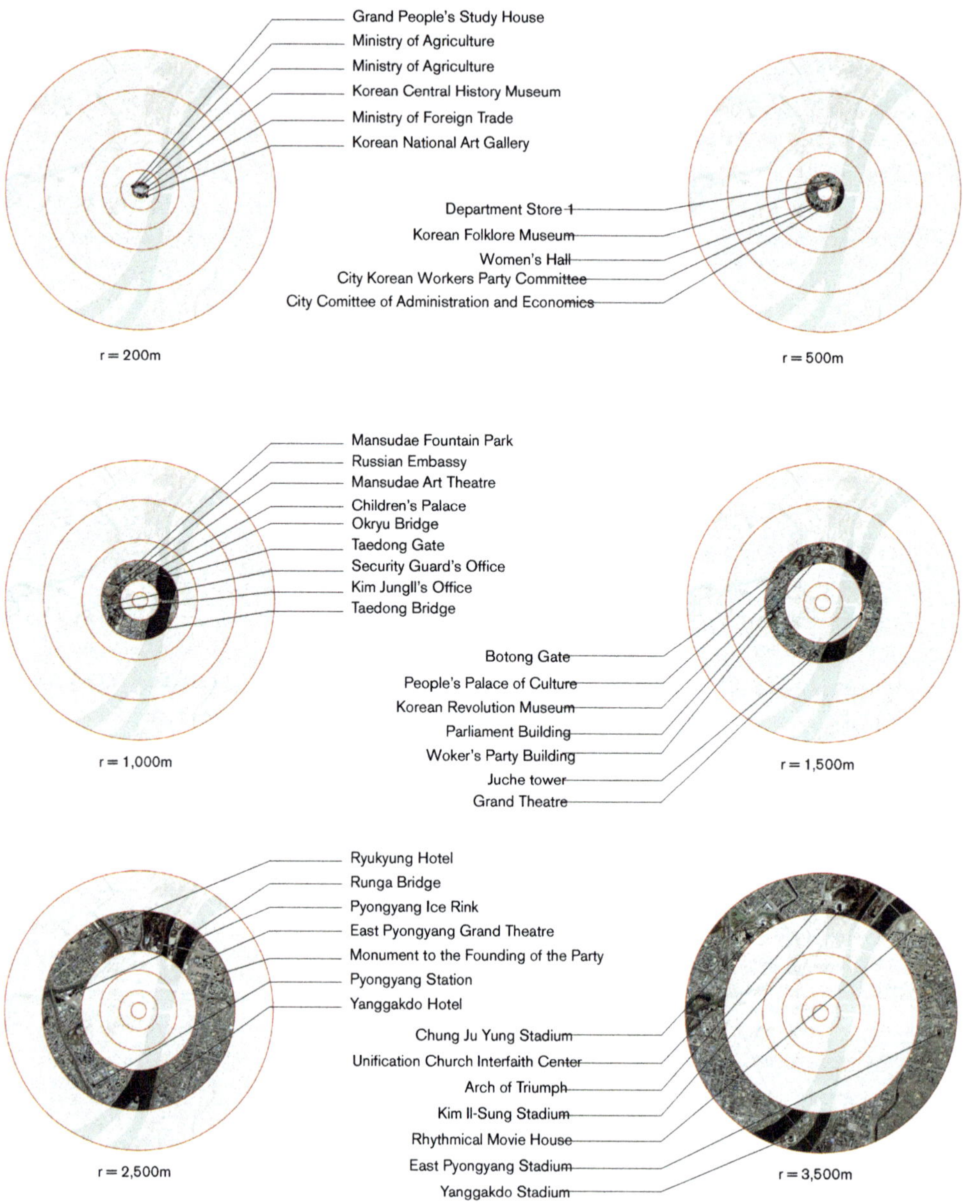

Key artifacts near KIS Square

urban transformation of Pyongyang may also start from the city center and this will both impact and generate the transformation of other urban areas. In short, three major types of transformation are expected in this area: change of program, diverse use of surface, and redevelopment of monumental spaces and buildings.

Since it was reconstructed after the Korean War in early 1950s, Pyongyang has a long tradition of monumentalization and symbolization. The 1953 Master Plan, which was strongly influenced by socialist urban planning, proposed inventing and developing major squares and edifices. Although various development strategies throughout different periods have influenced the formation of the urban structure of Pyongyang, the major monumental squares and structures are still realized based on the 1953 Master Plan. For instance, although Juche Tower and Ryukyung Hotel were developed in the 1980s they are not like the Kim Il Sung Square, developed in the 1950s according to the 1953 Master Plan. Their locations, however, were still determined by the early master plan. Since these urban spaces are the most distinctive urban structures within a socialist city, it will be interesting to see what kind of transformation patterns will unfold in the new era and how the transformation of these spaces will influence and generate other urban transformations.

Kim Il Sung Square without Grand People's House

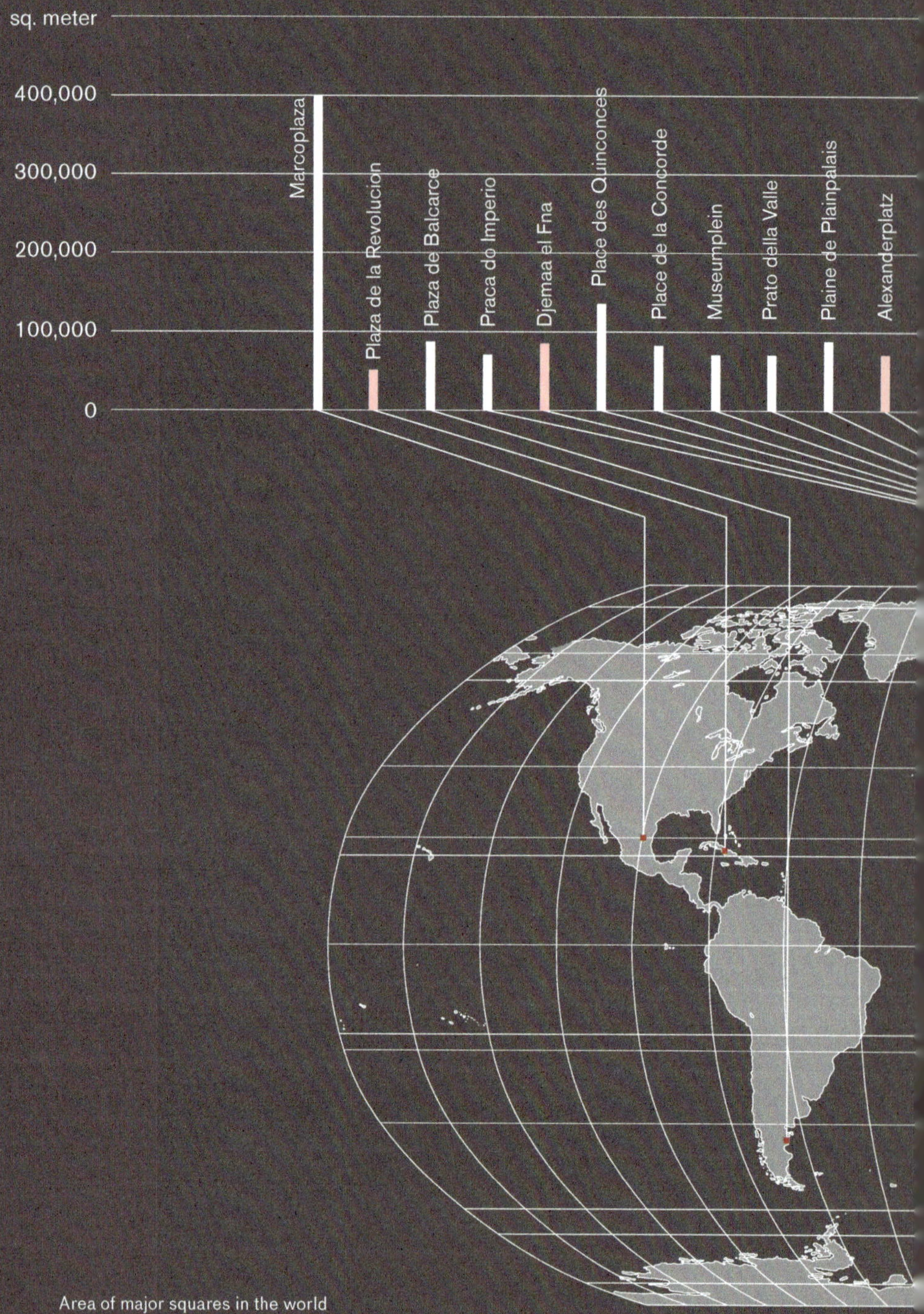

Area of major squares in the world

Victory Square
Moskovskaya Square
Freedom Square
Kuybyshev Square
Naghsh-i Jahan Square
Sukhebaatar Square
Sanam Luang
Tiananmen Square
Bayi Square
Kim Il-sung Square

Grand People's House Interior

The Grand People's Study House: change of program

> ... in city centres the institution of a private market in land and rising land prices leads to a new pattern of land usage. Many public institutions and ex-state socialist retail establishments are forced to move out, unable to pay rising rents, while Western-style offices, leisure and other commercial developments take their place.[12]

Program rearrangement happens very easily in the city center. Since even program distribution is an important logistic issue of socialist urban planning, there are facilities that cannot be easily found in central district of a capitalist city such as institutions, residences, and even, in some cases, light industries, that on the contrary, appear in the city centre of a socialist city. And as Häussermann points out, an institution located in a city centre has a weaker capital value than a business cooperation; thus, when there is a competition between them, the weaker capital power should move out because it cannot afford the increased land value.[13]

The Grand People's Study House is a major institution built in 1982 in honor of Kim Il Sung's 70th birthday. Juche Tower, located directly across the Kim Il Sung Square, was also constructed in 1982, and these two major

Grand People's House Interior

artefacts create a central axis of Pyongyang with Kim Il Sung Square and the Taedong river in the middle. The Great People's Study House delimits Kim Il Sung Square with the Ministry of Foreign Trade, Ministry of Agriculture, Korean Central History Museum, and Korean National Art Gallery. Based on the Juche Idea, which urges people to study while they are working, this monumental artefact is used as a library instead of a government building, and now houses more than 30 million volumes.

However, despite its large scale political and ideological effect on society, this institutional program can easily be replaced by another program in the market-oriented era. As already mentioned, this area is considered the center of Pyongyang, and this symbolic meaning allows to have an institutional building reflecting the ideology of North Korea in the central area, that had no land value in the capitalist sense. As a result, there was hardly any competition between institutional and commercial programs. However, because of its strong locational advantages, The Grand People's Study House can be transformed to uses different than a library. Located next to the House, the Ministry of Foreign Trade and Ministry of Agriculture may also be relocated after the transition due to their weakness of capital power. As seen through many other examples of former socialist cities, they could be renovated as cultural facilities, more open to the flow of public, such as museums.

Kim Il Sung Square: diverse use of surface

> the local elections brought up an even more bizarre idea on how to use the ultimate public space of Romania's capital... the huge Constitution Square in front of the People's House - an empty territory preceding the ample denced park of the building - is used for various celebrations of consumerism. Beer festivals are most popular, but auto shows are also frequent quests to this very official location. The ministerial buildings and the House provide a posh background for all sorts of events.[14]

A large public square in the city centre is a very important potential area for transformation. In a socialist city, a city of symbolism, forming open spaces for large parades and memorandums was one of the chief criteria when structuring a city, and they are mainly located in city centre. These are the places where people gather and major public facilities revolve around, and thus, they become perfect places for retail in market-oriented economy.
In the beginning of a transition, numbers of mobile trade form and kiosks, emerge first to fill the gap between the demand of consumers and the lack of retail distribution in the socialist period.[15] Further, these places where people gather and the flow of pedestrians is high, provide perfect locations for these flexible trade stalls.

> First, kiosks and mobile trade forms were the first to explore and introduce the market to a new system of commercial space that is of no less value to the contemporary market. Second, they influenced the character of the trading forms that emerged later to replace them. Third, they led to the emergence of shopping practices that have become accepted by the majority of the population and have, as a result, affected location decision-making, in terms of the demands and expectations to be met by a retail location. Fourth, entrepreneurs who started out in kiosks and mobile forms have graduated to become the larger operators and real estate owners in the city's retail trade and services sector. These entrepreneurs now constitute probably the major share of local retail capital in the market. [16]

Kim Il Sung Square is the major square that was constructed in 1954 following the 1953 Master Plan. It is located on the west bank of the Daedong River, directly opposite the Juche Tower and recognized as the "centre" of Pyongyang. According to the 1953 Master Plan, the square is formed to indicate the center of the city, and with the symmetric square on the other side, later developed as the Juche Tower site, it ties the development of the East

Potential development underneath the square

Collage image of Kim Il Sung square being "public space"

side of Daedong River with the old part of Pyongyang. Moreover, it gives the directionality of development axis of Pyongyang. It is the biggest symbolic urban space in the city where major parades and demonstrations take place and represents Pyongyang as well as the social and political system of North Korea. It is approximately 75,000 sqm, which is 16th largest square in the world, and can accommodate nearly 100,000 people in the square.

The square is formed with a couple of symbolic buildings around it; the Grand Peoples' Study House, Ministry of Foreign Trade, Ministry of Agriculture, Korean Central History Musem, and Korean National Art Gallery. These edifices are mostly occupied by public programs that can bring people into the square. Additionally, Department Store number 1, the biggest and the first retail store in Pyongyang, near the square is another strong attraction for the people. It was first built during the Japanese colonial era, but later in the early 1980s, was redeveloped and expanded to be twenty-five times bigger than the previous department store. It is a nine story building with nearly 40,000 sqm of interior floor area . Also, Sungni Street, one of the major boulevards in Pyongyang, and Sungni subway station around it, are infrastructural features that give strong advantages to the square. High-rise residential buildings as well as major public buildings are distributed along the 2.4km-long Sungni Street.

Having both locational and infrastructural advantages, Kim Il Sung Square has a strong potential to undergo a programmatic transformation in the future. Like the case of Constitution Square in Bucharest, the square can be used for various consumerist activities.[17] The Square is now used as a field for various festivals as well as shows. Not only the size of Kim Il Sung Square but also public oriented programs will attract people and generate various forms of commercial activities. Already are there emerging mobile vendors on the square selling street foods to pedestrians. Additionally, depending on investment scale and type, there are possibilities for public buildings around the square to be transformed to other use. Especially Department Store 1, which already has a 'commercialized' program, can attract huge investment for new mixed-use type development. Eventually, the transformation of Kim Il Sung Square may generate new developments in other places near it.

Ryukyung Hotel; redeveloping a monumental building

> Icon-driven projects, particularly those that go beyond "logo" architecture, open a new dimension in the restructuring of a city. They provide new spaces that, if crafted correctly, can be significant contributors to the urbanity of a city at large. More importantly, icon-driven projects have the ability to operate at multiple levels and scales, and to endow diverse geographies with significant worldwide recognition.[18]

> In the case of Sofia's central core, the expansion of retail and office functions since the early 1990s has been assessed to clear up to 40 percent of the built residential space, pushing over 50,000 residents out of the downtown area. This process has been carried out through three types of development schemes. The first one is through redevelopment of existing buildings. The process most often involves ground floor conversions, primarily to retail functions but also to restaurants, coffee houses, art galleries, banks, beauty salons, or travel agencies. Upper floor conversions are less common and are concentrated in buildings flanking the main boulevards. The most frequent non-residential uses inserted on these floors include office and service functions - medical and law offices, architecture and engineering studios, travel and real estate agencies, and some offices with unidentifiable nature of business.[19]

With the same reason as programmatic and usage change, large-scale development occurs in public and monumental spaces where infrastructures are well developed, and they have locational advantages. For instance, Alexanderplatz in Berlin was used as a showcase of socialist architecture in German

Democratic Republic's period. A couple of symbolic buildings as well as monuments were built around the square during the socialist era. However, after the German reunification, a major redevelopment plan including several skyscrapers was proposed in 1993. The square has now become one of major retail complexes in Berlin. Because of their locational advantage and ideological significance, monumental spaces and buildings of the socialist period can easily maintain higher recognition even after the transition, and this fact provides a strong impetus for new investment.

Ryukyung hotel was originally planned as a generator for foreign investment and expected to attract $230 million with the project, and started its construction in 1987.[20] It was designed as a 105-story building having 3,000 rooms, covering a total 360,000 sqm floor area. It rises to a height of 330m and is currently the 28th tallest building in the world. If it had actually been built when planned, it would have been the tallest hotel in the world at the time. However, as financial crisis hit North Korea, its construction ceased in 1992.

Ryukyung Hotel is located northwest from the city centre where the area is surrounded by Potong River. It was originally planned as one of main squares in the 1953 Master Plan to function at the core of the satellite district. Due to the close distance to the central district, the area has been developed from the early 1970s as a residential zone. The hotel creates a strong urban axis with Potong Gate, which was originally built in the sixth century and rebuilt in 1473. Kunsul subway station is located on the edge of the axis and residential mid-rise and high-rise are distributed throughout the area.

Because of its scale, as Busquets mentioned, Ryukyung hotel has strong impact potential over the urbanity of Pyongyang. As the master plan showed, it's surrounding area is designated as a major public space in the city and therefore, the transformation of the hotel may impact the transformation of the areas nearby. Recently an Egyptian development company re-engaged the hotel construction in 2008, and it is expected to be completed by 2012.[21] This investment will clearly attract other investments into the area. Especially, for its locational advantage, the surrounding area has the strong possibility to be transformed as the major CBD of Pyongyang. Unlike the "central district" area around Kim Il Sung Square, this area barely has administrative programs, which are not easy to relocate even after the transition, and is mostly developed as residential district that has less capital power than business or commercial. Therefore, the renovation of Ryukyung Hotel, which is closely related to business and commercial development, will influence the relocation of residents and replace them with office and retail programs.

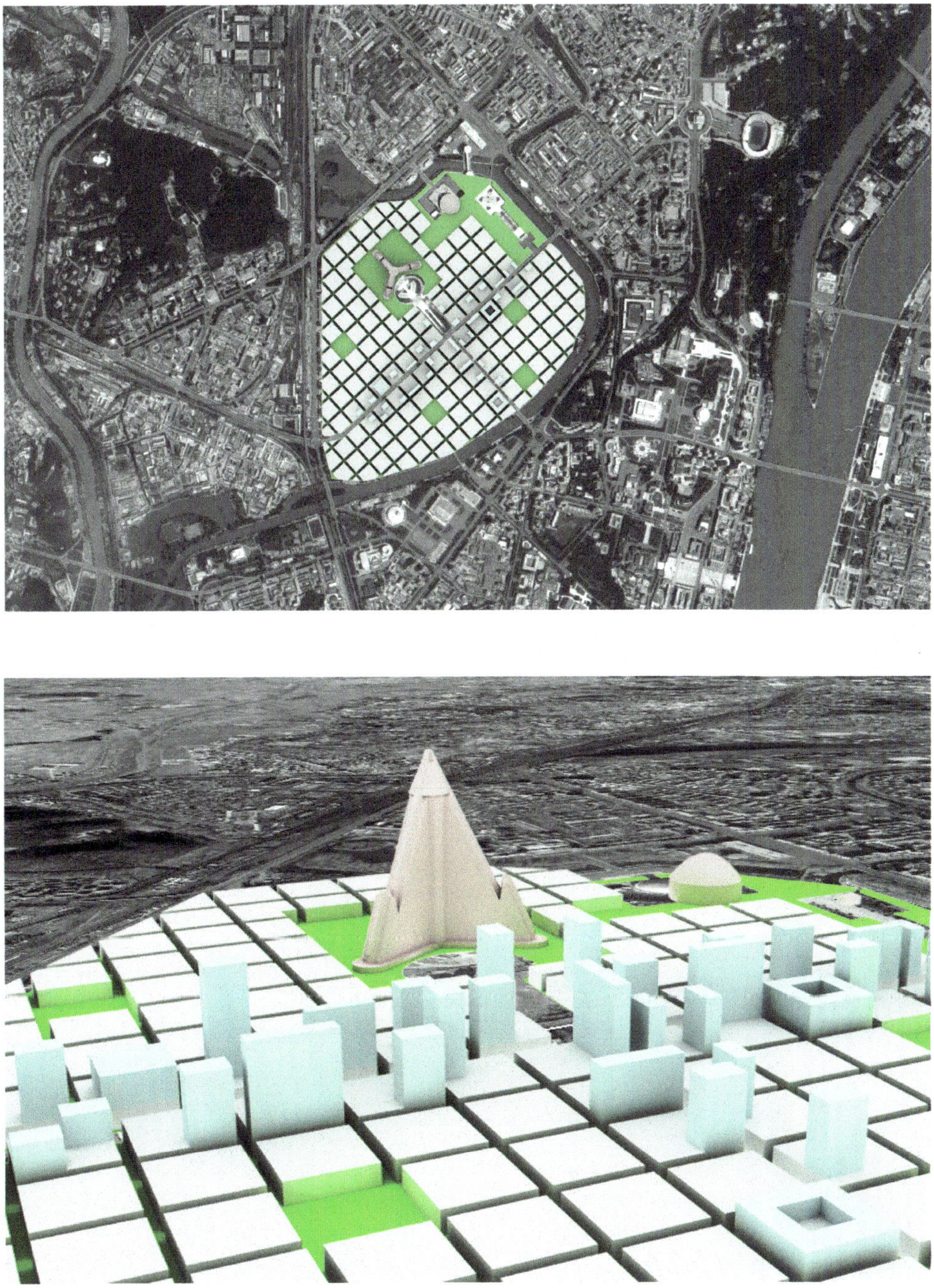

Urban developments around Ryukyung Hotel

Transformation @ Production Space

To meet the demand of the housing and land markets in the new transitional economy, residential development tends to be located in good neighborhoods away from industrial areas. Many large-scale housing projects are developed at the periphery of the city, especially near sub-centers outside the city.[22]

The shift from planned to market economy since 1978 has created new opportunities for the implementation of the microdistrict scheme. With a series of reforms targeting housing commodification, the task of residential development was gradually transferred from the government to private developers.[23]

Micro-district

The micro-district system is a basic self-sustainable unit in a socialist city that includes both residential and light industry workshops to achieve the socialist goal of combining production with consumption.[24] It is a socialist type of mixed-use development and the size of the block is determined by walking distance to improve productivity and generate use of public transportation instead of private vehicles. Therefore, the micro-district area has a well developed public transportation system with well-organized block structure. These features may become strong advantages for new investments in a market-oriented economy system.

In Pyongyang, micro-districts are easily visible on the east side of Daedong River, directly opposite Kim Il Sung Square. The area is structured with a maxi-grid system with a block size of 250m X 250m. This area was first planned in the colonial era as a new expansion of the city mostly for Japanese residents. Then, in the 1953 Master Plan, it was designated as one of the central districts amongst several satellite districts. However, the area was not well-developed until major developments of Pyongyang turned their focus to the east side of Daedong River.

The micro-district area is confined within four major infrastructures of Pyongyang; Saesallim Street, Tapje Street, Samwon Street, and Daedong River. Saesallim Street and Tapje Street are two main arteries that connect the west and east side of Pyongyang. These infrastructures contain the main axis of Pyongyang and therefore, are considered to be the backbone of the urban expansion of Pyongyang. Since the area is developed within a grid system (unlike other new high-rise residential development areas such as districts along Tongil Street or Gwangbok Street that have a linear structure), it has a systematized infrastructure as well as public transportation. For instance, Chungnyun Street, which is one of the major boulevards in Pyongyang, runs through the micro-district area, accompanied by subway and tram lines. As in many micro-districts in other socialist cities, mid-rise and high-rise residential developments are laid out at the periphery of each block. They are mostly 10 to 15-story apartment buildings with few retails on the ground floor, and some of them continue all the way along one side of the block, covering almost the full length of 250m. As mentioned, the micro-district is designed as a public transportation oriented development, so that secondary streets for service and private vehicles that cut in through the block are not well-developed. This feature makes a long snake-like residential development possible along the periphery of the block. Light industry facilities, work studios, and common facilities are distributed inside of it. These facilities are considered to be the main feature of micro-district because of their character of "production." This work-living environment is well structured in micro-district and it has a huge possibility for future transformation.

Light industry and work studios that existed in micro-districts as common labour facilities have strong potential to be transformed by new development. In a market-oriented society, privatization of property is allowed and there is no restriction of migration; thus, residents can have stronger opinions about the quality of their housing. The owner's demand generates new investment so, when a new residential development happens in the district, light industries and work studios, which are considered as disadvantageous factors for a residential area, are forced to move out leaving the space for new types of activities to fill the area.

Also, the increase of private vehicles in a market-oriented economy strongly influences the structure of the micro-district, designed as a walking-distance block based on use of the public transportation, and with less developed inner block, streets. However, as a number of private vehicles increase in new housing complexes, parking lots for residents as well as vehicle access become critical factors in structuring the block.

As the original micro-district is not structured with private lots but rather one single ownership, the new construction is always on a large scale. Mostly, in socialist cities, tenants have rights to reside in their units, but they do not own the land itself. Therefore, in the face of new development, they are relocated to other places and the area is developed by a single developer. This is similar to redevelopment or gentrification patterns in capitalist cities. And mostly, since the district is in or close to the city center, they are developed in large-scale condominiums instead of low-density collective housing.

> The high demand for office space in the city center resulted in a sharp increase of property values in the urban core. Owners of residential units in these areas capitalized on this opportunity, either by selling their property to commercial developers and users, or by increasing rents to levels which could be afforded only by prosperous businesses. The process of dwelling unit conversions in the city center was considered part of exercising the newly acquired (or restored through restitution) private property rights, and there was practically no control over the extent of these conversions.[25]

The micro-district area of Pyongyang has strong locational and structural advantages. Located directly opposite to the central administrative zone, the area could potentially be developed as a business-residential mixed-use complex. In a market oriented economy system, a mixed-use development

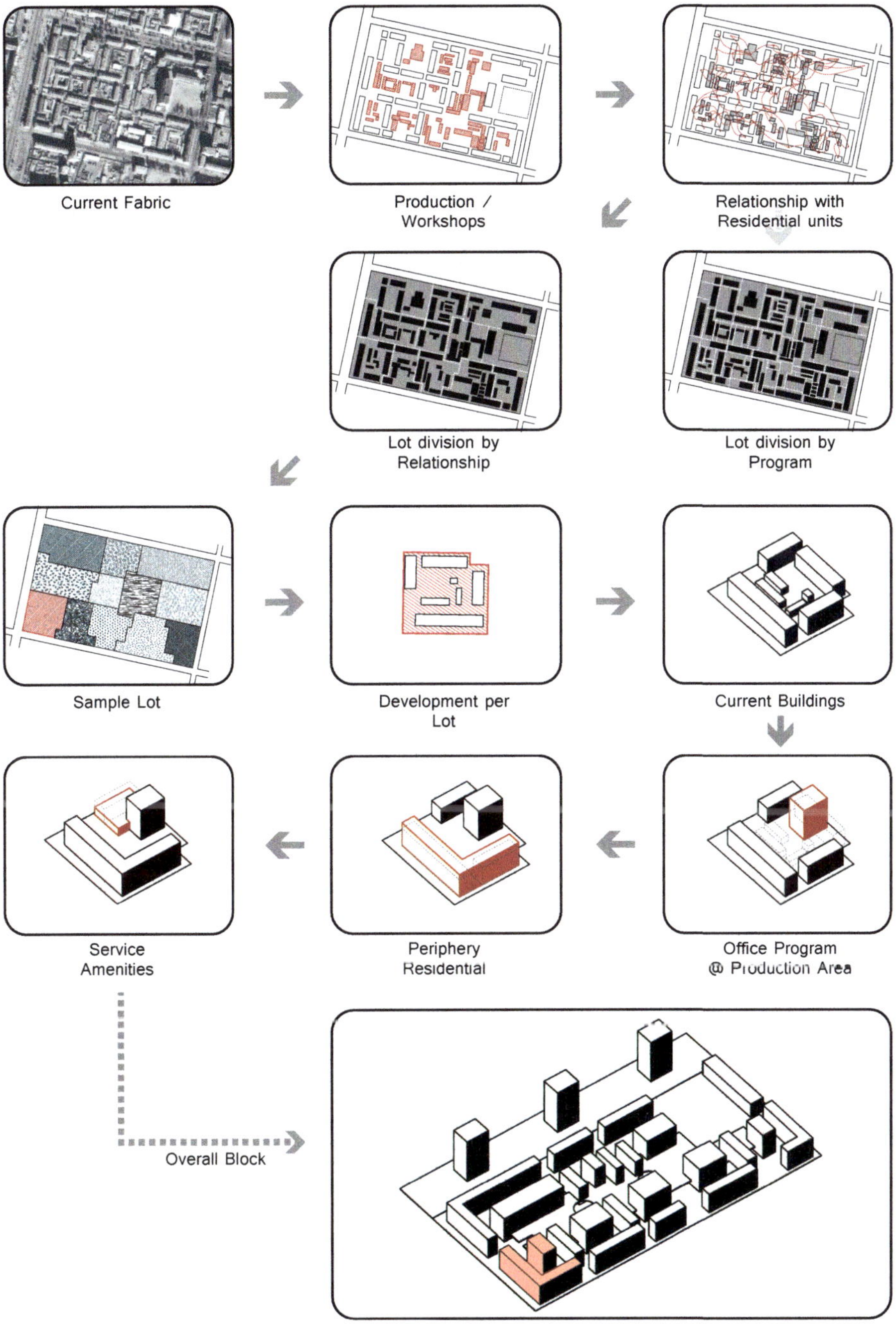
Current Fabric
Production / Workshops
Relationship with Residential units
Lot division by Relationship
Lot division by Program
Sample Lot
Development per Lot
Current Buildings
Service Amenities
Periphery Residential
Office Program @ Production Area
Overall Block

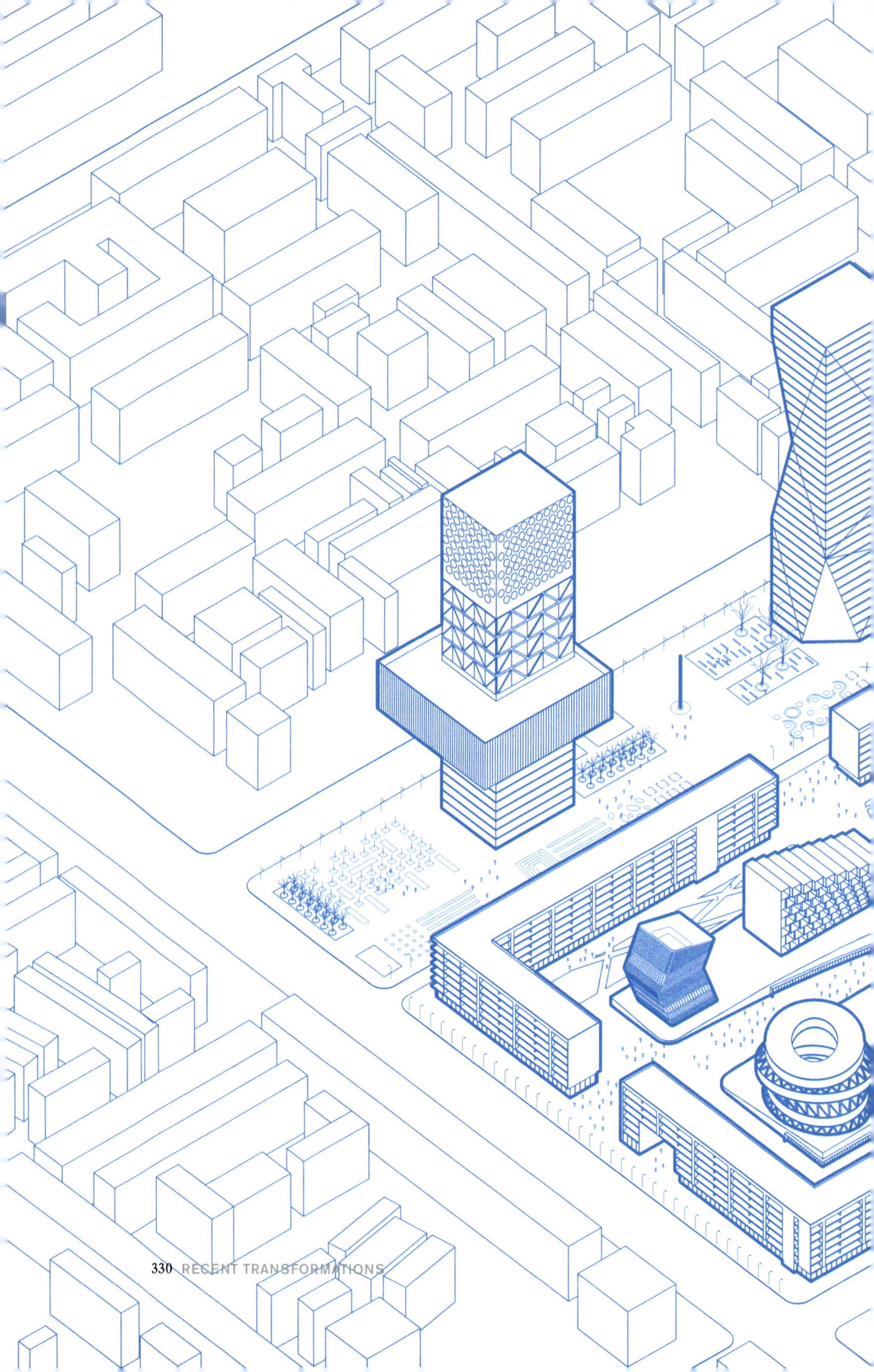

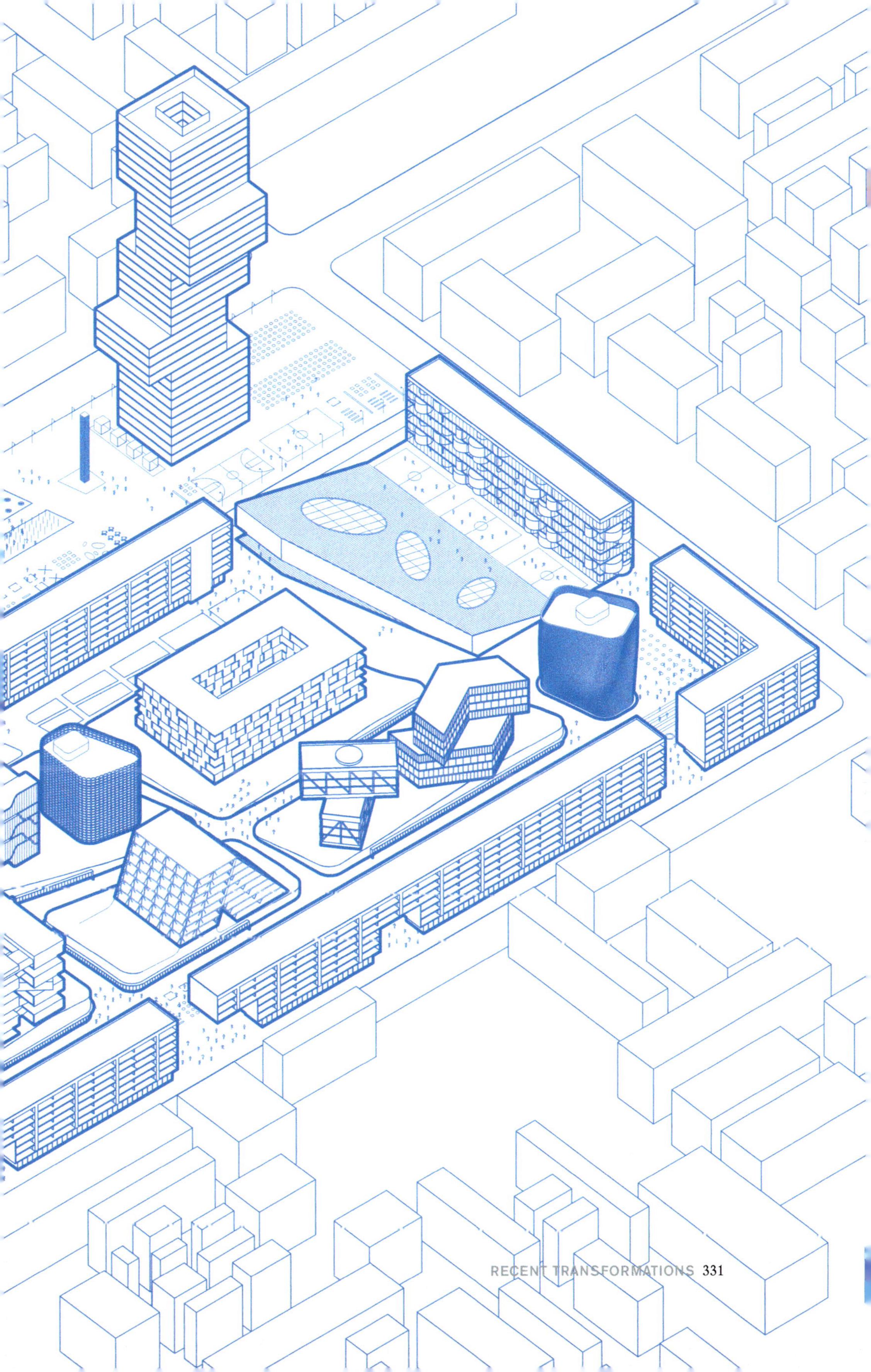

is its own way of work-living environment which is similar with the socialist urban concept of the micro-district. The difference, however, lies in the fact that in a market-oriented economy system, business and enterprise fields are major "work" fields instead of manufacturing industries. Also, during the transition period a socialist city experiments a shortage of office spaces because private businesses as well as enterprises were extremely limited in the state controlled economy. This lack of office spaces will be perceived in Pyongyang as well, and it is predictable that the micro-district's close distance to the central administrative area might attract major investment for office spaces.

On the other hand, residential programs in the micro-district will possibly remain after the transformation of the district. With the allowance of private property and assets typical for a market economy, individuals wield power to significantly influence the distribution of programs. Whether an individual owns or occupies a residential unit, North Korea also allows the "right of residency", that is usually transformed into "a preference for purchase" for tenants. Therefore, over the transformation process of the micro-district, this right of residency will play a strong role in keeping residential program within the district. In turn, the question of how new development conditions the implementation of the parcel system on the district must also be considered.

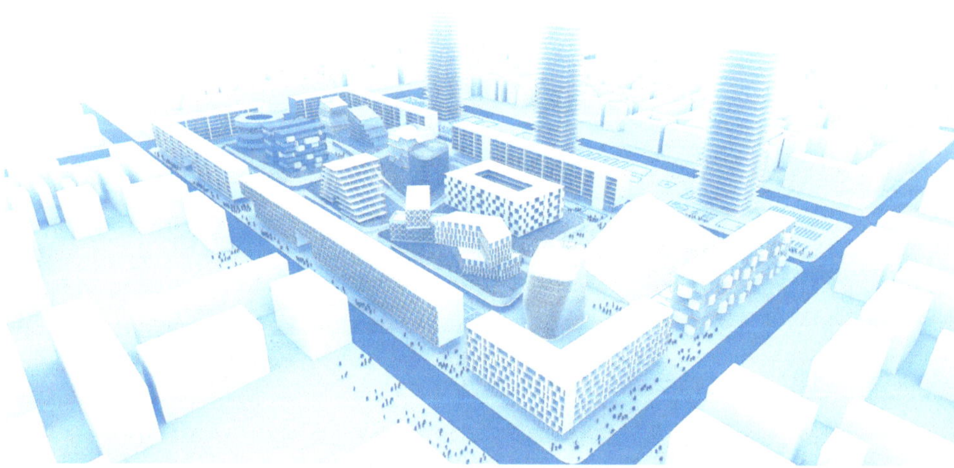

New Microdistrict Proposal

Since the whole district was developed by the government and private ownership is extremely limited, there is no existing parcel system in the micro-district in Pyongyang. Thus, the possibilities are to either convert the whole block into one mixed-use development or to subdivide the block into several parcels. When a block is subdivided, part of the residences at the periphery of the block and part of the "production" facilities inside the block can be mixed together within a parcel so that the transformation of the block does not necessarily need large scale investment but still generates mixed-use development. Therefore, it can follow incremental growth pattern without the major relocation of residents.

Industrial Facilities

> Another practice concerning the location of hypermarkets has been mentioned already. This is the tendency of retailers to seek a location that combines the public transport accessibility with proximity to major highways. The most attractive locations for this practice are areas around metro stations in the largest residential areas. Normally, such sites can provide sufficient space for the hypermarket building and parking, as well as guaranteeing potential customers from the daily flow of commuters using the transportation node. The third trend in

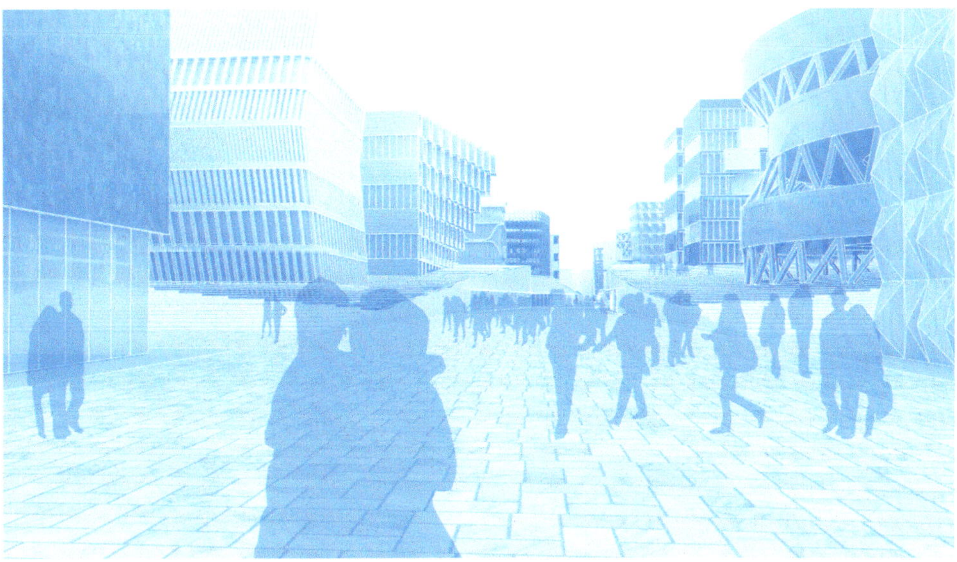

Street view of New Microdistrict

hypermarket location is the redevelopment of old industrial facilities all around the city. The most actively sought-after locations are those in proximity to transportation nodes, as in the above case, and those in the inner industrial belt close to the city center.[26]

Another potential area for the transformation of production space is the industrial district in the city. Like in capitalist cities and the post-industrial society, industrial facilities in a socialist city have strong potential to be transformed into other programs. As both the market-oriented economic city and voices of citizens grow, industrial areas, which do not necessarily have to be located inside the city, are relocated or abandoned. Not only because of the large size of the lot and facilities, but also because of its well-developed infrastructure, a former industrial zone becomes the most flexible area during the transition. In a city based on the socialist idea of abolition of the distinction between town and countryside, the aim to improve the city's

productivity renders the expansion of the industrial zone a very important factor in structuring the city. In fact, most cases exhibit a higher ratio of industry than a capitalist city. And these industrial facilities, not only because of the end of the industrial era, but also because of their weak capital power, are transformed into other programs in a market-oriented economic society.

There are several factories areas located within 5km distance from Kim Il Sung Square, the central point of Pyongyang, such as the Pyongyang Silk Factory, 3.26 Factory, Pyongyang Textile Factory, and Botong Shoe Factory. They are mostly located along the railway line constructed during the colonial era. Pyongyang used to be a major heavy industrial city under Japanese rule, and after the independence proclamation and the Korean War, North Korea put major efforts into reconstructing those industrial facilities in Pyongyang. This was in line with the socialist urban planning intent to make it the city of production instead of one of consumption. Unlike the capitalist city, these industrial facilities remained important urban programs

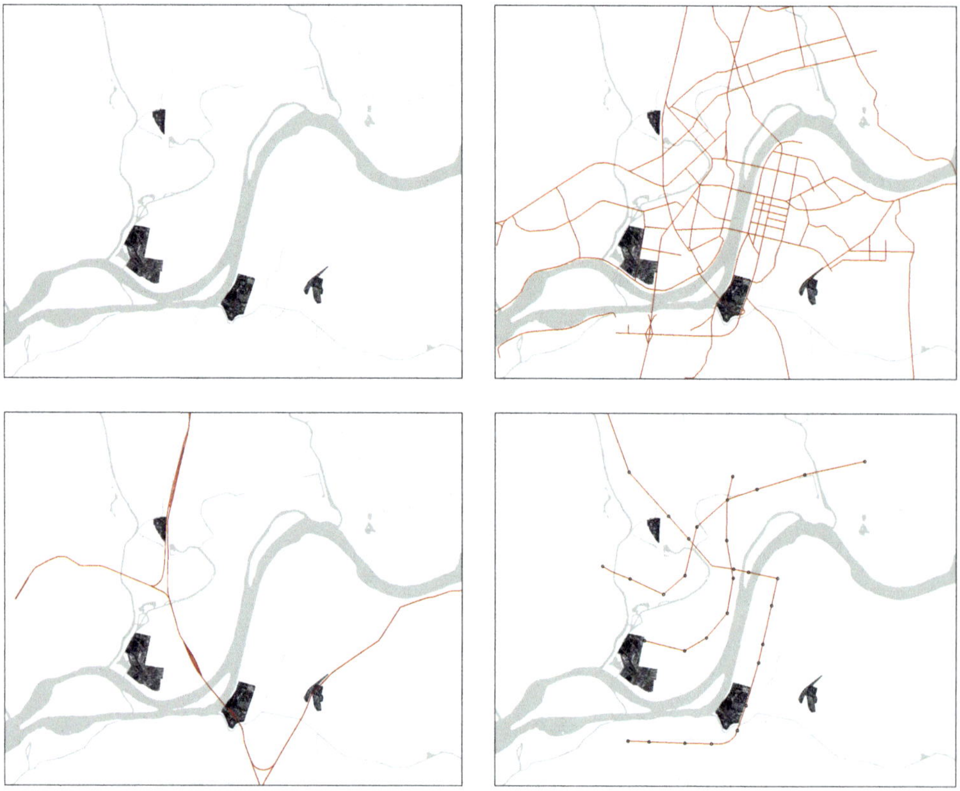

Infrastructure Network around Industrial Zones; Street, Railway, and Subway

in Pyongyang even when the city was expanding. In a capitalist city, on the other hand, industrial facilities, especially heavy industries that have less capital power and cause environmental problems, are systematically relocated outside the city when the city expands and needs more areas for new housing developments. Therefore, when Pyongyang adopts a market-oriented economic system and new developments emerge, those heavy industrial areas will be transformed into other types of developments or programs.

> We used to have a colourless land with everybody waiting to get something they needed or for something to happen. It was a grey place where time got stuck. The film opens with black-and-white reminders of the omnipresent police, slogans everywhere and people standing in queues waiting … waiting for a kilo of bananas, half a kilo of oranges. The clever ones, the well informed, those who bribed and had the money knew when and where to be to get what everybody wanted but not everybody could have. Suddenly, with the velvet revolution in 1989, colour, sound and life broke into the country. Markets, supermarkets and hypermarkets were standard-bearers of this new life and more welcome than anyone in the west can probably imagine, because of the freedom and prosperity they symbolised. But where do we find ourselves fifteen shopping years on? [27]

One possibility lies in the transformation of heavy industrial areas into large-scale retail shops or shopping malls. In a controlled economic system, retail existed only to distribute products to people, and therefore, there was no competition between various types of retail to match people's tastes. However, in a market-oriented system, retail becomes the most competitive field, and thus, various forms of retail emerge to meet people's taste while the number of retail outlets increase radically. 'Big box" type retail stores are one of the new retail typologies in a former socialist city, and this type of retail currently plays a major role in the commercial activity of most capitalist cities, as well as in post-socialist cities. Retail centers are usually located on a large site where the land value is low, such as former industrial areas, so the cost of products can be lowered.

As mentioned, heavy industry areas in Pyongyang are located along the railway that runs through whole North Korea, and this is a very strong infrastructural advantage for these areas. Regions where infrastructure for distribution is well-developed and public access is convenient, are perfect location for large-scale retail. Also, since they are located in the city, these current industrial areas in Pyongyang are close to main residential areas, meaning that they have solid customers nearby. For instance, Pyongyang Silk Fac-

Industrial area in Pyongyang

tory is situated just across the Daedong River from the high-rise residential district along the Tong-Il Street. Therefore, these locational advantages may stimulate the area to be developed as large-scale retail district when the demand of various retails emerges in a market-oriented economy.

Another possibility of these former industrial areas is their transformation into art galleries and studios. Since industrial facilities have large indoor spaces and lower land value, they potentially become artist areas. This renovation happens not only in post-socialist cities, but also in most post-industrial cities. After relocating major industrial facilities outside of the city, these large and vacant spaces are filled with other programs such as artist studios and exhibition galleries. Also, art industry in market-oriented society is much bigger than controlled economic society, and thus, it has higher demand from the public than heavy industry in the city. For example, Factory 798 (798 Art District) in Beijing used to be a military industrial facility from the 1950s until the early 1990s. However, during the economic transition process, the industry began to decline and artists took over the area. This

Potential development of industrial areas

may as well happen in Pyongyang. Currently, most of the artists' works are sponsored and controlled by the state, severely hampering the free market for art. However, after the transition, as in the Chinese case, individual artists in Pyongyang will seek their own studios for work and exhibition.

Transformation @ Green Space

Abolition of difference between town and countryside is one of the major socialist urban planning goals so landscape areas inside the city as well as agricultural areas on the periphery are well-structured as integral parts of a socialist city. The concept is strongly influenced by Howard's Garden City concept, and captures a major structural difference from capitalist cities. In a capitalist country, city and rural area are strictly separated and it is the rural area that is largely encroached upon as the city expands. Also, because of taxation issue, as Banik-Schweitzer pointed out, landscape areas are hard develop in a capitalist city.[28]

Green infrastructure in Pyongyang was first proposed in the 1953 Master Plan. Influenced by the socialist urban planning concept, the master plan designated green infrastructure as a buffer zone for limiting the expansion of the city. It is integrated with existing topography and laid out between satellite districts so that it can limit the size of each district. However, as the city grew radically and had several other development strategies conflicting with the master plan, the green infrastructure concept was not implemented entirely in Pyongyang. On the other hand, landscape areas along the river and agricultural areas at the periphery of Pyongyang were largely realized through out the planned period. In the 1980s, Pyongyang focused on improving planting as well as landscaping to donate the city the international character, and most improvements were concentrated along the Daedong River. Also, all agriculture areas are well developed at the periphery of the city. Because the size of Pyongyang is strictly limited, the border between the city and agriculture area is especially small: the countryside takes over from less than 10km from Kim Il Sung Square, the center of the city.

When the transition to market-oriented economy unfolds, these landscape and agricultural areas will have strong potential for transformation. As mentioned before, in a market-oriented economy, these areas have less capital power than other programs such as retail, residences, or offices. Also, the new influx of investment into the city can generate the expansion of the city either horizontally or vertically. Therefore, those landscape and agricultural areas that have low land value can be a "blue ocean" for new developers seeking the most profitable areas. In Eastern European cities, the surrounding agriculture suburbia has in a relatively short time been transformed into light industry private complexes, quarters of warehouses and large commercial establishment.

Taedong Riverfront

> Many successful riverfront developments are in larger cities, where more people use the space and support the businesses that exist there. The local government also has a larger tax base to provide funding for development. The city governments began to use riverfront development as a tool in economic development. The river connects a city. If a city has something special to draw a business or corporation, then that business in more likely to locate and stay in that particular city. [29]

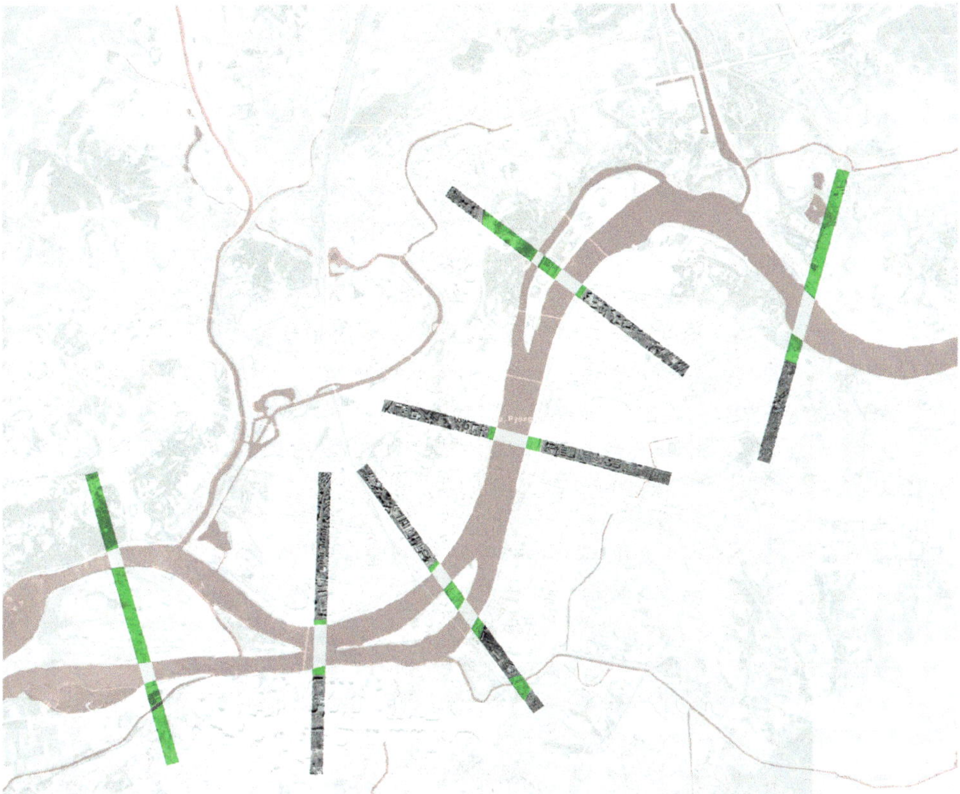

Landscape band along the Taedong River

Landscape along the Taedong River was mostly developed in the 1980s with the idea of making Pyongyang into international city. Juche Tower, one of the major monuments of Pyongyang, and parks surrounding it, were constructed in the early 1980s along the Taedong River directly opposite Kim Il Sung Square. Also, some leisure facilities such as Okryu Restaurant and Songyo Restaurant were developed to draw the public to the riverfront. Nonetheless, to address a strong goal such as making a "city in the park," the riverfront developments in terms of office and residential developments have never been considered. Another reasons for lack of riverfront development is that Pyongyang is not highly dense and, unlike capitalist cities, it does not focus on special and intense development in the city center.

However, after the economic transition, Taedong Riverfront area shows strong potential to be developed as office spaces or residential units.

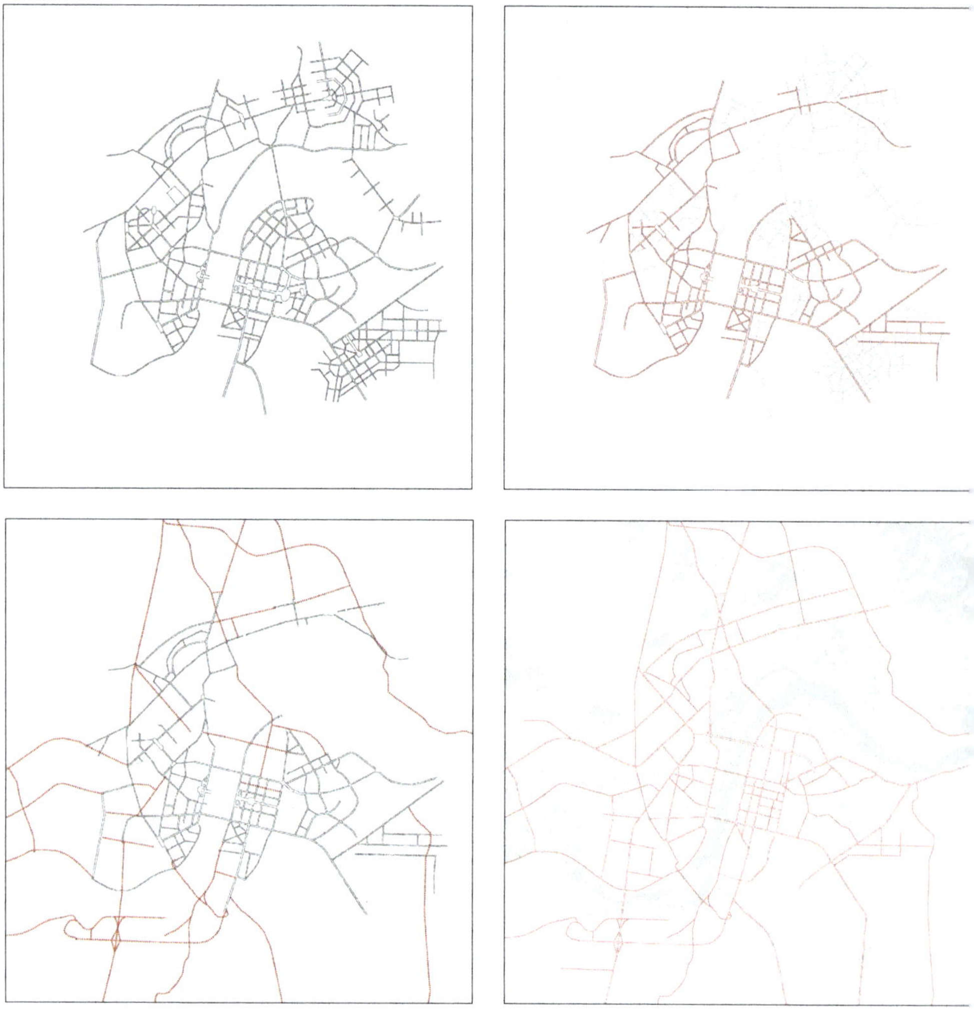

Developable area along the river

As mentioned, the investment flow in the capitalist economy generates active businesses and stronger demand for quality housing that reinforces the need for attractive spaces and locations, preferebly close to the city center. Therefore, the Taedong Riverfront, especially the parks around Juche Tower, could be the most profitable site for the riverfront developments. Currently, the area is not occupied by any specific program and is close to the micro-district as well as the "city center." Also, it is located in between two major bridges, the Okryu Bridge and the Taedong Bridge, that connect the West and East of Pyongyang and can easily be accessed by subway.

There are plenty of different riverfront development models that could be applied to the Taedong Riverfront. However, it is likely to be more construction works to satisfy the demand for new spaces, instead of landscape development. This is not only due to the plentiful landscape areas in available in Pyongyang, but also because the developmental pressure placed on this landscape area, which is very close to city center, might be high. The micro-district that is right next to the area could be easily extended towards the riverfront, and an institutional facility, the "Korea Documentary Film Studio," which is right behind the Juche Tower, could be transformed into a different program or redeveloped due to its weakness of capital power. These forces might generate the strong new development at the riverfront.

Duru Island

> The housing market in Moscow in the twenty-first century is characterized by a boom in the upscale segment of the market. The demand for luxury residences continues to grow faster than the supply. Most residents of Moscow, or at least those who can afford it, are driven by a desire to escape the drab environments of the Soviet mass-produced housing estates and move as quickly as possible to new or renovated upscale dwellings. [30]
>
> The suburbanization has become one of the most visible features of the process of spatial restructuring rearranging the urban patterns of the post-socialist city. While the spread of housing beyond the urban border was observed in small numbers during the socialist period, large expanses of land covered with detached houses have become a typical sight for metropolitan areas throughout Central and Eastern Europe today. [31]

Duru Island is a large island at around 3.2 sqkm located on the Taedong River where the Taedong River and Botong River meets. With exception to a small part, most of the island is developed as an agricultural area for mostly rice and vegetable farming. Because of its fertile crescent, it has been

Mirae Science Street Development, photo by Calvin Chua

a major agricultural area since the Koryo Dynasty in the tenth century. Currently, there is no infrastructure connecting the island to other parts of the city. However, there are two major boulevards right across Duru Island that could be expanded in the future; Chungchun Street and Tongil Street. It is now almost at the periphery of the development areas in Pyongyang.

The island has the potential to attract new investment after Pyongyang adopts the market-oriented economy. Agricultural areas at the periphery of the city transform dramatically not only because the expansion of the city but also because of a new suburban type of development. Increasing numbers of private vehicles make it easier for people to commute and generate migrations to new areas where better living environments are offered. In a market-oriented economy, class segregation occurs based on their capital and properties, and similar to suburbanization in capitalist cities, in former socialist cities, the class of citizens that can afford their own cars and houses move out and settle in suburbs. For example, in Beijing where post-socialism and globalization are happening at the same time, new types of townhouses called "villas" (due to their low density) are emerging in outer areas of 4th ring road.[13] This kind of new development is mostly set aside for the middle class drawn to the higher quality of living environment and lower density.

As mentioned before, Duru Island has the locational advantage of being in the middle of Pyongyang. Moreover, there is a major high-rise residential development on each side of the river: Tongil Street District and Gwangbok Street District. The disconnection between the island and land was the key feature in keeping the island as an agricultural area, yet a strong demand for expansion triggered by the emergence of high-rise residential districts will likely result in the connection of the two major boulevards. This infrastructural improvement will, in turn, generate a radical development of Duru Island. Since it has no urban structure, the island can be urbanized as a new type of suburban development of Pyongyang without any constraints.

> While it is clear that economic development imperatives and consumer preferences for greater shopping opportunities have supported these new forms of retail development, the challenge for planners and public officials is how to incorporate them successfully in the existing urban fabric, avoiding the adverse effects on the environment.[32]

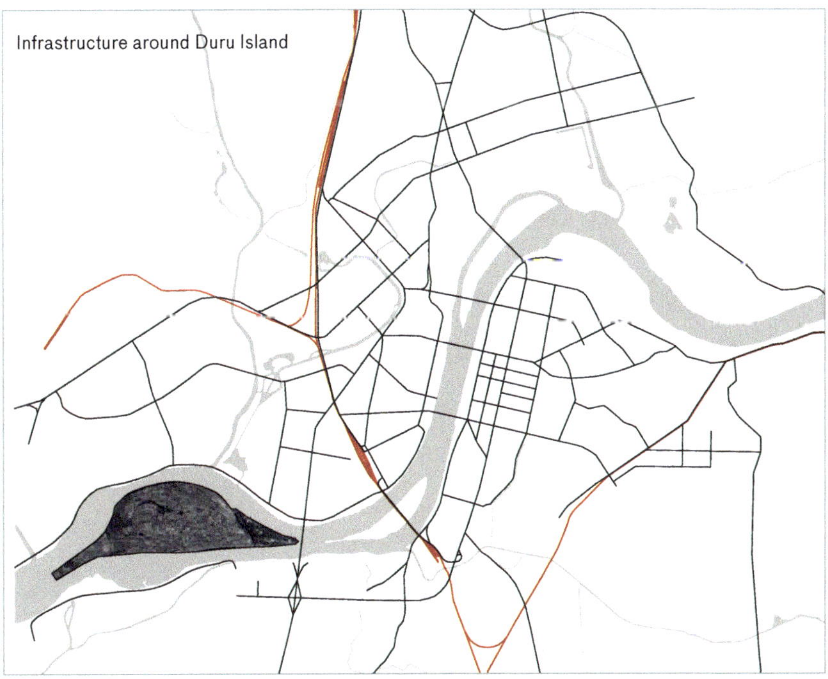

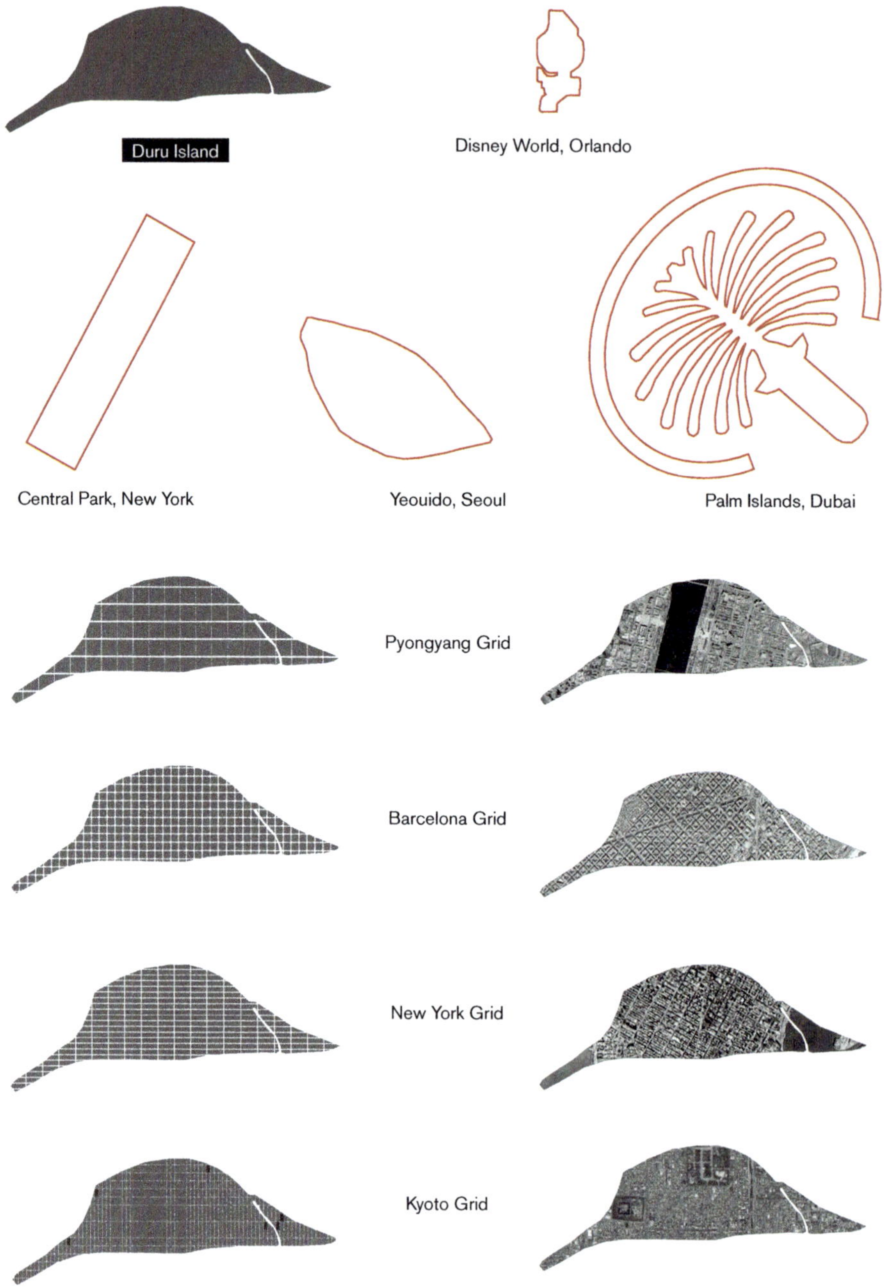
Duru Island
Disney World, Orlando
Central Park, New York
Yeouido, Seoul
Palm Islands, Dubai
Pyongyang Grid
Barcelona Grid
New York Grid
Kyoto Grid

In addition to residential developments, Duru Island can attract new types of emerging large-scale retail stores. As mentioned before, new retail must have vast lots of low land value and improved infrastructure. In addition to the former industrial areas in the city, new areas at the periphery of the city are also good locations for large-scale retails. It has large number of potential customers from new housing developments and an easy access from the highway that connects the city center to the suburbs. Therefore, large-scale retail stores will prove to be a catalytic force generating and attracting future developments in the area. Duru Island, with its major high-rise residential districts on both sides of the island and new residential developments in the island, could be a perfect location for large-scale retail stores after the implementation of a new infrastructure that connects the island to the land.

Endnotes

1 Blau, Eve, Ivan Rupnik, and Ivan Rogić Nehajev. *Project Zagreb: Transition as Condition, Strategy, Practice*. Barcelona: Actar D, 2007.

2 Wu, Fulong, Jiang Xu, and Anthony G. O. Yeh. *Urban Development in Post-reform China: State, Market, and Space*. Abingdon, Oxon: Routledge, 2007.

3 *Harloe, Michael, Iván Szelényi, and Gregory D. Andrusz. Cities in the Transition. Oxford: Blackwell, 1996.*

4 Faiola, Anthony. "A Capitalist Sprout In N. Korea's Dust; Industrial Park to Broach Free Market." *The Washington Post*, May 23, 2004.

5 Nam, Sung-wook. "Chinese Capital Preoccupying Pyongyang Economy." Pressian. 2005. Accessed August 04, 2016. http://m.pressian.com/m/m_article.html?no=46319.

6 *Cho, Myŏng-ch'ŏl. 7·1 Kyŏngje Kwalli Kaesŏn Choch'ı Hyŏnhwang P'yŏngka Wa Kwaje: Pukhan Kyŏngje Kaehyŏk Ŭi Chŏnmang. Sŏul T'ŭkpyŏlsi: Taeoe KyŏngjeChŏngch'aek Yŏn'guwon, 2003.*

7 *Axenov, Konstantin, Isolde Brade, and Evgenij Bondarchuk. The Transformation of Urban Space in Post-Soviet Russia. Abingdon Oxon: Routledge, 2006.*

8 *Ellin, Nan. Integral Urbanism. New York: Routledge, 2006.*

9 *Ellin, Nan. Integral Urbanism. New York: Routledge, 2006.*

10 Engel, Barbara. "Public Space in the "blue Cities" of Russia." In *The Post-socialist City: Urban Form and Space Transformations in Central and Eastern Europe after Socialism*. Dordrecht, the Netherlands: Springer Verlag, 2007.

11 Glabau, Leonie. *Plätze in Einem Geteilten Land: Stadtplatzgestaltungen in Der Bundesrepublik Deutschland Und Der Deutschen Demokratischen Republik Von 1945 Bis*

1990. Frankfurt, M.: Lang, 2010.

12 Häussermann, Hartmut. "From the Socialist to the Capitalist City: Experiences from Germany." In *Cities after Socialism: Urban and Regional Change and Conflict in Post-socialist Societies*. Oxford: Blackwell, 1996.

13 *Wu, Fulong, Jiang Xu, and Anthony G. O. Yeh. Urban Development in Post-reform China: State, Market, and Space. Abingdon, Oxon: Routledge, 2007.*

14 *Ioan, Augustin. "The Peculiar History of (post) Communist Public Places and Spaces: Bucharest as a Case Study." In The Post-socialist City: Urban Form and Space Transformations in Central and Eastern Europe after Socialism. Dordrecht, the Netherlands: Springer Verlag, 2007.*

15 *Axenov, Konstantin, Isolde Brade, and Evgenij Bondarchuk. The Transformation of Urban Space in Post-Soviet Russia. Abingdon Oxon: Routledge, 2006.*

16 *Ibid.*

17 *Ioan, Augustin. "The Peculiar History of (post) Communist Public Places and Spaces: Bucharest as a Case Study." In The Post-socialist City: Urban Form and Space Transformations in Central and Eastern Europe after Socialism. Dordrecht, the Netherlands: Springer Verlag, 2007.*

18 Busquets, Joan, and Felipe Correa. *Cities X Lines: A New Lens for the Urbanistic Project = Ciudades X Formas ; Una Nueva Mirada Hacia El Proyecto Urbanístico*. Cambridge, MA: Harvard University, Graduate School of Design, 2006.

19 Hirt, Sonia, and Kiril Stanilov. "The Perils of Post-socialist Transformation: Residential Development in Sofia." In *The Post-socialist City: Urban Form and Space Transformations in Central and Eastern Europe after Socialism*. Dordrecht, the Netherlands: Springer Verlag, 2007.

20 *Ngor, Oh Kwee (1990-06-09). "Western decadence hits N. Korea". The Japan Economic Journal: 12.*

21 *Demick, Barbara (27 September 2008). "North Korea in the midst of mysterious building boom". Los Angeles Times. Retrieved 14 December 2008.*

22 Wu, Fulong, Jiang Xu, and Anthony G. O. Yeh. *Urban Development in Post-reform China: State, Market, and Space*. Abingdon, Oxon: Routledge, 2007.

23 Lu, Duanfang. *Remaking Chinese Urban Form: Modernity, Scarcity and Space, 1949-2005*. London: Routledge, 2006.

24 *Ibid.*

25 Stanilov, Kiril. "The Restructuring of Non-residential Uses in the Post-socialist Metropolis." In *The Post-socialist City: Urban Form and Space Transformations in Central and Eastern Europe after Socialism*. Dordrecht, the Netherlands: Springer Verlag, 2007.

26 Axenov, Konstantin, Isolde Brade, and Evgenij Bondarchuk. *The Transformation of Urban Space in Post-Soviet Russia*. Abingdon Oxon: Routledge, 2006.

27 *Czech Dream: C eský Sen*. Directed by Vít Klusák and Filip Remunda. United Kingdom: Hypermarket Films Ltd, 2007.

28 *Renate Banik-Schweitzer, "Urban Visions, Plans, and Projects: 1890–1937", in Eve Blau and Monika Platzer, eds, Shaping the Great City: Modern Architecture in Central Europe 1890–1937, Munich, Prestel, 1999.*

29 Angelina V., Butler. *Successful Riverfront Development.* Master's thesis, Ball State University, 2001.

30 Medvedkov, Yuri. "Upscale Housing in Post-Soviet Moscow and Its Environs." In *The Post-socialist City: Urban Form and Space Transformations in Central and Eastern Europe after Socialism*, edited by Olga Medvedkov. Dordrecht, the Netherlands: Springer Verlag, 2007.

31 Stanilov, Kiril. "Housing Trends in Central and Eastern European Cities during and after the Period of Transition." In *The Post-socialist City: Urban Form and Space Transformations in Central and Eastern Europe after Socialism.* Dordrecht, the Netherlands: Springer Verlag, 2007.

32 Schwedler, H. U., Greenfield development versus inward urban development - challenges in sustainable development in central and eastern Europe, European Academy of the Urban Environment, available at: http://www.eaue.de/Vortrag/Greenfield.htm

IMAGE CREDITS

pp. 4,5_ https://www.flickr.com/photos/fljckr/

pp. 6,7_ John Pavelka_https://www.flickr.com/photos/28705377@N04/4610975882

pp. 8,9_ Nicor - Own work, CC BY-SA 3.0, _https://commons.wikimedia.org/w/index.php?curid=21296140

pp. 10,11_ Stefan Krasowski_https://www.flickr.com/photos/rapidtravelchai/9465931714/

pp. 22_ https://commons.wikimedia.org/wiki/File:Gangnam_Station_and_Samsung_Headquarters,_Seoul,_South_Korea.jpg

pp. 23_ https://upload.wikimedia.org/wikipedia/commons/5/50/Kim_Il-Sung_Square_overview.jpg

pp. 30_ Gabriel_Bucharest, Romania_https://www.flickr.com/photos/cod_gabriel/2788949359

pp. 32_https://commons.wikimedia.org/wiki/File:Map_of_Manchester_1801.PNG

pp. 34_ Ebenezer Howard (1850-1928) Public Domain_Garden City Diagram, E. Howard https://commons.wikimedia.org/w/index.php?curid=6085014

pp. 36 Above_ Edition A. S. Suvorin_Public Domain. Moscow Plan, 1917_https://commons.wikimedia.org/w/index.php?curid=554752

pp. 36 Below_Архитекторы В. Н._Public Domain_Moscow General Plan, 1935 https://commons.wikimedia.org/w/index.php?curid=17458605

pp. 39_ Waldemar Titzenthaler_Public Domain_Potsdamer Platz_https://commons.wikimedia.org/w/index.php?curid=3095466

pp. 40_ Paata Vardanashvili from Tbilisi, Georgia - gldani, CC BY 2.0,_Microdistrict, Gldani, Georgia_https://commons.wikimedia.org/w/index.php?curid=3242734

pp. 42_ Fyodor Alekseyev_Public Domain_Red Square, 1801_https://commons.wikimedia.org/w/index.php?curid=2994221

pp. 43_ Bart Slingerland (Rex) - Own work,_CC BY-SA 3.0,_Red Square, 2000s https://commons.wikimedia.org/w/index.php?curid=2674399

pp. 80,81_ Yim, Dongwoo, and Rafael Luna._"Administrative Structure of Pyongyang." In North Korean Atlas. Seoul: Damdi, 2014.

pp. 84,85_ Kok Leng Yeo, CC BY 2.0_View of Eastern Pyongyang_https://commons.wikimedia.org/w/index.php?curid=4962461

pp. 86-95_ Yim, Dongwoo, and Rafael Luna. "Administrative Structure of Pyongyang." In North Korean Atlas. Seoul: Damdi, 2014.

pp. 98-99_ Raw data from National report DPR Korea 2008 population census

pp. 114_ Yim, Dongwoo, and Rafael Luna. "Major Cities in North Korean Territory in History." In North Korean Atlas. Seoul: Damdi, 2014.

pp. 115 Above_ Kim Hong-d_Public Domain Feast for the Pyongyang Governor, Kim Hong-do1593_https://commons.wikimedia.org/w/index.php?curid=25653842

pp. 115 Below_ Public Domain. Pyongyang, 1593. https://commons.wikimedia.org/w/index.php?curid=25909916

pp. 117 Above_Public Domain Jangdaehyun Church, 1900s

pp. 117 Below_Site of Jangdaehyun Church now https://commons.wikimedia.org/wiki/File:Murals_of_Kim_Il-sung_and_Kim_Jong-il_01.JPG

pp. 120_George Rose_Public Domain

pp. 121 Above_Public Domain. Pyongyang during the Colonial Period_https://commons.wikimedia.org/w/index.php?curid=3293596

pp. 121 Below_Public Domain. Pyongyang Tram during the Colonial Period_https://commons.wikimedia.org/w/index.php?curid=4568300

pp. 122_Public Domain. Pyongyang Map, 1930 https://commons.wikimedia.org/w/index.php?curid=7683135

pp. 123_Pusey Library, Harvard University Pyongyang Master Plan by Japan in 1930s

pp. 124_https://www.flickr.com/photos/alfblume/15538828003/

pp. 126 Left_Kim, Wŏn. Sahoejuŭi Tosi Kyehoek (Socialist Urban Planning). Seoul: Posŏnggak, 1998._1950 Master Plan

pp. 126 Right_Kim, Wŏn. Sahoejuŭi Tosi Kyehoek (Socialist Urban Planning). Seoul: Posŏnggak, 1998._1953 Master Plan

pp. 128,129_Pyogyang. Pyogyang: Foreign Languages Pub. House, 1961_View of Pyongyang, Sketch, 1950s

pp. 153_Pyogyang. Pyogyang: Foreign Languages Pub. House, 1961_Pyongyang during the reconstruction, 1960s

pp. 155_Pyogyang. Pyogyang: Foreign Languages Pub. House, 1961_Pyongyang Station, 1960s

pp. 162_Pyogyang. Pyogyang: Foreign Languages Pub. House, 1961_Construction Site in Botong Plain

pp. 163_Pyogyang. Pyogyang: Foreign Languages Pub. House, 1961_Concrete Block Factory

pp. 170_Pyogyang. Pyogyang: Foreign Languages Pub. House, 1975_Pyongyang, 1975

pp. 172_Chosŏn Minjujuŭi Inmin Konghwaguk. Pyongyang: Chosŏn Hwabosa, 1986. Pyongyang, 1980s

pp. 173_Chosŏn Minjujuŭi Inmin Konghwaguk. Pyongyang: Chosŏn Hwabosa, 1986. Pyongyang, 1980s

pp. 72-75, 79, 80, 86-94, 294-297_Yim, Dongwoo, and Rafael Luna. North Korean Atlas. Seoul: Damdi, 2014.

pp. 26-27, 146-147, 276, 279, 282, 286, 289, 300-306, 309, 314, 316_Yim, Dongwoo. P'yŏngyang Kŭrigo P'yŏngyang Ihu. Kyŏnggi-do P'aju-si: Hyohyŏng Ch'ulp'an, 2011.

REFERENCES

Andrusz, Gregory D., Michael Harloe, and Iván Szelényi. Cities after Socialism: Urban and Regional Change and Conflict in Post-socialist Societies. Oxford: Blackwell, 1996.

Angelina V., Butler. Successful Riverfront Development. Master's thesis, Ball State University, 2001.

Axenov, Konstantin, Isolde Brade, and Evgenij Bondarchuk. The Transformation of Urban Space in Post-Soviet Russia. Abingdon Oxon: Routledge, 2006.

Axenov, Konstantin, Isolde Brade, and Evgenij Bondarchuk. The Transformation of Urban Space in Post-Soviet Russia. Abingdon Oxon: Routledge, 2006.

Axenov, Konstantin, Isolde Brade, and Evgenij Bondarchuk. The Transformation of Urban Space in Post-Soviet Russia. Abingdon Oxon: Routledge, 2006.

Axenov, Konstantin, Isolde Brade, and Evgenij Bondarchuk. The Transformation of Urban Space in Post-Soviet Russia. Abingdon Oxon: Routledge, 2006.

Bater, James H. The Soviet City: Ideal and Reality. Beverly Hills, CA: Sage Publications, 1980.

Bater, James H. The Soviet City: Ideal and Reality. London: E. Arnold, 1980.

Bater, James H. The Soviet City: Ideal and Reality. London: E. Arnold, 1980.

Blau, Eve, Ivan Rupnik, and Ivan Rogic_ Nehajev. Project Zagreb: Transition as Condition, Strategy, Practice. Barcelona: Actar D, 2007.

Bonino, Michele, and Filippo De Pieri. Beijing Danwei: Industrial Heritage in the Contemporary City.

Bray, David. Social Space and Governance in Urban China: The Danwei System from Origins to Reform. Stanford, CA: Stanford University Press, 2005.

Busquets, Joan, and Felipe Correa. Cities X Lines: A New Lens for the Urbanistic Project = Ciudades X Formas ; Una Nueva Mirada Hacia El Proyecto Urbanístico. Cambridge, MA: Harvard University, Graduate School of Design, 2006."

Cho, Myŏng-ch'ŏl. 7·1 Kyŏngje Kwalli Kaesŏn Choch'i Hyŏnhwang P'yŏngka Wa Kwaje: Pukhan Kyŏngje Kaehyŏk Ŭi Chŏnmang. Sŏul T'ŭkpyŏlsi: Taeoe Kyŏngje Chŏngch'aek Yŏn'guwon, 2003.

Crowley, David, and Susan Emily. Reid. Socialist Spaces: Sites of Everyday Life in the Eastern Bloc. Oxford: Berg, 2002.

Demick, Barbara (27 September 2008). "North Korea in the midst of mysterious building boom". Los Angeles Times. Retrieved 14 December 2008.

Demko, George J., and Joanna Regulska. "Socialism And Its Impact On Urban Processes And The City." Urban Geography 8, no. 4 (1987): 289-92. doi:10.2747/0272-3638.8.4.289."

Dormels, Rainer. North Korea's Cities: Industrial Facilities, Internal Structures and Typification = Pukhan Ŭi Tosidŭl: Sanŏp Inp'ŭra, Naebu Kujo Wa T'Ŭkching.

Ellin, Nan. Integral Urbanism. New York: Routledge, 2006.

Engel, Barbara. "Public Space in the blue Cities of Russia." In The Post-socialist City: Urban Form and Space Transformations in Central and Eastern Europe after Socialism. Dordrecht, the Netherlands: Springer Verlag, 2007.

Engels, Friedrich. The Housing Question. New York: International Publishers, 1935.

Enyedi, Gy^rgy. "Urbanization Under Socialism." In Cities after Socialism: Urban and Regional Change and Conflict in Post-socialist Societies. Oxford: Blackwell, 1996."

Faiola, Anthony. "A Capitalist Sprout In N. Korea's Dust; Industrial Park to Broach Free Market." The Washington Post, May 23, 2004.

Faiola, Anthony. "For North Korea, Openness Proves a Two-Way Street; As Increased Trade and Communication Bring Outside World In, More Citizens Are Spurred to Leave." The Washington Post, December 13, 2004. Accessed 2016. http://www.highbeam.com/doc/1P2-228101.html?refid=easy_hf.

Fedchenko, G. Irina., ìSocial Accessibility in the Large Post-Industrial City: From Traditional Planning of Microdistrict to Newest Demandsî, http://www.livablecities.org/downloads/49th-Portland/Fedchenko_Irina.pdf

Fisher, Jack C. Planning the City of the Socialist Man. Ithaca, NY: Center for Urban Development Research, Cornell University, 1962.

French, R. A. Plans, Pragmatism and People: The Legacy of Soviet Planning for Today's Cities. London: UCL Press, 1995.

Glabau, Leonie. Pla_tze in Einem Geteilten Land: Stadtplatzgestaltungen in Der Bundesrepublik Deutschland Und Der Deutschen Demokratischen Republik Von 1945 Bis 1990. Frankfurt, M.: Lang, 2010.

Han, Pon-jo. Pyongyang, a Park City. Pyongyang: Korea Pictorial, 2002.

Harloe, Michael, Iva_n Szele_nyi, and Gregory D. Andrusz. Cities in the Transition. Oxford: Blackwell, 1996.

H‰ussermann, Hartmut. "From the Socialist to the Capitalist City: Experiences from Germany." In Cities after Socialism: Urban and Regional Change and Conflict in Post-socialist Societies. Oxford: Blackwell, 1996.

Hirt, Sonia, and Kiril Stanilov. "The Perils of Post-socialist Transformation: Residential Development in Sofia." In The Post-socialist City: Urban Form and Space Transformations in Central and Eastern Europe after Socialism. Dordrecht, the Netherlands: Springer Verlag, 2007.

Ioan, Augustin. "The Peculiar History of (post) Communist Public Places and Spaces: Bucharest as a Case Study."In The Post-socialist City: Urban Form and Space Transformations in Central and Eastern Europe after Socialism. Dordrecht, the Netherlands: Springer Verlag, 2007.

Jeong, Eunmee. "Food, Clothing and Housing of North Koreaís Residents and Social Changes." The World Conference on North Korean Studies, 2014.

Joung, Eun-Lee. "An Analysis on the Status of a Real Estate Investment in North Korea." The World Conference on North Korean Studies, 2014.

Kang, KŬn-jo, Kyŏng-hye Yi, and Ch'un-hŬi Yi. P'yŏngyang Ŭi Ŏje Wa OnŬl. Chosŏn, P'yŏngyang: Sahoe Kwahak Ch'ulp'ansa, 1986.

Kim Il-sŏng, Uri nara sahoejuŬi nongch'on munje e kwanhan t'eje (Theses on the socialist rural question in our country), P'yŏngyang, Chosŏn Rodongdang Ch'ulp'asa, 1964

Kim, Chŏng-il. Kŏnch'uk Yesullon: 1991-yŏn 5-wŏl 21-il. P'yŏngyang: Chosŏn Nodongdang Ch'ulp'ansa, 1992.

Kim, Hyun-soo, Kim, Kyung-suk. "Nam-Pukhan Tosi Kyehoek Ŭi Pigyowa Chŏnmang." Korea Planning Association 1 (1998): 3-12.

Kim, Hyun-soo. Pukhan Ŭi Tosi Kyehoek E Kwanhan Yŏn'gu (A Research on North Korean Urban Planning). Master's thesis, Seoul National University. 1994.

Kim, Il Sung. In Glorious 50 Years. Pyongyang: Korea Pictorial., 1995.

Kim, Il-sŏng. Kim Il-sŏng Chŏnjip. P'yŏngyang: Chosŏn Nodongdang Ch'ulp'ansa, 1992.

Kim, Pok Rok. Glorious 50 Years. Pyongyang: Korea Pictorial, 1995.

Kim, Wŏn. "A Study on the Urban Development Policy in North Korea." The Korea Local Administration Review 4 (1990): 4123 - 4142

Kim, Wŏn. SahoejuŬi Tosi Kyehoek (Socialist Urban Planning). Seoul: Posŏnggak, 1998.

Kim, Youngkyu. T'ongil Han'guk, 1988.

Kliems, Alfrun, and Marina Dmitrieva. The Post Socialist City: Continuity and Change in Urban Space and Imagery. Berlin: Jovis Verlag, 2010.

Ko, Yu-hwan, and Dongwoo Yim. HamhŬng Kwa P'yŏngsŏng: Konggan, Ilsang, Chŏngch'i Ŭi Tosisa = Hamhung and Pyeongsung. P'aju: Hanul Ak'ademi, 2014.

Ko, Yu-hwan. Pukhan Tosi HamhŬng, P'yŏngsŏng Charyo Haejejip.

Langdon Winner, ëDo Artifacts Have Politics?í, Daedalus,109, no.1(Winter 1980), reprinted in Donald McKenzie and Judy Wajcman, eds, The Social Shaping of Technology (London: Open university Press, 1985)

Leung, Chi-Keung, and Norton Sydney. Ginsburg. China: Urbanization and National Development. Chicago: University of Chicago, Dept. of Geography, 1980.

Lu, Duanfang. Remaking Chinese Urban Form: Modernity, Scarcity and Space, 1949-2005. London: Routledge, 2006.

Lu, Duanfang. Remaking Chinese Urban Form: Modernity, Scarcity and Space, 1949-2005. London: Routledge, 2006.

Lü, Xiaobo, and Elizabeth J. Perry. Danwei: The Changing Chinese Workplace in Historical and Comparative Perspective. Armonk, NY: M.E. Sharpe, 1997.

Mao, Zedong. "Turing a City of Consumption to a City of Production." People's Daily, March 17, 1949.

Marcus, S. Reading the Illegible. Barrett, G, 2001.

Marx, Karl, Friedrich Engels, Samuel Moore, Edward Aveling, Marie Sachey, and Herbert Lamm. Karl Marx: Capital: Edited by Friedrich Engels ; And, Manifesto of the Communist Party by Karl Marx and Friedrich Engels. Chicago: Encyclopaedia Britannica, 1990."

May, Ernst. City building in the USSR. In Russia: An Architecture for World Revolution. Edited by Lissitzky, El. Cambridge: M.I.T. Press, 1970.

Medvedkov, Yuri. "Upscale Housing in Post-Soviet Moscow and Its Environs." In The Post-socialist City: Urban Form and Space Transformations in Central and Eastern Europe after Socialism, edited by Olga Medvedkov. Dordrecht, the Netherlands: Springer Verlag, 2007.

Meuser, Philipp. Architectural and Cultural Guide Pyongyang. Berlin: Dom, 2012.

Mumford, Lewis. The Culture of Cities. New York: Harcourt, Brace and, 1938.

Nam, Sung-wook. "Chinese Capital Preoccupying Pyongyang Economy." Pressian. 2005. Accessed August 04, 2016. http://m.pressian.com/m/m_article.html?no=46319.

Ngor, Oh Kwee (1990-06-09). "Western decadence hits N. Korea". The Japan Economic Journal: 12.

Obraztsov, A. "What Will our Future Cities Look Like," Soviet Review, II, No. 4 (April, 1961), 34-37

Pukhan Ŭi Tosi Mit Chiyŏk Kaebal. Sŏul T'ŭkpyŏlsi: Posŏnggak, 2009.

Qualls, Karl D. "Accommodation and Agitation in Sevastopol: Redefining Socialist Space in the Postwar 'City of Glory'" In Socialist Spaces: Sites of Everyday Life in the Eastern Bloc. Oxford: Berg, 2002.

Renate Banik-Schweitzer, "Urban Visions, Plans, and Projects: 1890ñ1937", in Eve Blau and Monika Platzer, eds, Shaping the Great City: Modern Architecture in Central Europe 1890ñ1937, Munich, Prestel, 1999.

Saunders, Peter. Social Theory and the Urban Question. New York, NY: Holmes & Meier, 1981.

Schwedler, H. U., Greenfield development versus inward urban development - challenges in sustainable development in central and eastern Europe, European Academy of the Urban Environment, available at: http://www.eaue.de/Vortrag/Greenfield.htm

Son, Chŏng-mok. Han'guk Kaehanggi Tosi Pyŏnhwa Kwajŏng Yŏn'gu: Kaehangjang, Kaesijang, Chogye, Kŏryuji. Seoul: Ilchisa, 1982.

Springer, Chris. Pyongyang: The Hidden History of the North Korean Capital. Budapest: Entente Bt., 2003.

Stanilov, Kiril. "Housing Trends in Central and Eastern European Cities during and after the Period of Transition." In The Post-socialist City: Urban Form and Space Transformations in Central and Eastern Europe after Socialism. Dordrecht, the Netherlands: Springer Verlag, 2007.

Stanilov, Kiril. "The Restructuring of Non-residential Uses in the Post-socialist Metropolis." In The Post-socialist City: Urban Form and Space Transformations in Central and Eastern Europe after Socialism. Dordrecht, the Netherlands: Springer Verlag, 2007."

Treadgold, Donald W. Twentieth Century Russia. Chicago: Rand McNally, 1964.

Wu, Fulong, Jiang Xu, and Anthony G. O. Yeh. Urban Development in Post-reform China: State, Market, and Space. Abingdon, Oxon: Routledge, 2007.

Wu, Fulong, Jiang Xu, and Anthony G. O. Yeh. Urban Development in Post-reform China: State, Market, and Space. Abingdon, Oxon: Routledge, 2007.

Yi, Hwa-sŏn. Chosŏn Kŏnch'uksa (North Korean Architectural History). Seoul: Parŏn, 1993.

Yi, Hwa-sŏn.Chosŏn kŏnch'uksa, Kwahak Paekkwa Sajŏn Chonghap Ch'ulp'ansa, 1989

Yi, Ok-hŭi. Puk, Chung Chŏpkyŏng Chiyŏk: Chŏnhwan'gi Puk, Chung Chŏpkyŏng Chiyŏk Ŭi Tosi Net'ŭwŏk'ŭ. Sŏul-si: P'urŭn Kil, 2011.

Yi, Sun-gŏn, and Wan-gi Paek. Chut'aek Soguyŏk Kyehoek. P'yŏngyang: Kungnip Kŏnsŏl Ch'ulp'ansa, 1963.

Yi, Wang-gi. Pukhan Esŏ Ŭi Kŏnch'uksa Yŏn'gu (Research on Architectural History in North Korea). Seoul: Parŏn, 1994.

Yi, Wang-gi. Pukhan Kŏnch'uk, Tto Hana Ŭi Uri Mosŭp (North Korean Architecture). Seoul: Seoul Forum, 2000.

Yim, Dongwoo, and Rafael Luna. North Korean Atlas. Seoul: Damdi, 2014.

Yim, Dongwoo. P'yŏngyang Kŭrigo P'yŏngyang Ihu: P'yŏngyang Tosi Konggan E Taehan Tto Tarŭn Sigak, 1953-2011. Kyŏnggi-do P'aju-si: Hyohyŏng Ch'ulp'an, 2011

Zhao, Liang. Modernizing Beijing: Moments of Political and Spatial Centrality. 2005.

Dongwoo Yim

Dongwoo Yim is an architect as well as an urbanist. He is the co-founder of PRAUD, a visiting professor at Washington University in St. Louis and an adjunct professor at Rhode Island School of Design. He is a PhD candidate from RMIT, received Master of Architecture in Urban Design from Harvard University, and bachelor's degree from Seoul National University.

Dongwoo's research and design focus on relationship between urban morphology and architectural typology, and he tries to bridge global conversation in urbanism to local architectural dialogues. Branched out from his original research on socialist city and architecture, his current interest is in how recent maker movement culture will influence housing typology and structure of a city in near future.

He is the winner of Architectural League Prize 2013, and the author of "Pyongyang, and Pyongyang After," and the co-author of "North Korean Atlas" and "I Want to be Metropolitan" His works have been exhibited worldwide including the award winning Korean Pavilion in Venice Biennale 2014, Museum of Modern Art in New York, DNA Galerie in Berlin. Dongwoo has lectured in various institutions including Harvard University, Columbia University, Dartmouth College, Freie Universität Berlin, University of Vienna, China Academy of Art, University of Queensland, AHO in Oslo and Seoul National University among others.

Jelena Prokopljević

Jelena Prokopljević (Belgrade, 1972) is Barcelona based architect and researcher in the field of socialist architecture and urbanism and their relation with the general history of modern architecture. Graduated from the University of Belgrade (1998), with PhD from the Polytechnic University of Barcelona (2006). Co-author of the book on North Korean architecture "North Korea, the Concrete Utopia", published in Spain, 2012. Collaborations with CCCB, URBS, Arquia, Autònoma University Barcelona- Research Group of Contemporary History, with Korean Pavilion for the Venice Biennale 2014. Co-curator and designer of "Aftermath", the Catalan Pavilion exhibition for the Venice Biennale 2016. Lectures and papers on socialist and North Korean architecture at different Universities in Spain, Europe and Asia. Currently teaches the course of urban history at Barcelona Architecture Centre (BAC).

Rafael Luna

Luna is a co-founder of PRAUD. He received a Master of Architecture from Massachusetts Institute of Technology and is an adjunct professor at the Rhode Island School of Design since 2012. Luna's current teachings focus on hybrid architecture as an adaptive reuse programming strategy for interior urbanism. Luna is the award winner of the Architectural League Prize 2013, and has international professional experiences in Japan (Toyo Ito), UK (KPF), France (Ateliers Jean Nouvel), and the US (Martha Schwartz Partners, dECOI, Sasaki Associates, and Machado and Silvetti). He is currently pursuing his Ph.D. research on Infra-architectural typologies. He is the co-author of, "I Want to Be Metropolitan," and editor of "North Korean Atlas."

(UN)PRECEDENTED PYONG YANG,
CAPITAL OF NORTH KOREA

Author
Dongwoo Yim

Editor
Dongwoo Yim
(email contact : dyim@praud.info)

Graphics
Rafael Luna, Heidi Cho, Sunjin Kim,
Chong Ho Park

Research Sponsored by
Design Beyond East & West

Graphic Design
Papersdoc SL

Copy-editing and proofreading
Jelena Prokopljević
Rafael Luna

Published by
Actar Publishers, New York, Barcelona
www.actar.com

Distributed by
Actar D Inc.

New York
440 Park Avenue South, 17th Floor
New York, NY 10016
T +1 212 966 2207
salesnewyork@actar-d.com

Barcelona
Roca i Batlle 2
08023 Barcelona
T +34 933 282 183
eurosales@actar-d.com

ISBN: 978-1-940291-35-2
Library of Congress Control Number:
2016960635

A CIP catalogue record for this book is available from the Library of Congress, Washington D.C., USA.